PLANNING
AND PERFORMANCE
IN
SOCIALIST ECONOMIES

PLANNING AND PERFORMANCE IN SOCIALIST ECONOMIES

The USSR and Eastern Europe

Abram Bergson

Harvard University

Boston
UNWIN HYMAN
London   Sydney   Wellington

Unwin Hyman, Inc.
8 Winchester Place, Winchester, MA 01890, USA

Published by the Academic Division of
Unwin Hyman Ltd,
15/17 Broadwick Street, London W1V 1FP, UK

Allen & Unwin Australia Pty Ltd,
8 Napier Street, North Sydney, NSW 2060, Australia

Allen & Unwin (New Zealand) Ltd,
in association with the Port Nicholson Press Ltd, 60 Cambridge Terrace,
Wellington, New Zealand
First published in 1989

Library of Congress Cataloging-in-Publication Data

Bergson, Abram, 1914 –
    Planning and performance in socialist economies.
    HC336.25.B454 1988   338.947   88–10712
    HC336.25.B454 1988   338.947   88–10712
    1. Soviet Union—Economic conditions—1976–
2. Central planning—Soviet Union. 3. Europe, Eastern—
Economic conditions. 4. Central planning—Europe,
Eastern. I. Title.
HC336.25.B454 1988   338.947   88–10712
ISBN 0-04-445115-6

British Library Cataloguing in Publication Data

Bergson, Abram, 1914–
    Planning and performance in socialist
    economies: the USSR and Eastern Europe.
1. Eastern Europe & Soviet Union.
Economic conditions
I. Title
330.947
ISBN 0-04-445115-6

Set in 10 on 12 point Garamond by Grove Graphics, Tring Herts
and printed in Great Britain at the University Press, Cambridge

Contents

List of Tables

Chapter 2

Chapter 2: Appendix Tables

Chapter 3

Chapter 4

Chapter 5

Chapter 6

Chapter 7

Chapter 8

Chapter 9

Chapter 10

Chapter 11

Chapter 12

Preface

Of the twelve studies collected in this volume, nine were published previously and are reproduced here essentially without change. In a tenth study, appearing here as Chapter 4, "Soviet Consumption in Comparative Perspective," I have revised a previously published essay to take into account further results of the ongoing World Bank-United Nations International Comparison Project. Chapter 2, "Comparative Productivity: The USSR, Eastern Europe, and the West," also provided a more substantial basis than had been previously available for relating Soviet consumption to output per worker.

In republishing, in Chapter 2, the study on productivity, I have added a number of related tables that the reader may find of value. The tables are taken from an appendix providing detailed explanations of sources and methods used in deriving the more basic statistical data in the text. Of interest primarily to specialists, this appendix has been and continues to be available to readers upon request from the author.

Chapter 8, "The Soviet Slowdown: Can It Be Reversed?" was prepared originally as a conference paper and has appeared only in an abbreviated form. Chapter 10, "Annual Plan Fulfillment in Soviet Industry, 1961–1985," is printed for the first time in this volume.

I am much indebted to Mary Towle and Rose di Benedetto for their skillful aid in preparing the studies for publication. Use of the facilities of the Russian Research Center at Harvard has also been helpful.

Abram Bergson
Cambridge, Massachusetts
November, 1987

1

Introduction

While the studies gathered together in this volume were written over a period of nearly a decade, and almost inevitably have diverse concerns, all relate to the functioning of contemporary socialist economies—mainly that of the USSR, but also those of several of its Eastern European associates. Practically all of the studies also bear, at least obliquely, on a grand theme in comparative economics: The contrasting economic merits and deficiencies of socialist societies, where ownership of the means of production is predominantly public, and Western capitalist economies, where ownership of the means of production may be quite mixed but is still primarily private.

The present volume can be viewed as a companion volume to a previous collection of mine addressing the comparative economic merit of the two systems (Bergson 1978), and as similarly related to a still earlier study (Bergson 1968). No occasion has been found now to revise in any consequential way the view reached previously that socialist economic performance tends to be undistinguished by Western standards. Fresh evidence to that effect is offered here.

In assessing economic merit previously I usually took production efficiency as a normative standard, referring thereby both to the "static" variety observable in productivity levels and the "dynamic" variety seen in productivity growth.[1] Since one of the studies included in the present collection deals with income distribution, it may facilitate application of the related standard of equity to assessment of relative economic merit.

While the studies in this volume generally bear on comparative economic merit, a number of the studies are otherwise preoccupied. A word or two may be in order on the contents of the different essays and their relation to each other.

In Chapter 2, I focus on efficiency—in this case of the "static" variety. In particular, I attempt to gauge the causes and extent of differences in output per worker between four socialist countries (the USSR, Hungary, Poland and Yugoslavia) and seven Western mixed economy (WME) countries. With available data, comparison of the socialist countries among themselves is felt to be insecure, but, in light of the WME performance, productivity levels in all the socialist countries are seemingly substandard, and indicate reduced efficiency.

One source of difference in productivity between socialist and WME countries could be a difference between the volume of inventories required to produce and distribute any given output. How the two systems compare on this score is also a matter of separate interest—as a summary indicator of potentially significant differences in their manner of operation. It is also a matter on which there has been much speculation and some illuminating, quantitative research. By drawing on data compiled for Chapter 2, I have been able, in Chapter 3, to provide a firmer and more inclusive empirical basis for appraising the question at issue than has hitherto been available.

Consumer standards are ultimately delimited by productivity, but, in Chapter 4, it still seemed of interest to see how the USSR contrasts with WME countries in that regard. I draw heavily here, however, on previous Western research on comparative consumption levels. For that reason, the inquiry may be of more value because it attempts to delineate systematically the relation between per capita consumption and productivity in the USSR and in WME countries. A curious result is that the notably low per capita consumption in the USSR is a near reflection of depressed output per worker there. While nonconsumption (that is, defense and investment) absorbs an inordinately large share of the Soviet output, the resulting adverse effect on per capita consumption is largely offset by the low population–employment ratio associated with the proverbially high Soviet labor participation rate.

The essay on income distribution alluded to above, appears as Chapter 5. In exploring income inequality in the USSR, and also the inevitable additional question concerning social stratification in that country, I do not seek especially to plow new ground. The essay delineates the burden, for those topics, of a by now voluminous Western literature.

In view of their interconnectedness, I have grouped the foregoing studies into the first of four parts into which this volume is divided. The three studies that constitute the second part are closely related to those in the first, as well as to each other. In Chapter 6, I examine afresh the recurring question of the sources of Soviet output growth. The contribution of the increase of "factor productivity" in general, and of "technological progress" specifically, are of particular concern in this study. Those matters are immediately pertinent to dynamic efficiency, and, as in previous inquiries, the Soviet performance appears to be less than exemplary, judging by that yardstick. In respect of the USSR, the inquiry into productivity growth also helps to put the substandard socialist productivity levels of Chapter 2 into perspective. The study may also be of methodological interest for its unusually systematic decomposition of sources of Soviet output growth.

Methodology is also the subject of Chapter 7, which appraises the import, for analysis of Soviet growth, of diverse and often conflicting econometric studies of the so-called "production function" in Soviet industry. Completed before the study which appears here as Chapter 6, this essay served as a point of departure for that study.

Growth continues to be the theme in Chapter 8. I focus here particularly on the twelfth five-year plan (1986–1990) of the USSR. Essentially this essay was written soon after the Communist Party adopted that program, on March 9, 1986.[2] At that time a dynamic new leadership was still at an early stage in its efforts to "restructure" the Soviet economy and social life in general. For that reason this essay is somewhat dated. It may still retain interest, however, because it elucidates the long-range economic goals of the new administration as well as the deep-seated difficulties that have confronted it in seeking to realize those goals.

In the third part of the volume I turn from the quantitative assessment of performance, in terms of productivity levels, growth, and the like, to a consideration of underlying mechanisms, beginning, in Chapter 9, with those of Yugoslavia. Inquiring into the famous Yugoslav system of labor "self-management" represented for me a process of self-education. But others too may find useful this attempt at relating the burgeoning—and often quite abstract—theoretic literature on the labor-managed economy to available—often sparse—empirical information on the Yugoslav experience. The specific occasion for which the essay was written dictated a focus on entrepreneurship. Happily this is topic of particular interest that seems to have been relatively neglected in Western research. While the essay is not primarily normative in purpose, its incidental result may be to underline dysfunctional features in Yugoslav labor self-management that do not always seem sufficiently considered.

There follows, in Chapter 10, a brief inquiry into trends in annual plan fulfillment in the USSR and the possible causes of the striking shifts that seem to emerge therein. Chapter 11 inquires into COMECON trade. The main concern is to interpret exchanges between the USSR and its Eastern European associates in the light of Western international trade theory. Adam Smith held that both sides may gain from trade. At least in the pre-oil-shock years in question, COMECON appears to provide an illustration of how both sides may well lose. That finding probably will be no great surprise to the more informed reader, but the essay may serve to elucidate more clearly some underlying theoretic and empirical considerations.

In trying to quantify socialist economic performance in many of the foregoing studies, I necessarily seek to take account of deficiencies in relevant statistical data, both Eastern and Western. In Chapter 12, which initiates the volume's final section, I address the controversial issue of the reliability of one important type of relevant statistical data the data of the Soviet Central Statistical Administration and the United States Central Intelligence Agency on Soviet investment volume. In conclusion, in Chapter 13, I address a methodological issue which is raised by the CIA's index numbers of comparative volume of Soviet and United States defense expenditures. The novel approach to such measurements advanced in this study may have some general application to index number computations.

As this volume goes to press, the world's socialist economies are much in the news. A chief reason is, no doubt, the quite novel reforms lately initiated in their planning systems. The rearrangements have been especially dramatic in China, and are apparently now projected to be sweeping also in the USSR. Elsewhere as well, however, economic institutions, policies, and procedures, long considered as essentially settled, seem to be increasingly open to experimentation.

This volume does not concern itself especially with such rearrangements. Of all the essays included, only one, that on the twelfth five-year plan, touches on planning reform, and only in a limited way. The system that is being reformed in the USSR and often elsewhere, though, has proved remarkably durable. The so-called centralist planning scheme, with its stress on bureaucratic as distinct from market processes of economic coordination and direction, is today, despite numerous reformist initiatives, still substantially the system that Stalin established in the USSR under the early five-year plans. It may be too early to suppose that that system at long last has seen its day.

Whatever the prospect in that regard, however, the studies collected here, by expatiating on centralist planning, may help provide a needed perspective on ongoing and projected planning rearrangements. Among other things, quantitative assessments of performance such as those made in different spheres, would seem indispensable in understanding why socialist governments are now pursuing planning reform, with an apparently particular urgency; as well as for understanding the scale of the task that they are grappling with.

While centralist planning is still the rule in the socialist world, two outstanding deviants emerged even before the latest shifts. Moreover, the relatively extensive rearrangements that were made in Yugoslavia, beginning in the 1950s, and have been in progress in Hungary since 1968, are clearly now influencing planning reform elsewhere. By elucidating, if only in a limited manner, the experience under those shifts, the essays are thus addressing the very pertinent question of what the pursuit of such options might offer. In that way they may provide perspective on current planning reforms.

Footnotes

[1] On normative criteria for appraising economic merit, Bergson (1968: 15–19; 1978: 1–2, 92).
[2] The plan was then approved, with some changes, by the Supreme Soviet on June 19, 1986.

References

Bergson, Abram (1968). *Planning and Productivity under Soviet Socialism*. New York: Columbia University Press.

——(1978). *Productivity and the Social System: The USSR and the West*. Cambridge, Mass.: Harvard University Press.

Part I

Productivity and Welfare

Comparative Productivity: The USSR, Eastern Europe, and the West*

In previous writings,[1] I compared in a more or less aggregative way output per worker in the USSR and several Western mixed-economy (WME) countries in 1960, and explored sources of observed differences in that aspect. Focusing on a more recent date, 1975, this essay attempts to extend this earlier work in order to embrace, in addition to the USSR, several Eastern European countries: Poland, Hungary, and Yugoslavia. I am also able to consider more WME countries than before, and to take account of further thoughts on methodology.

Among the possible sources of productivity differences between the groups of countries in question, one of particular interest is the difference in prevailing economic sys-

tems. The issue concerning the comparative efficiency of socialism that is posed is notably complex, but my previous studies may have limited speculation on it. Hopefully this one will serve in the same way.

An attempt to update and extend the reach of my previous studies seemed in order in view of the completion of another major phase (III) of the ongoing World Bank International Comparison Project (ICP) on relative national income. The latest work (Irving Kravis et al., 1982) provides systematic data on comparative real national income of the sort needed here for 1975, for numerous socialist as well as WME countries. The USSR is not among the socialist countries considered in ICP–III, but a careful inquiry into the relative national income of that country and the United States for a recent year, 1976, has become available elsewhere.

The ICP has compiled comparative data on national income not only for Poland, Hungary, and Yugoslavia, but for Romania. Because of limitations of available statistics on related matters of concern, I reluctantly omitted that country from this inquiry. Among WME countries covered by ICP–III, I limit myself to seven that are OECD members: the United States, Germany (the Federal Republic), France, Japan, the United Kingdom, Italy, and Spain. These countries do not vary as widely as might be desired regarding their development stage (the possible import of that matter will become evident), but inclusion of still other OECD members covered by ICP–III would have magnified an already onerous undertaking

*Harvard University, Cambridge, MA 02138. A separate Appendix, giving details on sources and methods for deriving basic data, is available to readers upon request. I am indebted to Zvi Griliches and anonymous readers for helpful comments on earlier versions, and have also benefited from discussion with Michael Keren and Gur Ofer. In utilizing national statistics for different countries, I have been aided in more than one way by numerous persons and agencies. Particular thanks are due to Edmond Malinvaud of INSEE, Paris; the Statistisches Bundesampt, Wiesbaden; Takao Fukuchi of the Economic Planning Agency, Tokyo; Thad P. Alton, of L. W. International Financial Research, New York; Ivo Vinski and Michael L. Boyd. Mary Towle has provided her usual sterling secretarial assistance. Daniel Quah and Marc Rebick also served by carrying out regression computations.
[1] Chiefly 1971 and 1972 studies, reprinted in somewhat revised form in my book (1978). See also my studies (1964; 1968), and, on methodological aspects, my paper (1975).

without much substantive gain. I also pass by a number of Third World countries that the ICP covers.

Since the completion of ICP–III, results of other related calculations, chiefly in connection with the still ongoing Phase IV of that program, have already begun to appear. For various reasons, comparison with the results of phase III is difficult, but may shed some light on the reliability of the latter.

A socialist economic system is understood here in the conventional, though admittedly controversial, way as one where ownership of the means of production is predominantly public. Among the countries in question, though, economic working arrangements (i.e., institutions, policies, and procedures determining resource use) often differ from one country to another. Thus, despite numerous highly publicized reforms, planning in the USSR and Poland in the mid-1970's was still broadly of the centralist sort, stressing bureaucratic as distinct from market coordination of production units, that originated in the USSR under Stalin. In Hungary that form of planning has given way, since 1968, to one stressing market processes, though probably not to the degree often supposed. Yugoslavia's economic system seems almost continually in flux, but here, too, market processes have tended to be in the ascendant. Also, under so-called industrial self-management, workers, at least in principle, are ultimately in control of the production unit (for which reason, Yugoslavs prefer to refer to their system as one where there is "social" rather than "public" ownership of the means of production). In both Poland and Yugoslavia, agriculture is still predominantly of the peasant as distinct from collectivized sort. Such facts should be borne in mind. Of course, economic working arrangements also often differ markedly among WME countries, and that, too, must be considered.

Also to be noted is the fact that in 1975 a poor harvest probably cost the USSR a few percent of its GNP. The year 1975 also tended to be a recession one in the West. Among countries considered, output and employment responded variously. Three countries, the United States, Germany, and Italy,

suffered absolute declines in GDP of 0.9, 1.8, and 3.6 percent, respectively.

Methodology

Resistant as comparative efficiency is to measurement, it is still advisable to be clear that I focus, as before, on production efficiency as manifest in realization of production possibilities. In the case of labor, however, attention is directed only to the use made of employed endowments, and my findings will have to be read accordingly.

In seeking insight into intersystem differences in efficiency, as so understood, I focus on this equation:

$$(1) \quad \log y = A \log k + B \log l + Md + Q.$$

Here, A, B, M and Q are constants; y is output per worker, relatively to that in the United States; k and l are capital and land per worker, similarly calculated; and d is a dummy variable denoting socialism or its absence. The constants in (1) are to be evaluated by regressing y on k, l, and d, in the light of available observations on their magnitudes. Of the different constants, M, the coefficient of d, is necessarily of particular interest. I interpret the regression relation that is obtained, however, and hence also M, in a rather novel way.

In applying (1), I evidently assume that production both in the WME countries and under socialism conforms to a log-linear version of the Cobb-Douglas formula. According to the usual understanding, that would mean determining the contribution (positive or negative) of socialism to y after normalizing, in conformity with that formula, for differences in factor inputs, as represented by k and l. The constants A and B are seen correspondingly as having the familiar status of output elasticities or comparative "earning shares" imputable to capital and land, respectively. And that is also the understanding here, but in the present context k is viewed not only as the input of capital per worker but as an indicator—it is an appealing one, I think—of a country's stage of development. In normalizing for k, therefore, I allow not only for differences in per worker capital as such, but also for additional forces affecting output per worker that are associated with the development stage.

Such forces must sometimes affect output per worker rather than efficiency; for example where, as commonly must be so, the technological knowledge of a less advanced country lags behind that of a more advanced one because of its tendency to borrow rather than generate new knowledge. Such a lag has an interest of its own, but would not exemplify efficiency in the usual sense envisaged here. Sometimes, though, efficiency too must be affected, as where a historically distorted resource allocation can be remedied only as the development process unfolds. But for our purposes, normalization is appropriate in either case, and that seemingly is accomplished by inclusion of k as an independent variable. With that, should M differ significantly from zero, that should testify that, depending on its sign, socialist countries tend to be more or less efficient than WME ones at the same stage.

Development stage is open to more than one construction, and capital per worker is not the only criterion that might be used to gauge it. That measure has a distinct advantage here, however, over a rival often employed, agriculture's share of the labor force. Thus, it does not itself depend on efficiency, as the agricultural share in the labor force clearly does. Other familiar criteria, such as output per worker and output per capita, evidently cannot serve us at all.

Formula (1) presupposes that each of the three inputs embraced is homogeneous, but in principle is easily elaborated to allow for heterogeneity. As usually so in computations such as in question, however, we must settle for something less than the ideal kind of data required, which for each input, including labor, entails the same sort of earnings-share-weighted logarithmic aggregation of varieties as that which is in effect applied in (1) in totalling the inputs of capital and land. Thus, labor will be calculated simply in physical units, though an attempt is made to allow in a conventional way for quality. Land here reduces to that employed in agriculture,

and that, too, will be computed in physical units. I try, however, to allow for quality in one outstanding case, the USSR.[2] I refer, as usually done, to a linear sum of the price-weighted volumes of different capital items.

For capital, the volumes in question properly are not of stocks but of services, and correspondingly reference should be not to the prices of capital goods but to rental rates. In practical work, however, one is usually offered a choice between two procedures, neither one of which is entirely satisfactory: to take services as proportional to gross assets, on the one hand, or to net assets, on the other. Partly because of the greater availability of relevant data, I opt for the former course, but we cannot ignore altogether that services tend to decline with age, even if not always commensurably with depreciated value. The rate of utilization also matters, though here, too, quantification is difficult.[3]

---

[2] Farm land may perhaps be viewed here as representing not only itself but other nonreproducible capital, which is not otherwise accounted for. As between the socialist and WME countries studied, in any event, there is little basis to suppose that such capital is relatively much more abundant in one case than in the other.

[3] Intercountry differences in utilization of the capital stock are manifest in diverse ways, but principally in differing shares of capacity that may be completely inoperative, and, for capacity that is in any degree operative, in differing labor hours and use of shift work. Productivity is calculated in this essay by reference to employed workers only. In the case of the capital stock, arguably a parallel treatment calls for adjustment to allow for disparities in services on all of the indicated counts. While relevant to efficiency, the import of the differences in question from that standpoint would then be reserved for separate inquiry.

Logical as it is, such procedure can be only very partially applied here. But a principal limitation is probably our inability to allow, except in respect of the resultant shortening of hours, for the reduction in capital services employed in WME countries that was associated with the 1975 recession. Perhaps it is as well, though, to have WME productivity levels deflated in that way by inclusion of recession-induced underutilization of capital.

However that may be, a question remains as to how capital services vary with indicators of utilization such as in question. If only for illustrative purposes, I shall take the relation to be one of proportionality. While often done, that is likely to overstate the variation in

I have construed the Cobb-Douglas formula in the usual way, excluding economies of scale. So far as scale economies are realized, they are reflected in output per worker, and what remains to be accounted for here is differential opportunities for such economies. Development stage apart, such opportunities presumably depend in a degree on country size. In applying (1), I accordingly explore a variant where an additional parameter, population, is introduced. The regression computation also allows another useful modification: rather than assigning but one dummy variable for all socialist countries together, such a variable is assigned separately to each.

With available data, each country's output can be compared with that of the United States in terms of both its own and U.S. prices (similarly for each country's capital stock). While prices nowhere conform fully to well-known theoretic desiderata for computations such as ours (compare my paper, 1975), they often diverge egregiously from such desiderata under socialism. It thus seems best to focus here primarily on calculations where valuations are in U.S. prices, but it will still be of interest to see how the results are affected when valuation is in other country prices.[4]

With only 11 observations, opportunities to explore alternatives to the Cobb-Douglas production function are limited. I nevertheless experimented with a partial shift to a CES formula, specifically one entailing retention of Cobb-Douglas to aggregate capital and land, but leaving the elasticity of substitution (σ) unconstrained otherwise. The resulting σ turns out, however, to be oddly negative, and not surprisingly fails to be significantly different from unity at the 10 percent level; or at the 20 percent level when labor is adjusted for quality. Reassuringly, though, results in respect of M are fully in accord with those from application of (1), to be presented below.[5]

I consider performance in the economy generally, but for familiar reasons exclude the services of personnel engaged in the provision of education and health care, and delimit correspondingly inputs of capital. In the WME, labor and capital employed in government administration, including defense, and the resultant output, are also

---

services. As easily seen, that follows from the fact that the appropriate rental rate for any given asset is given ideally by the sum of interest and depreciation on it, while any capital gain, if of an expected sort, is to be deducted (compare Laurits Christensen et al., 1981). The volume of services rendered by any given gross stock, it must also be considered, might be affected by differences in the physical structure of the capital stock, and resulting differences between relative prices and gross rentals.

Formula (1) also presupposes that output in each country is a single homogeneous product. So far as there are many products, theory allows for more than one kind of aggregation (my paper, 1975), but I must in any event opt for the usual price-weighted linear form.

[4] I am thus in effect exploring implications of both Laspeyres and Paasche index numbers—to give them their proper names. That is a somewhat cumbersome procedure, but, given the highly dubious nature of the socialist prices, it seems preferable to the alternative of focusing simply on one or another summary composite such as Fisher's "ideal" index or the relatively novel multilateral "superlative" index. The latter measures are

nevertheless still of interest but results of use of the ideal index must fairly clearly be more or less congruent with those indicated by our Laspeyres and Paasche indexes. As for the superlative index, at least at levels now of interest, resultant measures of output appear to conform quite well to those obtained by use of the ideal formula: see, for example, Christensen et al. (p. 89) and further ideal indexes in the source of ICP–II data cited there.

[5] I applied this formula:

(a) $\log y = (1/\alpha)\log[\,C + (1 - C)\bar{k}^\alpha\,] + Md + Q.$

Here $\bar{k}$ is the indicated composite of reproducible capital and land. In aggregating the two inputs, I take the needed output elasticities to be proportional to those obtained by application of (1). The terms y, d, M, and Q are understood as in (1), while α is a parameter, such that

(b) $\sigma = 1/(1 - \alpha).$

These are the resulting magnitudes of α and, for later reference, those for M, with associated T values indicated parenthetically: with labor not adjusted for quality, α, 2.425 (1.73) and M, -0.363 (8.81); with labor so adjusted, α, 2.448 (1.13); M, -0.300 (6.09). In inferring significance levels, I reduce degrees of freedom by one in order to allow for the use of previously derived factor coefficients in calculating the capital-land composite.

Table 1—Gross Domestic Material Product (GDMP), Gross Reproducible Capital Stock (GRCS), and Farm Land, per Worker, Specified Countries, 1975[a]
(USA = 100.0)

Country	Per Worker, Adjusted for Nonfarm Hours			Per Worker, Adjusted for Labor Quality		
	GDMP	GRCS	Farm Land	GDMP	GRCS	Farm Land
USA	100.0	100.0	100.0	100.0	100.0	100.0
FRG	94.1	111.0	15.4	108.3	127.8	17.7
	(76.9)	(89.0)		(88.5)	(102.4)	
France	90.7	81.7	39.4	104.4	94.0	45.4
	(71.6)	(69.3)		(82.4)	(79.7)	
Italy	71.0	71.4	28.8	81.6	82.0	33.1
	(56.7)	(68.2)		(65.2)	(78.3)	
UK	68.6	78.7	14.8	75.0	86.1	16.2
	(57.0)	(68.5)		(62.4)	(75.0)	
Japan	56.9	65.4	3.7	64.1	73.8	4.2
	(41.4)	(50.3)		(46.7)	(56.7)	
Spain	56.0	41.3	58.1	67.8	50.0	70.3
	(40.7)	(31.9)		(49.3)	(38.7)	
USSR	47.4	57.8	81.8	57.6	70.3	49.7[b]
	(30.8)	(45.2)		(37.5)	(54.9)	
Hungary	43.4	50.4	42.6	52.8	61.3	51.7
	(31.6)	(41.2)		(38.4)	(50.1)	
Poland	36.2	34.1	33.2	44.7	42.1	41.1
	(26.2)	(28.8)		(32.4)	(35.5)	
Yugoslavia	33.9	29.3	37.3	42.0	36.3	46.2
	(26.4)	(26.7)		(32.7)	(33.1)	

[a] For GDMP and GRCS, each comparison with USA is in U.S. prices; the comparisons in other countries' prices are shown in parentheses. For concepts more generally, and sources and methods, see text and the Appendix (available upon request).
[b] Farm land as well as labor adjusted for quality; see text.

properly omitted. By reference to the funding involved, particularly whether financing is through the so-called "government" budget, one can delineate and exclude labor and capital employed and the associated output in an essentially similar sphere in the socialist economies studied. So as to allow, if only arbitrarily, for the productive use of highways and streets, I omit only one-half the capital of those funds, although that is in the WME almost entirely and in our socialist economies entirely, of a governmental kind.[6]

[6] More generally, while excluding government administration from the scope of my calculations, I try, data permitting, to include in their entirety, and without regard to their ownership or administrative status, all transportation infrastructures other than highways and streets, and also the stocks employed in irrigation and conservation; and urban water supply. Urban sewage works, however, are omitted. On the scope of government administration, compare Kravis et al. (pp. 66–68).

Because of the special nature of housing services, I also omit them from output, and exclude from inputs the capital involved in their provision. No attempt is made, however, to omit from labor inputs the relatively limited number of workers so employed. I understand by "selected services" the foregoing diverse omissions. The economy generally, exclusive of those aspects, is referred to as "material sectors," though services apart from selected ones are, of course, included.

II. The Data

I have assembled here (Table 1) the basic data on output and inputs in 1975 to which (1) is to be applied. For all countries, I refer to output in material sectors; hereafter gross domestic material product (GDMP). The gross reproducible capital stock (GRCS) is of corresponding scope, and so too is the level of employment to which output, the

TABLE 2—GROSS DOMESTIC PRODUCT (GDP), GROSS DOMESTIC MATERIAL PRODUCT (GDMP),
EMPLOYMENT AND GROSS REPRODUCIBLE CAPITAL STOCK (GRCS), AND FARM LAND, PER CAPITA,
SPECIFIED COUNTRIES, 1975[a]
(USA = 100.0)

Country	GDP per Capita	GDMP per Capita	Employment per Capita				GRCS per Capita	Farm Land per Capita
			All Sectors	Material Sectors	Material Sectors Adjusted for NFH	Material Sectors, Adjusted also for Labor Quality		
USA	100.0	100.0	100.0	100.0	100.0	100.0	100.0	100.0
FRG	88.3	90.9	100.6	101.4	96.6	84.0	107.3	14.8
France	89.5	92.2	99.1	100.2	101.7	88.3	83.0	40.1
Italy	60.7	61.3	87.4	87.9	86.4	75.2	61.6	24.9
UK	73.5	67.2	109.4	102.1	98.0	89.6	77.2	14.5
Japan	75.5	82.8	115.0	128.6	145.5	129.0	95.2	5.4
Spain	62.0	64.6	91.3	101.0	115.4	95.4	47.7	67.0
USSR	60.2	60.0	125.2	132.0	126.5	104.1	73.2	103.5
Hungary	56.3	61.1	120.1	135.1	140.6	115.6	70.9	59.8
Poland	54.2	54.8	126.7	143.2	151.5	122.7	51.6	50.4
Yugoslavia	41.2	41.5	107.3	121.0	122.4	98.8	35.9	45.6

[a] Output and capital stock in U.S. prices. For concepts more generally and sources and methods, see text and the Appendix.

capital stock and farm land are related. That is so whether employment is adjusted for differences in nonfarm hours (NFH) or further adjusted for differences in labor quality.

Details on sources and methods used in compiling those data are set forth in an Appendix (available upon request); a summary account of their provenance, however, will serve among other things to bring out limitations that must be considered in applying (1). Sources and methods are much the same whether GDMP and GRCS are valued in U.S. or other country prices, but it facilitates discussion if I focus on data where the former valuation is used, and where related elements underlying Table 1 are as shown (Table 2).

Output. For all countries, GDMP is calculated by exclusion of services from GDP. For the GDP, for all countries other than the USSR, as indicated, I draw on ICP–III. The GDP of the USSR, relatively to that of the United States, is derived essentially from Imogene Edwards et al. (1979). The ICP calculations have been widely greeted as of outstanding merit, and those of Edwards et al. are also the result of an unusually systematic inquiry. In comparing Soviet and U.S. output in terms of U.S.

prices, though, Edwards et al. had to grapple somehow with the notable volume of defective or otherwise substandard goods that are produced in the USSR, apparently often to be sold at prices of standard products. Careful as the computations were, it seems doubtful that they could have allowed sufficiently for that feature. More generally, because of residual qualitative deficiencies in Soviet products that couldn't be accounted for, as the authors themselves acknowledge, their calculations could significantly overstate Soviet output.[7]

The production of substandard goods in Eastern Europe has yet to be explored in any depth. Such production on some scale has apparently been a feature wherever centralist planning prevails, and that scheme still operates in Poland. Performance regarding prod-

[7] In addition to Edwards et al., on the question of product quality as it affects calculation there of the comparative volume of Soviet output, see the sources cited in the Appendix on the ruble-dollar ratios compiled for investment goods, and Gertrude Schroeder and Edwards (1981) on those for consumer goods. On the consumption component of GDP, I have revised Edwards et al. to conform to Schroeder and Edwards.

TABLE 3—COMPARATIVE GROSS DOMESTIC PRODUCT AND EXPENDITURE PER CAPITA,
ALTERNATIVE COMPUTATIONS, SELECTED COUNTRIES, 1975[a]
(AUSTRIA = 100.0)

Country	Prices: ICP–III, 1975				Prices: APC, 1975		ICP–IV, 1980 Extrapolated to 1975
	U.S.	International	Austrian	Other Country's	Austrian	Other Country's	
GDP, less Net Exports, per Capita							
Austria			100.0	100.0	100	100	
Poland			80.9	64.9	67	54	
GDP per Capita							
Austria	100.0	100.0	100.0	100.0			100.0
Hungary	73.6	71.3	79.0	64.1			58.6
Poland	70.8	72.0	77.3	60.9			60.1
Yugoslavia	53.9	51.9	55.7	49.1			45.5
FRG	115.4	119.2					116.0
							(119.5)
France	117.0	117.7					115.2
							(117.6)
Italy	79.3	77.3					89.6
							(83.5)
UK	96.1	91.9					103.7
							(100.7)
Spain	81.0	80.3					81.7

[a]*Sources*: For ICP–III, Kravis et al.; for APC, A. Franz et al. The ICP–IV data for 1980 are from UN Statistical Commission and Economic Commission for Europe (1985), retrapolated to 1975 by reference, for WME countries, to GDP and population in OECD (1982a); for Poland and Hungary, to GNP and population in Thad Alton et al. (1983) and SEV (1981), and for Yugoslavia, to GNP in OECD (1982b) and to de facto population in Appendix Table 1 and as inferred from OECD (1982b). On ICP–III international prices, ICP–IV prices, and alternative figures in parentheses, see fn. 8.

uct quality in Hungary and Yugoslavia, though, is often assumed to have benefited from the increased reliance there on market processes.

We must also consider, however, further calculations of comparative output in Austria and Poland (APC) made collaboratively by the national statistical offices of the two countries; and of comparative output in Austria, Poland, Hungary, and Yugoslavia, made as part of ICP–IV. The latter calculations likewise involved a joint effort on the part of the countries concerned, though with Austria exercising primary responsibility. Because of the different valuation standards applied, and, in the case of ICP–IV, the focus on 1980, the import of these further inquiries for the reliability of our ICP–III data on comparative GDP in East European countries and the United States in 1975 in U.S. prices is not easy to judge. Juxtaposition of the alternative measures with related ICP–III results, however, seems to underline

for Hungary and Yugoslavia as well as Poland, that the ICP–III data on GDP per capita are more likely to err in the direction of over- than of underestimation (Table 3). Further ICP–IV measures for Western European countries seem more or less consistent with those of ICP–III. For Italy and the United Kingdom, though, ICP–III may have underestimated GDP per capita somewhat in relation to other European countries.[8]

[8] In ICP–IV, comparative Austrian-Eastern European output is calculated essentially in terms of a weighted average of relative prices in the three Eastern European countries, Austria, and Finland. ICP–IV comparative data for Austria and Western European countries are calculated essentially in terms of average relative prices of ten EEC member countries. ICP–III international prices purportedly represent similar averages of global scope. While ICP–IV data for 1980 are retrapolated to 1975 by reference to comparative trends in real GDP (GNP) per capita, I also show parenthetically corresponding measures obtained after partial adjustment for

Employment. I utilize here data on numbers employed and NFH drawn mainly from OECD, other Western and socialist official sources, and ICP–III. The results are unavoidably inexact, but there is no basis to suppose a bias here might offset that very possibly affecting socialist GDP per capita. I allow in a usual, Denison-like way for labor quality, as that is affected by differences in hours, sex structure, and educational attainment, and also draw on Edward Denison (1979) for earnings weights needed in the computations. As is well-known, such calculations even at best have their limitations; because of deficiencies in available data, they are not at their best here.[9] For that reason, I apply (1) to data on output and inputs both before and after adjustment for labor quality.

Capital Stock. In calculating GRCS in terms of U.S. prices of 1975, I apply to data on stocks in national currencies purchasing power parities (*PPP*s) relating to producer's durables, construction and the GDMP generally that were used in the calculation of output in U.S. prices of 1975. The data on socialist output in terms of U.S. prices of 1975, though, may well be overestimates. If they are, the cause should be the overvaluation of socialist currencies in terms of dollars. Such an overvaluation, then, may also occur at this point, and correspondingly

an overstatement of socialist stocks of reproducible capital per worker.

As for the gross reproducible capital stocks in national currencies, the dominant element here is fixed capital. For all Western countries except Spain, I could draw on results of substantial inquiries, usually of the perpetual inventory sort. While that procedure is subject to familiar limitations, resultant errors need not be in one direction rather than the other.[10] For Italy, gross stocks had to be estimated from data computed on net stocks. For Japan, I extrapolate from results of an official wealth survey for December 31, 1970. No data are at hand on Spain's fixed capital stock. Relatively to that of the United States, I take Spain's stock to be of the same magnitude as its aggregate 1960–74 volume of investment in fixed capital (excluding housing) is relatively to the corresponding U.S. total. Fixed capital investment (excluding housing) has lately been growing rapidly in Spain—over the decadal interval 1960–64 to 1970–74, by 10.6 percent yearly. In taking comparative investment volume during 1960–74 as a yardstick, I may have overestimated Spain's terminal stock.

For socialist countries, I draw on official data that derive in each case primarily from *ad hoc* surveys of fixed assets on hand at particular dates. The statistical agencies concerned apparently expand the survey results into serial data by reference to current new investment and retirements. Asset surveys such as are in question have, in the case of the USSR, been subject to close Western scrutiny with results that are reassuring as to their substantial reliability. More generally, the socialist official data have their limitations, but there should not be any systematically consequential overstatement.[11]

---

disparate volume trends in final use categories: see Eurostat (1983, p. 115); as confirmed by Hugo Krijnse Locker (letter of April 25, 1984), relevant figures cited there for Germany and Italy should be corrected to read (−) 2.9 and (+) 7.3, respectively.

Compared to ICP–III, both APC and ICP–IV have the virtue of using more voluminous price data in deriving *PPP*s needed to translate outlays from one currency to another. In ICP–III, though, a novel "country product dummy" (CPD) method was used to augment price quotations.

[9]Among other things, for Spain I assume average educational attainment of male workers is the same as for Italy. While the adjustment for labor quality, where GDMP and GRCS are in U.S. prices, has its limitations, the earnings weights at least properly reflect U.S. values. Where GDMP and GRCS are in other country prices, corresponding earnings weights are not at hand, so I apply again those reflecting U.S. values. One might wish to derive weights for different qualitative features, along with constants such as in (1), by regression analysis, but that is not feasible here.

[10]Among the more troubling features is the introduction, either implicitly or explicitly, of assumptions as to asset longevity that are often of doubtful validity. Simulations made for the United States and United Kingdom, however, suggest that resulting stocks are probably not as sensitive as might be supposed to error at this point: see U.S. Department of Commerce Bureau of Economic Analysis (1982, pp. T–13ff, 1, 197); J. Hibbert et al. (1977, pp. 124–25).

[11]On Soviet surveys of the fixed capital stock, see Raymond Powell (1979) and the sources cited there.

(Continued)

Although capital services cannot be expected to correspond to the depreciated value of an asset, as noted, they tend to decline to some extent with its age. Hence, relatively to the gross values that I record, services can be expected to vary so far as the assets in question differ in age. Such variation could be material here, since service lives of capital goods appear to be relatively lengthy in

---

Granting that these inquiries inspire confidence, the official data drawn on here for 1975 had to be derived from a survey for 1971–72. The official measures of "real" investment volume that must have been used in such a calculation have lately been held likely to overstate growth in that aspect. Very possibly, they do in a degree (see my forthcoming study), but for the 3–4 year interval for which their use is in question here, the effect on the official stock data for 1975 must have been quite limited.

The last fixed capital stock survey date before 1975 was for Hungary, 1968; Poland, 1960; and Yugoslavia, 1953. Should there be any upward bias in official data for real investment volume for these countries, it might seem the cumulative effect on stocks reported for 1975 could be significant. In official serial data, however, while stocks are initially valued at prices prevailing around the date of a survey, they subsequently are adjusted for price level changes. The adjustment seems clearly to have involved application of price index numbers that are complementary to the official measures of "real" fixed investment: compare with due allowance for presumable aggregation differences, the implied deflators for capital formation and stocks in UN national accounts yearbooks and successive editions of the statistical yearbooks on which I draw for capital stock data in the Appendix. In finally translating the official stock data, as necessary, to 1975 prices, I myself essentially apply implied investment deflators.

Should official measures of real investment volume be subject to an upward bias, therefore, the price index numbers used to update capital stock values must be subject to a downward one. On balance, as readily seen, the result should be an understatement of the fixed capital stock in 1975 prices. I have, nevertheless, been informed by Leszek Zienkowski of the Polish statistical office (letter of October 28, 1982) that the official data overstate Polish stocks. The grounds for that opinion are not clear. Possibly the Polish capital stock is relatively aged (see below). For Yugoslavia, the correspondence of capital stock inflation and investment deflation could be established only in respect of a capital stock revaluation from 1966 to 1972 prices, but judging from calculations of Ivo Vinski (see the Appendix), the fixed capital stock of 1975 could be some 8.8 percent greater than has been estimated here. While I rely primarily on official data, I have referred to Vinski to fill in some gaps.

socialist countries. The resultant disproportion between services and gross capital stock, though, should not be too great, for at relevant tempos of growth the share of superannuated goods in the capital stocks of the socialist countries must be rather limited. There is more than that to the question of comparative services and gross capital stocks, but further biases that can be discerned in my measures of capital inputs at this point are by no means unidirectional. Overall, however, some relative overestimation of socialist capital services is not precluded.[12]

Farm Land. Understood essentially as arable land, including land under permanent cultivation, this is represented simply by its acreage as determined from standard sources. In calculating factor productivity with labor adjusted for quality, however, I also reduce farm land in the USSR by one-half, that discount being suggested by reference to U.S. climatic analogues (see my study, 1964, p. 379).

Comment. Relatively to each other, output and employment per capita have been found sometimes to vary rather differently for the whole economy and material sectors (Table 2). Such incongruities must be read, however, in the light of the relatively high U.S. prices of selective services employment, which in a number of countries tends markedly to inflate their product relatively to that of material sector workers (compare Kravis et al., pp. 191 ff.). The notably high socialist ratios of employment to population that are observed are, of course, mainly an expression of the well-known tendency in socialist countries to high rates of labor par-

---

[12] Differences in the relation of services to gross stocks also result from differences in the use of shift work and in working hours, and the inclusion in gross stocks, as calculated, of varying amounts of unfinished construction. From often notional calculations, I judge that with allowance for those aspects our measures of GRCS per worker, adjusted for NFH, might have to be further adjusted by these amounts, in percentage points with the United States as 100.0: FRG (−) 6.7; France (−) 0.8; Italy (−) 2.9; U.K. (−) 4.2; Japan 3.5; Spain 4.0; USSR (−) 0.6; Hungary 3.6; Poland 2.8; Yugoslavia 0.8. On the foregoing, and on services more generally, including the possible import of differences in service lives and growth, see fn. 3 and the Appendix.

ticipation.[13] Employment per capita is also high in Japan, however, and the relative labor input in that country is the greater because of the long hours there. Hours are also long in Spain, but overall hours are not too different in WME and socialist countries. Owing chiefly to their comparatively limited educational attainment, all countries other than the United States—both socialist and WME—experience a decline in per capita labor inputs compared to the USA when an adjustment is made for quality (Table 2). Here too, though, Japan is rather special since educational attainment there compares favorably with that everywhere but in the United States.

Much has been written lately about the so-called "second economy" of the socialist countries. As not always made clear, many of the undertakings referred to are quite legal, but by all accounts there has been a proliferation in the course of time of diverse quasi-legal (i.e., not officially approved or disapproved) and illegal economic activities. The under coverage of economic data that almost inevitably results, however, apparently affects inputs as well as outputs. Also, activities in question relate solely to private enterprise, while reported statistics are inclu-

sive of the socialized sector which is of primary concern here. Of course, underreporting is not confined to socialist countries, but for the WME, too, the reported data retain interest.[14]

III. Results

With GDMP valued in U.S. prices, output per worker is found to vary widely among both WME and socialist countries, but for all the latter it falls distinctly short of levels attained in the former. With employment adjusted for NFH, output per worker among WME is at the least 56.0 percent of that of the United States, while among socialist countries it varies from 33.9 to 47.4 percent of the United States (Table 1). With employment adjusted also for quality, the corresponding minimal WME level is 67.8 percent, while among socialist countries output per worker ranges from 42.0 to 57.6 percent of the U.S. level. Chiefly because of the possible overvaluation of socialist currencies in terms of dollars, my calculation may understate the margin between WME and socialist countries in respect of output per worker.

Among diverse regressions computed on sources of that gap, I refer first to a number where employment has been adjusted for NFH but not for quality. Of these, priority is accorded one (Table 4, I–1) simply applying formula (1) to relevant data (Table 1).

[13] In this essay employment is understood to be of the domestic sort in the country concerned, and thus inclusive of foreign workers employed there. That is as it should be where employment is juxtaposed with "domestic," as distinct from "national," output. The corollary, though, is that employment for a country excludes its workers abroad. That should be considered in construing the cited data on employment per capita, especially those for Italy, Spain and Yugoslavia. In the case of the latter, workers abroad are particularly numerous.

Prescribed Western national income accounting procedures for dealing with earnings of foreign workers (UN, 1968, p. 93) are rather complex, and can hardly be adhered to always, even among Western countries. Available employment data also seem unlikely to be entirely congruent with GDP as actually computed. Among socialist countries, however, workers abroad are consequentially only for Yugoslavia, and such workers are known to be generally excluded from Yugoslav employment data as recorded in this essay. Any error to speak of here thus should be on the side of improper inclusion of remittances in, and hence of overstatement of, Yugoslav GDP, and presumably of GDMP per worker.

[14] At least for the USSR, the undercoverage due to second-economy activities probably is not as great as often imagined. Taking retrospective emigre budgets for 1972–74 as a point of departure, Gur Ofer and Aaron Vinokur (1980, p. 51) conclude that omissions from urban household incomes may come to 3–4 percent of the GNP. The cited figures would not reflect significant illegal rural activities (probably mainly distilling), but second-economy output must often be overpriced. For Hungary there are indications that at the time studied, activities such as in question may have been relatively to GNP much more extensive than in the USSR. While our data should be inclusive in respect of the socialized sector, they must understate productivity there to some extent so far as socialist inputs are reportedly sometimes appropriated for private use, for example, state materials are pilfered for use in private construction.

TABLE 4—ALTERNATIVE REGRESSIONS WITH OUTPUT PER WORKER, ADJUSTED FOR NFH, AS DEPENDENT VARIABLE, 1975[a]

Regression	Scope of Dummy Variable	R^2	Regression Coefficient				
			A	B	M	N	Q
I–1	Socialist Countries	.970	.560 (8.22)	.092 (3.85)	−.351 (5.77)		−.001 (0.018)
I–2	Socialist Countries	.976 ⎫			−.397 (6.01) ⎫		
I–3	Socialist Countries	.976 ⎭	.560 (8.22)	.092 (3.85)	−.331 (4.58) ⎭		.001 (0.018)
I–4a	USSR ⎫				−.409 (5.38) ⎫		
I–4b	Hungary				−.343 (4.54)		
I–4c	Poland	.972	.644 (8.08)	.101 (4.27)	−.247 (2.67)		.036 (0.76)
I–4d	Yugoslavia ⎭				−.227 (2.24) ⎭		
I–5	Socialist Countries	.969	.589 (7.60)	.096 (3.86)	−.351 (5.64)	−.023 (0.85)	−.013 (0.28)
I–6	Socialist Countries	.949	.645 (6.27)	.102 (2.63)	−.410 (4.20)		−.075 (1.01)

[a] The T-statistics are shown in parentheses, each having the sign of the coefficient to which it relates. R has been adjusted. For purposes of the computations, output and inputs per worker and population are expressed in relation to USA = 1.000.

The striking result is that with R^2 as high as .970, a dummy variable standing for socialism has a negative coefficient, M, significant at the 1.0 percent level. Judging from the magnitude of the coefficient, −.351, output per worker under socialism, tends to be 29.6 percent below that in a WME country.

The two other variables considered, capital and farm land per worker, also have the regression coefficients, A and B, respectively, that are significant at the 1.0 percent level. The coefficient for capital, .56, is distinctly larger than the corresponding "earnings share" that is often imputed to capital in factor-productivity studies for the more advanced WME countries. That is not surprising, since capital per worker represents here not only the corresponding input but also the stage of development. An increase in capital per worker thus predictably has a more pronounced impact on output per worker than factor earnings imputable to capital in an advanced WME country might indicate.

In I–2 and I–3 (Table 4) all is as in I–1, except that I now allow illustratively for the possible overvaluation of socialist national currencies in U.S. dollars. I consider here that as a result socialist capital stocks as well as outputs may be overstated. In I–2, I reduce both the output and capital per worker of socialist countries by 10 percent. In I–3, their output per worker is cut by 10 percent and their capital per worker by 20 percent. With either adjustment, all is essentially as in I–1, with the dummy variable for socialism still having a negative coefficient significant at the 1.0 percent level. The coefficient, however, is now a somewhat larger negative in I–2 and a somewhat smaller negative in I–3 than it was in I–1. Consequently, while socialism in I–1 underperforms a WME country by 29.6 percent, the corresponding shortfall under I–2 is 32.8 and under I–3, 28.2 percent. Not shown in the table is another computation which, while allowing for possible overvaluation of socialist national currencies, also adjusts, often

TABLE 5—ALTERNATIVE REGRESSIONS WITH OUTPUT PER WORKER, ADJUSTED FOR NFH AND LABOR QUALITY, AS DEPENDENT VARIABLE, 1975[a]

Regression	Scope of Dummy Variable	R^2	Regression Coefficient				
			A	B	M	N	Q
II–1	Socialist Countries	.962	.567 (7.87)	.098 (3.98)	−.304 (5.45)		.047 (1.14)
II–2	Socialist Countries	.971	.567 (7.87)	.098 (3.98)	−.350 (5.73)		.047 (1.14)
II–3	Socialist Countries	.971			−.283 (4.20)		
II–4a	USSR				−.320 (3.89)		
II–4b	Hungary	.950	.637 (6.13)	.101 (3.56)	−.324 (3.73)		.063 (1.26)
II–4c	Poland				−.228 (2.13)		
II–4d	Yugoslavia				−.208 (1.76)		
II–5	Socialist Countries	.958	.585 (7.04)	.098 (3.78)	−.304 (5.17)	−.014 (0.55)	.034 (0.69)
II–6	Socialist Countries	.954	.631 (6.76)	.115 (3.44)	−.386 (5.00)		−.032 (0.54)

[a] See Table 4. In the case of the USSR, land as well as labor has been adjusted for quality.

speculatively, for possible divergencies between capital stocks and services. That computation too hardly improves the socialist performance.[15]

In I–4a to I–4d (Table 4), I again repeat the calculations made for I–1, but separate dummy variables are assigned to the different socialist countries. With this, R^2 and the results for capital and land are more or less comparable to what they were in I–1. In all cases, too, socialism still has a negative

[15] The calculation allows as before for an overestimation of socialist GDMP by 10 percent and an overestimation of socialist capital inputs by 20 percent. The latter distortion could again be due simply to overvaluation of socialist currencies, but possibly it reflects also some comparative superannuation of socialist capital assets, with a resultant impairment of services. Additionally, I allow, for all countries, as in fn. 12 above, for differences in hours, shift work, and unfinished construction. The dummy variable for socialism, again significant at the 1.0 percent level, is now of a magnitude, (−) .309, implying a 26.6 percent shortfall of socialist output per worker below WME levels. For the rest, the results are essentially as before, though the coefficient for capital per worker increases to .620.

coefficient. The magnitude of the latter varies, the negatives obtained for Poland and Yugoslavia being smaller than those for Hungary and the USSR. With the marked reduction in degrees of freedom, however, significance levels for the socialist coefficients decline, and for Yugoslavia the negative coefficient is reliable at little better than the 10 percent level. Intriguing as such contrasts are, note that they are especially affected by data limitations.

None of the regressions considered thus far allows for the possibility that output per worker might be affected by differing opportunities to exploit economies of scale. In a further computation (Table 4, I–5), I try to test that possibility by introducing into (1) an additional term, $N \log P$, where P is population and N is a coefficient to be determined. Evidently N has the wrong sign and is not significant at any interesting level. Other results, though, are almost the same as in I–1.

I have referred to regressions where labor is adjusted for nonfarm hours. When allowance is made also for labor quality, and

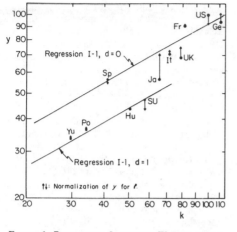

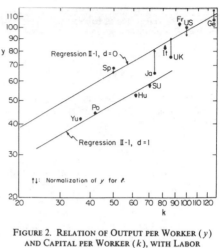

FIGURE 1. RELATION OF OUTPUT PER WORKER (y) TO CAPITAL PER WORKER (k) WITH LAND PER WORKER (l) ADJUSTED TO MEAN VALUE

FIGURE 2. RELATION OF OUTPUT PER WORKER (y) AND CAPITAL PER WORKER (k), WITH LABOR ADJUSTED FOR QUALITY AND LAND PER WORKER (l) ADJUSTED TO MEAN VALUE

each computation is repeated, the results are much as before (Table 5). Socialism, however, now performs somewhat better than previously, for example, with labor adjusted for quality, as in II–1, output per worker under socialism is found to fall short of the WME level by 26.2 percent, instead of 29.6 percent as in the corresponding regression I–1, without such adjustment. The result is again significant at the 1.0 percent level. When separate dummy variables are assigned to the different socialist countries (II–4a to II–4d), they are again negative in all cases, but for Poland only at a 10 percent level and for Yugoslavia not even at that significance level.

With other country prices superseding those of the United States, GDMP per worker for WME countries other than the United States tend to compare less favorably with that country than they did before (Table 1). But, despite limitations of socialist prices, that familiar index number effect also holds for socialist countries. Hence, output per worker there continues to fall distinctly below WME levels. When (1) is applied, the dummy variable standing for socialism is again negative at the 1.0 percent level, and indicates a shortfall in socialist performance

somewhat greater than that observed previously: by 33.6 percent when employment is adjusted for NFH and by 32.0 percent with further adjustment of employment for quality (Table 4, I–6; Table 5, II–6). Coefficients for capital and land per worker are much the same as before, though that for land now falls somewhat short of the 1.0 percent significance level.

By normalizing for land per worker, we can graph in two dimensions relations between output and capital per worker that have been described. With particular reference to regressions I–1 and II–1, the result (Figures 1 and 2) underlines what was already evident, that the calculated regression relations fit strikingly well the data they summarize. Interestingly, land, despite its relatively modest coefficient, turns out to be a consequential source of deviant productivity levels in some countries, especially the United Kingdom and Japan. The charts also illustrate, however, a feature alluded to at the outset: the lack of observations for WME countries at lower socialist levels of capital per worker. Granting the notably favorable T-statistics, my findings at such levels represent an extrapolation that remains to be tested by further observations for WME countries. The same sort of caveat applies also where reference is to very high levels of capital per worker not yet experienced in the socialist world.[16]

IV. Conclusions

My principal conclusions are already fairly evident. Essentially, output per worker under socialism, as exemplified by the USSR, Hungary, Poland, and Yugoslavia, is found systematically to fall short of that in Western mixed-economy (WME) countries, such as the United States, the FRG, France, Italy, the United Kingdom, Japan, and Spain. I refer to output per worker in "material sectors," that is, the economy generally, exclusive of diverse services and housing; and to a residual discrepancy in that aspect that remains after allowance for differences in reproducible capital and land per worker.

As indicated by regression computations, the shortfall of socialist output per worker relative to that in WME countries is significant at the 1.0 percent level and of a magnitude ranging from 25 to 34 percent, the precise figure depending on whether allowance is made for differences in labor quality and possible data deficiencies, and also whether output and capital are valued in U.S. prices or, in each comparison with the United States, in the prices of the other country.

While comparative productivity is the immediate concern, the more ultimate one is comparative efficiency. The observed difference in performance between socialist and WME countries regarding output per worker should reflect any difference in efficiency between the two sorts of economic systems represented. In my regression calculations, however, I in effect normalize for conventional inputs, but fail to allow for a possible difference in technological knowledge. Reflecting variations in generation and borrowing of new knowledge, such a difference

would not connote a difference in efficiency in the accepted sense understood in this essay. Once available in one country, however, technological knowledge seems soon to become available in another, and where it varies must often do so in dependence on a country's development stage. So far as it does, my calculations should in fact discount for it appropriately.

Thus, reproducible capital per worker, while representing the comparative inputs of the two factors, may also be viewed as an indicator of the development stage. Normalization for that coefficient, then, in effect normalizes as well for related differences in technological knowledge. The further result, also to the good, is normalization for the development stage more generally.[17]

The foregoing are results of regression computations where a single dummy variable stands for socialism in all four such countries considered. In further computations, where separate dummy variables are assigned to different socialist countries, the corresponding coefficients are still all negative. While with the reduction in degrees of freedom significance levels also deteriorate, the results appear to be consistent with those

---

[16]Judging from the graphs, output per worker under socialism not only falls short of but also may increase less rapidly with capital per worker than in WME countries.

[17]In seeking to acquire advanced technologies, the socialist countries in particular have doubtless been impeded by Western strategic controls, especially in some high-technology sectors. But the controls, directed primarily at military related technologies, have by all accounts been rather leaky. True, if the USSR is at all indicative, the socialist countries tend to lag behind the West in respect of civilian technologies, and perhaps more than might be expected of countries at their stage. But they have been able to obtain Western technologies on a vast scale, and if their technological levels tend to be unduly low, reasons enough can be found in the limitations of their own innovation processes. See my study (1983) and further works cited there on the Soviet experience in that sphere.

Economic advance results, among other things, from learning by doing. That is a process that takes time. May not our normalization, after all, be faulty so far as socialist countries, while accumulating capital relatively rapidly, have in effect had less time to learn? To a degree perhaps it is, but among WME countries, capital stock growth has been notably speedy in Japan and probably also in Spain. Yet output per worker in Japan falls but 2.1 percent below the norm for its input levels (under regression I–1). For Spain, too, there is a shortfall, but only of 3.3 percent.

of my earlier inquiry (1978, ch. 7) indicating that in respect of productivity the USSR was distinctly outclassed by a number of Western countries. My findings are still to be validated, however, by observations on WME performance at relatively early and on socialist performance at late development stages. The results for different socialist countries, in any event, differ to some extent, and divergencies in their economic working arrangements could be a cause. Without further inquiry, extension of our findings to other very different schemes could be hazardous.

I have assumed throughout that economic performance depends only on economic working arrangements. In complex ways still only imperfectly understood, such performance must also depend on the social system more generally—and that, Marx notwithstanding, can vary in a degree independently of the economic system. Quite similar economic systems might conceivably prevail and perform differently in different social contexts. The socialist schemes represented here thus might possibly perform better in another milieu. Such a qualified potentiality, however, is not what proponents of socialism have usually claimed for that system.

REFERENCES

Alton, Thad P. et al., *Economic Growth in Eastern Europe, 1965, 1970 and 1975–1982*, Occasional Paper 75, New York: L. W. International Financial Research, 1983.

Bergson, Abram, *Economics of Soviet Planning*, New Haven: Yale University Press, 1964.

_____, *Planning and Productivity under Soviet Socialism*, New York: Columbia University Press, 1968.

_____, "Index Numbers and the Computation of Factor Productivity," *Review of Income and Wealth*, September 1975, *21*, 259–78.

_____, *Productivity and the Social System —The USSR and the West*, Cambridge: Harvard University Press, 1978.

_____, "Technological Progress," in his and Herbert S. Levine, eds., *The Soviet Economy: Toward the Year 2000*, London: Allen and Unwin, 1983.*

_____, "On Soviet Real Investment Growth," *Soviet Studies* (forthcoming).**

Cristensen, Laurits R., Cummings, Dianne and Jorgenson, Dale W., "Relative Productivity Levels, 1947–1973: An International Comparison," *European Economic Review*, May 1981, *16*, 61–94.

Denison, Edward F., *Accounting for Slower Economic Growth*, Washington: The Brookings Institution, 1979.

Edwards, Imogene, Hughes, Margaret and Noren, James, "U.S. and U.S.S.R. Comparisons of GNP," in Joint Economic Committee, U.S. Congress, *Soviet Economy in a Time of Change*, Vol. 1, Washington: USGPO, 1979.

Franz, A. et al., "Comparison of Prices and Levels of Gross Domestic Expenditures between Austria and Poland (APC), 1975 and 1978," *Statistical Journal of the United Nations Economic Commission for Europe*, 1982, 125–41.

Hibbert, J., Griffin, T. J. and Walker, R. L., "Development of Estimates of the Stock of Fixed Capital in the United Kingdom," *Review of Income and Wealth*, September 1977, *23*, 117–35.

Kravis, Irving B., Heston, Alan and Summers, Robert, *World Product and Income*, Baltimore: Johns Hopkins University Press: 1982.

Ofer, Gur and Vinokur, Aaron, *Private Sources of Income of the Soviet Urban Household*, R-2359 NA, Santa Monica: Rand Corporation, August 1980.

Powell, Raymond P., "The Soviet Capital Stock from Census to Census," *Soviet Studies*, January 1979, *31*, 56–75.

Schroeder, Gertrude E. and Edwards, Imogene, *Consumption in the USSR, An International Comparison*, Joint Economic Committee, U.S. Congress, Washington: USGPO, 1981.

European Economic Community Statistical Office, (Eurostat), *Comparison in Real Values of the Aggregates of ESA 1980*, Luxembourg: Eurostat, 1983.

Organization for Economic Cooperation and Development, (OECD), (1982a) *National Accounts*, Vol. 1, *1951–1980*, Paris: OECD, 1982.

* See Chapter 6.
** See Chapter 12.

_____, (1982b) *Economic Surveys 1981–1982 Yugoslavia*, Paris: OECD, 1982.

Sovet Ekonomicheskoi Vzaimopomoshchi, (SEV), *Statisticheskii Ezhegodnik Stran-Chlenov Soveta Ekomicheskoi Vzaimopomoshchi 1981*, Moscow, 1981.

United Nations, *A System of National Accounts*, New York: United Nations, 1968.

_____, Statistical Commission and Economic Commission for Europe, *International Comparison of Gross Domestic Product in Europe 1980*, New York: United Nations, 1985.

U.S. Department of Commerce, Bureau of Economic Analysis, *Fixed Reproducible Tangible Wealth in the United States, 1925–79*, Washington: USGPO, 1982.

Appendix Tables

The tables following are taken from an appendix giving details of sources and methods for the more basic data in Chapter 2. The appendix is available upon request from the author.

Appendix Table 1
Population, Specified Countries, 1975 (millions)

Country	Population, mid-year
USA	213.566
Germany	61.829
France	52.748
Italy	55.830
UK	55.981
Japan	111.566
Spain	35.515
USSR	254.4
Hungary	10.541
Poland	34.022
Yugoslavia	20.110

Appendix Table 2
Gross Domestic Product (GDP), Selected Services, and Gross Domestic Material Product (GDMP), per Capita, Specified Countries, 1975 (U.S. 1975 dollars)

Country	GDP per capita (1)	Selected services per capita (2)	GDMP per capita (3)
USA	7,176.7	1,869.4	5,307.3
Germany	6,339.7	1,514.2	4,825.5
France	6,420.1	1,525.3	4,894.8
Italy	4,359.8	1,104.8	3,255.0
UK	5,271.9	1,706.8	3,565.1
Japan	5,415.8	1,024.2	4,391.6
Spain	4,446.1	1,014.1	3,432.0
USSR	4,307[a]	1,113[a]	3,194[a]
Hungary	4,041.7	800.5	3,241.2
Poland	3,890.0	979.0	2,911.0
Yugoslavia	2,955.8	751.2	2,204.6

[a] Data refer to GNP and are not fully comparable otherwise to figures cited for other countries. Corresponding per capita figures for the USA are: for GNP, 7,158; for selected services, 1,832; for GNP excluding selected services, 5,326.

Appendix Table 3
Elements in Calculation of Comparative Gross National Product (GNP), Excluding Selected Services, USSR, 1976 (billions of 1976 dollars)

Item	USSR (1)	USA (2)
GNP, unadjusted	1,253	1,700
Adjustment of consumption	(−) 31	(+) 15
GNP adjusted	1,222	1,715
Less labor services in:		
(1) Health care	89.5	77.5
(2) Education	91.2	81.9
(3) Government, other than defense	60.9	85.2
(4) Defense	43.4	24.4
(5) Housing[a]	30.7	169.5
(6) Selected services, all	315.7	438.5
GNP, less selected services	906	1,276

[a] Gross rent, excluding fuel and power.

Appendix Table 4
Employment in All Sectors, Selected Services, and Materials Sectors, Specified Countries, 1975 (thousands)

Country	Employment, all sectors (1)	Employment, selected services (2)	Employment, material sectors (3)
USA	86,963	18,547	68,416
Germany	25,323	5,232	20,091
France	21,280	4,339	16,941
Italy	19,868	4,145	15,723
UK	24,929	6,628	18,301
Japan	52,230	6,253	45,977
Spain	13,206	1,710	11,496
USSR	129,741	22,192	107,549
Hungary	5,157	596	4,561
Poland	17,549	1,941	15,608
Yugoslavia	8,783 (9,723)[a]	988	7,795

[a] The parenthetic figure includes 940,000 persons working abroad.

Appendix Table 5
Employment in Selected Services, Specified Countries, 1975 (thousands)

Country	All selected services (1)	Education and health care (2)	Government, including armed forces (3)
USA	18,547	9,874	8,673
Germany	5,232	1,990	3,242
France	4,339	2,363	1,976
Italy	4,145	1,990	2,155
UK	6,628	3,080	3,548
Japan	6,253	n.a.[a]	n.a.
Spain	1,710	n.a.	n.a.
USSR	22,192	13,551	8,641
Hungary	596	407	189
Poland	1,941	1,218	723
Yugoslavia	988	497	491

[a] n.a.: not available.

Appendix Table 6
Employment by Sector and Sex, Specified Countries, 1975 (thousands)

Country	All material sectors			Agriculture extended			Non-farm sectors		
	M+F (1)	M (2)	F (3)	M+F (4)	M (5)	F (6)	M+F (7)	M (8)	F (9)
USA	68,416	44,091	24,325	3,476	2,882	593	64,940	41,209	23,732
Germany	20,091	13,124	6,967	1,823	854	969	18,268	12,270	5,998
France	16,941	11,176	5,765	2,104	986	1,118	14,837	10,190	4,647
Italy	15,723	11,877	3,846	3,274	2,165	1,109	12,449	9,712	2,737
UK	18,301	12,236	6,065	668	534	134	17,633	11,702	5,931
Japan	45,977	29,160	16,817	6,610	3,300	3,310	39,367	25,860	13,507
Spain	11,496	8,505	2,991	2,872	2,140	732	8,624	6,365	2,259
USSR	105,549	55,278	52,271	28,453	13,515	14,938	79,096	41,763	37,333
Hungary	4,561	2,750	1,811	980	623	357	3,581	2,127	1,454
Poland	15,608	9,159	6,449	5,017	2,666	2,350	10,591	6,493	4,099
Yugoslavia	7,795	5,048	2,747	3,294	1,943	1,351	4,501	3,105	1,369

Appendix Table 7
Average Weekly Hours, Non-farm Workers, Specified Countries, 1975

Country	Average weekly hours (1)	Average weekly hours (USA = 100.0) (2)	Average weekly hours, adjusted for quality (USA = 100) (3)
USA	36.25	100.0	100.0
Germany	34.35	94.8	96.4
France	36.83	101.6	101.1
Italy	35.46	97.8	98.5
UK	34.77	95.9	97.1
Japan	41.81	115.3	110.7
Spain	43.10	118.9	113.2
USSR	34.23	94.4	96.1
Hungary	38.12	105.2	103.6
Poland	39.38	108.6	106.0
Yugoslavia	37.00	102.1	101.5

Appendix Table 8
Indexes of Educational Quality of Male Workers,
Specified Countries and Dates

Country	Date (1)	Index, male eighth-grade equivalent = 100.0 (2)	Corresponding US index (3)	Index USA = 100.0 (4)
USA	...[a]	...[a]	...[a]	100.0
Germany	1964	105.49	123.83	85.2
France	1968	110.82	125.65	88.2
Italy	1966	101.79	124.79	81.6
UK	1972	115.16	129.29	89.1
Japan	1970	116.25	125.99	92.3
Spain	...[b]	...[b]	...[b]	81.6[b]
USSR	1970	111.56	127.51	87.5
Hungary	1970	108.62	127.51	85.2
Poland	1970	108.36	127.51	85.0
Yugoslavia	1971	103.82	128.51	80.8

[a] For USA, date and index vary with the other country compared with it.

[b] Index, with USA = 100.0, assumed as for Italy.

Appendix Table 9
**Gross Stock of Reproducible Fixed Capital, Material Sectors,
Specified Countries, July 1, 1975, in National and U.S. Prices
of that Year (billions)**

Country	In national prices of 1975 (1)	In US prices of 1975 (2)
USA	2,752.6	2,752.6
Germany	2,123.5	868.9
France	2,562.1	533.5
Italy	281,857	426.8
UK	266.9	539.5
Japan	327,929	1,337.5
Spain	n.a.[a]	186.6
USSR	823[b]	2,176
Hungary	1,383.7	78.7
Poland	3,641	188.2
Yugoslavia	1,394.2	77.6

[a] n.a. = not available.
[b] In 1973 prices.

Appendix Table 10
**Inventories, Material Sectors, Specified Countries, July 1, 1975, in National
and U.S. Prices of that year (billions)**

Country	In national prices of 1975 (1)	In US prices of 1975 (2)
USA	332.4	332.4
Germany	244.3	89.7
France	442.8	99.3
Italy	39,015	70.2
UK	33.4	84.3
Japan	48,487	196.9
Spain	2,393	58.0
USSR	277.0	513.0
Hungary	366.0	29.2
Poland	1,060	65.5
Yugoslavia	310.2	26.6

Appendix Table 11
Gross Reproducible Capital per Worker, Adjusted for NFH, and Further Adjusted for Services (USA)=100.0)

Country	Gross reproducible capital per worker, adjusted for NFH (1)	Working hours (2)	Shift work (3)	Unfinished construction (4)
		After further adjustment for		
USA	100.0	100.0	100.0	100.0
Germany	111.0	105.8	103.3	103.3
France	81.7	82.5	89.9	80.9
Italy	71.4	70.1	68.5	68.5
UK	78.7	75.6	74.5	74.5
Japan	65.4	74.0	69.6	68.9
Spain	41.3	47.2	45.8	45.3
USSR	57.8	55.4	58.1	57.2
Hungary	50.4	52.5	55.4	54.0
Poland	34.1	36.0	38.3	36.9
Yugoslavia	29.3	29.7	31.4	30.1

Appendix Table 12
Farm Land Area, Specified Countries and Dates (millions of hectares)

Country and date	Area
USA, 1974	188.2
Germany, 1973	8.081
France, 1972	18.632
Italy, 1973	12.236
UK, 1973	7.164
Japan, 1972	5.296
Spain, 1973	20.979
USSR, 1973	232.1
Hungary, 1973	5.555
Poland, 1973	15.107
Yugoslavia, 1973	8.087

3

Inventories: East and West

In the perennial discussion of the economic merit of socialism, one of the more intriguing claims made for such a system is that concerning inventory control. With predominantly public ownership of the means of production, it has been held, a community should be able, through the planning thus made possible, to regulate relatively effectively the amount of goods held as stocks, and so to restrict below levels customary in the Western mixed economy (WME) the volume of resources that must be committed to such uses.

Economy of inventories, as the primers teach, need not be an unmitigated good. Carried to extremes it can be costly to resource use more generally. The proposition that socialism is a priori especially favorable to such economy is in any event hardly self-evident. Rather one might easily be led to a contrary view by familiar critical analyses of socialist planning.

But, in pondering the possible magnitude of inventories under socialism, we need not limit ourselves to theoretic speculation. That kind of economic system has now prevailed for more or less protracted intervals in a number of countries. There is, thus, an opportunity to inquire into inventory requirements under it in the light of experience.

That in fact has been done by Campbell (1959) and again by Schroeder (1972). Both conclude that, relative to output, inventories in the USSR have tended to be higher than those in the USA. Reference is particularly, in the case of Campbell, to comparative inventory-output ratios in industry and trade during pre- and early post-World War II years; and, in the case of Schroeder, to such ratios in industry during the sixties.

For further perspective on the question at issue, I present here the results of an attempt to compile comparative data on the relation of inventories to output for 1975, not only for the USSR and USA, but for a number of other socialist and WME countries (Table 1). While the data have limitations of their own, they relate virtually to the whole economy, and so should not be affected by incongruities that are difficult to avoid in purely sectoral comparisons.[1]

Gross domestic material product (GDMP) is understood to be the gross domestic product (GDP) less services engaged in the provision of health care, education and public administration, including the armed forces. Also deducted from the GDP are the services of housing, exclusive of fuel and power. Inventories are intended to represent stocks in "material sectors" as so delineated, and hence to correspond in scope to GDMP.

In the sources that I draw on here (see below), public administration in socialist countries is construed in a conventional way that should make that sphere more or less comparable there and in WME countries. Almost inevitably, though, the data for different countries are not always fully comparable in scope. Perhaps the most significant incongruity that results concerns livestock herds, which probably are partially omitted from inventories in the UK and may be omitted in part or in their entirety from inventories in Spain, Italy, Hungary and Yugoslavia. What is in question usually, however, is whether breeding stocks are included or omitted. The disparities that may result on that account would seem to be of a modest sort when we consider that all livestock herds constituted but 8.1 percent of all French material sector inventories; and that basic herds alone amounted to some 7.2 percent of the corresponding Soviet total.

In 1975, a poor harvest probably cost the USSR a few percent of national income growth, while inventories still grew more or less as before (CIA 1980: 56; TSSU 1976: 731). Coming as it did two years after the first oil shock, 1975 tended to be a recession year in the West. While output tended to grow relatively slowly or even to decline, inventories often grew less or fell more. In the case of the UK, the inventory-output ratio may have in consequence fallen by several percent. The ratio sometimes rose, however, as in Italy, where it probably increased by several percent. (OECD 1981; I refer to percent, not percentage points.) The tabulated ratios should be read in the light of those shifts.

The tabulated data all derive from a larger study, and sources and methods used in compiling them are explained there (Bergson forthcoming). I should note here, though, that for GDMP for all countries, other than the USSR, I take as a point of departure the well-known computations of Phase III of the International Comparison Project (ICP-III) and published in Kravis et al. (1982). For the USSR, the needed basic data on national output were found in Edwards et al. (1979), together with Schroeder and Edwards (1981).

In all cases, I could obtain in these sources data on output already computed in terms of the standard that I apply here: US prices of 1975. For inventories I first compile from diverse national and international sources data in terms of national prices, and then translate such prices into US 1975 dollars by reference to purchasing power parities implicit in the calculation of output in the sources drawn on for data on that aspect. More precisely, for each country inventories are translated from its national currency into US prices of 1975 by reference to a single purchasing power parity (PPP) corresponding to the comparative magnitudes of the GDMP in national and US prices of 1975.

Table 1
Gross Domestic Material Product (GDMP) and Inventories per Capita, and their Ratio: USSR, Eastern Europe and the West, 1975[1]

Country	GDMP per capita, US 1975 prices	Inventories per capita, US 1975 prices	Ratio: Inventories ÷ GDMP (%)
USA	5,307	1,556	29.3
France	4,895	1,883	38.5
FRG	4,826	1,451	30.1
Japan	4,392	1,765	40.2
UK	3,565	1,506	42.2
Spain	3,432	1,633	47.6
Italy	3,255	1,257	38.6
Hungary	3,241	2,770	85.5
USSR	3,194	2,016	63.1
Poland	2,911	1,925	66.1
Yugoslavia	2,205	1,323	60.0

[1] For source and scope of data, see text.

The ratio of inventories and output that is thus obtained might be viewed as representing the relation in question in terms of not only US but national prices. Valuation in the latter terms follows from the fact that, in effect, one and the same PPP applies in the translation of both output and inventories from national into US prices.

It must be observed, though, that on neither view is the result quite what one might wish. Where the national currency valuation obtains, the desideratum presumably is valuation at factor cost, or, in the case of the socialist countries (if I may have recourse again to the surrogate that I advanced long ago) "adjusted factor cost" (AFC). With such valuation, one might read the inventory-output ratios, as would be desirable, as indicating the volume of resources committed to inventories, relatively to that represented by current output.

The national prices that are in question here, however, are for the most part market prices, though in the case of inventories reference must often be to production costs. For WME countries, such prices diverge from factor cost because of commodity taxes and subsidies, but the impact on our ratios could only be consequential if, along with subsidies and taxes at very diverse rates, there should be a very marked difference in structure between inventories and the GDMP. Such a conjuncture does not seem very likely. For socialist countries, taxes and subsidies fall in a notable degree on consumers' goods, and there we must reckon with a further deviation from our desideratum so far as profits too may be notably high on such goods. If incomplete data for the USSR are at all indicative, however, our ratios should not diverge from corresponding ones in AFC by more than several percentage points in either direction.[2]

Ratios of inventories to output in dollar prices are also of interest so far as they indicate how different countries compare in respect of the physical volume of goods held in inventories relative to the corresponding volume of output. Here, too, application to inventories of single PPP that is implied by the conversion of GDMP from national to US prices is a possible source of error. Although that again appears unlikely to be very consequential, one would wish at this point to convert inventories by a more appropriate PPP.

I have tacitly assumed that the PPP applied is in any event accurate in respect of the category to which it purportedly relates, that is, the GDMP itself. Its accuracy turns essentially on that of the underlying data, on which I draw, on national output in national and US dollar prices. The inquiries from which these data are drawn, cited above, are notably substantial and systematic. The task undertaken is nevertheless an extraordinarily difficult one, and error is practically unavoidable. Among other things, for reasons elaborated elsewhere (Bergson, forthcoming), the PPP's for socialist countries may well tend to overstate the dollar value of their currencies, and consequently also their national output. Since the same PPP applies here to inventories as to output, such an error would not affect our ratios, but the comparative levels of GDMP per capita that have been computed here (Table 1) would be affected. That has to be considered in connection with an aspect to which I now turn.

Why are inventories in socialist countries so high compared with those in the West? It seems difficult to avoid the conclusion that the difference in economic institutions must itself be a factor. At any rate, rudimentary regression analysis only underlines what inspection of the tabulated data suggests: a highly significant relation between the economic system and inventories remains even if one hypothesizes, as a further source of the observed differences in the latter, the stage of economic development. Relative to output, inventories, one might suppose, would tend for one reason or another to vary inversely with development stage. As represented by GDMP per capita, however, that factor seems to have no explanatory value to speak of. Not very surprisingly, that is still true even if one should allow for overestimation of socialist GDMP per capita by as much as, say, 20 percent.

Socialist planning imaginably might affect inventories not so much directly but indirectly via the impact of that scheme on, say, the economic structure. As represented by an outstanding feature, the relation of gross domestic capital formation to GDMP, the economic structure also appears to have no significant relation to the inventory-output ratio. The role of economic structure, however, doubtless merits further inquiry.[3]

If socialist planning should be conducive to notably high inventories, that at least in the case of the USSR is not very surprising. The tendency there of enterprises to hedge against the vicissitudes of an erratic supply system by accumulating inordinately large stocks is a familiar theme in Soviet as well as Western literature on planning in the USSR. Reports of empty shelves in retail shops are also familiar, but the resultant shortfalls in inventories are apparently only a partial offset to the excess holdings in industry. Relevant behavior patterns are not always as clearly documented for Poland as for the USSR, but in one country as in the other planning is of the proverbial centralist sort, stressing bureaucratic, as distinct from market, processes of enterprise coordination and direction. In the circumstances, notably high inventories in Poland are also understandable.

Less expected is the finding that inventories are also inordinate in Hungary, where centralist planning has been significantly modified, and in Yugoslavia, where it was effectively abandoned long ago. We must conclude that, while public ownership is still predominant, introduction of market processes provides by itself no assurance of inventory economy. Maybe requirements for stocks are even greater, as the result for Hungary suggests. But it probably burdens my flawed data unduly to make comparisons among socialist as well as between socialist and WME countries. In any event, causal factors shaping inventory requirements under Hungarian and Yugoslav socialism doubtless merit further inquiry.

Notes

1. For industry, both Campbell and Schroeder find it necessary, in the case of the USA, to refer to manufacturing alone. For the USSR, industry comprehends mining and electric power as well. Both writers also take the output of industry to be measured by its gross sales turnover, though as Campbell notes the resultant ratios could be affected by differences in industrial integration in the two countries. In respect of ratios such as in question, the comparative magnitudes obtained must also be affected should the two countries differ in respect of the degree to which finished products are held in stock in industrial enterprises rather than in wholesale or retail trade outlets. Campbell recognizes and tries to grapple with the problem that this poses for his comparative ratios.
2. Among other things, the share of consumers' goods in inventories is probably very similar to their share in the GDMP: TSSU (1976: 192, 731); CIA (1975: 11).
3. As implied, I experimented with two sorts of regression calculations. In the first, I refer to a relation of the form: Inventory-output ratio = A(GDMP per capita) + B (S) + D. Here S is a dummy variable standing for socialism or its absence, and A, B and D are regression constants. The resultant magnitude for B, 26.48, is significant at the 1.0 per cent level. As for A, that has a slight negative value ($-.0031$) that is not significant at any acceptable level.

   For the second kind of computation, I simply expand the above formula to include as an additional independent variable, with a coefficient C, the relation of gross domestic capital formation to GDMP. The magnitude of B, almost as before at 26.77, is significant at the 5.0 percent level; A remains slightly negative and not statistically significant, while C is also slightly negative ($-.0205$) and even less significant.

   Neither regression is materially affected if the GDMP per capita for socialist countries is reduced by 20 percent. Needed data on gross domestic capital formation are from Bergson (forthcoming) and sources cited therein. Mr. Daniel Quah kindly made the foregoing computations for me.

References

Bergson, Abram (1987, June). "Comparative Productivity: The USSR, Eastern Europe and the West" (forthcoming).

Campbell, Robert (1958, September). "Soviet and American Inventory-Output Ratios." *American Economic Review, 48* (4), 549–565.

CIA (Central Intelligence Agency) (1975, November). *USSR: Gross National Product Accounts, 1970.* A (ER) 75–76, Washington, D.C.: CIA.

CIA (1980). *Handbook of Economic Statistics 1980*, ER 80-10452, Washington, D.C.: CIA.

Edwards, Imogene, Margaret Hughes, and James Noren (1979). "US and USSR: Comparisons of GNP." In *Soviet Economy in a Time of Change.* Vol. 1. Issued by Joint Economic Committee, U.S. Congress, Washington, D.C.: GPO, 369–401.

Kravis, Irving B., Alan Heston, and Robert Summers (1982). *World Product and Income.* Baltimore, Md.: Johns Hopkins Univ. Press.

OECD (Organization for Economic Cooperation and Development) (1981). *National Accounts of OECD Countries (1962–1979).* Vol. 2, Paris: OECD.

Schroeder, Gertrude (1972, July). "The Reform of the Supply System in Soviet Industry." *Soviet Studies*, 24 (1), 97–119.

Schroeder, Gertrude, and Imogene Edwards (1981). *Consumption in the USSR: An International Comparison.* Issued by Joint Economic Committee, U.S. Congress. Washington, D.C.: GPO. TSSU (Tsentral'noe Statisticheskoe Upravlenie SSSR) (1976). *Narodnoe khoziaistvo SSSR v 1975 g. Moscow.*

* See Chapter 2.

4

Soviet Consumption in Comparative Perspective

Among the numerous virtues claimed for the novel social system that originated in Russia in 1917, a cardinal one is the unlimited abundance it is ultimately supposed to provide for consumers. Marx's economic utopia has, nevertheless, hardly been approached anywhere, but progress in consumption can be a principal yardstick for assessing the economic performance of the new system.

It is also a yardstick whose application could be a large task. But, thanks to not-widely-familiar Western research, much is known, or can readily be ascertained, concerning comparative consumption levels and trends in the country where the new social system was first established. While outlining those aspects, a summary review may also serve by exploring conditioning factors.

The social system in question continues to be referred to as socialism, though many observers, citing its authoritarian nature, call for another term. Even in a limited inquiry, we must remind ourselves that in the USSR socialism is organized economically in a particular way. The famous Soviet system of "centralist planning," however, has been widely copied in other socialist countries.

I shall note sources as I proceed, but should record here my particular debt to Schroeder and Edwards (1981), for comparative Soviet and U.S. data on consumption, and to Kravis et al. (1982) for comparative data on GDP by end use for the U.S. and other Western countries. On recent consumption levels, I do little more than collate the calculations of these studies. I often draw also on Edwards et al. (1979) for related Soviet and U.S data on GDP by end use.

Table 1
Consumption per Capita, USSR and Selected Western Countries, 1975[a]

	Consumption per capita	
Country	In ideal units (1)	USA = 100.0 (2)
United States	5,183	100.0
France	3,929	75.8
Germany	3,841	74.1
United Kingdom	3,452	66.6
Japan	3,053	58.9
Italy	2,866	55.3
USSR	1,788	34.5

[a] *Sources.* Col. (1): for USA, Kravis *et al.* (1982); for other countries, by reference to USA and col. (2). Col. (2): for Western countries, Kravis *et al.* (1982); for USSR, Schroeder and Edwards (1981: 20), with extrapolation from 1976 to 1975 by reference to Schroeder and Denton (1982: 367); USDC Bureau of Economic Analysis (1986: 387) and OECD (1981: 19, 20).

Per Capita Consumption

Comparative figures compiled on levels of per capita consumption (Table 1), refer, for both the USSR and Western countries, to all consumer goods and services provided to households, including both those privately acquired and those publicly supplied. The latter are principally in the form of educational and health services. For each country, per capita consumption is expressed in "ideal" units. For the United States, such units correspond to current dollar values. For other countries, a corresponding measure in ideal units is obtained in each case by application, to the U.S. measure, of the "ideal" index number of the relation of per capita consumption in the country concerned to that in the United States.

The ideal index is understood, in the usual way, as the geometric mean of two alternative index numbers relating per capita consumption in the country in question to that in the United States: one with consumption valued in U.S. prices (the Laspeyres index), the other with consumption valued in prices of the other country (the Paasche index). Hence, if C_k represents per capita consumption in country k in ideal units, we have

$$C_k \doteq 5,183 \ (L_{ku} \cdot P_{ku})^{1/2},$$

where L_{ku} and P_{ku} are the Laspeyres and Paasche index numbers in question.

The ideal index has been widely used to summarize the two measures obtained by applying the Laspeyres and Paasche formulas, but in focusing on the ideal index we should have in mind that the latter measures generally differ appreciably both from the ideal index and from each other (Table 2).

Table 2
*Alternative Index Numbers of per Capita Consumption, USSR
and Selected Western Countries, 1975ᵃ (USA = 100.0)*

Country	Ideal index (1)	With valuation in domestic prices (2)	With valuation in dollar prices (3)
United States	100.0	100.0	100.0
France	75.8	67.2	85.4
Germany	74.1	67.2	81.8
United Kingdom	66.6	60.7	73.0
Japan	58.9	50.6	68.6
Italy	55.3	49.2	62.1
USSR	34.5	27.7	43.0

ᵃ *Sources*: as for Table 1, col. (2).

Whichever measure is considered, however, different countries rank in essentially the same way. And, in all calculations, per capita consumption in the USSR is distinctly below that in any of the Western countries considered.

International comparisons of aggregates, such as per capita consumption, are unavoidably inexact. Careful as were the calculations on which I draw, they are not exceptions to that rule. What must be in question, though, is whether there may not be a systematic bias one way or the other in the calculations. Of particular interest is a possible bias affecting the standing of the USSR relative to the standing of other countries. One possible source of such a bias, illegal and underreported legal pursuits, practically defies accurate quantitative assessment. Although such "underground" activities are, by all accounts, widespread in the USSR, the resulting deficiencies in aggregative measures of Soviet consumption, may not be as great as is often supposed.[1] Moreover, the West has its "underground" economy, though perhaps less often than in the USSR does it go beyond merely underreported to embrace illegal activities.

Apart from the "underground" economy, there is an apparent bias in our comparative data. It is difficult to avoid the conclusion that Soviet per capita consumption, if anything, is even lower than what has been indicated.

The reasons for the bias are more or less familiar, but the nature of the resultant distortions of comparative measures is not always clearly grasped.[2]

(1) As calculated, consumption represents the volume of goods acquired by households, and no account is taken of concomitant services provided by trade and other enterprises supplying goods to consumers. That omission could be a source of distortion in measures of comparative consumption levels among Western countries. In the USSR, however, the services of retail distribution are notoriously meager. The deficiencies often appear to be a matter of organization and quality of service rather than a matter of sheer

volume of factor inputs employed,[3] but, the presumption is that Soviet per capita consumption, as computed, tends to be overstated relative to the per capita consumption of Western countries.

(2) As the primers teach, in order for index numbers of consumption to be fully meaningful, the prices used in aggregating different goods should correspond to scarcity values. This principle must often be breached even in the West, but under centralist planning the Soviet government responds at best only sluggishly to market disequilibria. As a result, supplies are again and again short at prevailing ruble prices. The proverbial Soviet queues are only the surface manifestation of pervasive imbalances.

Although some goods have been reported to be in excess supply, with resultant overstocks, the fact remains that for those supplies actually acquired by households ruble prices tend to be too low for the very goods that are especially sought. The volume of such goods must also frequently be limited relative to the volume of Soviet consumption generally. As the calculations of Schroeder and Edwards (1981:20–21) indicate, this observation egregiously applies to housing and passenger cars, but it must also frequently apply to goods in short supply more generally. From the standpoint of the Russians' own scarcity values, the corollary is that the Paasche index, as computed, must overstate Soviet per capita consumption. If that is so, the calculated ideal index should be similarly biased, though to a reduced degree.

(3) A cardinal problem in the compilation of comparative measures of consumption is the matching of product specifications and qualities between different countries. Where, for the measures in questions here, the underlying calculations proceed by deflation, such matching is needed to derive purchasing power parities appropriate to serve as deflators for different expenditure categories. The matching often can only be approximate, and the resulting measures are correspondingly inaccurate.

That is true of measures of comparative consumption for any of the countries, but, again, circumstances in the USSR seem rather special, for the quality of consumer goods there, even by the Russians' own admission, frequently leaves much to be desired. In the calculations relied upon here, every effort was made to be careful in dealing with this problem, but as the authors acknowledge, a bias in favor of the USSR was sometimes unavoidable. Both the Paasche and Laspeyres index numbers should have been affected and, correspondingly, the ideal index.[4]

(4) Closely related to the matching problems is that of representativeness. Here too error is unavoidable generally, but a distortion such as occurs in the comparison of the USSR with the United States seems unlikely to be as pronounced, if it occurs at all, in corresponding calculations for West European countries and Japan. I refer to the bias resulting from the fact that higher quality goods found in the United States are often not produced at all in the USSR. Hence, in matching ruble and dollar prices, reference can only be made to lower quality goods. The result, as readily seen, is a tendency for

the Paasche index to be overstated.

I referred above to the limited quality and volume of Soviet retail trade services and the pervasive market imbalances and associated queues. The costs that the deficiencies in Soviet consumer goods distribution impose on consumers are a closely related, though separate, issue. Such costs, consisting primarily of inordinate shopping time and effort, are conventionally omitted from index numbers of consumption, so their omission from the measures considered here cannot, strictly speaking, be viewed as a source of bias in such data. Given a more complete reckoning, however, shopping time and effort should be regarded as an offset to the otherwise realized consumer values. Consumers devote time and effort to shopping everywhere, and some find it pleasurable to do so, but our comparative measures could be misleading if we didn't consider that according to a Soviet estimate (Rutgaizer 1981), the Soviet population devotes 37 billion hours per year to shopping. Included in this time are 12 billion hours spent in selecting and paying for merchandise. The remaining 25 billion hours are spent in travel time and waiting in line.[5]

Conditioning Factors

In any country, how well or poorly consumers fare must depend finally on the productivity of labor in that country. Per capita consumption must also depend on other factors, in particular the share of consumption in the country's output as well as the comparative numbers of dependents and gainfully employed in the population. Further data (compiled in Table 3) allow us to gauge how these diverse factors operate to determine comparative consumption levels in the USSR and the West.

GDP per employed worker

As with our measures of consumption per capita, in the case of each country compared with the United States, GDP per worker is calculated from an ideal index number of output.[6] Like the former measures, GDP per worker among Western countries varies over a wide range, but in the USSR it is outside and below that range. Among Western countries, Japan somewhat unexpectedly turns out to have the lowest GDP per worker, though only by a narrow margin. The Soviet GDP per worker, however, is markedly below that of Japan.

Table 3
Elements in Relation of Consumption per Capita to GDP per Employed Worker, USSR and Selected Western Countries, 1975[a]

Country	GDP per employed worker, ideal index, USA = 100.0 (1)	Consumption share of GDP[b] (2)	Consumption per worker, ideal index, USA = 100.0 (3)	Population/ employment (4)	Consumption per capita, ideal index, USA = 100.0 (5)
United States	100.0	.722	100.0	2.46	100.0
France	81.9	.674	76.5	2.48	75.8
Germany	80.4	.662	73.7	2.44	74.1
United Kingdom	61.1	.720	60.9	2.25	66.6
Japan	57.9	.639	51.2	2.14	58.9
Italy	63.4	.721	63.2	2.81	55.3
USSR	38.8	.513	27.6	1.96	34.5

[a] *Sources.* Col. (1): for GDP per capita, ideal index, for Western countries, Kravis et al. (1982); for USSR, Bergson (1987). For employment per capita, see col. (4). Col. (2): for consumption, Table 1, col. (1); for GDP in ideal units, for Western countries, Kravis et al. (1982); for the USSR, Bergson (1987). Col. (3): for consumption, Table 1, col. (2); for employment, Bergson (1987). Col. (4): Bergson (1987). Col. (5): Table 1. Discrepancies between indicated numbers and results of computations referred to in text due to rounding.

[b] Both consumption and GDP in ideal units.

Consumption share of GDP

I properly consider here the ratio of consumption in ideal units to GDP in ideal units. Such a ratio is rather novel, but it corresponds broadly to ratios indicated by more familiar calculations in domestic and dollar prices (Table 4).[7]

Consumption apart, the GDP is devoted to government administration, defense, and investment. The varying consumption-GDP ratios cited for Western countries reflect differences in allocations to government administration and defense (the two categories are bracketed into one in the calculations I draw upon) but they primarily reflect the further differences in the investment share. For Japan in particular the low ratio for consumption mirrors an exceptionally large investment share in that country. The Japanese allocation to government administration and defense is quite modest.

For the USSR, though, consumption is an even smaller share of the GDP than it is for Japan. That apparently results from superimposing notably large outlays for government and defense on a no less notably large investment share.[8]

Consumption per employed worker

In this case I refer not to actual consumption of workers, but to the relation of consumption of the whole population to total employment. For each country, therefore, the cited magnitude (Table 3) corresponds to the GNP per worker, after reducing the latter to conform with the consumption share.

Table 4
Consumption Share in GDP, USSR and Selected Western Countries, 1975, Alternative Valuations[a]

| Country | Consumption share with valuation in | | |
	Ideal units (1)	Domestic prices (2)	U.S. dollars (3)
United States	.722	.722	.722
France	.674	.653	.690
Germany	.662	.649	.669
United Kingdom	.720	.683	.718
Japan	.639	.621	.657
Italy	.721	.692	.738
USSR	.513	.584	.511

[a] *Sources.* Col. (1): see Table 3, col. (2). Cols. (2) and (3): for Western countries, Kravis *et el.* (1982); for the USSR, for GDP, Bergson (1987); for consumption, Schroeder and Edwards (1981: 20), with extrapolation from 1976 to 1975 as in Table 1.

Relative to the United States, consumption per worker in Western Europe and Japan tends to be below GDP per worker. That is because consumption shares in the latter countries are lower than that of the United States. Since the consumption share is particularly low for Japan, the shift in criterion from GDP per worker to consumption per worker is especially unfavorable to the comparative standing of that country. As we saw, though, the consumption share is even lower in the USSR than in Japan. The shift in criterion from GDP per worker to consumption per worker, therefore, is even more markedly unfavorable to the USSR.

Population/employment

These measures vary inversely with the share of the population that is of working age, and the rate of labor participation, understood as the relative number of working-age persons who are actually employed. Curiously, the share of population of working age varies little between countries. In all countries, including the USSR, it falls within a range of five percentage points. The rate of labor participation, however, varies widely, and the diverse ratios of population to employment (Table 3) should be read accordingly. Among Western countries, the participation rate is relatively high for Japan and quite low for Italy, so the population–employment ratio is comparatively low for the former and high for the latter. As is commonly known, the participation rate is especially high in the USSR, so the population–employment ratio is unusually low for that country.[9]

Consumption per capita

For each country, the cited figures (Table 3) correspond to consumption per employed worker after deflation of the latter by the population–employment ratio. Among Western countries, the low population–employment ratio for Japan is thus seen to translate itself into a relatively increased per capita consumption. With a high population–employment ratio, Italy suffers a relative reduction in per capita consumption at this point. As for the USSR, since the population–employment ratio there is especially low, that country gains much from the shift from consumption per worker to consumption per capita. Judging by consumption per capita, though, the USSR is still below all of the Western countries under consideration.

   In sum, per capita consumption varies more or less with GDP per worker, but the impact of the latter is sometimes compounded, sometimes offset, by further variations in the consumption share and the population–employment ratio. Relative to consumer standards in other Western countries, those in

Italy, for example, are markedly reduced as a result of the high population–employment ratio there. In Japan, on the other hand, that ratio is comparatively low, and partially offsets the effect on per capita consumption of the low consumption share.

Compared with that of Western countries, per capita consumption in the USSR is relatively low, primarily because of the low GDP per worker there. Owing to the very low Soviet consumption share, per capita consumption might have been reduced much further if it were not largely offset by an equally low Soviet population–employment ratio.

In the foregoing, consumption per employed worker appears as a link in the chain connecting GDP per worker with consumption per capita. Viewed as a summary measure of the relation between the community's current effort and its current material compensation, consumption per employed worker is also of interest in itself. It merits note, therefore, that in terms of this coefficient the Soviet rating is but 27.6 percent of that of the United States, and but 53.9 percent of that of Japan. Among the Western countries considered, consumption per worker is lowest in Japan.

As before, our comparative measures of consumption probably unduly favor the USSR. If so, that should also be true of the corresponding measures of consumption per worker, though the data considered on employment are also inexact. Insofar as consumption is a major component of the GNP, one is led to suppose that the comparative data on GDP per worker are also biased in favor of the USSR. When productivity is in question, however, valuation is often properly in terms of "factor cost" rather than market price. Use of the "factor cost" standard would, by itself, probably tend to somewhat raise GNP per worker in the USSR relative to Western levels.[10]

Trends

Ideal indexes of Soviet and Western per capita consumption, such as we considered previously for 1975, are also available for 1955. By juxtaposing the two sets of measures (Table 5), we may gauge comparative gains in consumption standards in the USSR and the West during the two post-World War II decades ending in 1975. The United States enjoyed the highest standards in 1955, as it did in 1975, but other Western countries, not including the United Kingdom, gained markedly on the United States in the interval between these two dates. The gain was especially great for Italy and Japan, both of which initially enjoyed consumption standards that were well below those of other Western countries. While their consumption levels were still relatively low in 1975, they had by then gained not only on the United States, but also on other Western countries.

The USSR also gained on the United States between 1955 and 1975, but

Table 5
Consumption per Capita, USSR and Selected Western Countries, 1955 and 1975[a]

| | Consumption per capita, ideal index, USA = 100.0 | | Ratio of ideal indexes |
| | 1955 | 1975 | 1975/ 1955 |
Country	(1)	(2)	(3)
United States	100	100.0	1.00
France	51	75.8	1.49
Germany	48	74.1	1.54
United Kingdom	59	66.6	1.13
Japan	25	58.9	2.36
Italy	29	55.3	1.91
USSR	24	34.5	1.44

[a] *Sources.* Col. (1): for Western countries, other than Japan, Gilbert *et al.* (n.d.: 36); for Japan, see text; for USSR, Bergson (1978: 50). Col. (2): see Table 1.

in view of the pattern of shifts that apparently prevailed among Western countries, it is of interest that the Soviet advance was little greater than that realized in France and West Germany—two Western countries where consumption standards were initially at a much higher level. The Soviet advance also fell below advances in Japan and Italy, where consumption was initially at low levels similar to those of the USSR.

The ideal index cited for Japan for 1955 is a crude estimate, but the resultant error is more likely to make for an understatement than an overstatement of the gain in Japan's comparative standing from 1955 to 1975.[11] More generally, our measures of consumption in 1955 are affected by limitations much like those discussed above, relating to our data for 1975. For the USSR, the error in measuring per capita consumption is, again, probably, in the direction of overstatement, but for all countries alike the margin for error is necessarily widened when consumption levels are compared at two different dates. The comparative data presented must be read accordingly.

As might have been expected, gains in per capita consumptions over time, were broadly comparable to those in output per worker (Tables 3, 6 and 7).[12] Relative to the United States, however, the expansion of per capita consumption in other Western countries is sometimes adversely affected by reductions in the consumption share of output. That is especially true of Japan, where the consumption share falls from .746 in 1955 to .639 in 1975. Since per capita consumption was already restricted by a high population–employment ratio in 1955, and that ratio became even higher by 1975, Italy's per capita consumption, when compared with that of the U.S., grows distinctly less than output per worker over this twenty-year span.

Table 6
Elements in Relation of Consumption per Capita to GNP per Employed Worker, USSR and Selected Western Countries, 1955[a]

Country	GDP per employed worker, ideal index, USA = 100.0 (1)	Consumption share of GNP[b] (2)	Consumption per employed worker, ideal index, USA = 100.0 (3)	Population/ employment (4)	Consumption per capita, ideal index, USA = 100.0 (5)
United States	100	.657	100	2.54	100
France	43	.684	45	2.23	51
Germany	43	.618	41	2.16	48
United Kingdom	47	.680	49	2.11	59
Japan	19	.746	21	2.18	25
Italy	28	.657	28	2.46	29
USSR	25	.543	21	2.21	24

[a] *Sources.* Col. (1): GNP per capita for Western countries other than Japan, from Gilbert, *et al.* (n.d.: 36), and for USSR, from Bergson (1978: 50). For Japan, see text. GNP per capita adjusted to per worker basis by reference to col. (4). Col. (2): Derived from indexes of consumption per capita in Table 5 and of GNP per capita noted above, and corresponding data on U.S. consumption and GNP per capita in current dollars. On the latter, see Gilbert *et al.* (n.d.: 82, 168). Col. (3): Table 5, col. (1) and this table, col. (4). Col. (4): See Bergson (1974) and Bergson (1978: 242–243). Soviet employment, as previously estimated, is reduced by 5.0 million, or 5.3 percent, in order to allow, perhaps excessively, for double-counting of socialized and private agricultural employment. Compare Bergson (1987). Col. (5): see Table 5.

Discrepancies between indicated numbers and results of computations referred to in text due to rounding.

[b] Consumption, ideal units/GNP, ideal units.

Table 7
Variations in per Capita Consumption and in Conditioning Factors,
USSR and Selected Western Countries, 1955–1975[a]

Country	Increase in per capita consumption: ideal index, 1975, less ideal index, 1955 (1)	Increase in Output per Worker: ideal index, 1975, less ideal index, 1955[c] (2)	Increase in consumption share (3)	Decrease in population–employment ratio (4)
United States	...[b]	...	.065	.08
France	25	39	(−).010	(−).25
Germany	26	37	.044	(−).28
United Kingdom	7	14	.040	(−).14
Japan	34	39	(−).107	.04
Italy	26	35	.064	(−).35
USSR	10	14	(−).030	.25

[a] Sources. Tables 3 and 6.
[b] ... = nil.
[c] For 1975, GDP per worker; for 1955, GNP per worker.

In the USSR, on the other hand, the population–employment ratio of 1955 was already low by U.S. standards, and it became still lower by 1975. But relative to the gains in output per worker, those in consumption per capita were somewhat depressed by a decrease in the consumption share of output.[13]

Consumption in the USSR in 1975, as we saw, was especially low when related to the level of employment there. In 1955, too, consumption per worker in the USSR tended to be low relative to that of the West, but this gap has seemed only to widen in more recent years (compare Tables 3 and 6).

For 1955, as for 1975, limitations in our measures of consumption per capita also affect those of consumption per worker, while employment data considered are likewise inexact.

Conclusions

At 34 percent of the U.S. level, per capita consumption in the USSR in 1975 was well below that in a number of Western countries. The low standards essentially reflected a correspondingly low level of output per worker in the USSR. Although the consumption share in Soviet aggregate output was also exceptionally low, its adverse impact on Soviet per capita consumption was largely offset by a likewise exceptionally low population–employment ratio.

Compared to the United States, whose standards throughout were the highest in the West, the USSR scored a distinct gain in per capita consumption from 1955 to 1975. Numerous Western countries other than the United States, however, also tended to gain on the latter country in terms of per capita consumption. Their gains often were practically as great as those of the USSR. In Japan and Italy, where 1955 consumption levels were, like those in the USSR, especially low, the gains exceeded those achieved in the USSR.

Of the two years under consideration, 1955 represents an early post-World War II date. By that time, all the countries in question were operating above their pre-World War II levels; in those countries ravaged by war, however, resultant damages often remained to be made good.[14] For the USSR, the year 1955 also followed soon after the death of Stalin (March 5, 1953). Coming in the second year after the OPEC "oil shock," 1975 fell in a period of slowing growth for Western countries, but Soviet growth had also been slowing for some time. The comparisons that have been made must be seen accordingly.

Although Soviet consumers have hardly fared well relative to those in Western countries, an inevitable question concerns the role of the Soviet social system in that experience. The question is also complex, but the reader does not have to be told how to view from that standpoint the restricted share of consumption in Soviet output, reflecting as it does a relatively high rate of investment compounded, according to all accounts, by substantial defense expenditures. There is also little need to expatiate here on the relatively low Soviet population–employment ratio. The high rate of labor participation has been a characteristic feature under authoritarian socialism and centralist planning, such as that of the USSR.

More basic to the Soviet consumption experience has been the low initial level of output per worker and the relatively modest increase in that level compared with increases achieved not only in Western countries that were initially at similar levels but, indeed, also in some Western countries that were more advanced at the outset. Judging from somewhat dated research (Bergson 1978: Chs. 7, 9, 10), Soviet productivity growth might be explicable in more than one way, but socialism and centralist planning probably contributed significantly to results that are subnormal by Western standards.[15] It is hoped that further research, taking into account the most recent, as well as earlier experience, will shed more light on this fundamental question.

If authoritarian socialism and centralist planning do not work well in the USSR, of course, that does not preclude that the same institutions might work well elsewhere. Indications, nevertheless, abound that this is not the case; this, too, is a matter calling for further inquiry.[16]

While attention has centered on per capita consumption, the analysis has brought into focus a cognate measure, summarizing the relation of the community's aggregate consumption to the total labor performed. As so understood, consumption per worker in the USSR varies with per capita consumption there, but with consumption per worker in 1975 amounting to but 27.6 percent of consumption per worker in the United States, the Soviet standing, according to that yardstick, is inferior to its standing where per capita consumption is the criterion. What might be said here as to the relationship between that result and the Soviet social sysem is already evident and need not be labored here.[17]

Notes

[1] Judging from retrospective emigre budgetary data for the years 1972 through 1974, compiled by Ofer and Vinokur (1980: 54ff), perhaps not much more than 6–9 percent of the total. See also Schroeder and Edwards (1981:5).

[2] As will appear, I refer to the accuracy of our measures of per capita consumption as representations of index numbers, such as theory prescribes. Even if the index numbers were fully accurate from that standpoint, of course, they would be expected to be subject to error in a deeper sense, also familiar in theory. How comparisons among many countries might be affected by such error, however, is difficult to say.

[3] Compare Nove (1977:256ff).

[4] In matching Soviet and U.S. products, Schroeder and Edwards availed themselves of expert guidance, and were even able to bring many Soviet products covered in their inquiry to the United States for expert evaluation. One wonders, however, to what extent they were able to allow for the extraordinary volume of defective or otherwise substandard goods produced, and apparently often sold, at prices of standard goods in the USSR. In any event, as Schroeder and Edwards make clear, they were not able to allow at all for such elusive matters as style, design, and limitations in training of service personnel. There are reasons to think Soviet goods are often inferior to those of the West in respect to such matters.

On the quality of Soviet consumer goods and the problems posed at this point for compilation of comparative measures of Soviet consumption, see Bergson (1964:287ff); Schroeder and Severin (1976:632ff); Bergson (1978:53ff); Schroeder and Edwards (1981:4, 34–35, 52–53, 70–71).

[5] Shopping time per adult inhabitant in the USSR may not be especially great in absolute terms compared with that in Western countries, but it must be large relative to the volume of goods purchased. Compare Ofer (1973:116–117). The USSR must also be notable for its amount of non-pleasurable shopping, such as where there are queues.

[6] In the USA–USSR comparison, reference is to GNP. The Soviet index, I suspect, might increase, though by not much more than a percentage point, if the calculations related instead to GDP.

[7] As seen from the table, though, the ratio in ideal units is sometimes, but not always, bracketed by the alternative measures. It should also be noted that components of the GDP in ideal units cannot be expected to sum precisely to the GDP in ideal units.

[8] On comparative investment shares in different countries, the following data representing 1975 shares of gross fixed investment in the GDP in domestic prices are indicative: United States, .163; France, .233; West Germany, .207; United Kingdom, .196; Japan, .324; Italy, .206. I cite investment rates indicated by OECD data. For the USSR, data in Edwards et al. (1979: 378), after adjustment as in Bergson (1987), indicate a corresponding 1976 share of .275.

[9] These indexes represent the comparative ratios of employment to working age population, with United States, 100.0; France, 102.1; Germany, 101.1; United Kingdom, 112.5; Japan, 109.3; Italy, 88.0; USSR, 124.1. Employment as in Table 3; population of working age (15–64 years), OECD (1980); United Nations (1979); USDC Bureau of Census (1979).

[10] Some sources of bias affecting consumption measures, such as the deviation of ruble prices of consumers' goods from clearing levels, would also no longer apply. On the effect of a revaluation of Soviet GDP in factor cost, and limitations affecting comparative data on Soviet GDP in

terms of that standard, see Bergson (1978:Ch. 5).

[11] For Japan, I extrapolate to 1955 the ideal index for 1975. That is done by reference to conventional indexes for consumption volume in national prices. Use of that procedure for other countries would have yielded these ideal indexes for consumption per capita in 1955; with United States, 100, France, 53; Germany, 52; United Kingdom, 71; Italy, 39; USSR, 26. Judging from these results, my extrapolation for Japan could significantly overstate the 1955 ideal index for that country, and correspondingly understate the improvement that it achieved in comparative standing from 1955 to 1975.

On trends in per capita consumption in national prices for Western countries, see Bergson (1974); OECD (1982); for the USSR, Schroeder and Denton (1982:365ff). Consumption for Western countries excludes publicly supplied education and health care; for the USSR these are included.

For technical reasons relating to the procedure for valuing farm income in kind, the ideal index for Soviet consumption in 1955 in Bergson (1978:50), that is cited here, I believe, may be understated relative to that for 1976. If it is, of course, the Soviet gain in standing from 1955 to 1975 would be correspondingly overstated.

[12] For Japan, GNP per worker in Table 6 is derived from GNP per capita as is done for other countries. As for GNP per capita, a 1975 index of per capita GDP in Kravis et al (1982) is extrapolated to 1955 by sources and methods such as were used to extrapolate corresponding 1975 per capita consumption indexes to 1955. See above, note 11.

[13] As the data in Table 6 suggest, regarding labor participation, as represented by the rates of employment to the population of working age (15–64 years), the USSR compares somewhat differently with Western countries in 1955 than it did in 1975. Here are the ratios in question, with that of the United States, 100.0; France, 109.7; Germany, 105.8; United Kingdom, 112.8; Japan, 118.5; Italy, 93.4; USSR, 107.7. Data on employment are as in Table 6. Population data for Western countries are from OECD sources; for the USSR, I use U.S. Department of Commerce data.

[14] In terms of national income per capita, Japan in 1955 probably was only barely above the 1939 level. On early post-World War II economic levels in the USSR and the West, see Bergson (1971):586, 613) and OECD population data.

[15] The analysis in Bergson (1978) appears to confirm what has been suggested here, that productivity growth in the West has tended to vary inversely with the initial level. More basically, the stage of development is doubtless a factor in the level as well as the growth of productivity, but the Soviet performance still seems unimpressive when such a consideration is taken into account. See also Bergson (1987).

[16] See, however, Bergson (1978: ch. 11); Bergson (1987).

[17] While consumption per worker is of interest, so, too, would be a variant where employment is adjusted for working hours. Judging from not entirely appropriate data on non-farm working hours compiled for Bergson (1987), adjustment of consumption per worker for differences in such hours might raise the corresponding index for the USSR for 1975 (with the United States = 100) by one percentage point, while lowering that for Japan by six percentage points. Other Western countries in question would either gain somewhat in comparative standing or be hardly affected by such an adjustment.

References

Bergson, Abram (1971, July). "Development under Two Systems: Comparative Productivity Growth Since 1950." *World Politics*, 23, (4), 579–617.
—— (1964). *The Economics of Soviet Planning*. New Haven, Conn.: Yale University Press.
—— (1974). *Soviet Post-War Economic Development*. Stockholm: Almquist and Wicksell.
—— (1978). *Productivity and the Social System: USSR and the West*. Cambridge, Mass.: Harvard University Press.
—— (1987, June). "Comparative Productivity: USSR, Eastern Europe and the West." *American*

Economic Review, 77, (3), 342–347.

Edwards, Imogene, Margaret Hughes and James Noren (1979). "U.S. and U.S.S.R.: Comparisons of GNP." In *Soviet Economy in a Time of Change,* vol. 1, 369–401. Joint Economic Committee. Washington, D.C.: GPO.

Gilbert, Milton and Associates (n.d.). *Comparative National Products and Price Levels.* Paris.

Joint Economic Committee, U.S. Congress (1959). *Comparisons of the United States and Soviet Economies,* Part II. Washington, D.C.: GPO.

—— (1976). *Soviet Economy in a New Perspective.* Washington, D.C.: GPO.

—— (1979). *Soviet Economy in a Time of Change,* Vol. 1, Washington, D.C.: GPO.

Kravis, Irving B., Alan Heston and Robert Summers (1978). *International Comparisons of Real Product and Purchasing Power.* Baltimore, MD.: Johns Hopkins University Press.

—— (1982). *World Product and Income.* Baltimore, MD: Johns Hopkins University Press.

Nove, Alec (1977). *The Soviet Economic System.* London: Allen and Unwin.

Ofer, Gur (1973). *The Service Sector in Soviet Economic Growth.* Cambridge, Mass.: Harvard University Press.

——, and Vinokur (1980). *Private Sources of Income in the Soviet Urban Household,* R-2359 NA. Santa Monica, Calif.: RAND Corporation.

Organization of Economic Cooperation and Development (OECD) (1980). *Labor Force Statistics,* 1967–78. Paris: OECD.

—— (1981). *National Accounts of OECD Countries, 1962–79.* Paris: OECD.

—— (1982) *National Accounts, 1951–1980.* Paris: OECD.

Rutgaizer, V. M. (1981). "Chelovek truda v sfere raspredeleniia i potrebleniia." *Ekonomika i organizatsiia promyshlennogo proizvodstva,* 9, 46–62.

Schroeder, Gertrude E., and Barbara S. Severin (1976). 'Soviet Consumption and Income Policies in Perspective." In *Soviet Economy in a New Perspective,* 620–660. Joint Economic Committee. Washington, D.C.: GPO.

——, and Imogene Edwards (1981). *Consumption in the USSR: An International Comparison.* Issued by Joint Economic Committee, U.S. Congress. Washington, D.C.: GPO.

United Nations (1979). *Demographic Yearbook, 1978.* New York: United Nations.

United States Department of Commerce (USDC), Bureau of the Census (1979). *Population Projections by Age and Sex: For the Republics and Major Economic Regions of the U.S.S.R. 1970 to 2000.* Washington, D.C.: GPO.

——, Bureau of Economic Analysis (1986). *The National Income and Product Accounts of the United States, 1929–82.* Washington, D.C.: GPO.

5

Income Inequality
under Soviet Socialism*

I. *Introduction*

S OCIALISM, according to its proponents, has diverse virtues, but not least is the notable degree of equity that it is seen as assuring in the assignment of claims to the community's income. With the substantial replacement of private by public ownership of the means of production, it is held, a cardinal source of inequity in incomes under capitalism ceases at once to be operative. Under socialism the intimate relation between income and work done that prevails under the rival system supposedly will also give way soon or late to the alternative principle, proclaimed long ago as the only equitable one, of distributing the community's output simply according to need.

In the socialist world today, as no one must be told, incomes hardly conform to need anywhere. The question remains, though, as to how far socialist countries may have progressed toward implementation of that norm. That is a matter of inter-

est even to those who do not subscribe to such an egalitarian principle. What is essentially at issue, however, is the extent of income inequality in socialist countries and how such countries compare in that regard with the mixed economy countries of the West. Those are matters on which socialist countries have not always been especially forthright. That is an interesting fact in itself, but it necessarily obstructs accurate appraisal of income inequality. Even where relevant data on incomes are available, their meaning is often obscured by complexities of prevailing commodity distribution arrangements. Pervasive imbalances in the retail market are the best known but not the only example of such complexities.

These difficulties are encountered in inquiring into comparative income inequality under socialism everywhere. They seem especially pronounced, however, in the case of the chief country where that system prevails. The USSR, though, is of particular interest as the country where

* Simon Kuznets helpfully read and commented on an earlier draft, and so too did Janet G. Chapman, Gur Ofer, Gregory Grossman and an anonymous reader. Barry J. Eichengreen provided useful advice on the Addendum, and Clint Cummins kindly made the computations there. Mary Towle exercised her usual skill in transforming my not always legible handwriting into a presentable typescript.

socialism has been experienced for by far the longest period. Income inequality there has by now been the subject of a good deal of Western research, often with an emphasis on comparisons with the West. As those responsible would be the first to acknowledge, the results are hardly conclusive. Indeed, in view of the considerable effort that has been exerted, one must be struck at how much remains conjectural. A survey of Soviet income inequality in the light of that work, however, may facilitate appraisal of an important theme, and also usefully underline significant knowledge gaps.

In inquiring into income inequality in the USSR, Western scholars have sought to clarify not only the comparative degree of inequality but the process of income formation that underlies it. The latter as well as the former aspect is properly of concern here. While I focus primarily on recent Soviet circumstances, trends over time have also been explored in Western writings and they too will be of interest. Although relatively familiar, some attention must be paid even to the earliest post-Revolutionary experience.

I consider the USSR as "socialist" on the understanding that reference is essentially to a feature already alluded to: the predominantly public ownership of the means of production. In view of the proverbially authoritarian nature of Soviet politics, though, that customary usage understandably has often been challenged. Some who consider themselves socialists are also deeply concerned that, more than six decades after the Revolution, incomes still diverge from need.

While ownership of the means of production is predominantly public, cooperative ownership also prevails in the USSR on some scale. The outstanding instance, though not nearly as important as it once was, is the collective farm that Stalin imposed on the countryside, but cooperative ownership is also found elsewhere, principally in housing and retail trade. Private ownership too continues to prevail, chiefly in housing and on the small plots that the government allows collective farm and other households to cultivate individually. Such plots might be viewed as the remnants of the peasant farms, which prior to the wholesale collectivization of the early thirties, had predominated in Soviet agriculture. The alternative forms of ownership, especially the cooperative variety, seem often more formally than practically different from that of a public sort, but the distinction is still of interest for this inquiry.[1]

Also fundamental here is the nature of Soviet planning. I refer to the familiar system of centralist planning, with its extensive reliance on physical controls, through bureaucratic structures, as a means of coordinating and directing operational decisions. That form of coordination and direction, however, is not universal. Among other things, some use is made of alternative procedures stressing market processes in two spheres that will be of particular interest to us: labor recruitment and disposition of consumers' goods among households.

Central planning in a sense had its beginnings almost with the Revolution, but the urgent improvisations of the first post-Revolutionary years (1918–1920) have properly been called War Communism, and that experience was followed in turn by the New Economic Policy (1921–1928), with its renewed emphasis on market processes. It was not until after the five year plans had commenced, in 1928, that centralist planning really came into being. Since Stalin died (March 5, 1953) that scheme itself has been in flux, but the suc-

---

[1] The alternative forms prevail only in the case of reproducible capital. All land was declared to be public property at the time of the Revolution, and has remained so ever since. On the nature and roles of different forms of ownership in the USSR, see Abram Bergson 1964, ch. 2; Alec Nove 1977, ch. 1.

cessive revisions made are only of limited import here.

The reader is also reminded that under War Communism the economy approached utter collapse, that being the cumulative result of three years of World War, two revolutions and a civil war. NEP, however, brought rapid recovery, and in 1928, as the First Five Year Plan was being initiated, output in different sectors approached and sometimes exceeded pre-World War I levels. Under the plans, the government embarked on its famous drive for accelerated industrialization, with its stress on sharply increased capital formation and self-sufficiency, and the associated emphasis on heavy industry and defense. Wholesale collectivization was essentially a further corollary. With an interruption for the War, that so-called Soviet "growth model" remained in operation until Stalin's death. Since then the model appears to have been modified to a degree to allow increased attention to consumer wants, though defense clearly still claims high priority.

While the USSR is the outstanding case, the reader will wish to know that, in respect of income distribution, it may not always be especially representative of socialist countries more generally. Thus, inequality there may be greater than is usually so elsewhere (Frederic Pryor 1973, pp. 80–85; Peter Wiles 1974; Janet Chapman 1977a, and the Addendum).

II. *Conceptual Aspects*

How is inequality of income to be measured? Where the more ultimate concern is with equity, a formula that essentially generalizes one proposed by Anthony Atkinson (1970; 1975, p. 48; compare Dale Jorgenson and Daniel Slesnick 1983) seems especially apt:

$$I = 1 - (\overline{Y}/Y). \qquad (1)$$

Here Y is the community's total income while $\overline{Y}$ is the corresponding sum that would be required to attain the same level of social welfare should income be optimally distributed. I, the shortfall of the ratio $\overline{Y}/Y$ from unity, is an index of inequity.

That is still not income inequality, and depending on the underlying social welfare function (SWF), that might be one thing and inequity quite another. The SWF is manifestly to be construed here, however, in an egalitarian way, so it is not incongruously taken to be of the familiar Benthamite form, and for simplicity such that the satisfactions of each and every household are representable by one and the same utility function. Then, as Atkinson (1970) has shown, alternative income distributions rank in just the same way in terms of inequity, as just defined, as in terms of the proverbial Gini coefficient of income inequality.

I refer to alternative income distributions having the same mean. Should the means be different, the desired correspondence of inequity and the Gini coefficient still obtains if the SWF is such that relative incomes alone count for equity, though not necessarily otherwise. As an indicator of equity, the Gini coefficient must be read in that light. As we must also consider, inequity and inequality can be expected to be congruent only if the Lorenz curves in question do not intersect. Should they intersect, alternative income distributions might rank differently depending on the precise shape of the households' common utility function.[2]

[2] The utility function in any event is supposed to be concave and such that the marginal utility of income is positive. What Atkinson (1970) demonstrates is this: Assume a Benthamite SWF, with all households having one and the same utility function possessing the foregoing properties. For any two income distributions with the same mean that have nonintersecting Lorenz curves, social welfare is less for the one whose Lorenz curve is further from the diagonal.

In sum, the Gini coefficient taken by itself could be misleading. In inquiring into income inequality from the standpoint of equity, one must consider as well observations on at least a few points on the underlying Lorenz curve. We focus, though, on income inequality in the USSR. For that country, Lorenz curves are not always easy to come by, and neither are Gini coefficients. If we bear in mind the relation of such curves and coefficients to inequity, however, we will be able to see in perspective other measures, such as percentile ratios, that are often considered as indicators of income inequality. Although we can often refer to several percentiles in any given income distribution, such measures leave something to be desired as observations even on the Lorenz curve and Gini coefficients, never mind inequity. That sort of limitation of such data will have to be considered.[3]

While favoring the Lorenz curve and Gini coefficient, a concern with equity also argues for casting the income distribution in a particular form: one where reference is not to individual income recipients and their incomes but to households and their incomes. Households or preferably household members, it is understood, are to be classified according to household income per capita, or better yet, according to household income per adult equivalent, as given by some appropriate convention. Measures of inequality would be computed from such a distribution. Here too data available for the USSR are less than ideal, and will have to be seen accordingly.

In addition to differing for different individuals, income often fluctuates over time for any one individual. In available data on inequality, such fluctuations have usually been averaged out in some degree, but, so far as the averaging is incomplete, inequality as recorded is necessarily affected—it is almost inevitably greater than it would be if the averaging were more complete. That fact too must be kept in mind, but whether income fluctuations are averaged out or not, it should also be observed that they are apt in themselves to be a source of inequity. That would be so even should all income levels be equally affected.

The inequity, however, results mainly from differential access to accumulated liquid assets and loanable funds, and should be more pronounced in a Western market economy than in the USSR. There all individuals alike are allowed to accumulate liquid assets, but essentially in only two forms, cash and savings deposits (on which interest rates have invariably been almost nominal). Opportunities for consumer borrowing seem to be strictly limited though loans can be obtained to finance acquisition of housing and some durables.

Fluctuations apart, an individual's income tends almost everywhere to vary over his life span. Such variation, which

---

The congruence in ranking in terms of I in formula (1) and the Gini coefficient, though not entirely explicit in Atkinson, follows at once. Should the means be different, such congruence still obtains provided the SWF is such that I is unaffected by a proportional shift in all incomes.

[3] As rarely considered, the relation of percentile ratios to the corresponding Lorenz curve can sometimes be rather complex. Consider two cumulative frequency distributions, $f(y)$ and $g(y)$, with a common median, Me, in terms of which income is scaled. Let P_i^f and P_i^g represent the magnitudes of the ith percentiles (reading from low to high incomes) of the two distributions. Since the percentiles are likewise scaled in terms of the median, they also represent percentile ratios, the denominator percentile in all cases being the median.

Suppose that for all $i < 50$, $P_i^f \leq P_i^g$; and that for all $i > 50$, $P_i^f \geq P_i^g$. One might think that the Lorenz curve corresponding to $f(y)$ would everywhere be no closer than $g(y)$ to the diagonal. That need not be the case. Suppose in particular that for a range of incomes at the lowest level and for all incomes above Me, $P_i^f = P_i^g$, but that for all other incomes $P_i^f < P_i^g$. Suppose also that for $f(y)$, the mean, $M^f = Me$. In that case $M^g > Me$ and, as readily seen, the share of income accruing to a given proportion of income recipients at the lowest levels must be greater for $f(y)$ than for $g(y)$.

could be expected to occur even if there were no concomitant shift in incomes in the community generally, introduces a further familiar complexity into the interpretation of measures of income inequality. If the period to which income relates is at all limited, measured inequality may vary because of differences in age structure and lifetime earnings profiles, and hence without any corresponding difference in inequality of lifetime income.

In the circumstances, for purposes of inequality measurement, some sort of normalization of income for career stage or age has sometimes been suggested (Simon Kuznets 1966). If equity is the concern, however, inequality in incomes relating even to limited intervals would also seem to be of interest. The case for normalization at this point, therefore, is less compelling than it might be otherwise. In any event, it has yet to be attempted on any scale for the USSR. Lacking such inquiries, it is not easy to judge how available measures of income inequality might be affected.

A household's income, the primers tell us, comprises all current receipts that it might spend while leaving its total assets unchanged. Although not always made explicit, it is understood that the receipts may be in kind, in which case it is consumption rather than money expenditure that is in question. As so construed, household income in the USSR has diverse forms and sources, some familiar and others not so familiar in the West (Section IV). As in the West, however, income currently earned differs from income disposed of since there are both transfer receipts and transfer payments. Income disposed of clearly must be the category of prime interest here, although available data are not always favorable to that emphasis.[4]

[4] As often understood, income includes capital gains. In the USSR, there are still some privately owned goods, such as apartments and automobiles

Income, according to an argument espoused long ago by Irving Fisher, is properly viewed as constituted of consumption alone.[5] However questionable such a construction may be generally, from the standpoint of equity consumption has an interest of its own as representing the household's actual current withdrawals from the community's output. It is in the sphere of consumption that conflicting claims to output are finally adjudicated.

The distinction that is indicated between the distribution of consumption and the distribution of income may gain in interest in an inquiry such as this where inequality is compared in the USSR and the West. As between any two Western countries, as we may infer from usual household budget data, inequality in consumption is likely to differ less than inequality in income. Presumably that is also true when the USSR is compared with one or another Western country, but one wonders whether inequality in consumption and in income would differ as markedly under Soviet circumstances as is typical in the West. That is an as yet unexplored question, however, which I cannot pursue.

A question of scope is of unusual interest in this essay. Data on income distribution in Western countries, such as are to be considered, almost invariably omit institutionalized persons. Although rarely explained even in Western sources, that is almost certainly true as well regarding available data on income distribution in the USSR. That on the face of it might seem to make for comparability, but the institutional population includes penal workers. In terms of the numbers of persons involved, at least in earlier periods, and surely also in terms of their material

on which capital gains might be earned, but such gains must be relatively unimportant, if they figure at all, in available income data.

[5] Or so Irving Fisher (1906, pp. 101ff) has often been construed. In fact, he apparently limits income to services to consumers, and also diverges from conventional usage in other ways.

lot, it is not easy to think of likely parallels in the West to such workers in the USSR. The resultant incongruity in our data is not easy to correct, but it should be noted that the penal labor force of the USSR, according to relatively conservative estimates, numbered circa 1940, some 3.5 million persons, or 4.5 percent, and in recent years, some 2.0 million persons or 1.6 percent of all Soviet workers.[6]

III. *The Consumers' Goods Market*

In the appraisal of equity, incomes that are compared, while expressed in monetary terms, are supposed to represent commensurate differences in real income. Income, that is, should ideally be received in a monetary form, and be freely exchangeable for goods and services at established prices that are uniform for all households in any market area.

The ideal is hardly realized anywhere, but in inquiring into income inequality in the USSR we shall have to consider that the shortfall from the ideal has been notably marked. Soviet households do in fact receive the great bulk of their income in monetary form. That is so whether reference is to income currently earned or to income disposed of.[7] Negative transfers

apart, Soviet households may also use their money income to purchase consumers' goods. They may do so in a complex of retail shops, service facilities and the like that are operated by government agencies and cooperatives, and also in the collective farm markets where collective farms and their members may dispose of surplus produce. They may also be able to purchase goods and services from various quasi-legal and illegal sources. Such "second economy" transactions are a principal source of private entrepreneurial income that still survives in the USSR.[8]

But, granting the predominance of money income and the opportunities to spend it, how nearly real corresponds with money income in the USSR is another matter. In order for household money income to be freely exchanged for consumers' goods at established prices, such prices must limit household demand at least to levels corresponding to available supplies. Prices of consumers' goods in the USSR apparently are again and again below such levels. That prices are often of such a disequilibrium sort is readily acknowledged in the USSR itself. That, for example, must be the burden of consumer complaints, noted by L. I. Brezhnev (*Pravda*, Nov. 28, 1979) concerning "in-

---

[6] The cited estimates purportedly refer to inmates of so-called correctional labor camps. Recently many more persons—possibly as numerous as penal labor camp inmates—have apparently been subject, as "parolees" and "probationers," to compulsory labor of one sort or another without confinement. On the number of penal workers: Naum Jasny (1951); CIA (1982); Steven Rosefielde (1981); Stephen Wheatcroft (1981, 1983), and Robert Conquest (1982). In saying that data on income distribution in Western countries omit institutionalized persons, I refer particularly to data such as will be presented on the distribution of households by income. Institutionalized persons, I suspect, are usually excluded also from further statistics to be considered on the distribution of employees by earnings. Corresponding data to be presented for the USSR may safely be assumed to omit such persons.

[7] As will appear, income in kind is essentially of a conventional sort, comprising mainly, for farm households, own consumption of output, and for households generally, transfer receipts in the form

of educational services and health care. Subsistence, of course, is also provided members of the armed forces. While the volume of income in kind overall is now relatively modest (Section IV, Table 2), that consisting of farm consumption of own output was necessarily important in early years. Because of the nature of the data on income inequality that are to be considered, the question posed concerning the valuation of income in kind nevertheless tends to be rather academic for purposes of this essay. I comment on it at a later point, however, where it is of some practical interest.

[8] In respect of the USSR, the term "second economy" is often understood to embrace legal activities, though of a private sort, the most important case in point being production on household farm plots (Gregory Grossman 1977, 1979). To avoid ambiguity, I shall refer to income from both legal private and quasi-legal and illegal sources as "private income"; and to income from the latter sources as "second-economy income."

terruptions" in supplies of such products as "medicine, soap, detergents, toothbrushes and toothpaste, needles, thread, diapers and other goods produced in light industry."

Disequilibrium prices are also indicated by recurring reports of Western observers as to the frequency of empty shelves and queues in retail shops. With due allowance for possible differences in quality of the commodities supplied, the persistently high though fluctuating premia over prices in official retail outlets that prevail for food products sold in collective farm markets also points in the same direction (Bergson 1964, pp. 53ff; Nove 1977, p. 247). Collective farm market prices are substantially free to respond to market conditions.

It is also easy to read the prevalence of disequilibrium prices into some of the second-economy activities alluded to: payment of "tips" to retail shop employees supplying scarce consumer goods; diversion of such supplies for sale at enhanced prices in black markets (the diverted supplies, as might be expected, sometimes go at a discount); moonlighting of services at a premium, and so on (Gregory Grossman 1977, 1979; Hedrick Smith 1976, ch. 3). The apparently wide prevalence of such practices is the more striking in view of the forbidding powers of Soviet law enforcement agencies.[9]

With prices so often in disequilibrium, just how is real related to money income? Such prices prevail, as indicated, for very diverse goods. While shortages persist for some goods, they are apparently intermit-

tent for others. In any event, there is no basis to suppose that they are confined to products favored by any one income group; rather, the presumption is that they are experienced by both low- and high-income households. If so, the shortages manifestly should tend to dampen real relatively to money income differentials. With prices below clearing levels, money income ceases to be the sole determinant of capacity to acquire goods; to a degree, fortitude in searching out supplies and standing in queues, and plain luck, become consequential.[10]

True, where there are shortages in the USSR, goods are often sold at two prices rather than one. Such prices may be legal, as in the collective farm market, or illegal, as where there are "tips" or black market sales. In either case, the tendency towards dampening of real relatively to money income differentials should be mitigated but not eliminated.

But in the USSR, real and money income diverge not only because of disequilibrium prices. While less familiar, another consequential source of such divergence is the notable variety of discriminatory marketing practices. Although the Soviet government has been especially reticent regarding such practices, they must often offset, in part if not entirely, the egalitarian effects of disequilibrium prices. As will appear, individuals at the very highest levels of Soviet political and social life enjoy correspondingly high money incomes. At least relatively, their real incomes can only have been all the higher as a result of the discriminatory practices.

Thus, at least for such individuals, there are "closed shops" supplying select categories of customers with deficit goods, possibly at reduced prices (Mervyn Matthews 1978, pp. 38ff). Closely related in nature

9 I have been referring to partial disequilibrium. It has often been held that the Soviet retail market is in fact in general disequilibrium. A corollary, though, should be a tendency for household savings in the USSR to be inordinately large. Empirical inquiries into Soviet household savings do not seem to substantiate that inference (Joyce Pickersgill 1976, 1980; Gur Ofer and Pickersgill 1980). For a recent statement of the view that demand is generally excessive, Igor Birman (1980).

10 Of course, the effort expended in seeking supplies and standing in queues might be considered as something of an offset to the resultant gain in real income, but a gain there is nonetheless.

and effect, though not the same thing, are restricted outlets which provide special services (home delivery to order, special weekly allotments, etc.) to different occupational groups. Under centralist planning, by all accounts, a remarkable volume of goods is produced that are defective or otherwise substandard even according to the government's own norms (Bergson 1964, pp. 292ff). Not the least of the privileges enjoyed by persons in favored posts must be their superior access to better-quality products.

Differentiation of restaurant services for employees of an institution or enterprise apparently proceeds in a highly refined way:

> The Central Committee building in Moscow, for example, possesses at least three dining rooms, on different floors. These evidently serve different categories of officials, and the most select room has a militiaman at the door . . . . The range and quality of food seems to be comparable to that in very good restaurants outside, but the prices are considerably lower [Matthews 1978, p. 40].

At the prevailing depressed rental rates, housing has been a proverbially scarce good in the USSR. Here too, well-placed individuals seem in one way or another very often to be accorded priority either regarding the quantity of space or its quality or both.[11] And the discrimination sometimes again assumes a rather developed form, as in Akademgorodok, the research complex near Novosibirsk, where an academician is allotted a cottage; a professor

[11] The resultant relative gains for higher income groups were for long somewhat mitigated by the practice of progressively discounting the already low rentals for low-income households. For some time, workers and employees have practically all been at income levels subject to the maximum rate, but increased rates are still charged for extra space beyond a standard per capita norm, while that norm is reduced for individuals in the "free professions" (doctors, writers, et al.) whose income derives primarily from self-employment (Ministerstvo kommunal'nogo khoziaistva RSFSR 1947, pp. 145ff; Alfred DiMaio 1974, pp. 116ff, 144ff; Murray Yanowich 1977, pp. 40–43; Matthews 1978, pp. 42–46).

or senior scientific worker, an apartment with 97 square feet per family member, plus an extra family allotment of 216 square feet, an engineer or junior scientific worker, an apartment with 97 square feet per family member and a construction or service worker, an apartment with at least 77 feet per family member (Bernard Frolic 1971, p. 238).

Although demand for autos much exceeds supply, they are by Soviet standards by no means inexpensive, so not surprisingly supplies tend to gravitate to more affluent households. For many in high posts, a car (with a chauffeur) is apparently a fringe benefit (Yanowich 1977, pp. 44–45; Matthews 1978, p. 46). Upper income groups might also be favored in other ways through access to superior vacation resorts administered by prestigious institutions, highly-valued foreign travel privileges, and so on.

In the West too, of course, recipients of high incomes are often favored as well with nonmonetary rewards. Such fringe benefits are doubtless sometimes consequential, but they seem unlikely to compare in volume to the privileges enjoyed by advantaged groups, especially at the highest levels, in the USSR.

It remains to refer to still another aspect of the relation of real and money income in the USSR: the Soviet price structure. That, it is often suggested, could be rather special, and in a way that affects the real value of money income differentials. Such real value, it is supposed, may well be systematically deflated by a tendency of "necessities" to be notably cheap and of "luxuries" to be notably expensive.

Although long current, the supposition is rarely tested in any systematic way. Judging from limited data at hand (Table 1), the ruble price structure is perhaps not as odd as assumed. It does differ, though, from the price structures of two Western countries, the United States and Italy, and sometimes in the way suggested. Most im-

TABLE 1

RUBLE-DOLLAR RATIOS, 1976 AND LIRA-DOLLAR RATIOS, 1975. SELECTED CATEGORIES OF CONSUMERS'
GOODS, IN RELATION TO CORRESPONDING RATIO, ALL HOUSEHOLD CONSUMPTION[a]
(RATIO, ALL HOUSEHOLD CONSUMPTION, EQUALS UNITY)

Consumers' good category	Ruble-dollar ratio	Lira-dollar ratio	Consumers' good category	Ruble-dollar ratio	Lira-dollar ratio
Food	1.23	1.10	House furnishings	1.00	.83
Bread, cereals	.79	1.02	Furniture	.83	.68
Meat	1.62	1.42	Appliances	1.67	1.86
Fish	.45	1.81			
Milk, eggs, cheese	1.29	1.17	Transport, communications	.52	.81
Oils, fats	1.97	1.24			
Vegetables, potatoes	1.58 ⎱	.78	Auto	2.52	1.55
Fruit	2.65 ⎰		Auto services	1.13	.94
Sugar, confectionaries	1.37	1.02	Bikes, motor bikes	.55	n.a.
			Transport, public	.44	.32
Beverages	1.42	1.11	Communications	.53	1.11
Alcoholic	1.52	n.a.[b]	Publications, school supplies	.35	n.a.
Inc. Spirits	1.79	1.27			
Wine	1.44	.96	Publications	.26	n.a.
Beer	.94	1.60	Paper supplies	1.01	n.a.
Nonalcoholic	.80	n.a.	School supplies	.75	n.a.
Inc. Tea	1.44	2.00	Books, paper, magazines	n.a.	1.02
Coffee	1.00	2.94	Stationery	n.a.	1.26
			Educational books, supplies	n.a.	1.09
Tobacco	1.66	1.09	Recreation	.58	1.18
Clothing, footwear	1.75	1.24	Hotels, entertainment	.25	.53
			Radios, TV	3.87 ⎱	1.46
Clothing	2.04	1.30	Musical instruments	1.00 ⎰	
Footwear	1.15	1.02	Photo supplies	.50	n.a.
			Sports equipment	2.07	2.14
Gross rent, utilities	.34	.94	Toys	1.05	n.a.
Gross rent	.24	.85			
Utilities	.53	1.42			

[a] Compiled from data in Gertrude Schroeder and Imogene Edwards (1981) and Irving Kravis et al. (1982, pp. 208ff, 264). Ruble-dollar and lira-dollar ratios calculated respectively with Soviet and Italian weights, though alternative procedures sometimes used for subcategories. Ruble-dollar and lira-dollar ratios may not fully correspond in scope. Designations for different categories and subcategories usually, though not always, taken from Schroeder and Edwards.

The overall ruble-dollar and lira-dollar ratios considered, .654 and 543.3 respectively, relate to all household consumption except health care and education. In the case of the ruble-dollar ratio, though, household purchases of medical and school supplies are included. As indicated, the ruble-dollar price ratio for any commodity is expressed in relation to the overall ruble-dollar ratio; similarly, for the lira-dollar ratio for any commodity and the overall lira-dollar ratio.

[b] n.a. = not available

portantly, the low level of housing rentals, already noted, is here underlined. Associated utilities are apparently also very inexpensive in the USSR, and so too is public transportation. Relatively to the United States, however, public transportation is also very cheap in Italy.

Housing, associated utilities and public transportation are properly viewed as "necessities." I have in mind the usual standard for delineating such goods that relates to the comparative structure of consumption at different income levels. In the USSR, in terms of the same standard, autos, TV and possibly radios as well might be considered "luxuries." Autos, and in the aggregate, TV and radios, are apparently relatively expensive in the USSR. Some goods, such as hotels and entertainment, and possibly publications, however, are probably more nearly luxuries than necessities and yet are comparatively inexpensive.

For present purposes, relative prices within consumption classes such as those tabulated probably are often more interesting than those between them. On limited inquiry (see the sources cited in Table 1) circumstances here too appear rather complex. Lower income groups, however, are doubtless sometimes favored.[12]

Of the two Western countries in question, Italy is probably the more interesting one to compare with the USSR, for it is at a more or less similar stage of economic development (Section IV). Two countries, however, hardly represent an adequate sample for purposes of seeing the Soviet price structure in Western perspective. Granting that that structure may tend to favor lower income groups, the effect must frequently be dampened by other

features of the Soviet consumers' market already discussed: the disequilibrium prices and discriminatory practices.

I have been focusing on the Soviet consumers' goods market as it has been recently. As for earlier years, suffice it to say that disequilibrium prices have tended to be a feature of the Soviet consumers' goods market at least from the beginning of the five year plans. During the earliest plan years, consumers' goods were in any case supplied to households to a great extent through a system of rationing or otherwise restricted distribution rather than through an open market. These arrangements should have tended to mitigate money income inequality, though probably not as much as might be supposed. That should also have been the effect of similar arrangements for consumers' goods distribution that prevailed during WWII and immediately thereafter (Bergson 1944, pp. 36–43, 1964, ch. 4; Chapman 1963, ch. 2; Nove 1969, pp. 201ff; Matthews 1978, pp. 104ff).

Rationing of a more or less egalitarian sort had also been the rule under War Communism. Many supplies were simply distributed free of charge (Nove 1969, ch. 3; Margaret Dewar 1956, pp. 65ff). Considering the important role of private trade during subsequent years under the NEP, one might suppose, prices at least then should have tended relatively often to be at clearing levels. The functioning of the NEP consumers' goods market, however, has yet to be systematically explored from that standpoint.

Factual information about discriminatory practices such as have been described has become available to Western scholars only in the course of time. Very possibly the practices have become more consequential than they were formerly, although they are by no means novel (Matthews 1978, chs. 3, 4). How the consumers' goods price structure has evolved must be left to separate inquiry.

---

[12] Thus, it is TV sets, as distinct from radios, that are especially expensive in the USSR. Children's things, it is often supposed, are particularly cheap in the USSR. Among clothing articles, those for children do appear often to be somewhat less expensive relatively in the USSR than in the U.S.

IV. *Comparative Inequality: Wages and Salaries*

In inquiring into income inequality in the USSR, Western scholars have tended to focus on one or another facet of that matter and only rarely deal with it in a comprehensive way. One such facet addressed, though, is that concerning inequality of pay among public sector employees. That is of central interest in a country where government employment is predictably a preponderant source of household earned income (Table 2). That is so even if, as Soviet statistical usage mandates, collective farmers are treated as other than government employees (they are at least nominally cooperative producers). Although the sometimes crude data drawn on here probably understate some of the diverse prevailing forms of private income (Table 2, items 6, 7 and 8, and so far as they derive from household farm plots, items 3 and 4), the predominance of earnings from public sector employment remains pronounced.[13]

Turning first to such earnings, I cite (Table 3) ratios of different percentiles of frequency distribution of wage earners and

---

[13] In particular, the cited data probably understate income from activities of a private entrepreneurial sort other than that from household farm plots (item 6): see Section V. The almost nominal figure for imputed net rent on private housing, of course, reflects the proverbially low level of rental charges in the USSR that were noted above. "Other income currently earned" (item 9), however, should not be thought of as representing a corresponding amount of private income. It may consist primarily, if not exclusively, of a statistical discrepancy; see the notes to the table.

While collective farmers are not included here among public sector employees, such employees are engaged in agriculture on a considerable scale in the so-called state farms. Inclusive of pay to workers in diverse auxiliary state agricultural enterprises, their earnings represented 7.2 and 9.2 per cent, in 1960 and 1980 respectively, of all civilian public sector wages and salaries (TSSU 1961, p. 521; 1971, p. 519; 1981, pp. 282, 364). Note, too, that household plots are operated by not only collective farmers but also state farm workers and to some extent even urban employees.

TABLE 2

HOUSEHOLD INCOMES IN THE USSR, 1960 AND 1980
(BIL. RUBLES)

	Item	1960	1980
1.	Wages and salaries, civilian employees, public sector	60.1	229.3
2.	Money payments to collective farm members by collective farm	4.4	16.5
3.	Net income of farm households from sale of farm products	5.4	14.3
4.	Net farm income in kind	9.1	19.2
5.	Income of armed forces		
	a. Pay and allowances	2.3	4.9
	b. Subsistence	1.6	4.0
	c. All	3.9	8.9
6.	Net money income from privately supplied services and construction, imputed value of owner supplied construction services	4.5	4.8
7.	Imputed net rent	.8	1.2
8.	Interest income	.2	3.6
9.	Other income currently earned	9.7	12.6
10.	Income currently earned, all	98.2	310.5
11.	Money transfers		
	a. Money receipts (pensions, allowances, stipends)	10.3	46.5
	b. Direct taxes; other outlays	6.9	29.0
	c. Net transfers	3.4	17.5
12.	Net income disposed of	101.6	328.0
13.	Educational services; health care, other transfers in kind	9.7	33.8
14.	Net income disposed of, including transfers in kind	111.3	361.7

Source: CIA, March 1983. Wages and salaries, civilian employees, public sector, include the pay of Party and trade union staff, and also that of employees of consumers' cooperatives. A small sum paid hired labor by collective farms is also included. Interest income includes a minute amount of consumers' coop dividends. Some items treated in the source as transfers have been reclassified here as earned income, or (in the case of "net new bank loans") have been omitted from income altogether. "Other payments to the state" in the cited source are treated here as transfer payments, though they may include some fees for services. Other income currently earned includes a statistical discrepancy emerging in a national accounting context. Discrepancies between sums of items and indicated totals are due to rounding.

TABLE 3

SELECTED PERCENTILE RATIOS, DISTRIBUTIONS OF WAGE EARNERS AND SALARIED WORKERS BY EARNINGS, AND GDP PER CAPITA, USSR AND WESTERN COUNTRIES, SPECIFIED YEARS

Country and Year	Real GDP per capita (U.S. 1975 = 100)	Percentile Ratio			
		P_{10}/P_{50}	P_{90}/P_{50}	P_{95}/P_{50}	P_{90}/P_{10}
USSR: 1961	31	.50	2.0	2.4	4.0
1966	36	.55	1.8	2.2	3.3
1968	40	.56	1.8	2.1	2.8
1970	43	.58	1.7	2.0	
1972	45				3.1
1976	50				3.4
1981	55				3.0
Spain: 1964	27		2.0	2.4	
Austria: 1957	28		1.8	2.3	
Argentina: 1961	31		1.8	2.3	
Japan: 1968	47	.52	1.9	2.3	3.7
Canada: 1950–1951	47		1.6	1.9	
1960–1961	54		1.8	2.1	
France: 1963	49		2.0	2.7	
U.K.: 1964–1965	49	.48	1.6		3.5
1976	66	.60	1.7	2.0	2.8
Belgium: 1964	53		1.6	2.0	
U.S.: 1949	58		1.7		
1959	72		1.8	2.2	
1972	99	.47	2.1	2.6	4.5
1975	100	.45	1.8		4.0

Sources: See text for the nature and scope of data on wages that underlie the cited percentile ratios. The sources of the ratios as well as of real GDP per capita follow:

Real GDP per capita. Soviet versus U.S. GNP in 1976, as in Edwards et al. (1979), adjusted chiefly to conform to consumption calculations in Schroeder and Edwards (1981) and extrapolated to earlier years by use of standard sources, including for Soviet GNP Rush Greenslade (1976) and CIA (Nov. 1981; Sept. 1983). For Western countries, see Robert Summers et al. (1980). U.S. 1949 and 1959 and Austria 1957 extrapolated from corresponding data for 1950 and 1960 in ibid.
Percentile ratios. USSR: P_{90}/P_{10} for all years except 1981, N. E. Rabkina and N. M. Rimashevskaia (1978). For 1981, E. Alexandrova and E. Federovskaia (1984). For all other ratios, see Chapman (1977b).
Spain: Lydall (1968, p. 342).
Austria: Lydall (1968, p. 289).
Argentina: Lydall (1968, p. 287).
Japan: Calculated from Ministry of Labor, Japan (1969, p. 172).
Canada: Lydall (1968, p. 301).
France: Lydall (1968, pp. 142, 143, 312).
U.K.: 1964–1965, Chapman (1977a); 1976 calculated from Department of Employment, U.K. (1978, p. 39).
Belgium: Lydall (1968, p. 292).
U.S.: 1959, Lydall (1968, p. 362); 1949, 1972 and 1975, Chapman (1977a, 1979a).

salaried workers (WESW) classified by their pay.[14] Percentiles are numbered beginning with that referring to the lowest paid workers. Earnings are as reported in Soviet March surveys of employees of public enterprises and institutions. The armed forces are excluded, however, and so too are employees of quasi-public agencies such as the Communist Party and trade unions (Chapman 1977b, p. 258).

Or rather, to be precise, the cited indicators are assumed to characterize frequency distributions resulting from the Soviet March surveys. The caveat is needed, for the Soviet government has not released any of the frequency distributions in question. The fact that the indicators characterize those distributions, thus, has to be inferred, but the inference seems inevitable when we consider that all the cited magnitudes for the decile ratio (P_{90}/P_{10}) have been reported in Soviet sources. Moreover, the nature of the underlying frequency distributions has been the subject of much rather sophisticated techni-

---

TABLE 4

SELECTED PERCENTILE RATIOS, DISTRIBUTIONS OF SOVIET WAGE EARNERS AND SALARIED WORKERS BY EARNINGS, SOVIET DATA, ALTERNATIVE WESTERN ESTIMATES

Year and Nature of Data	Percentile Ratio		
	P_{10}/P_{50}	P_{90}/P_{50}	P_{90}/P_{10}
1961			
Soviet release			4.02
Chapman estimates	.50	1.98	3.92
1966			
Soviet release			3.26
Chapman estimates	.55	1.83	3.36
Wiles estimates	.58	1.88	3.26
McAuley estimates	.58	1.91	3.30
1968			
Soviet release			2.83
Chapman estimates	.56	1.78	3.17
McAuley estimates	.61	1.70	2.78
1970			
Chapman estimates	.58	1.73	3.00
McAuley estimates	.59	1.84	3.15

Sources: For Soviet data, see Table 3; Chapman (1977b, p. 261); Wiles (1974, p. 24); McAuley (1979, p. 222).

---

[14] It is time to explain that reference to wages *and* salaries or to wage earners *and* salaried workers serves to underline what reference to wages or wage earners alone might obscure, that the data to be considered extend to the earnings of not only production workers but technical, administrative and office personnel. As the context will make clear, though, I sometimes use the term wages elliptically to embrace the earnings of all workers, including the latter sorts. Sometimes too I must make a distinction between "wage earners" and "salaried workers." That can be done in terms of different categories of workers that are delineated in Soviet Labor statistics: i) "ordinary laborers" (*rabochie*), who comprise all production workers below the rank of foremen, except two further categories, ii) custodial and other service personnel, and iii) apprentices; iv) "engineer-technical personnel" (*inzhenerno-tekhnicheskie rabotniki*), comprising the administrative and supervisory staff, as well as engineers and other specialists; and v) clerical and similar office workers (*sluzhashchie*).

According to a usual Western convention, the first three groups of workers have come to be referred to as wage earners and the last two as salaried workers. I conform to this usage where a definite one is needed. Soviet statistical practice regarding the classification of different kinds of labor has evolved somewhat in the course of time (Bergson 1944, pp. 213–14).

cal discussion in the USSR. Evidence has been presented showing that the distributions are closely approximated by a log normal curve.[15] Utilizing in an ingenious way that fact, and diverse data released

[15] A "coefficient of similarity" of the log normal and the actual distributions is calculated to be in 1956, 96.1; 1961, 95.1; 1964, 96.0; 1966, 95.7 and in 1968, 91.6. The coefficient is obtained by taking for each class interval the lesser of the actual and the corresponding theoretic frequency and summing. The frequencies are apparently expressed initially as percentages, the lesser being related in each case to the larger one (N. E. Rabkina and N. M. Rimashevskaia 1972, pp. 193, 195; Chapman 1977b, pp. 261–62).

on relevant parameters, Chapman (1977b) was able to derive the indicated magnitudes for percentile ratios other than P_{90}/P_{10}. Estimates derived for the latter decile ratio by a somewhat different procedure closely approximate the corresponding reported Soviet figures. There appears to be an appreciable over-statement, however, in 1968 (Table 4).

According to an informational device, which in respect of the resultant frustration of Western scholars is exceptional even by Soviet standards, the Russians have also released charts of the frequency distributions resulting from the March surveys, but without any numerical scales on the axes! Not to be daunted, though, Wiles (1974) and Alastair McAuley (1979, ch. 9), by reference to diverse clues, and following a trail blazed by Wiles and Stefan Markovski (1971), have managed somehow to decipher the charts. They arrive at estimates for percentile ratios that tend to be closely in accord with Chapman's. In contrast to Chapman, however, McAuley closely approximates the reported Soviet decile ratio for 1968 (Table 4).[16]

In carrying out special surveys of wages,

[16] The import, for the reliability of the Western estimates of percentile ratios generally, of the relation between those estimates for P_{90}/P_{10} and corresponding Soviet figures is regrettably not all that it might seem. As indicated, Chapman computes P_{90}/P_{10} by a rather different procedure from that used to calculate other percentile ratios. Wiles apparently imposes on his computations for 1966 the reported Soviet decile ratio for that year, so the resultant identity of his estimate and the Soviet figure signifies nothing as to the reliability of his calculations more generally. McAuley appears to have used one and the same procedure to derive all of his percentile ratios, including P_{90}/P_{10}, but to what extent the computations were independent of the reported Soviet decile ratios is difficult to judge from his abbreviated explication.

Granting the ambiguity of the relation of the Western and reported Soviet decile ratios, however, it is reassuring that separate Western computations utilizing (in the case of Chapman, on the one hand, and Wiles and McAuley, on the other) different methods, are so substantially in accord.

the Soviet government has apparently resumed a practice which was regularly followed in the late twenties and early thirties. In contrast to its present policy, however, it released in substantial detail results of those previous investigations, thus providing the basis for an early Western inquiry into Soviet wage inequality (Bergson 1944). Summary measures now being released for early years differ to some extent from, but need not be inconsistent with, results obtained in that work (Section VII).

In that study and often in later Western ones on the same theme, inequality in the USSR is compared with that in the U.S. Comparisons are also sometimes made with other Western countries. For an early year, 1959, however, Pryor (1973, pp. 74ff) has extended the scope of such comparisons by drawing extensively on the work of Harold Lydall (1968). Proceeding in good part in the same way, I have juxtaposed with the indicators computed for the USSR corresponding measures for a number of Western countries (Table 3).

What emerges is a rather striking similarity in inequality, as measured, between the USSR and Western countries. Inequality in the USSR fluctuates in the course of time, but only rarely does any particular percentile ratio fall outside the range delineated by corresponding measures for Western countries.

According to a familiar finding, due mainly to Kuznets (1963; 1966, pp. 206ff, 420ff), however, income inequality tends to vary with the stage of development. Referring particularly to the distribution of wages and salaries among recipients, Lydall (1968, pp. 215–18) also found such a relation, with the degree of inequality tending to decline with the development stage. Among countries that are at all advanced, the tendency is rather weak, and that is so among the Western countries in question here. With development stage represented by GDP per capita (Table 3), any systematic connection one way or the other between that and earnings inequality is not readily apparent. The import of the development stage for our comparison of Soviet and Western wage inequality is thus not too clear.

But what is posed is a larger issue: regarding inequality in pay, after appropriate normalization of the measures considered, how does Soviet socialism compare with Western mixed economies? That is a matter that seems to have been little explored, and I cannot adequately explore it in this survey, but a brief appended inquiry suggests that the development stage is properly included among the conditioning factors for which our comparison of Soviet and Western wage inequality is normalized, and that with such normalization, wage inequality in the USSR, especially in the early seventies, may have been somewhat low relatively to that in the West. The relations disclosed, though, leave much to be desired statistically.

Measures of inequality of wages for different countries are apt to be less than fully comparable statistically. Although I have sought to avoid egregious incongruities, residual divergencies doubtless are a reason why the data compiled here are as resistant to statistical analysis as suggested. Judging from available evidence, the divergencies are unlikely to distort the comparison of the USSR and the West radically in any systematic way, but that is a complex matter on which further research could be rewarding.[17]

[17] To be more explicit, while the Soviet March surveys do not extend to collective farmers, they do cover state farm workers constituting in 1970 some ten per cent of persons in enterprises covered by the surveys. For Western countries, reference is most often to nonfarm employees, but farm employees as well are covered in the case of Australia, Belgium, Canada and, I believe, the United Kingdom. The Soviet March surveys cover only workers who were employed a full month. Workers who worked part-time for a full month may also have been included, though that is not clear (Chapman 1977b, p. 263; McAuley 1979, p. 219). For Spain and Argen-

According to Soviet sources, as we saw, the distribution of WESW by earnings tend to be log-normal. Even without normalization, such a distribution might already betoken some compression of differences in pay. Among Western countries, at least for adult male workers, distributions of recipients by labor earnings apparently manifest an excess of frequencies in upper-income brackets over those called for by the log-normal curve (Lydall 1968, pp. 60–68).

V. *Comparative Inequality: Household Income per Capita*

Statistical heterogeneity apart, the measures considered thus far are still wanting for present purposes. They are incomplete in their coverage of both the gainfully employed and household income. The deficiencies vary in importance even among Western countries, but in view of the differing economic institutions, necessarily do so in a dramatic way as between the USSR and the West. The measures also relate to incomes of income recipients,

tina, reference is to all workers employed during a reporting period, the period for Spain being one month in each of three quarters and for Argentina, a year. For Japan reference is to "contractual" earnings of "regular" employees during a reporting period of one month. For all other countries, the data relate to employees who worked during an entire reporting period. That is sometimes as long as a year, though (as is possibly so for the USSR) part-time workers who worked during the entire interval are included in some cases. For Britain, reference is to adult workers (in 1964–1965, 18 years and over; in 1976, males 21 and over, females 18 and over.)

On the possible impact of statistical divergencies such as the foregoing, see the illuminating comparative data in Lydall (1968, pp. 142–44, 153), and in Christopher Saunders and David Marsden (1981, pp. 64ff). To my regret, the latter study became available to me too late to be fully taken into account.

For his purposes, Lydall finally adjusts his percentile ratios to refer to a "standard" earnings distribution, i.e., one referring to full-time male workers. It is the adjusted ratios that he juxtaposes with the development stage, and it is to the result of that inquiry that I refer above. In Table 3, however, I cite Lydall's ratios as they were prior to adjustment. See also the Addendum.

TABLE 5

SELECTED PERCENTILE RATIOS, SPECIFIED INCOME DISTRIBUTIONS AND YEARS, USSR

Distribution and Year	P_{10}/P_{50}	P_{90}/P_{50}	P_{95}/P_{50}	P_{90}/P_{10}
Nonfarm households, by pre-tax household income per capita, McAuley, 1967	.59	1.77	2.08	3.01
Nonfarm household members, by pre-tax household income per capita, McAuley, 1967	.58	1.79	2.29	3.11
Total population, by pre-tax household income per capita, McAuley, 1967	.54	1.72	2.20	3.21
Urban households, by post-tax household income per capita, Ofer and Vinokur, 1972–1974	.54	1.92	2.32	3.56
Urban household members, by post-tax household income per capita, Ofer and Vinokur, 1972–1974	.56	1.78	2.16	3.18

Sources: Percentile ratios for McAuley distributions taken from or calculated from frequency distributions in McAuley (1979, pp. 57, 65). For total population, reference is to his frequency distribution "B." For Ofer and Vinokur ratios, see their 1980a essay.

rather than as is desired here, consumer units. What of the distribution of income in a more or less inclusive sense among consumer units?

The answer for the nonfarm population of the USSR, according to findings of McAuley (1979, ch. 3), is that, in terms of percentile ratios, inequality of per capita incomes is much the same as inequality of wages and salaries. That is so whether reference is to the distribution of income among nonfarm households or among nonfarm household members (Table 5). In both cases, the cited data relate to household income per capita.

The percentile ratios now in question are of similar provenance to those considered previously for wages and salaries. For the latter, however, the underlying Soviet surveys are of a census sort and essentially comprehensive of workers in sectors covered. For income distribution among nonfarm families and the nonfarm population, use is made of results of a Soviet sample survey, whose representativeness, as McAuley points out, is questionable; results,

that is, which as with those of surveys of wages and salaries have in any event to be inferred from restricted releases.

On Soviet income inequality, however, we may also refer to another and quite different source. In arriving at measures of urban income inequality in the USSR (Table 5), Gur Ofer and Aaron Vinokur draw on a survey of retrospective household budgets of some 1,200 families of Jewish emigrés from the USSR to Israel. Under intensive interviews conducted in 1976 and 1978, the emigrés were asked to recall their incomes and outlays during their last year of "normal" residence in the USSR. That generally turned out to be a year during the period 1972–1974. The sample thus obtained was systematically inflated so as to conform in terms of occupation (blue collar vs. white collar; active vs. inactive), education, sex and family structure, to the Soviet urban population generally.

Such an inquiry too is not exactly what one might wish for, but both it and McAuley's reconstruction of the Soviet survey results, I believe, merit careful attention. A word first regarding the nature of a household. Soviet statisticians refer rather to "family" (*sem'ia*), which is understood to be "a group of individuals not necessarily related by blood or marriage who share a common budget" (McAuley 1979, p. 15). This is apparently the usage underlying the Soviet income survey. It is also the meaning of household for Ofer-Vinokur, though in practice individuals grouped as such were almost always related.

Although the two inquiries are thus in conformity in that regard, in comparing their results we must consider: i) the difference in dates to which they refer; ii) the fact that income for McAuley is gross and for Ofer-Vinokur, net of direct taxes (in both cases, however, it includes money transfer receipts and excludes imputed rents), and iii) the apparent inclusion by McAuley and exclusion by Ofer-Vinokur of the rural nonfarm population.

With due allowance for these incongruities, inequality of incomes, particularly among households, is probably greater for Ofer-Vinokur than for McAuley.[18] The inflated Ofer-Vinokur sample could somewhat overstate urban income inequality. Among other things, transfers in the form of pensions and the like that are relatively consequential for low income groups may be underestimated.[19]

[18] Judging from the trends in percentile ratios for wages and salaries (Tables 3 and 4), the difference in dates should have made for less inequality in McAuley than in Ofer-Vinokur. But, while Soviet direct taxes are only mildly progressive, the difference in that regard should have had a contrary effect (fn. 32). That must have been the case also for the further difference regarding the rural, nonfarm population.

[19] On the transfers in question, see Section VI, particularly fn. 33. Transfers apart, one feature of the Ofer-Vinokur inflated sample must cause an understatement rather than overstatement of inequality. This is the practical omission of "elite" households. But, while as will appear, this could appreciably affect Lorenz-type data on income distribution, the number of persons involved is too small for percentile ratios in question to be noticeably distorted. Here, as well as in respect of the Lorenz-type data to be considered later, however, a further upward

There are also reasons to think, however, that the McAuley measures are subject to a contrary bias. The Soviet 1967 income survey on which he relies apparently omitted entirely families with no gainfully employed members (i.e., predominantly families of pensioners), and tended systematically to underrepresent single-member households and households with only one worker. As reflected in McAuley's measures, these deficiencies should have tended markedly to reduce inequality. The measures for households should have been especially affected.[20]

To what extent the Soviet 1967 survey

bias in the Ofer-Vinokur inequality measures, though of a very limited sort, must result from a technical limitation of their data. I refer to the fact that, in inflating their sample, Ofer-Vinokur do not attempt to adjust for differences in money income levels depending on which year during the period 1972–1974 the different emigré households took as "normal." During 1972–1974, money wages were rising by 4.1 per cent yearly.

While computing data on the distribution of income among households, Ofer-Vinokur also inflate their sample to represent the distribution of WESW by earnings from their main public sector job. Resulting magnitudes of percentile ratios, after approximate adjustment to a pre-tax basis (fn. 32)—for P_{10}/P_{50}, .51; P_{90}/P_{50}, 1.82 and P_{90}/P_{10}, 3.53—seem to indicate a greater dispersion than do corresponding ratios considered above (Table 3) relating to Soviet census-type distributions of wage earners and salaried workers by earnings. Comparison of the alternative measures in question is made difficult, however, by uncertainties as to the precise treatment accorded in the Soviet census-type data to such aspects as part-time labor and secondary public sector employment.

[20] The omission, from the Soviet survey, of households with no active members must in itself have significantly depressed McAuley's inequality measures. Of this we may judge from further data compiled by Ofer-Vinokur. For the distribution of income among households, the decile ratio of 3.56 (Table 5) falls to 3.31 when reference is made to active households alone. For the distribution of income among household members, there is a corresponding reduction of the decile ratio from 3.18 to 3.05. The downward bias in the McAuley measures, for both households and household members, probably was compounded by the omission or underrepresentation of part-time workers. Following McAuley, I assume that the 1967 Soviet survey was patterned methodologically after an earlier one carried out in 1958. A cardinal feature of that was to use enterprise employment rolls to select households to be covered. On the 1967 survey: McAuley 1979, pp. 53ff; Rimashevskaia 1965, pp. 46ff.

covered private income, particularly of the second-economy sort (fn. 7), is conjectural. Most likely it did so at best only very partially. In Ofer-Vinokur (1980a; also 1980b), where such coverage should have been more nearly complete, private income is found to constitute 11–12 per cent of all household income. Their more complete coverage of private income probably affects their percentile ratios in complex ways, but overall the tendency here too should be for inequality to be understated in the McAuley data.[21]

In brief, Ofer-Vinokur may somewhat overstate Soviet income inequality, but should be closer to the mark than McAuley could be on the basis of the flawed Soviet survey data on income distribution.[22]

I have been referring to income distribution among urban and nonfarm households and their members. The cited McAuley measures of income inequality among the Soviet population more generally (Table 5) result from the aggregation, with the distribution of nonfarm household members by household income per capita, of a further distribution for the farm population. The latter originated in another Soviet sample survey, which as McAuley indicates, is less reliable than that on nonfarm households. The Soviet releases on it, furthermore, are even more than usually enigmatic.[23] McAuley's findings merit attention, however, as the results of the one systematic Western inquiry to date into income inequality among the Soviet population generally by household income per capita.[24]

---

[21] Of that we may judge by comparing the Ofer-Vinokur ratios in Table 5 with corresponding incomes, which omit private earnings: P_{10}/P_{50}, .52; P_{90}/P_{50}, 1.77; P_{95}/P_{50}, 2.28, and P_{90}/P_{10}, 3.40. For the distribution of public sector incomes among the urban household members, Ofer-Vinokur arrive at these further results: for P_{10}/P_{50}, .52; for P_{90}/P_{50}, 1.68; P_{95}/P_{50}, 1.96; P_{90}/P_{10}, 3.26.

For Ofer-Vinokur income inequality among urban household members is markedly less than that among urban households. For McAuley, income inequality among nonfarm household members is, if anything, somewhat greater than that among nonfarm households. Without further information, however, there is no basis to choose between the alternative calculations at this point.

[22] Note must be taken of a related computation by Wiles (1974). His point of departure is the frequency distribution of WESW by their earnings, that he derives in the manner already described. Referring to the magnitudes of the various deciles in that distribution, Wiles adjusts them to obtain corresponding deciles of a distribution of wage earners, salaried workers and their families by household income per capita. Adjustment coefficients applied, taken from Rabkina and Rimashevskaia (1972, pp. 212–15), are supposed to reflect Soviet experience.

Wiles interprets the result as relating to the distribution of the employee population qua individuals by household income per capita. As described in the cited Soviet source, they could equally relate, I think, to the distribution of employee households by per capita income.

In any event, his decile ratio for 1966 is 3.5–3.7, or about the same as the corresponding Ofer-Vinokur ratio for income distribution among urban households in 1972–1974. It is markedly higher, however, than the Ofer-Vinokur decile ratio for income distri-

bution among urban household members and also higher than that ratio for the McAuley distributions for nonfarm households and household members (Table 5).

[23] The survey relates only to the collective farm population. In Table 5, I give percentile ratios relating to a frequency distribution in which income distribution among the collective farm population is allowed to represent that among state farm employees and their families. An alternative computation of McAuley where income distribution among such persons is represented by that for the nonfarm population yields essentially the same results.

Income-in-kind is still a significant element in farm household income in the USSR. In the survey of collective farm household income according to McAuley (1979, p. 53), such income most likely was valued at state retail shop prices. David Bronson and Constance Krueger (1971, p. 225), however, hold that it was valued at average farm realized prices, which is not the same thing.

[24] The decile ratio of the distribution of household members by income per capita in the USSR in 1972 has been reported in a Soviet source (L. A. Migranova and N. E. Rabkina 1976, p. 62) as 3.59. This apparently is indicated by a survey of income in September 1972, which like that of 1967 was a sample sort, but covered families of not only nonfarm WESW but collective farmers and presumably also state farm workers (McAuley 1979, p. 54; V. G. Kriazhev 1973, pp. 182–83). Whether the cited ratio also relates to all such persons is less clear; in the context it might be construed as relating only to families of WESW, including those of state farm workers. On any construction, though, it appears to signify a greater degree of inequality than McAuley's calculations do. Note, however, that the September 1972

TABLE 6

INCOME SHARES OF SELECTED PERCENTILE GROUPS AND GINI COEFFICIENTS, DISTRIBUTIONS OF HOUSE-
HOLDS BY PER CAPITA HOUSEHOLD INCOME, AND GDP PER CAPITA, USSR AND WESTERN COUNTRIES,
SPECIFIED YEARS

Distribution, Country and Year	GDP per capita (U.S. = 100)	Income Share (%) of				Gini Coefficient
		Lowest 10%	Lowest 20%	Highest 20%	Highest 10%	
Nonfarm households, pre-tax						
USSR, 1967 (McAuley)	38	4.4	10.4	33.8	19.9	.229
Urban households, post-tax						
USSR, 1972–1974 (Ofer-Vinokur)	48	3.4	8.7	38.5	24.1	.288
All households, pre-tax						
Australia, 1966–1967	56	3.5	8.3	41.0	25.6	.317
Norway, 1970	64	3.5	8.2	39.0	23.5	.306
U.K., 1973	66	3.5	8.3	39.9	23.9	.308
France, 1970	68	2.0	5.8	47.2	31.8	.398
Canada, 1969	74	2.2	6.2	43.6	27.8	.363
U.S., 1972	99	1.8	5.5	44.4	28.6	.376
All households, post-tax						
Sweden, 1972	80	3.5	9.3	35.2	20.5	254

Sources: GDP per capita as in Table 3. Income shares for USSR 1967 calculated from frequency distribution
in McAuley (1979, p. 57); for USSR, 1972–1974, see Ofer and Vinokur (1980a). For all Western countries,
income shares from Sawyer (1976, p. 17). For comparability, all Gini coefficients computed from income
shares of decile groups. Ofer-Vinokur coefficient in source, apparently calculated from frequency distribution,
was .293

To turn finally to the inevitable question concerning comparative Soviet and Western income inequality, gauging that is unfortunately obstructed by limitations in available data for Western countries as well as the USSR.

For the USSR, the Lorenz-type measures cited for urban households (Table 6) correspond to those of Ofer-Vinokur just considered. Judging from data in Ofer-Vinokur (1980a, 1982), adjustment

survey was reportedly more inclusive than that of 1967 of low income families (Migranova and Rabkina 1976, p. 57). On recent Soviet income inequality, see also A. Aleksandrova and E. Federovskaia 1984, p. 21.

for the underestimate of pensions referred to above might raise the income share of the lowest fifth by, say, 1.0 percentage point. As Ofer has informed me, he was unable to include in his sample any "elite" households. Since such households could account for but a fraction of one per cent of households supposedly represented by the sample, their omission hardly matters for inequality measures such as discussed above. Inclusion of their income, however, might raise the income shares of the highest fifth and tenth by some 1.5 percentage points.[25] Overall, though, Ofer-

[25] I allow for elite households numbering 0.3 per cent of the urban population, and having a per capita income of five times the urban average (Section IX).

Vinokur here as before could overestimate inequality among Soviet urban households (fn. 19).

While Ofer-Vinokur refer only to such households, that is not all to the bad where Soviet inequality is compared, as is done here, with that for households generally in the most industrialized Western countries. In those countries, the rural sector tends in any case to be quite small. Should the Ofer-Vinokur calculation be extended to include rural households as well, that by itself should make for greater inequality.[26]

McAuley does not undertake to cast in Lorenz form frequency distributions from which his percentile ratios are calculated. For completeness I have made the necessary translation. This involved dealing with an all-over class containing 3.5 per cent of the households, but the resulting measures, like the corresponding McAuley percentile ratios, must significantly understate inequality.[27]

For Western countries, I draw (Table 6) on the very useful report prepared by Malcolm Sawyer (1976) for the OECD. As in Ofer-Vinokur and McAuley, household income is understood to include transfer receipts as well as earned income, but the scope of income, as noted later, differs to some extent not only between the USSR and the West but also between different Western countries. Probably more important, as Sawyer (1976, pp. 12–13, 33–34) makes clear, the indicated Lorenz-type measures for Western countries are all affected by unevenness in reporting, in relevant statistical sources, of major types of income. Although adjustments could sometimes be made for resulting deficiencies, coverage of property and entrepreneurial income in particular is often comparatively limited. Entrepreneurial income includes earnings of self-employed who are not always prosperous. Perhaps on that account the impact of underreporting for the United States, according to calculations by Edward Budd (1970, pp. 256–57) for 1964, must have been rather complex and limited. When the incomplete Current Population Reports data that are in question are adjusted to assure totals for different types of income that conform to national accounts data, the income shares of both the lowest and the highest fifths of households increase, the former by 0.3 and the latter by 0.6 per cent. The Gini coefficient rises from .423 to .424.[28] More generally, however, as Sawyer indicates, underreporting seems likely often to result in a nonnegligible downward bias in his inequality measures.[29]

Among Western countries, except for Sweden, the tabulated inequality measures relate to the distribution of households by pre-tax per capita income. Corresponding comparative data that Sawyer

---

[26] That is suggested by the comparative data compiled by McAuley for income distribution among the nonfarm and all-USSR population (Table 5), but for Ofer-Vinokur, the extension in question should have a greater impact, for it would involve coverage of rural nonfarm as well as farm families. The Soviet figure on P_{50}/P_{90} that is cited above, fn. 24 is also illuminating at this point. The cited measures for Australia relate only to urban households.

[27] The calculation for the all-over class takes such households as having a per capita income of 2.5 times the average of all households. That should be conservative.

[28] Like income in the Ofer-Vinokur and McAuley data for the USSR, that in Current Population Reports omits imputed rent on owner-occupied dwellings. Since Budd presumably adjusts for that among other things, he goes beyond what would be desirable for purposes of a comparison with the USSR. Imputed rent is generally omitted from income in the income distribution data, but Sweden and the United Kingdom, at least, are exceptions to that rule. Hence, for those countries, there is a divergence at this point from our income distribution data for the USSR. For one country or another, there are sometimes also such divergencies at other points, but that is a matter that need not, I think, be pursued further here.

[29] That appears so for France, for example, but Sawyer's measures for that country have been held to overstate comparative inequality for reasons other than underreporting (Jean Bégué 1976).

TABLE 7

INCOME SHARES OF SELECTED PERCENTILE GROUPS AND GINI COEFFICIENTS, DISTRIBUTIONS OF HOUSE-
HOLDS BY TOTAL HOUSEHOLD INCOME, PRE- AND POST-TAX, SELECTED COUNTRIES

Country and Distribution	Income Share (%) of				
	Lowest 10%	Lowest 20%	Highest 20%	Highest 10%	Gini Coefficient
Australia, 1966–1967					
Pre-tax	2.1	6.6	38.9	23.8	.313
Post-tax	2.1	6.6	38.8	23.7	.312
Norway, 1970					
Pre-tax	1.7	4.9	40.9	24.5	.354
Post-tax	2.3	6.3	37.3	22.2	.307
U.K., 1973					
Pre-tax	2.1	5.4	40.3	24.7	.344
Post-tax	2.5	6.3	38.7	23.5	.318
France, 1970					
Pre-tax	1.5	4.3	47.0	31.0	.416
Post-tax	1.4	4.3	46.9	30.4	.414
Canada, 1969					
Pre-tax	1.2	4.3	43.3	27.1	.382
Post-tax	1.5	5.0	41.0	25.1	.354
U.S., 1972					
Pre-tax	1.2	3.8	44.8	28.4	.404
Post-tax	1.5	4.5	42.9	26.6	.381

Source: Sawyer (1976, pp. 14–16).

compiles for the distribution of households by their pre- and post-tax *total* income (Table 7) indicate that direct taxes make for greater equality in the countries considered, most markedly in Norway, the United Kingdom and Canada.

For Western countries (Norway is a lone exception), income is apparently exclusive of capital gains. For the USSR, such gains are not unknown, but if included at all in income, the amounts must generally be minimal. Since in the West capital gains must accrue more than proportionately to higher income households, their inclusion as income would tend to increase income inequality in the West compared to that in the USSR. Capital losses also occur,

however, and judging from limited inquiries into the British and U.S. experience, while the inclusion of capital gains might increase inequality markedly in some years, the impact on the average over a period of years appears to be minimal (Atkinson 1975, pp. 59–60).

For the cited measures, a household is usually understood in more or less the same way for Western countries as for the USSR. As well known, however, such measures are apt to be affected even so by differences in household structure. Among other things, measured inequality may be greater or less depending on the share of single-members in the total number of households. Such variations might reflect institutional or cultural factors that are rather peripheral to comparative income inequality in any consequential sense. It should be observed, therefore, that in Ofer-Vinokur, as inflated, single-member households constitute 22.5 per cent of all households. That is much the same as the share of single-member in all households, in the income distribution data for almost all the Western countries considered. A very low share (9.5 per cent) for Australia, however, might have reduced and a very high figure for Sweden (37.6 per cent) might have increased the inequality recorded for those countries.[30] That appears to follow from further calculations of Sawyer standardizing income distribution for household structure.

I have been referring to the distribution of households by household per capita income. I must focus exclusively on that classification, for systematic comparative data have yet to be compiled on the alternative one, where household members are distributed by household per capita income. That is regrettable. The household member is probably of more normative interest than the household distribution.[31]

[30] The corresponding figures for other countries are: Norway, 25.1; United Kingdom, 18.9; France, 21.4; Canada, 26.4, and the United States, 19.1 (Sawyer 1976, p. 18).

In view of the housing shortage in the USSR, the figure cited for that country is surprisingly large. Although reference is only to the urban population, for the USSR as a whole single-member households constitute 20.2 per cent of the total. In respect of household structure, Ofer and Vinokur inflate their sample to conform to the Soviet 1970 census. That is also the source of the figure just given on the all-USSR share of single-member households in the total.

[31] For the USSR, in the inflated Ofer-Vinokur sample, inequality is somewhat reduced by a shift from a distribution of households to one of household members by household per capita income, with the Gini coefficient falling from .288 (Table 6) to .268. Judging from data for alternative distribution in Table 6, Sawyer (1976, pp. 14–17), and Kuznets (1976, p. 37), a corresponding shift for the United States probably would have only a very limited impact on measured inequality. On household structure and measured income inequality, see also Kuznets (1981).

Like our data for the USSR, those for Western countries almost always rest on sample surveys. Here too, then, sampling error is doubtless a factor.

In sum, any definitive judgment on comparative income inequality in the USSR and the West is obviously excluded, but Soviet income inequality probably has been found to be greater than often supposed. It is very possibly as great as or greater than that in Sweden, and not much less than that in some other Western countries such as Norway and the United Kingdom. Income inequality in the USSR is commonly assumed to be less than that in the U.S. That is doubtless so, though not by as wide a margin as sometimes imagined. Elsewhere in the West, however, inequality is sometimes greater than in the United States. That appears to be true, for example, of France, though Sawyer has been challenged on that matter (fn. 29).

With the data at hand, an attempt at normalization for conditioning factors would be pointless, but I have referred only to relatively advanced Western countries. Related data in Sawyer (1976, pp. 14ff) suggest that income inequality in Spain in 1973 (per capita GDP index of 44) and Italy in 1969 (per capita GDP index of 44) may well have been greater than in the USSR. In Japan in 1969 (per capita GDP index of 51), however, income inequality may not have been much greater than that in the USSR. For purposes of appraising Soviet income inequality, one wishes especially for more and better data on income distribution for such countries.

VI. *Transfers*

I have sought, in the light of incomplete and imperfect data, to compare inequality in the USSR and the West in respect of disposable income of households, that is income gross of transfer receipts and net of direct taxes. From available statistics, it is still more difficult to judge a further interesting question concerning the degree to which, in the USSR and the West, the distribution of earned income is modified by net transfers. Very likely the resultant redistribution tends to be less pronounced in the USSR than in the West, at least in relatively advanced countries.

Thus, direct taxes, as indicated, tend to have only a rather limited impact on income distribution in such countries, but in the USSR they must be even less consequential. Although there is an income tax there, total revenues are modest (Section IV, Table 2). For the great bulk of household income consisting of wages and salaries, the rate schedule is only mildly progressive. The rate is nul on incomes up to a legal minimum, while beyond that level it typically rises to a maximum of but 13 per cent of income.[32]

In the Ofer-Vinokur inflated sample, transfer receipts contribute especially to income at low-income levels, but that generally must be so also in the West. Overall, transfer receipts are a significant source of income in the USSR, but do not appear inordinately large or redistributive by

Western standards. Very possibly, they are, if anything, like taxes, less consequentially redistributive than is often the case in the West.[33]

I have been referring to income and hence to transfers of an essentially monetary sort. As so understood, income and transfers fail to include benefits from goods and services that are publicly supplied without charge. Since in the USSR practically all education and health care are made available as such "public goods"[34] and the expenditures involved are sizable (Section IV, Table 2), their impact on income distribution is of decided interest. Judging from data compiled by Ofer-Vinokur (1982) for 1,016 two-parent families that are included in their sample, the effect of such benefits is material: rela-

---

[32] I cited above percentile ratios for an Ofer-Vinokur distribution of wage earners and salaried workers by pre-tax public sector earnings. We may judge the impact of the income tax on income inequality if we consider that corresponding ratios for post-tax public sector earnings were for P_{90}/P_{50} and P_{90}/P_{10}, 1.8 and 3.8 respectively.

I refer to earnings from main public sector jobs, and consider tax rates normally applicable for workers with one to three dependents. Earnings from a second public sector job would have been taxed separately. Bachelors of ages 20 to 50 years were subject to a surcharge, while the income tax was reduced for persons with more than three dependents.

Taxes on other incomes, such as royalties from literary works, were more or less comparable to those on wages and salaries, though there was no exemption for earnings below a legal minimum. Higher rates applied, however, to private earnings such as those of doctors and dentists from private practice.

I refer to income taxes, which are by far the most important direct taxes in the USSR. There were, however, other direct taxes, including one on the collective farm household plot. On Soviet direct taxes, see T. V. Koniukhova 1980, pp. 233ff.

[33] In the inflated Ofer-Vinokur (1980a) sample, money transfer receipts account for 7.8 per cent of disposable income. That seems to be an understatement. I cited above (Section IV) data from CIA (March 1983) on money transfer receipts and outlays in relation to household income in 1960 and 1980. From corresponding figures for 1970 and 1976 in the same source, and further data in TSSU (1976, pp. 568, 742), I estimate that in 1973 money transfer receipts amounted to 10.8 per cent of household net income disposed of. For purposes of comparison with Ofer-Vinokur, I exclude here from transfer receipts 4.3 billion rubles of sick pay (Gertrude Schroeder and Barbara Severin 1976, p. 653). Such receipts are treated by Ofer-Vinokur as wages and salaries.

Note that the indicated share of transfers in household net income disposed of relates to the entire population. For the urban population, on which Ofer-Vinokur focus, the share presumably would be higher. McAuley (1979, p. 35) cites still higher figures than I have calculated for transfers, but he apparently includes in such receipts "holiday pay and premia" as well as sick pay.

As for transfers in the West, such receipts in 1973 amounted to 11.1 per cent of all household receipts, less direct taxes, in the United States. I cite data on social security benefits and social assistance grants that may not be fully comparable to transfers in the USSR, as given above. For Canada, the corresponding figure was 13.6 per cent and for France, 17.9 per cent (OECD 1981).

On the redistributive impact of transfer receipts (with due regard to the indicated underestimate) Ofer and Vinokur (1980a, 1982) Sawyer (1976, pp. 34–35).

[34] In the case of education, that has not always been so (fn. 52; for health care fn. 47).

tively to all household income, including money transfers, publicly supplied education and health care are estimated at 14.7 per cent at the P_{10} and 4.1 per cent at the P_{90} income level. Thus, P_{90}/P_{10} would fall by 9.2 per cent if household income were extended to include such benefits.

For Western countries, our income data also omit publicly supplied education and health care. Where privately supplied, such services are generally still omitted if they are publicly funded. Curiously, according to data compiled by Richard and Peggy Musgrave (1980, p. 273), the impact of inclusion of such outlays in the U.S. in 1968 was probably not very different from that of the inclusion of corresponding outlays in the USSR.[35] Data are not at hand to indicate how typical the U.S. is of Western countries in that respect.

The low rates of direct taxation in the USSR, of course, have a mirror image in the often notably high indirect taxes there. In 1975, the famous turnover tax accounted for 30.4 per cent of all revenues in the Soviet government budget, while withdrawals from government enterprise profits accounted for another 20.5 per cent (TSSU 1976, p. 743). There are also sizable receipts from equalization of domestic and world prices in foreign trade. Direct taxes, in contrast, amounted to but 8.4 per cent of the total budget revenue.

In appraising the redistribution of earned income through transfers in the USSR, arguably we should consider not only such payments as usually understood, but also indirect taxes. Subsidies, which have always been significant for housing

[35] According to Musgrave and Musgrave, the ratio of benefits from U.S. public expenditures on education and health care to family income in 1968 was, for incomes under $4,000, 13.7 per cent; for incomes of $4,000–$5,700, 18.4 per cent; of $12,500–17,500, 6.7 per cent; of $35,000–92,000, 1.8 per cent. The first decile of family incomes in 1968 was below $4,000, while the ninth should have been between $15,000 to $25,000 (USDC, Bureau of the Census 1973a).

and lately have also become sizable for some foodstuffs, particularly meat, presumably should likewise be considered.

Under Soviet centralist planning, transfers in that extended sense are not always easy to delineate meaningfully from factor charges, but it is still of interest that, according to an analysis by Franklyn Holzman (1955, pp. 284ff), such transactions may tend to equalize incomes, but if they do the effect is apparently very limited. Holzman refers to pre- and early post-World War II years. An analysis of more recent circumstances has yet to be made; one wonders whether the redistributive effects in question could be very different now, though sizable food subsidies, as indicated, are rather novel. The data presented above on the Soviet price structure (Table 1) might be read as indicating obliquely a somewhat egalitarian impact of indirect taxes and subsidies. If the Soviet price structure is so oriented, however, indirect taxes and subsidies are doubtless not the only reason. Computations concerning transfers in an extended sense for the U.K. and U.S. seem to indicate that there too there is a modest egalitarian effect (Atkinson 1975, pp. 70–72).

I conclude that for the USSR as well as Western countries, though possibly to a greater degree, the distribution of income among households is dominated by that of the households' earned income. As for the households' earned income, in the USSR as we saw the great bulk of that consists of wages and salaries paid employees of state enterprises and institutions. Such payments are made for services rendered, and one need not prejudge the manner of their determination to view them as in effect payments for labor. Another major source of household earned income is the collective farm. Always akin to wages, collective farm payments to its members have become even more so as a result of recent reforms (McAuley 1979, pp. 28ff); it is not much amiss to regard such payments too as labor earnings. Household earned income, for the rest, has diverse sources, but on any accounting it clearly derives overwhelmingly from the rendering of labor services.[36]

If available data permitted, then, it would be interesting to compare the distribution of labor earnings alone in the USSR and the West. I refer particularly to the distribution of such earnings among households. Recalling our findings on related aspects, particularly the comparative inequality of wages and salaries, one surmises that inequality in the distribution of labor earnings among households in the USSR might be more or less similar to that in the West. Should that be so, a further result would follow: where incomes are distributed more unequally in the West than in the USSR, that must be due primarily to the greater inequality in the distribution of nonlabor than of labor income in the West. That is not a very surprising finding, but it may have emerged more clearly here than it has hitherto.

In the West, transfers serve diverse purposes, but a principal one is to impose political imperatives on an earned income distribution determined in the first instance by economic forces. Income redistribution for political ends must be especially characteristic in the case of transfers other than those of an indirect sort. Such direct transfers apparently tend overall to be more or less egalitarian. Though probably in a less degree, that is also true in the USSR, but there the government also exercises substantial direct control over the earned income distribution. Under the circumstances, where economics ends and

politics begins is no longer very clear, but our inquiry may already have provided some insight into the possible comparative roles of economics and politics in earned income. The sections following hopefully will illuminate that interesting matter further.

VII. *Trends*

I cited above a contribution by N. E. Rabkina and N. M. Rimashevskaia to the analysis of Soviet distributions of WESW by earnings. Those writers are also the chief source on which I drew (Table 3) for Soviet data on the decile ratios of such distributions during the period 1961–1981. In the same essay, Rabkina and Rimashevskaia also report decile ratios for the corresponding distributions for earlier post-World War II years.

From these ratios together with those for 1961–1981 (Table 8; for convenience I repeat the 1961–1981 ratios here), inequality of wages and salaries is seen to have been extraordinarily great in 1946. A decade later, however, it had markedly decreased. The decline continued until around 1968. More recently, there has been something of a reversal, though the inequality still does not compare with that of 1956, never mind that of 1946.[37]

Interesting as they are, decile ratios do not suffice for delineation of trends in equality, but computations by Chapman (1977b, pp. 257ff) such as already ex-

---

[36] In Table 2, revenues that are explicitly attributed to nonlabor factors amount in 1960 to 1.0 and in 1980 to 1.5 per cent of all household earned income. I refer to imputed net rent and interest income and co-op dividends. Income earned privately from other sources and recorded under various headings in the table must to a considerable extent represent payments for labor services, but nonlabor factors are often employed as well.

[37] As Chapman (1977b, p. 258) indicates, the wage survey from which the 1946 decile ratio derives may not have been fully comparable to those of later years. The cited decile ratio for 1981, 3.0, was released in Aleksandrova and Federovskaia (1984) with no indication of its provenance. The corresponding ratio for 1972 is said there, however, to be the same as that for 1981. That agrees essentially with the figure that I have cited for 1972, 3.10, which is taken from Rabkina and Rimashevskaia. Moreover, Chapman (1983) already cautioned against extrapolating to later years the increase in inequality observed in the early seventies. On her reasoning, the reduction from the 1976 level that the Aleksandrova-Federovskaia figure for 1981 indicates is not implausible.

TABLE 8

DECILE RATIOS, DISTRIBUTION OF WAGE EARNERS AND SALARIED WORKERS BY EARNINGS, USSR AND
RUSSIA, VARIOUS YEARS

Year	Wage Earners and Salaried Workers, All Sectors, by Monthly Earnings, Soviet Data	Wage Earners, Industry, by Monthly Earnings		Wage Earners, Industry by Daily Earnings, Bergson
		Soviet Data	Bergson	
1914				5.55
1924		4.47		
1927		3.6		
1928			3.66	3.49
1930		3.33		
1934		3.16	3.74	
1946	7.24	5.43		
1956	4.44	3.36		
1959	4.21	3.31		
1961	4.02	2.82		
1964	3.69	2.67		
1966	3.26	2.78		
1968	2.83	2.50		
1972	3.10	2.63		
1976	3.35			
1981	3.0			

Sources: Rabkina and Rimashevskaia (1978, p. 20); Aleksandrova and Federovskaia (1984); Bergson (1944, p. 128).

plained yield, as before, decile ratios approximating those presented by Rabkina-Rimashevskaia and also other percentile ratios that manifest essentially the same evolution.[38]

Rabkina-Rimashevskaia have also compiled decile ratios for the distribution of industrial wage earners by wages for the entire period 1924–1972. For years since 1946, these measures show much the same trends as do the decile ratios for wage earners and salaried workers in all sectors. The decile ratios for industrial wage earners thus may indicate trends in such mea-

[38] Because of the appreciable overstatement, already noted, in the decile ratio for 1968, however, the reversal in trend in that year is not apparent in the Chapman compilations.

sures for WESW in the economy generally for years prior to 1946. If they do, and if here too other percentile ratios should vary similarly, inequality in the mid-twenties was less than that of 1946, though still very marked, and subsequently declined in pre-war years, at least to 1934.

The suppositions are nevertheless of uncertain validity, and they seem the more so when we consider that Rabkina-Rimashevskaia do not explain the provenance of their pre-World War II data. The figures presumably relate to frequency distributions of workers by earnings that are derived from pre-war wage and salary surveys referred to earlier. Unlike the wage and salary surveys which Soviet scholars have been able to draw on for post-World War II years, those for pre-war years, in the case of industry, covered only large-scale enterprise, and even in that sphere were in effect only sample inquiries (Bergson 1944, pp. 60ff, 99ff).

The latter feature may be a factor in the apparent divergence in trends, from the eve of the plans to 1934, between the decile ratios of Rabkina-Rimashevskaia and corresponding measures compiled by Bergson (1944, p. 128). Although in that study I utilized data on wages that must be the same as those underlying Rabkina-Rimshevskaia, I attempted to inflate the survey materials to represent large-scale establishments generally. Rather than cover all large-scale industry, though, I limited myself to 26 branches for which inequality in wages could be compared individually in 1928 and 1934. That too could have been a source of divergence between me and Rabkina-Rimashevskaia. Then too, my data refer to all workers below the rank of foreman. Theirs refer to "ordinary workers" (*rabochie*), who according to the conventional Soviet usage include all wage earners except custodial and other service personnel, and apprentices (fn. 14).

In a word, the precise evolution of earnings inequality in pre-World War II years must be uncertain, but circumstantial evidence to appear (Section VIII) allows little doubt that the late twenties and early thirties witnessed a distinct reduction in inequality. The egalitarian drift, however, was abruptly reversed as early as 1931. Bergson (1944) is not inconsistent with such a shift, though it seems distorted in Rabkina and Rimashevskaia. The marked inequality of 1927, furthermore, emerged during the NEP after an initial radical reduction in differentials in the earliest post-Revolutionary years. Contrary to a common view, inequality in Soviet wages and salaries, rather than evolving in a linear way, has fluctuated. Since the Revolution there have been no less than three cycles

of differential leveling and its opposite.[3]

So much for trends in inequality of earnings among WESW. Trends in income distribution among such workers and their families are still a relatively unexplored theme, which I cannot hope to clarify here, but it should be observed that WESW already received at the outset of the plans appreciable benefits in the form of transfers in money and in kind, and were also subject to modest direct taxes. Among WESW, such taxes in early years, as lately, appear to have been only mildly progressive.[40]

On trends in income inequality among the population generally, we are still less well informed. With agriculture still predominant, public sector wages and salaries could constitute only a relatively limited share of household earned income in early years, so the lacunae in knowledge at this point are large indeed. A cardinal issue, though, is that concerning comparative income trends among the farm and nonfarm population. We perhaps need not await a still lacking statistical inquiry to conclude that by the eve of the plans farmers and nonfarmers alike must have recovered substantially from the extremes of privation experienced under War Com-

[39] To return to decile ratios, note that for pre-war as well as post-war years the Soviet wage surveys in question related to monthly rather than annual earnings, but only for workers on the payroll for an entire month. Also, among the 26 industries on which I focused in Bergson (1944), seventeen show an increase in inequality (as measured by the quartile ratio, i.e., P_{75}/P_{25}) from 1928 to 1934. Only in three industries is there a pronounced change in the opposite direction. For all 26 industries considered as a group, inequality increased among wage earners and salaried workers together as well as among wage earners alone. That is indicated by Lorenz-type data as well as by decile ratios (Bergson 1944, pp. 101, 120ff).

[40] In the late twenties income tax rates even on wages and salaries rose to relatively high levels (up to 30 per cent on the excess of earnings over 2,000 rubles monthly) but for WESW such levies must have been operative only very rarely (Holzman 1955; Bergson 1944, pp. 33–34; 1951; Koniukhova 1980, pp. 233ff; on early transfer payments generally, Oleg Hoeffding 1954).

TABLE 9

URBAN AND RURAL FOOD CONSUMPTION PER
CAPITA, USSR, 1928 AND 1932
(KILOGRAMS)

Item	Urban		Rural	
	1928	1932	1928	1932
Bread grains	174.4	211.3	250.4	214.6
Potatoes	87.6	110.0	141.1	125.0
Meat and lard	51.7	16.9	24.8	11.2
Butter	2.97	1.75	1.55	0.7

Source: Nove (1969, p. 177).

munism, and that subsequently both hardly prospered as Stalin pursued accelerated industrialization cum collectivization. At least initially, however, the farmer must have fared much worse than the industrial worker, as appears graphically in rare Soviet archival materials, on urban and rural consumption, that Nove (1969, p. 177) found in a release of the sixties (Table 9). In the USSR, the period 1932–1933 was one of extensive famine, which by all accounts affected especially the rural population. It is not clear how, if at all, the millions of so-called kulaks and their families, who were being deported from the countryside at the time, are treated in data such as shown.

Stalin died on March 5, 1953. Deficiencies in available data notwithstanding, we may also infer, I think, that farm income per capita was still well below that of the nonfarm population at that time,[41] but has risen markedly in relation to the latter since then. As a result, whatever gap remains between the two strata in per capita income has appreciably narrowed (Bronson and Krueger 1971; McAuley 1979, pp. 28ff).

To return to industrial wage earners, an attempt in Bergson (1944, pp. 57ff, 120ff) to compare inequality of earnings

[41] Which was itself still depressed (Chapman 1963).

of such workers in the USSR in 1928 and Russia in 1914 may provide further perspective on comparative Soviet and Western differentiation. For workers distributed according to their average daily wages during a single month, the decile ratio was 3.49 in 1928 compared with 5.55 in 1914. Lorenz-type data show the same pronounced reduction in inequality. For both 1914 and 1928, I drew here on results of sample surveys relating mainly to larger establishments in eight industries. While resultant errors could be in either direction, diverse differences in the data probably contribute to the apparent decline in inequality. Bergson (1944) concluded, however, that the decline is not just apparent. Industrial wages were significantly less unequal on the eve of the plans than before World War I.

Further calculations in Bergson (1944, pp. 78ff) indicate that inequality of wages, as measured by the quartile ratio in various industries in the USSR in 1928 tended to be less than that in the U.S. in 1904, though probably not as markedly so as between the USSR in 1928 and Russia in 1914.

VIII. Income Formation

In the USSR as in the West, inequality of income is dominated by the distribution of earned income as distinct from transfers. In the USSR, earned income consists almost exclusively of labor earnings. In inquiring into the process of income formation that underlies Soviet material inequality, Western scholars have properly focused on such earnings. They have addressed particularly the determination of comparative rewards among industrial WESW for different kinds of work. Determination of relative pay is not all there is to the distribution of labor earnings among Soviet households, but it is a cardinal aspect. Among WESW, principles of relative wage determination in industry, it seems clear, have been more or less paradigmatic of those applying more generally. Especially in recent years, as was suggested, they have also been not at all foreign to the collective farms, whose staff represents the only consequential form of civilian nonprivate employment other than that of WESW. Collective farms, in any event, have lately accounted for less than one sixth of all such employment.[42]

Under socialism, as the primers teach, relative wages might conceivably be determined entirely through a market process. Indeed, that is possible even under centralist planning. Such a process, according to further familiar reasoning, could be a highly efficient one with relative wages tending simply to conform to "scarcity values," those being the values indicated by forces of "demand" and "supply" that reflect worker freedom of choice, on the one hand, and unrestricted cost minimization in enterprise labor staffing on the other (Oskar Lange 1938; Bergson 1944, 1966, ch. 8).

For purposes of determining relative wages, the system's directors of the USSR nevertheless have opted rather for a predominantly bureaucratic process, and in Western discussion attention has understandably been directed especially to the system of wage administration immediately involved. That scheme is better understood, however, if we consider that the Soviet industrial worker was subject to stringent controls, amounting often to practical, if not actual, militarization under War Communism, and then again during World War II and for some time thereafter (Dewar 1956; Bergson 1944, pp. 234–40; 1964, pp. 93ff). Except during those periods, though, he has enjoyed substantial discretion regarding his occupation and place of work. The government

has obviously not been exactly at ease with the results, particularly the frequently high labor turnover, and with varying stress has sought to restrict that phenomenon in one way or another: in more recent years, by use of labor books as a control, graduation of bonuses, and social insurance and other benefits with length of uninterrupted service, enterprise administration of housing, and the like.[43] Free choice of employment has also been impeded in diverse other ways.[44]

Workers have continued to shift jobs, however, on some scale (Bergson 1944, pp. 143–53, 1964, pp. 93–104; Feshbach and Rapawy 1973, 1976), and despite efforts to systematize labor recruitment through labor exchanges, 68.1 percent of all newly recruited industrial workers were still in 1976 hired independently "from the gate." Use of the exchanges has in any case been generally voluntary for both the worker and the enterprise (Feshbach and Rapawy 1973, p. 143; Chapman 1982).

Also of interest here is the fact that, almost from the earliest post-Revolutionary years, the Soviet enterprise has been expected to economize on money costs. Under centralist planning, such economy has invariably been the subject of a plan target, and performance in that regard in one way or another has been a cardinal factor affecting managerial rewards. There have been other managerial "suc-

---

[42] State farm workers, who are included in WESW, accounted for 9.4 percent of the total (TSSU 1976, pp. 440, 532; fn. 13).

[43] Under a program to tighten labor discipline generally, the short-lived Andropov administration called for the establishment of further restrictions on voluntary departures and incentives for continuous service.

[44] Graduates of universities and advanced technical and vocational schools have long been subject to administrative assignment to particular jobs for a period of several years. The requirement, however, has sometimes been evaded (Philip Grossman 1979, pp. 44–45; Murray Feshbach and Stephen Rapawy 1973, pp. 532–33). For workers generally, movement into a number of larger cities has tended to be restricted under operation of an internal passport system.

cess criteria" as well, however, and one or another of these has often taken precedence over cost economy where, as might well be the case, the different criteria were in conflict. Since the mid-sixties managerial incentive arrangements have been almost continually in flux, with results that are still not too clear. In the upshot, cost economy directly or indirectly has probably gained in status (Bergson 1944, pp. 139–43; Joseph Berliner 1957, 1976, ch. 14; David Granick 1954, chs. 9–11; Jan Adam 1980). Although its autonomy has tended to be circumscribed, enterprise management has enjoyed substantial discretion regarding labor staffing. It has particular reason, however, to hesitate to initiate actions requiring staff curtailments (Bergson 1978, ch. 2; 1983, p. 61; Paul Gregory and Robert Stuart 1981, pp. 306ff).

In short, under Soviet centralist planning, there is in fact a recognizable market for labor. The forces of supply and demand that are manifest can hardly correspond fully to those that theory requires to be operative for efficient resource use, so there is already reason to doubt that relative wages could conform very closely to scarcity values. In administering relative wages, the Soviet system's directors nevertheless have had to reckon with supply and demand such as are operative in the market that actually prevails. Their mode of fixing relative wages must be seen in that light.

Turning to that, in briefest terms these appear to be the main Western findings on relevant aspects:

i) For purposes of determining relative wages, workers in an industrial branch in the USSR are classified in one or another bracket of a scale of basic wage rates, the particular bracket depending on the nature of the work performed: its complexity, the responsibilities involved, and other aspects such as are usually understood in the West as delineating skill.

While the resulting skill differentials are applied to workers generally, the basic rates are increased for workers engaged in especially arduous or unhealthy work, or who are paid by the piece (Bergson 1964, ch. 6; Leonard Kirsch 1972; Chapman 1970, 1979b). The latter have been notably numerous, constituting in 1965 some 58 percent of the industrial labor force. Among time-workers too, though, incentive pay has been the rule (Kirsch 1972, pp. 24–25, 27; TSSU 1968, p. 146).

The foregoing arrangements prevail for ordinary workers (*rabochie*). For supervisory and technical personnel, Soviet administrative practice is broadly similar, though in place of the scales of relative basic rates, the usual procedure is to fix at once absolute salaries for different occupations. Among managerial personnel at higher levels, salaries vary not only with the specific occupation, but with the complexity of the enterprise, and its importance as indicated by its size and other criteria (Bergson 1964, pp. 112ff; Chapman 1979b, pp. 156ff). For supervisory and technical personnel, as for ordinary workers, incentive pay is customary, with premia amounting in 1965 to 15.7 and in 1970 to 34.5 percent of their total earnings (Chapman 1979b, p. 163). Bonuses for individual supervisory and technical workers could run much higher. Wages of clerical workers and other personnel have been set under more or less similar procedures, though for them premia are comparatively limited.

The foregoing system of wage regulation had its beginnings in early post-Revolutionary years, and was already substantially in place under the early five year plans. While agencies responsible for its establishment and implementation have varied, much has generally been decided above the enterprise level. Such actions, however, have not always been definitive. Under a major reform initiated in 1956, for example, the government felt impelled to try to standardize differentials that had become very diverse for similar occupations, to tighten work norms that often had been markedly loose, and to make central controls more effective generally. The government at first met with considerable success in these endeavors, but its new arrangements have apparently been in process of erosion more recently (Bergson 1944, chs. 11, 12; 1964, pp. 116–18; Kirsch 1972; Nove 1977, ch. 8; Chapman 1979b).

ii) While seeking from early days to reward appropriately superior skill and more arduous and less healthy work, the government has in the course of time attached varying values to such aspects. That is already suggested by the data on inequality of pay set forth above (Table 8), but the reduction in inequality' from 1914 to 1928 observed there is properly viewed as originating in the initial Bolshevik scales of basic wage rates, such as those published in January 1919, which clearly entailed a radical contraction of differentials (Bergson 1944, pp. 180–82). Little more than a year later, though, in April 1920, new scales brought something of a reversal in that regard, and in 1922, after the NEP had succeeded War Communism the reversal became marked (Bergson 1944, pp. 180ff). Wage inequality in 1928, therefore, should have borne the imprint of these shifts towards wider differentials as well as the initial contraction. In a degree, it should also have been affected by still another turn towards narrowing differentials under a wholesale wage reform initiated in 1927. The effect of that further shift must have been compounded by restrictions imposed on premia and diverse supplements that had previously been grafted on to the wage scales (Bergson 1944, pp. 183ff).

The precise course of wage inequality under the early five year plans is left somewhat in doubt by available measures (Table 8), but the shift that commenced in 1927 is known to have been reversed under still another wholesale revision of wage scales initiated towards the end of the First Five Year Plan, in June 1931. Scales promulgated after that date were characterized by significantly widened differentials (Bergson 1944, pp. 177–79).

Rationing, which had become the rule under the First Five Year Plan, was abandoned towards the end of the Second, and with that a somewhat equalizing adjustment in wages was made to compensate for the restoration of the open market, but subsequent revisions in scales, at least in a number of industries, tended again to widen differentials (Bergson 1944, pp. 37ff; Chapman 1970, pp. 8–9). These developments must have contributed to the notably great inequality of pay observed in 1946, and they could only have been compounded by the increased stress, under the plans, on incentive pay, as indicated by the 76.1 percent of industrial wage earners already paid by the piece in 1936. The corresponding figure in 1928 was 57.5 percent (Bergson 1964, p. 110).

As reflected in our measures, wage inequality declined from 1946 through the late sixties. No wholesale reform such as occurred in pre-World War II years can be said to have initiated this trend. But rationing was again the rule during the war and immediately after, and, as in the mid-thirties, when the open market was restored, a partially compensatory wage adjustment had a significant equalizing effect (Chapman 1970, pp. 9–10).

The wage reform inaugurated in 1956, however, was of a wide-ranging sort, and brought both a further contraction in basic rate differentials and a restriction on incentive pay. The proportion of industrial wage earners paid by the piece had still been 77 percent in 1953, but as indicated, had fallen to 58 percent by 1965. The minimum wage, always somewhat ineffective, had become more so by the early fifties. In association with the new reform, however, its level was greatly increased, and additional increases that became operative in subsequent years should have acted further to narrow differentials (Chapman 1970; Kirsch 1972; McAuley 1979, ch. 8; also, however, Walter Galenson 1960).

The increase in inequality of pay that seems to take place in the early seventies (Table 8) occurred, despite a further rise in the minimum wage, in ways that are not too clear (Nove 1982; McAuley 1982; Chapman 1983). That trend, however, has apparently not continued.

iii) While rewards for skill and effort have been fluctuating, there have also been progressive changes in the relative pay of workers in different industries. Under Stalin, the changes were often dramatic. The earnings of coal miners and metal workers, for example, rose sharply in relation to the average pay of industrial workers generally, and even in relation to that of workers in other heavy industrial branches that were being expanded at a forced pace under accelerated industrialization, such as chemicals, machinery and electric power. On the other hand, wages in such low-priority industries as clothing, shoes, food processing and printing, initially at or above the average for all industry, tended to fall well below it. Concomitantly, the overall spread in pay between industries widened. Since Stalin, that trend has been checked, and there have been some gains in relative status in light industries and food processing (Bergson 1964, pp. 114–15; Chapman 1970, pp. 46ff; 1979b, pp. 169–71). Earnings inequality has tended to be relatively great in heavy industries (Bergson 1944, pp. 100–02; Chapman 1970, p. 26; Kirsch 1972, p. 73).

I have described summarily the nature of Soviet policies and procedures for determining relative wages in Soviet industry. In trying to understand that matter, we must also consider the fact noted earlier (Section IV) that among employees generally, including those not only in industry but in other sectors, inequality of pay in the USSR in recent years, while fluctuating, has tended to fall within the range of that observed in a number of Western countries. After appropriate normalization for relevant conditioning factors, though, inequality in the USSR, particularly in the early seventies, may be less than that in the West. What follows? Further inquiry into cited sources seems only to confirm what is suggested: the Soviet industrial wage structure has reflected a shifting mix of i) market forces that underly scarcity values; ii) political-ideological imperatives, and iii) planning distortions.

Under the last heading I refer to the impediments to freedom of choice of employment, sometimes severe, as under War Communism and during World War II and immediately after, and never entirely absent; the always qualified, though probably increasing, enterprise concern for labor cost economy and more or less persistent restrictions on managerial discretion to heed such concern; and deficiencies in wage administration, whether in the enterprise or at the center. Such deficiencies have yet to be explored systematically, but must be consequential.

The political-ideological imperatives in mind are of an egalitarian sort, and apparently were particularly influential in the earliest years. Thus, a principle concern of the drastic compression of wage differentials then projected was avowedly to assure that "the laborer of average qualification, at work of average injuriousness and intensity . . . be paid more justly" (report to Second All-Russian Congress of Trade Unions, quoted in Bergson 1944, p. 182). At a time when rationing was pervasive and money was falling into disuse, the resultant wage scales may only have been a demagogic gesture, but they could also have signaled a commitment to a common egalitarian aspiration.

The earliest scales, if operative at all, were short-lived, and differentials must have markedly widened by 1927, when further action was initiated to restrict them. After a reversal of that policy in 1931, the differentials increased still more, and were notably high in 1946 when in one way or another there was again a shift towards contraction, to be confirmed in major reforms and related actions of 1956 and later. Here too even the cynically inclined may find it difficult to discount completely the egalitarian rhetoric that has accompanied the more significant moves towards restriction of inequality, such as in 1927 and after (Bergson 1944, pp. 186–89) and in 1956 and after (Chapman 1970, pp. 18, 101ff).

But market forces manifestly have also had a place. Soviet reality has been far removed from the abstractions of economics primers, and the system's directors' responses to evolving conditions of supply and demand have necessarily had a judgmental quality not easily delineated analytically. But responses to market forces there doubtless have been, as the system's directors themselves have clearly affirmed; as when, with the shift from the egalitarian scales of War Communism to the more differentiated ones of the NEP, they declared that policy in that sphere must have "the aim of attracting into industry a qualified working force" (V. Shmidt, quoted in Bergson 1944, p. 184); and as when, under the extraordinary conditions of the First Five Year Plan, one of the system's directors in particular, Stalin, attacked the "egalitarianism" (*uravnilovka*) that had again been manifest since 1927, as among other things having the consequence "that the unqualified laborer is not interested in becoming a qualified laborer" (quoted in Bergson 1944, p. 178).

While sometimes impelling reversals of egalitarian trends, market forces probably have reinforced the latest egalitarian shift. Indeed, egalitarianism has been accorded

only limited stress in recent Soviet discussion of wage policy. Instead, the Soviet leadership appears to be primarily concerned with market developments. That could be due to the fierceness of Stalin's 1931 attack on egalitarianism, but increase in supplies of more qualified workers and slowing economic growth have been favorable to contracting differentials, that in any event had reached extraordinary levels at the end of the war (Chapman 1970, pp. 101ff).

Although their role in the overall spread of wage differentials has varied, market forces are not difficult to perceive throughout in the complex but purposeful procedures for rewarding different skills, working conditions and industries, and additional exertion. Even under the marked egalitarianism of War Communism, such aspects were never wholly without effect.

In brief, granting the planning distortions, in the seventh decade since the Revolution scarcity values are still very much in evidence in Soviet wage determination. Egalitarianism, however, could have caused a limited compression in differentials by Western standards.[45]

[45] The process of income formation that has been described, while determining relative pay generally, also settles that of male and female workers, but it should be noted that equal rights for women, including the right to equal pay for equal work, have long been enshrined as fundamental legal principles in the USSR. Yet women earn distinctly less than men. Among WESW, women lately have earned but two-thirds as much as men (Iu. B. Riurikov 1977, pp. 118–19; Chapman 1977c, pp. 225–26; Ofer and Vinokur 1981). Why?

Soviet wage administration apparently is sex-blind, in the sense that the rate structure (basic pay, piece rates, etc.) for any particular job does not depend on the sex of the person holding it (Chapman 1977c, p. 226), but women have gravitated to occupations where pay is relatively low. More basically, equal rights for women in the market place appear to be associated with unequal rights at home, with women still bearing the principal burden of childrearing and housekeeping. They may thus be unable to prolong their education or gain experience as readily as men, and often seek employment in services and other occupations where the intensity of work is relatively

IX. *A New Class?*

Who earns very high incomes in the USSR? How much do they earn? More may be known on these intriguing questions than might be supposed. If it is, that is due in no small part to Matthews' 1978 study supplementing sparse official releases with results of interviews that he conducted on Soviet "elite" groups. Those interviewed were almost all emigrés from the USSR, and only a minor fraction were of elite status, as seen by Matthews, but the great majority had a "professional" background in the USSR, and could report on other's as well as their own experience.

Matthews classifies as elite personnel individuals who earn at least 400–500 rubles a month. During 1971–1973, the period usually referred to, that would have been 3.1–3.8 times the average 1972 pay—130 rubles (TSSU 1976, p. 546)—of all Soviet WESW. The government was then in the process of raising the legally allowed minimum wage from 60 to 70 rubles a month, so the earnings needed to qualify for elite status came to 5.7–8.3 times the legal minimum. Although the legal minimum was supposedly obligatory, some 10 percent

of Soviet WESW earned less than that amount (McAuley 1979, pp. 200–01, 218–23).

As seen by Matthews, elite status is quite exclusive. In all, less than a quarter of a million persons (Table 10), or but 0.2 percent of all gainfully employed, are so classified. The cited estimates, though, are admittedly "hypothetical." More important, Matthews apparently applies his criterion for elite status primarily by reference to income from an individual's main job, as distinct from his total earnings, including those from a second public sector job and private activities. Especially at high income levels, the difference is not minor. Although the inflated Ofer-Vinokur sample accords no representation to speak of to elite personnel such as Matthews delineates, it seems to indicate individuals earning more than 450 rubles a month from all sources as much more numerous than Matthews' group.[46]

---

[46] In the inflated Ofer-Vinokur (1980a) sample, 2.7 percent of all wage earners and salaried workers earned more than 400 rubles monthly, or 2.6 times the average monthly earnings of all workers represented. Reference is to earnings from all sources, including second jobs and private activities. The corresponding figure for workers earning more than 400 rubles for pay from the main job alone was 0.4 percent, and for all public sector earnings, 0.9 percent.

Judging from these data, perhaps nearly as many as 1.0 percent of all WESW (apart from Matthews' elite personnel) could be earning more than 450 rubles a month gross of taxes from all sources. I consider these aspects: i) for Ofer-Vinokur, income is net of taxes. Before taxes, an individual with one to three dependents in order to have a net income of 400 rubles would have to earn 447 rubles, or again 2.6 times the corresponding average for all workers represented. ii) In view of the implied sample level of average earnings before taxes from the main job— 152 rubles monthly—the Ofer-Vinokur data could overstate incomes generally by, say, 10 percent (compare the indicated average wage with that in Ofer and Vinokur 1979, p. 75). Hence, what must be in question here is the numbers of persons indicated by Ofer-Vinokur as earning more than, say, 500 rubles monthly before or 440 rubles monthly after taxes. iii) The inflated Ofer-Vinokur sample relates only to the urban population. Among the rural population, constituting more than two-fifths of the total, very high earnings must be comparatively rare.

---

limited or the task convenient otherwise. A wife's mobility may also be constrained by the need to accord priority to her husband's locational choice. A degree of discrimination against women in one or another occupation, however, is not excluded (Ofer and Vinokur 1981; Chapman 1977c; Martin Lipset and Richard Dobson 1973, pp. 151ff; McAuley 1981).

Relative to the earnings of male workers, those of females appear to have been higher in the USSR than in the U.S. but little if at all higher than in a number of European countries (Edward Denison 1974, p. 187; Ofer and Vinokur 1981, p. 154; Saunders and Marsden 1981, pp. 218ff; McAuley 1981, ch. 2). The causal factors underlying such diverse relations have yet to be studied. Although the large share of women in the Soviet labor force (among wage earners and salaried workers, 51 percent in 1975, compared with a corresponding figure of 41 percent in the U.S.: TSSU 1976, p. 544; OECD 1980; also Marjorie Galenson 1973, pp. 18–19) must be a factor, there could be offsets, such as increased female entry into more remunerative occupations. The female share in employment nevertheless must be considered a possible basis for normalization of comparative wage distributions. See the Addendum.

TABLE 10

ELITE PERSONNEL BY OCCUPATIONAL STATUS, USSR, NOTIONAL ESTIMATES FOR THE SEVENTIES

Occupation	Number of Persons (thous.)
Enterprise directors	17
Intelligentsia, all	40
Academicians, university and institute directors, et al.	10
Leaders in arts and arts bureaucracy	4
Editors, senior journalists	17
Other	9
Government, komsomol and trade union officials	60
Military, police and diplomatic personnel	30
Party officials	80
All	227

Source: Drawn, with the permission of the author and publisher, from Matthews (1978, p. 31).

I would not urge, however, a more inclusive approach. Matthews probably has succeeded in delineating the more interesting occupations where high incomes are relatively frequent, and his estimate of the number of such persons there may well be of the right order. Elsewhere, such earnings testify as to the frequency of multiple jobs at high income levels in the USSR and, if we may judge from the Ofer-Vinokur data, even more to the powers of survival of private activities, but the individuals concerned for the most part must have been of doubtful distinction otherwise.[47]

One of the more significant of Matthews' elite occupations is that of enterprise director. The directors who qualify for elite status, however, constitute only a minor fraction of all persons occupying such a post. Even so, Matthews probably overestimates the earnings of the more

[47] Among the principal sources of private income at income levels in question probably are medical and dental practice, repair services and retail trade.

favored of such persons from their principal occupation. In category I enterprises in machine building, for example, such earnings of directors appear to have averaged somewhat less than the 516 rubles a month that he allows.[48]

Grouped together as "intelligentsia" by Matthews are elite individuals in diverse occupational categories of which a major one embraces academic and research pursuits. Here, salaries are found to have ranged up to 500–700 rubles a month, those being rates indicated for the director of a university or of a research institute. Should the individual in question, however, be one of the 2,521 full and corresponding members of the All-Union Academy of Sciences and related republican entities, he would receive an additional stipend of 350–500 rubles a month. He might also receive honoraria for technical and scientific publications. Extras might also be available on other accounts.

Persons classified as elite personnel in the arts might be serving in one or another capacity as salaried employees, with reported basic pay rates ranging up to 800 rubles a month. The first secretary of the Union of Composers, who earned that sum, was also earning an additional 600 rubles monthly from outside work.

Under long-standing arrangements for payment of royalties to creative workers (authors, playwrights, composers, et al.), such persons might qualify for elite status on the basis of such earnings alone: as witness the writer reported by Matthews to have a monthly income of 800–1,000 rubles, apparently derived mainly, if not exclusively, from royalties.

The writer in question is said to have been "well known" at the "all-union level," but there are reasons to doubt that he was among the most affluent in his pro-

[48] Rather than increasing from the 1960 levels, As Matthews supposes, basic rates for such directors seem to have remained constant until 1975 (Chapman 1979b, p. 157).

TABLE 11

MONTHLY EARNINGS FROM ROYALTIES, RUSSIAN REPUBLIC, 1936

Monthly earnings, rubles	Number of Persons
More than 1,000	14
600–1,000	11
200–300	39
100–200	114
50–100	137
Less than 50	(around) 4,000

Source: Reproduced from *Pravda,* June 27, 1937, in Bergson (1951). Ruble incomes in the source are divided by ten in order to make them comparable with contemporary data in rubles, reflecting the currency conversion of January 1961. The 300–600 ruble income class is omitted in the Soviet source without explanation.

fession. In 1936, according to a rare, if not unique, authoritative account, royalty incomes in the Russian Republic (by far the largest such entity in the USSR) varied over an extremely wide range (Table 11). Among recipients, we may infer that the great majority, earning royalties of less than 50 rubles a month, or but 2.2 times the 23.1 ruble average monthly wage of all workers (Bergson 1951), could not qualify, on the basis of such income alone, for elite status a la Matthews. Royalty incomes ranged upward, however, and at the highest levels, 14 persons were earning more than 1,000 rubles monthly, or 43 times the average wage.[49]

Royalties in the USSR are determined in a complex manner, and their trends over time are difficult to gauge. If since 1936, recipients failed at all to keep pace with the average worker, whose money

[49] Contained in a letter to the editor of *Pravda,* over the signatures of A. Tolstoi, the writer, and the playwright V. Vishnevskii, the cited data were said to be based on the annual accounts of the agency collecting royalties. The letter was apparently intended to "dispel the misunderstandings on the exceptionally high earnings, on the fantastic royalties." Could it possibly have accomplished that aim?

wage in 1972 had increased to 5.6 times the initial level, that is unlikely to have been by a wide margin (Bergson 1951; Matthews 1978, pp. 96–98).[50]

Among other elite intelligentsia, incomes are sometimes less than might be expected. The editor of a union-republican newspaper, for example, apparently did little better than qualify for elite status, with a reported monthly income of 500–600 rubles. That is often true also of elite personnel in other pursuits, though a marshal of the Soviet armed forces is cited as having an income of 2,000 rubles a month. Intermediate and higher officials in the Party, and possibly elsewhere, are said to receive as an addition to their usual pay a "thirteenth month," but the practice, often reported as prevailing under Stalin, of supplying such persons informally with sizable, supplementary pay "packets" has apparently been discontinued (Matthews 1978; Roy Medvedev 1971, p. 540).

The elite personnel delineated by Matthews, as we saw, constitute but a fraction of high-income earners in the USSR. For that reason, they are not readily compared with high-income earners in the West. It is still of interest, though, that in respect of occupational structure Soviet elite personnel are rather different from Western high-income recipients. Among other things, governmental, political and related pursuits constitute the bulk of elite personnel in the USSR. In the U.S., which is perhaps broadly illustrative of Western

[50] The writer Mekhty Hussein (as recalled by a former translator of his works now at the Harvard Russian Research Center, Kirill V. Uspensky) earned in the mid-sixties as much as 100,000 rubles a year. Some 86 times the average wage, that seems high even by 1936 standards. Hussein, in addition to being an eminent writer, however, was Chairman of the Writers' Union of Azerbaizhan and a secretary of the All-Union Writers' Union. He would have received additional income, beyond his royalties, from these posts. Note that royalties are no longer subject, as they were in 1936, to especially high income taxes such as apply to independent professions.

TABLE 12

OCCUPATIONS OF PERSONS EARNING OVER $50,000
PER YEAR, U.S., 1969

Occupation	Number of Persons (thous.)
Salaried managers, construction, manufacturing, transport, trade	49.6
Physicians, dentists, et al.	53.2
Lawyers, judges	18.8
Managers (self-employed)	12.5
Craftsmen and kindred workers	6.5
Brokers	5.8
Insurance, real estate and finance executives; sales employees	16.1
Sales workers, n.e.c.	11.8
Writers, artists, entertainers	5.0
Others	59.2
All	238.5

Source: USDC, Bureau of the Census (1973b, pp. 16ff) after Matthews (1978, p. 181).

circumstances, such occupations hardly rate separate listing among individuals with super-incomes (Table 12). On the other hand, production, trade and the like are the principal pursuits of super-income personnel in the U.S. and of relatively limited importance in the USSR. The contrast between the USSR and the U.S., as thus depicted, is doubtless overdrawn, for managerial staff at the highest levels in the U.S. must often be performing tasks that in the USSR fall to employees of superior economic agencies, e.g., ministries, that have the status of governmental departments, and to the staff of Party organizations. Although I refer for the U.S. to individuals whose incomes were seven or more times the average wage, those in question constituted but 0.28 percent of the U.S. labor force. They thus represent a group that seems properly compared with the elite personnel delineated by Matthews.

High incomes are not a novel feature in the USSR. They already prevailed there

long ago. I referred above to the extraordinary 1936 earnings of some recipients of royalties. Among WESW in large-scale industry in 1934, some 1.3 percent earned more than 3.8 and some 0.4 percent more than 5.1 times the average wage of all workers. At least for industrial WESW, similar differentials apparently prevailed also on the eve of the five year plans (Bergson 1944, pp. 227–28; TSUNKHU 1936, pp. 16–17).

The radical early post-Revolutionary shift towards income equality referred to above, however, affected not only workers generally but personnel at even the highest levels. According to a wage scale promulgated in June 1918 by the Council of Commissars over Lenin's signature, salaries of government employees were to range from 350 rubles a month for the lowest office worker, without previous experience, to but 800 rubles a month for the commissars themselves. Declaredly there were to be no extras, though specialists doing unusual work might be paid up to 1,200 rubles (Bergson 1944, p. 190; Matthews 1978, pp. 61–64).

For top personnel as for workers generally, however, such egalitarianism was soon breached. Just how elite income differentials varied subsequently is not very clear; probably they shifted more or less in step with differentials generally. There have, however, been incongruities as where for a protracted period, 1960–1975, the base salaries of some high-level personnel, e.g., directors of major enterprises, were frozen while wages generally rose (Chapman 1979b).

Not too much is known also about the determination of incomes of elite personnel. One might suppose that in principle the process of income formation here would be broadly similar to that prevailing in respect of incomes generally, a varying mix of market forces, political-ideological imperatives and planning distortions being operative in one case as in the other.

In a degree that must be so, but incomes in the occupations in question remain high. One wonders whether maintaining an appropriate supply of personnel really requires such differentials; whether, in other words, the differentials do not resolve in a significant degree into "rents." If so, the differentials call for further explanation, but that does not seem far to seek when we consider the nature of most of the occupations involved, and the importance to the system's directors of the loyalty of those who pursue them. Writers in particular can bolster the sense of legitimacy of a regime that is still unsure of itself.

I have been referring to the money incomes of elite personnel. Especially for such individuals, we must recall the limitations of money as a measure of real income (Section III). In view of the complex or privileges accruing to them, the residual influence of egalitarianism on the material status of elite personnel has surely become attenuated, if it exists at all.

The complex of privileges itself calls for explanation. Why not simply pay higher money incomes to the persons in question, and allow them to procure in the market the corresponding material benefits? One can only conjecture that the higher money incomes would likely make the privileged status of the elite groups more conspicuous, and hence politically disturbing. In order that the monetization be meaningful, it would be necessary to operate the consumer's goods market more effectively. Under centralist planning, that might not be easy to do. The complex of privileges also has the advantage that it reminds the recipient constantly of his special status and of his dependence on the continuing favor of those who grant it.

In the West, of course, material well-being at the highest levels has been in varying degrees self-perpetuating, in the sense of being passed on to children and

other relatives and connections. A principal object of radical criticism, that process probably has often been ameliorated through public action in democratic political systems; at least, the degree of self-perpetuation should have diminished relatively to other sources of material affluence. What of the USSR? In the West, a major source of self-perpetuation of material affluence has been inheritance of wealth. Despite its initial abolition in principle, inheritance has always been allowed in the USSR. For many years it has been subject at most to a charge of 10 percent of the estate. For many types of property, the charge is now nul (Vladimir Gsovski 1948, vol. 1, pp. 618ff; Matthews 1978, pp. 102–03; Koniukhova 1980, pp. 262ff). With preponderant public ownership of the means of production, though, accumulation of private wealth is limited (among the nonfarm population, savings deposits, government bonds and housing are the principal forms), and so too are the opportunities for transmission of affluence through inheritance.[51]

Children of Soviet elite personnel, however, fare quite well in admission to higher educational institutions. While "specialists" and their families constituted but one-seventh of the population, their children in the late sixties accounted for from 31.5 to 51.0 percent of the enrollment in a number of provincial universities for which such data are available. Relatively to their families' place in the population, children of nonmanual employees other than "specialists" also tended to be overrepresented in the student bodies in question. The share of children of manual workers in enrollment, concomitantly,

[51] The average savings deposit at the end of 1980 was 1,101 rubles (A. Shokhin 1981). Among the affluent, deposits must have been far larger than that, and wealth in that form must have been highly concentrated, but at the low interest allowed, even a deposit of 100,000 rubles would yield only 2,000–3,000 rubles a year, or 1.0–1.5 the average wage.

was less than one-half of their families' share in the population. Underrepresentation of children of collective farmers was even more marked. Children of manual workers and collective farmers fared better at a number of engineering and other advanced technical institutes, though their enrollment there too was disproportionately low (Yanowich 1977, pp. 88–91; see also Basile Kerblay 1983, pp. 163–64; Matthews 1982, pp. 158–61).

"Specialists," according to the Soviet usage understood here, are individuals engaged "in complex mental labor of high skills requiring . . . as a rule higher or specialized secondary education" (M. N. Rutkevich, quoted in Yanowich 1977, p. 108; also pp. 90–91). That presumably would include elite personnel as defined above, but also many other persons of lesser status. Children of elite personnel, however, have apparently been particularly well-represented in higher educational institutions, especially the more prestigious ones (Matthew 1978, pp. 47–49). Their superior status, like that of specialists generally, has reflected in good part the correspondingly advantageous position they enjoyed in secondary schools, and more basically a favorable parental background. As in the West, that has apparently been a consequential factor. Or so Soviet sociologists themselves have reported, and there is no basis to quarrel with them at this point (Rutkevich and F. R. Filippov 1973, pp. 255–56).

Applicants for university admission have come to exceed by far the number of available places. While providing a favorable environment for educational achievement generally, well-placed families, in order to enhance their children's prospects of university admission are often able to arrange special tutoring for them for the entrance examinations that are given, and sometimes resort to irregular procedures, including bribery, to the same end (Matthews 1978, pp. 47–48;

1982, p. 132; Yanowich 1977, p. 85; Lipset and Dobson 1973, pp. 175–77).

The disproportionately low enrollment of children of manual workers in the universities represents a dramatic denouement to early post-Revolutionary efforts to assure their predominance. After a protracted period of preoccupation with merit under Stalin, measures to "rectify" the university social structure were initiated by his successors, but seemingly with only limited effect.[52]

Interesting as their favored access to higher education is, what must finally be in question concerning Soviet elite children is the nature of the careers that they pursue. Data on the social origins of elite personnel that are needed for appraisal of that matter are very rare, but for the more inclusive category of specialists diverse tabulations indicate that recruitment is still substantially from other strata of Soviet society. Although often stressed by Soviet and Western scholars alike, that is not surprising when we consider the still limited fraction of the Soviet labor force (in 1970, 14.2 percent) that specialists constitute, and the fact that industrialization has until the last years still been proceeding in the USSR at a rapid pace. With the number of specialists likewise increasing rapidly (it nearly doubled during 1960–1970), a great many such persons had to be recruited from among the children of nonspecialists.

Of more interest, then, is the fact that 37.5 percent of the specialists in Kazan in 1967 were children of specialists. The

---

[52] One such action under Khrushchev was to abolish fees for secondary and higher education. Contrary to a common supposition, such fees, after being initially abolished, were reintroduced in the twenties, and after again being abolished in 1936 (under the new Stalinian constitution) were again reintroduced in 1940. For many years, though, the bulk of Soviet university students have received stipends for their maintenance (Bergson 1944, pp. 26–29, 234–35; Matthews 1978, pp. 78–80, 114–19; 1982, pp. 154ff; Yanowich 1977, pp. 79ff).

corresponding figure for Ufa in 1970 was 32.8 and for Leningrad in 1970, 31.3 percent (Yanowich 1977, pp. 108–11).

Something is known also about selected groups of specialists. Although reference is still not necessarily to elite personnel, it is illuminating that 62.9 percent of persons employed in "skilled mental work" or serving as "managerial personnel" in a Leningrad machinery factory in 1967 were children of specialists with higher education; 78.0 percent of the children of managerial personnel and 62.9 percent of the children of highly-skilled scientific-technical personnel in Leningrad machinery enterprises in 1970 were either specialists or full-time students in advanced institutions; and 49.0 percent of "highly skilled personnel in . . . creative occupations" and 45.8 percent of personnel in "highly skilled scientific and technical-work" in the city of Kazan in 1967 were children of employees in posts requiring specialized or higher education (Yanowich 1977, pp. 114ff; O. I. Shkaratan 1973, p. 297).

Not very surprisingly, the children of the most elite personnel of all, the members of the Politburo, and also their spouses have tended to find "jobs which place them in the upper ranks of the intelligentsia, but not necessarily over the elite threshold."[53]

Intergenerational mobility in the USSR begs for comparison with that in the West. Of particular interest would be a juxtapo-sition with the experience of a relatively open Western society such as that of the United States. Perhaps the comparison would not be unfavorable to the USSR. Data such as presented have been so read (Henry Phelps Brown 1977, pp. 192–93; see also Lipset and Dobson 1973, p. 185). For a socialist society, though, the data also seem to indicate stratification of a striking sort. With growth slowing, the stratification could become much more so in future. I have referred only to stratification in respect of the transmission of material status, but that is a cardinal sphere. Soviet socialism, as critics contend, has come to be a society with social classes of its own. Although still rather fluid, such strata could easily tend to congeal as time passes.

X. *Conclusions*

Concerning income inequality in the USSR, the Soviet government apparently prefers often to withhold rather than to release information. As this lengthy survey may testify, Western scholars have been able even so to compile much illuminating data on that matter. Although there are tantalizing gaps, much is known or can be surmised. The data seem illuminating even though they relate essentially to money income. Their real import is thus obscured by the proverbially flawed Soviet retail market. I try here to set forth summarily the more interesting findings.

Transfers apart, household income in the USSR consists preponderantly of wages and salaries paid employees of government enterprises and institutions. Among the more significant results of Western research are systematic data that have been compiled on the inequality of pay of such employees. As measured by selected percentile ratios of the distribution of wage earners and salaried workers (WESW) by earnings, inequality has varied over the last two decades, but appears

---

[53] Matthews (1978, p. 159). The majority of elite personnel, as we saw, are found in governmental, political and military organizations. One wonders how sources of recruitment there compare with those to other elite careers. In Kazan, children of employees in posts requiring specialized or higher education constituted but 19.3 percent of "executives of labor collectives and state organizations," or distinctly less than their corresponding shares of highly skilled scientific and technical workers and highly skilled personnel in "creative occupations." The import of this isolated and rather ambiguous datum relating to a provincial capital, however, is difficult to gauge.

to fall within the range delineated by corresponding measures for a number of Western countries at various dates. If we allow for relevant conditioning factors, including the development stage, inequality in the USSR in the early seventies may have been somewhat low by western standards.

The distribution of wages and salaries among recipients is one thing; that of income among consumer units could be quite another. That must be so for the USSR as well as the West, although in the former private income from property has been largely extinguished.

Concerning the distribution of income among consumer units in the USSR, there are diverse data, but probably nearest the mark are results of inflation of an emigré sample relating to the period 1972–1974. Among the urban households of the USSR, the highest tenth in terms of household income per capita is found to have received 24.1 percent of the income. The corresponding share of the lowest tenth was 3.4 percent. The income shares of the highest and lowest fifths were 38.5 and 8.7 percent respectively. The inflated sample may somewhat overstate income inequality among urban families, but for all Soviet households, rural as well as urban, inequality must be greater than for urban households alone.

International comparison of inequality in distribution of income among consumer units are proverbially difficult to make. An attempt to compare inequality in that regard in the USSR with that in the West exemplifies that rule. Among Western countries for which Lorenz-type data at all comparable to those available for the USSR are at hand, Sweden could well be one where inequality as so represented is no greater or less than in that country. Inequality in the USSR may not be much less than that in Norway and the United Kingdom, but is no doubt less than that in the United States and France. According-

ing to especially incomplete data, inequality in the USSR could sometimes fall short of that in countries at a comparable development stage, though that need not be markedly so in the case of Japan.

The indicated comparisons are intended to refer to disposable household income, that is, essentially money income including not only that earned but money transfer receipts (for the USSR, chiefly pensions, allowances and stipends) and less direct taxes. There are such taxes in the USSR, but they are only mildly progressive, and, compared with indirect taxes, of only very limited fiscal importance. While money transfer receipts, like those in the West, tend to favor low income groups, the redistributive impact of such receipts together with direct taxes most likely is less than is usually so in the West. Further transfers in the form of free educational and health services also tend to be equalizing in the USSR, but apparently little, if at all, more so than are comparable transfers in the United States.

Incomes in the USSR, it is often assumed, were radically equalized in the earliest post-Revolutionary years, but have become progressively more unequal ever since. In fact, available information on trends in Soviet income distribution is particularly meager, but the inequality in pay among WESW, while doubtless minimal initially, has subsequently varied in a complex manner. Indeed, there have been three cycles, rather than just one, of contraction of inequality and its opposite. The initial one occupied essentially the first decade after the Revolution, thus embracing first the years of War Communism and then those of the New Economic Policy (NEP). The second cycle occurs during the first two decades of five year plans and war, under Stalin. Having become extraordinarily marked by the early post-World War II years, inequality in pay has again tended to decline since then.

In the latest years, though, that trend has been checked.

The Soviet retail market is flawed, for one thing, in the familiar sense that prices are again and again below clearing levels. As a result, the real value of money income differentials must tend to be reduced. That must be considered in interpreting data, such as have been cited, on money income inequality. It must also be considered that higher income groups have often been shielded, if not more than shielded, from the resultant shortages by a complex of discriminatory distributional arrangements. I refer to more recent circumstances. The Soviet retail market has evolved in the course of time in ways not easily delineated summarily, but the meaning of money income differentials, it should be noted, was made especially problematic by pervasive rationing under War Communism, much of the first two five year plans, and then again during World War II and immediately after.

While seeking to measure income inequality in the USSR, Western scholars have also explored the process of income formation that underlies it. Here too they have focused on wages and salaries of government employees, particularly in industry. Under Soviet centralist planning, superior political and bureaucratic authorities necessarily play a major role in that process, but they have operated within the framework of institutions, which though of their own creation have had distinct market-like features. Thus, workers have been able to exercise discretion as to the work they do and where they do it. Their discretion has always been constrained, and at times in the past severely so, but the supply of labor in different occupations and industries must usually have depended consequentially on the prevailing wage structure. Enterprise managers too have had in varying degrees authority to determine the occupational structure of their labor force, and in doing

so have been induced to consider the costs involved. Economy of costs, though, has only been one of diverse success criteria motivating them.

The market forces that have manifested themselves in such complex circumstances have inevitably been distorted, and, whether because of inordinate controls above or evasive initiatives below, the system's response to such forces in determining the wage structure has often had a rather aberrant character. In exercising their responsibilities for wage determination, superior authorities apparently have also been influenced by political-ideological imperatives. Of an egalitarian sort, such imperatives probably contributed to the contraction of inequality in each of the cycles noted above.

Peculiar as the Soviet labor market may be, however, one still sees the imprint, on the resultant wage structure, of "scarcity values" such as might be encountered in a Western mixed economy. The scarcity values are necessarily those reflecting Soviet circumstances, as where the entire interindustrial wage structure was abruptly revised under Stalin to accommodate his growth model, and associated shifts in priorities. But they are scarcity values nonetheless. In the seventh decade since the Revolution, they still play a major, if not finally decisive, part in Soviet wage determination.

The Soviet government has been especially reticent as to who earns very high incomes in the USSR and how much they earn. In the early seventies, however, individuals earning more than 400–500 rubles monthly, or 3.1–3.8 times the average wage and 5.7–8.3 times the legal minimum, are known not to have been at all unusual. Such high earnings, though, often reflect income from a second public sector job or private activities. Of more interest are relatively restricted elite groups who achieve high incomes essentially from their main occupation, and who, through that work or through supplementary earnings or both, are frequently able to boost their incomes to high levels indeed. Among the principal groups involved are enterprise directors, high officials of the government and party, high level military and police staff and leading personalities engaged in diverse more intellectual pursuits (scholars, writers, journalists).

High as they are, the incomes of such elite personnel are the more impressive since the individuals in question are frequently among those especially favored by the discriminatory distribution arrangements noted above.

High incomes of individuals such as indicated are not novel in the USSR. Egalitarianism appears to have had for such persons a varying impact, to some extent paralleling that for industrial wages and salaries generally, but here too, scarcity values have manifestly also been consequential. Judging by the incomes earned, they should still be so. The high incomes earned, though, must often resolve in part into "quasi-rents" which the government could extract for public use without adverse effects on supply. That it has not done so on any scale, either by foreswearing inordinate income differentials or by levying more progressive taxes, is presumably to be read in the light of the critical importance of the personnel in question for the security of the regime. That must be a factor also in the curious arrangements by which elite personnel are sheltered from the vicissitudes of a malfunctioning retail market.

In contrast to the Western experience, high incomes do not appear to be perpetuated on any scale through inheritance in the USSR, though the intergenerational transmission of such wealth as is privately owned is permitted. Children of elite personnel and of better-placed individuals generally, however, are inordinately represented in admission to higher educational institutions. They also appear to be so represented in posts such as their parents occupied. Children of manual workers often have also been able to make careers in nonmanual pursuits, but rapid economic growth has hitherto created opportunities for advancement generally. Lately growth has been slowing. In the seventh decade since the Revolution, besides a marked income inequality, Soviet socialism manifests social strata that are still rather fluid but easily could become less so.

I have characterized the USSR as socialist in view of the predominance of public ownership there. On the official Soviet view, Soviet society is not only socialist in that sense but destined to become fully egalitarian. That follows at once from Marx' famous scheme of post-Revolutionary social evolution, application of which to the USSR is deemed canonical. Thus, the USSR is admittedly still in Marx' inegalitarian "lower" stage but is seen as bound to advance in time to his egalitarian "higher" one. Confronted by the Soviet experience to date, one imagines, Marx himself might have been surprised at how protracted the lower stage is proving to be, and disconcerted by currents manifestly at odds with attainment of the higher one.

Addendum: Note on Normalization

I refer here to the question raised in the text concerning the appropriate normalization of comparative data, such as in Table 3, on inequality of wages and salaries in the USSR and the West. For purposes of a limited inquiry into that matter, I have derived three regression relations.

The first, based on the data in Table 3, is of the form:

$$\log (P_{90}/P_{50}) = a \log (\text{GDP per capita}) \\ + cS_{61} + dS_{70} + eS_{76} + f. \quad \text{(A)}$$

Here reference is made to a single normalization parameter, development stage, as indicated by GDP per capita. The terms S_{61}, S_{70} and S_{76} are dummy variables standing for Soviet socialism as represented by P_{90}/P_{50} for the USSR for 1961, 1970 and 1976 (the magnitude of P_{90}/P_{50} for the latter year is extrapolated from that for 1968 by reference to P_{90}/P_{10}).

TABLE 13

COEFFICIENTS FOR ALTERNATIVE REGRESSION RELATIONS FOR P_{90}/P_{50} FOR SOVIET AND WESTERN
EARNINGS DISTRIBUTIONS[a]

Formula	Coefficient					
	a	*b*	*c*	*d*	*e*	*f*
A	0.0070		0.1124	−0.0524	0.1579	0.5565
	(0.1143)		(1.1458)	−(0.5594)	(1.6980)	(2.2794)
B	−0.0971	0.0506	−0.0196	−0.1558	0.0674	0.7737
	−(1.2065)	(1.8143)	−(0.1697)	−(1.5124)	(0.6824)	(3.0493)
C	−0.1480	0.0246	0.0146			1.0243
	−(2.3790)	(1.3299)	(0.1445)			(4.1846)

[a] Figures shown parenthetically are T statistics. In applying formula A there were 12 degrees of freedom; in applying formulas B and C, 11 in each case. For formula C, the regression coefficient c relates to the Soviet P_{90}/P_{50} for 1959, taken as a dummy variable.

As thus determined, P_{90}/P_{50} hardly varies one way or the other with the development stage, but the negligible coefficient in question is in any case not statistically significant (Table 13). Except for the intercept, that is also true of all the other coefficients in formula A, though the positive coefficient for S_{76} begins to be interesting.

The second regression relation derived is of the form:

$$\log (P_{90}/P_{50}) = a \log (\text{GDP per capita})$$
$$+ b \log (\text{pop.}) + cS_{61} \quad\quad\text{(B)}$$
$$+ dS_{70} + eS_{76} + f.$$

Here the additional parameter, population, is taken as a surrogate for a country's size. Population is taken from standard sources. Otherwise, I again draw on Table 3 for relevant data.

Under formula B there is a perceptible negative relation between P_{90}/P_{50} and the development stage, but the relevant coefficient is still of doubtful reliability (Table 13). There is now, however, a positive relation of P_{90}/P_{50} with country size, and the indicated coefficient is significant at the 0.10 level. All of the coefficients for the dummy variables indicate a substandard level of P_{90}/P_{50} for the USSR. Only that for 1970, however, approaches statistical significance by usual standards.[54]

Development stage and size are both considered by Lydall (1978, pp. 202ff) as among the more significant factors affecting observed intercountry differences in earnings inequality. Although Lydall does not test such relations statistically, Pryor (1973, pp.

[54] Formula B, as readily seen, comes to the same thing analytically as one in which GNP and population are taken as the normalization parameters, but that seems less easily interpreted than the version that I have considered.

80–85, 448–49), drawing heavily on Lydall's data, does do so, and finds inequality of earnings, as indicated by selected percentile ratios, to vary negatively with development stage and positively with country size, as represented by GDP per capita and population respectively. Following Lydall, Pryor focuses on standardized earnings distributions relating to male adult workers working full-time for a full period. His use of such relatively homogeneous data presumably has something to do with the fact that both of the regression coefficients in question are significant at the 0.05 level.

In inquiring into the factors affecting observed earnings inequality generally, Pryor also explores how such inequality in earnings compares for seven socialist countries, on the one hand, and fourteen Western ones, on the other. With due regard to development stage and country size, he finds socialism, as represented by a single dummy variable, to be associated with reduced inequality. Here too regression coefficients in question are significant at the 0.05 level.

Interesting as that result is, of more interest here is the fact that one of the socialist countries considered is the USSR. Pryor refers only to a single year, 1959, and is not very explicit as to how he derives for it, from available earnings distributions for the USSR, a standardized one.

Using Pryor's percentile ratios for male workers alone, though, I have made still another regression calculation, applying formula C. Not shown, this corresponds to B, except that there is now only a single dummy variable, representing Soviet socialism as indicated by the Soviet P_{90}/P_{50} for 1959. Here again P_{90}/P_{50} varies negatively with development stage and positively with country size. The coefficient for the former, however, is now significant at the 0.05 level, while that for the latter is less reliable than formerly (Table 13). Curiously the coefficient for Soviet socialism is now positive, though not statistically significant. That need not be inconsistent with Pryor's finding for socialism more generally, for among his socialist countries P_{90}/P_{50} is clearly greatest for the USSR. Recall, too, that in the USSR earnings inequality was still relatively marked in 1959.[55]

A standardized earnings distribution such as Lydall and Pryor consider has the virtue that it facilitates analysis of earnings inequality. For present purposes, however, the distribution, by earnings, of workers more generally must be the primary concern. One is led to wonder, therefore, what the result might be if still another variable, say, the share of female workers in employment, were taken as a parameter for purposes of normalization. That share, as noted, is relatively high in the USSR, but, without further inquiry that is beyond the scope of this survey, it seems difficult to gauge the effect of normalization for that aspect.

Still other candidates for normalization parameters come readily to mind, such as industrial structure, particularly the employment shares of heavy and light industry, and the average level and dispersion of educational attainment. From facts set forth in this survey and others generally known, the differential inequality attributable to Soviet socialism, I suspect, would be reduced by inclusion of branch employment shares as a parameter. Inclusion of the level and dispersion of educational attainment, however, should have a contrary effect. But these matters too must be left to separate inquiry.

The addition of parameters such as the female share in employment, branch employment shares and the level and dispersion of educational attainment, it should be observed, significantly changes the meaning of regression coefficients for Soviet socialism. For any given country size and development stage, the additional parameters might be viewed as encapsulating inter-country differences in supply and demand that affect earnings inequality. Without inclusion of such parameters, the coefficients for Soviet socialism hopefully represent the differential impact of that system on earnings inequality. With their inclusion, such coefficients could at best indicate how, if at all, the response in respect of earnings inequality to given market conditions differs under Soviet socialism from that in the West. Soviet socialism manifestly must also affect earnings inequality through its impact on the additional parameters, and hence market conditions, but such effects become embedded in the coefficients and magnitudes of those variables.

Normalization such as has been discussed represents an attempt to explain inter-country differences of earnings inequality. While all the parameters considered may in fact have explanatory value, it should also be noted that from a normative standpoint one of them, country size, has a rather special character. I described in the text the complex procedures through which political and bureaucratic authorities seek to control Soviet wage differentials. Such efforts extend to regional differentials, and not surprisingly the result has been a notable degree of uniformity. Wages in different regions necessarily differ so far as they relate to different industries. There are also sometimes quite sizable regional differentials as such, for example for the far North, but in 1960 some two-thirds of Soviet industrial wage earners were located in Zone 1, and subject to one and the same "regional wage coefficient" (Chapman 1970, pp. 37–45).

How regional wage differentials as so determined compare with those in the West has yet to be studied, but the resultant variation seems likely to be less than is usual in Western countries. After adjustment for country size, it also follows, earnings inequality in the USSR must tend to be depressed compared to that in the West because of the reduced regional variation.

And that, it might be thought, would normatively be of a piece with any other cause of differential earnings inequality in the USSR. But in the West regional wage differentials in part simply compensate for differences in prices. That seems to be so also in the USSR. Indeed, the uniformity in wages there is apparently associated with a substantial uniformity in prices. So far as earnings inequality in the USSR reflects a reduced regional variation, the resultant compression must often relate to money rather than real earnings. To that extent, any normative gains must be illusory.

REFERENCES

Abbreviations:

CIA:	Central Intelligence Agency
JEC:	Joint Economic Committee, United States Congress
TSSU:	Tsentral'noe Statisticheskoe Upravlenie
TSUNKHU:	Tsentral'noe Upravlenie Narodnokhoziaistvennogo Ucheta
USDC:	United States Department of Commerce

ADAM, JAN. "The Present Soviet Incentive System," *Soviet Stud.,* July 1980, *32*(3), pp. 349–65.
ALEKSANDROVA, A. AND FEDEROVSKAIA, E. "Mekhanizm formirovaniia i vozvysheniia potrebnostei," *Voprosy ekonomiki, 1,* 1984, pp. 15–25.
ATKINSON, ANTHONY B. "On the Measurement of Inequality," *J. Econ. Theory,* Sept. 1970, *2*(3), pp. 244–63.
———. *The economics of inequality.* Oxford: Clarendon Press, 1975.
BÉGUÉ, JEAN. "Remarques sur une étude de l'OCDE concernant la répartition des revenus dans diverse

pays," in *Économie et statistique*. Institut National de la Statistique et des Études Économiques, Dec. 1976, pp. 97–104.

BERGSON, ABRAM. *The structure of Soviet wages*. Cambridge, MA: Harvard U. Press, 1944.

———. "On the Inequality of Incomes in the USSR," *Amer. Slavic East Europ. Rev.*, Apr. 1951, *10*(2), pp. 95–99.

———. *The economics of Soviet planning*. New Haven: Yale U. Press, 1964.

———. *Essays in normative economics*. Cambridge, MA: Harvard U. Press, 1966.

———. *Productivity and the social system—The USSR and the West*. Cambridge, MA: Harvard U. Press, 1978.

———. "Technological Progress," in *The Soviet economy: Toward the year 2000*. Eds.: ABRAM BERGSON AND HERBERT S. LEVINE. London: Allen & Unwin, 1983, pp. 34–78.

BERLINER, JOSEPH. *Factory and manager in the USSR*. Cambridge, MA: Harvard U. Press, 1957.

———. *The innovation decision in Soviet industry*. Cambridge, MA: MIT Press, 1976.

BIRMAN, IGOR. "The Financial Crisis in the USSR," *Soviet Stud.*, Jan. 1980, *32*(1), pp. 84–105.

BRONSON, DAVID W. AND KRUEGER, CONSTANCE B. "The Revolution in Soviet Farm Household Income, 1953–1967," in *The Soviet rural community*. Ed.: JAMES R. MILLAR. Urbana, IL: U. of Illinois Press, 1971, pp. 214–58.

BROWN, HENRY PHELPS. *The inequality of pay*. Oxford: Oxford U. Press, 1977.

BUDD, EDWARD C. "Postwar Changes in the Size Distribution of Income in the US," *Amer. Econ. Rev.*, May 1970, *60*(2), pp. 247–60.

CHAPMAN, JANET G. *Real wages in the Soviet Union since 1928*. Cambridge, MA: Harvard U. Press, 1963.

———. "Wage Variation in Soviet Industry: The Impact of the 1956–1960 Wage Reform." The RAND Corp., R–6076–PR, Santa Monica, CA, Feb. 1970.

———. "The Distribution of Earnings in Selected Countries, East and West." Presented at symposium on "Technology, Labor Productivity and Labor Supply," Racine, Wisconsin, Nov. 1977a.

———. "Soviet Wages under Socialism," in *The socialist price mechanism*. Ed.: ALAN ABOUCHAR. Durham, NC: Duke U. Press, 1977b, pp. 246–81.

———. "Equal Pay for Equal Work," in *Women in Russia*. Eds.: DOROTHY ATKINSON, ALEXANDER DALLIN AND GAIL W. LAPIDUS. Stanford, CA: Stanford U. Press, 1977c, pp. 225–39.

———. "Are Earnings More Equal under Socialism," in *Income inequality*. Ed.: JOHN R. MORONEY. Lexington, MA: Lexington Books, 1979a, pp. 43–62.

———. "Recent Trends in Soviet Industrial Wage Structure," in *Industrial labor in the USSR*. Eds.: ARCADIUS KAHAN AND BLAIR RUBLE. NY: Pergamon Press, 1979b, pp. 151–83.

———. "Market and Administration in Improving Labor Allocation in the USSR." Presented at panel, American Association for Advancement of Slavic Studies, Washington, DC, Oct. 1982.

———. "Earnings Distribution in the USSR, 1968–1976," *Soviet Stud.*, July 1983, *35*(3), pp. 410–13.

CHILOSI, ALBERTO. "Growth Maximization, Egalitarianism and Wage Differentials in the Socialist Economy," *Z. Nationalökon.*, 1976, *36*(3–4), pp. 319–22.

CIA. *Handbook of economic statistics 1981*. Wash., DC: CIA, NF HES 81–001, Nov. 1981.

———. *The Soviet forced labor system*. Wash., DC: CIA, GI M 82–10241, Nov. 1982.

———. *Soviet gross national product in current prices, 1960–1980*. Wash., DC: CIA, SOV 83–10037, Mar. 1983a.

———. *Handbook of economic statistics 1983*. Wash., DC: CIA CPAS 83–10006, Sept. 1983b.

CONQUEST, ROBERT. "Forced Labor Statistics: Some Comments," *Soviet Stud.*, July 1982, *34*(3), pp. 434–39.

DEPARTMENT OF EMPLOYMENT, U.K. *British labour statistics yearbook 1976*. London: Her Majesty's Stationery Office, 1978.

DEWAR, MARGARET. *Labour policy in the USSR, 1917–1928*. London and NY: Royal Inst. of Int. Affairs, 1956.

DiMAIO, ALFRED J., JR. *Soviet urban housing*. NY: Praeger, 1974.

EDWARDS, IMOGENE; HUGHES, MARGARET AND NOREN, JAMES. "U.S. and USSR: Comparisons of GNP," in *Soviet economy in a time of change*. Vol. 1. JEC. Wash., DC: U.S. GPO, 1979, pp. 369–401.

ELLMAN, MICHAEL. "A Note on the Distribution of Earnings in the USSR under Brezhnev," *Slavic Rev.*, Dec. 1980, *39*(4), pp. 669–71.

FESHBACH, MURRAY AND RAPAWY, STEPHEN. "Labor Constraints in the Five-Year Plan," in *Soviet economic prospects for the seventies*. JEC. Wash., DC: U.S. GPO, 1973, pp. 485–563.

———. "Soviet Population and Manpower Trends and Policies," in *Soviet economy in a new perspective*. JEC. Wash., DC: U.S. GPO, 1976, pp. 113–54.

FISHER, IRVING. *The nature of capital and income*. London: Macmillan, 1906.

FROLIC, BERNARD MICHAEL. "Soviet Urban Sociology," *Int. J. Compar. Soc.*, Dec. 1971, *12*(4), pp. 234–51.

GALENSON, MARJORIE. *Women and work*. NY: NY State School of Ind. and Labor Relat., 1973.

GALENSON, WALTER. "The Soviet Wage Reform," in *Proceedings of the thirteenth annual meeting of the Industrial Relations Research Association*. St. Louis, MO, Dec. 1960, pp. 250–65.

GRANICK, DAVID. *Management of the industrial firm in the USSR*. NY: Columbia U. Press, 1954.

GREENSLADE, RUSH V. "The Real Gross National Product of the USSR, 1950–1975," in *Soviet economy in a new perspective*. JEC. Wash., DC: U.S. GPO, 1976, pp. 269–300.

GREGORY, PAUL R. AND STUART, ROBERT C. *Soviet economic structure and performance*. 2nd ed. NY: Harper & Row, 1981.

GROSSMAN, GREGORY. "The 'Second Economy' of the USSR," *Problems of Communism*, Sept.–Oct. 1977, *26*(5), pp. 25–40.

_____. "Notes on the Illegal Private Economy and Corruption," in *Soviet economy in a time of change*. Vol. 1. JEC. Wash., DC: U.S. GPO, 1979, pp. 834–55.

GROSSMAN, PHILIP. "The Soviet Government's Role in Allocating Industrial Labor," in *Industrial labor in the USSR*. Eds.: ARCADIUS KAHAN AND BLAIR RUBLE. NY: Pergamon Press, 1979, pp. 42–58.

GSOVSKI, VLADIMIR. *Soviet civil law*. Vols. 1 & 2. Ann Arbor: U. of Michigan Law School, 1948, 1949.

HOEFFDING, OLEG. *Soviet national income and product in 1928*. NY: Columbia U. Press, 1954.

HOLZMAN, FRANKLYN. *Soviet taxation*. Cambridge, MA: Harvard U. Press, 1955.

JASNY, NAUM. "Labor and Output in Soviet Concentration Camps," *J. Pol. Econ.*, Oct. 1951, 59(5), pp. 405–19.

JORGENSON, DALE AND SLESNICK, DANIEL T. "Inequality in the Distribution of Individual Welfare." Cambridge, MA: Harvard Inst. of Econ. Res., No. 987, June 1983.

KERBLAY, BASILE. *Modern Soviet society*. NY: Pantheon Books, 1983.

KIRSCH, LEONARD J. *Soviet wages: Changes in structure and administration since 1956*. Cambridge, MA: MIT Press, 1972.

KONIUKHOVA, T. V., ed. *Sbornik po finansovomu zakonodatel'stvu*. Moscow: Iuridicheskaia Literatura, 1980.

KRAVIS, IRVING B.; HESTON, ALAN AND SUMMERS, ROBERT. *World product and income*. Baltimore, MD: Johns Hopkins U. Press, 1982.

KRIAZHOV, V. G. "Metodologicheskie voprosy statistiki dokhodov semei trudiashchikhsia," in *Dokhody trudiashchikhsia i sotsial'nye problemy urovni zhizni naseleniia SSSR*. Ed.: G. C. SARKISIAN. Moscow, 1973, pp. 175–86.

KUZNETS, SIMON. "Quantitative Aspects of Economic Growth of Nations: VIII. Distribution of Income by Size," *Econ. Develop. Cult. Change*, Jan. 1963, 11(2, Part II), pp. 1–80.

_____. *Modern economic growth*. New Haven: Yale U. Press, 1966.

_____. "Demographic Aspects of the Size Distribution of Income. An Exploratory Essay," *Econ. Develop. Cult. Change*, Oct. 1976, 25(1), pp. 1–94.

_____. "Size of Households and Income Disparities," in *Research in population economics*. Vol. 3. Eds.: JULIAN L. SIMON AND PETER H. LINDERT. Greenwich, CT: JAI Press, 1981, pp. 1–40.

LANE, DAVID. *The end of social inequality?* London: Allen & Unwin, 1982.

LANGE, OSKAR. "On the Economic Theory of Socialism," in *On the economic theory of socialism*. Ed.: BENJAMIN E. LIPPINCOTT. Minneapolis: U. of Minnesota Press, 1938, pp. 55–143.

LIPSET, MARTIN AND DOBSON, RICHARD B. "Social Stratification and Sociology in the Soviet Union," *Survey*, Summer 1973, 88(3), pp. 114–85.

LYDALL, HAROLD. *The structure of wages*. Oxford: The Clarendon Press, 1968.

MCAULEY, ALASTAIR. *Women's work and wages in the Soviet Union*. London: Allen & Unwin, 1981.

_____. *Economic welfare in the Soviet Union*. Madison, WI: U. of Wisconsin Press, 1979.

_____. "Sources of Earnings Inequality: A Comment on A. Nove's Income Distribution in the USSR," *Soviet Stud.*, July 1982, 34(3), pp. 443–47.

MARX, KARL. *Critique of the Gotha Programme*. NY: International Pub., 1938.

MATTHEWS, MERVYN. *Privilege in the Soviet Union*. London: Allen & Unwin, 1978.

_____. *Education in the Soviet Union*. London: Allen & Unwin, 1982.

MEDVEDEV, ROY A. *Let history judge*. NY: Knopf, 1971.

MIGRANOVA, L. A. AND RABKINA, N. E. "Izmenenie differentsiatsii pri prevrashchenii zarabotnoi platy v dokhod sem'i," in *Sotsial'no ekonomicheskie problemy blagosostoianiia*. Ed.: N. M. RIMASHEVSKAIA. Moscow: Tsentral'nyi Ekonomiko-matematicheskii Institut, 1976, pp. 53–73.

MINISTERSTVO KOMMUNAL'NOGO KHOZIAISTVA RSFSR. *Zhilishchnye zakony*. Moscow, 1947.

MUSGRAVE, RICHARD A. AND MUSGRAVE, PEGGY B. *Public finance in theory and practice*. NY: McGraw-Hill, 1980.

MINISTRY OF LABOR, JAPAN. *Yearbook of labor statistics 1968*. Tokyo: Ministry of Labor, 1969.

NOVE, ALEC. *An economic history of the USSR*. London: Penguin Press, 1969.

_____. *The Soviet economic system*. London: Allen & Unwin, 1977.

_____. "Income Distribution in the USSR: A Possible Explanation of Some Recent Data," *Soviet Stud.*, Apr. 1982, 34(2), pp. 286–88.

OECD. *Labor force statistics 1967–1978*. Paris: OECD, 1980.

_____. *National accounts of OECD countries: 1962–1979*. Vol. 2. Paris: OECD, 1981.

OFER, GUR AND VINOKUR, AARON. "Family Budget Survey of Soviet Emigrants in the Soviet Union." The RAND Corp., P–6015, Santa Monica, CA. July 1979.

_____. "The Distribution of Income of the Urban Population of the Soviet Union." Presented at Second World Congress of Soviet and East European Studies, Garmisch, 1980a.

_____. "Private Sources of Income of the Soviet Urban Household." The RAND Corp., R–2359–NA, Santa Monica, CA, Aug. 1980b.

_____. "Earnings Differentials by Sex in the Soviet Union: A First Look," in *Economic welfare and the economics of socialism: Essays in honor of Abram Bergson*. Ed.: STEVEN ROSEFIELDE. Cambridge: Cambridge U. Press, 1981, pp. 127–62.

_____. "The Distributive Effects of the Social Consumption Fund of the Soviet Union." Presented at a Conference on Social Welfare and the Delivery of Social Services, USA-USSR, Berkeley, CA, Nov. 1982.

OFER, GUR AND PICKERSGILL, JOYCE. "Soviet Household Saving: A Cross Section Study of Soviet Emigrant Families," *Quart. J. Econ.*, Aug. 1980, 95(1), pp. 121–44.

PICKERSGILL, JOYCE. "Soviet Household Saving Behaviour," *Rev. Econ. Statist.*, May 1976, *58*(2), pp. 139–47.

———. "Recent Evidence on Soviet Household Saving Behaviour," *Rev. Econ. Statist.*, Nov. 1980, *62*(4), pp. 628–33.

Pravda. Moscow, June 27, 1937; Nov. 28, 1979.

PRYOR, FREDERIC L. *Property and industrial organization in communist and capitalist nations.* Bloomington: Indiana U. Press, 1973.

RABKINA, N. E. AND RIMASHEVSKAIA, N. M. *Osnovy differentsiatsii zarabotnoi platy i dokhodov naseleniia.* Moscow, 1972.

———. "Raspredelitel'nye otnosheniia i sotsial'noe razvitie," *Ekonomika i organizatsiia promyshlennogo proizvodstva,* 1978, No. 5.

RIMASHEVSKAIA, N. M. *Ekonomicheskii analiz dokhodov rabochikh i sluzhashchikh.* Moscow, 1965.

RIURIKOV, IU. B. "Deti i obshchestvo," *Voprosy filosofii,* No. 4, 1977, pp. 111–21.

ROSEFIELDE, STEVEN. "An Assessment of the Sources and Uses of Gulag Forced Labor 1929–56," *Soviet Stud.,* Jan. 1981, *33*(1), pp. 51–87.

RUTKEVICH, M. N. AND FILLIPOV, F. R. "Social Sources of Recruitment of the Intelligentsia," in *Social stratification and mobility in the USSR.* Eds.: MURRAY YANOWICH AND WESLEY A. FISHER. White Plains, NY: Int. Arts and Sciences Press, 1973, pp. 241–74.

SAUNDERS, CHRISTOPHER AND MARSDEN, DAVID. *Pay inequalities in the European community.* London: Butterworth, 1981.

SAWYER, MALCOLM. "Income Distribution in OECD Countries," *OECD Economic Outlook: Occasional Studies,* July 1976, pp. 3–36.

SCHROEDER, GERTRUDE E. AND EDWARDS, IMOGENE. *Consumption in the USSR: An international comparison.* JEC. Wash., DC: U.S. GPO, 1981.

——— AND SEVERIN, BARBARA S. "Soviet Consumption and Income Policies in Perspective," in *Soviet economy in a new perspective.* JEC. Wash., DC: U.S. GPO, 1976.

SHKARATAN, O. I. "Social Ties and Social Mobility," in *Social stratification and mobility in the USSR.*

Eds.: MURRAY YANOWICH AND WESLEY A. FISHER. White Plains, NY: Int. Arts and Sciences Press, 1973, pp. 289–319.

SHOKHIN, A. "Denezhnye sberezheniia naseleniia," *Ekonomicheskaia gazeta,* Aug. 1981, No. 35, p. 9.

SMITH, HEDRICK. *The Russians.* NY: Quadrangle, 1976.

SUMMERS, ROBERT; KRAVIS, IRVING B. AND HESTON, ALAN. "International Comparison of Real Product and Its Composition: 1950–77," *Rev. Inc. Wealth,* Mar. 1980, *26*(1), pp. 19–66.

TSSU. *Narodnoe khoziaistvo v 1960 g.,* Moscow: 1961, and other volumes for 1975 and 1980 in the same series.

———. *Trud v SSSR.* Moscow: 1968.

TSUNKHU. *Trud v SSSR.* Moscow, 1936.

USDC. *Surv. Curr. Bus.,* July 1982, *62*(7).

———. Bureau of the Census. "Money Income in 1972 of Families and Persons in the United States," in *Current population reports: Consumer income.* Series P-60, No. 87, June 1973a, pp. 1–7.

———. Bureau of the Census. *Occupations of persons with high earnings. Census of the population, 1970.* Vol. 1. *Characteristics of the population, subject report.* P.C. (2)–7F. Wash., DC: U.S. GPO, 1973b.

WHEATCROFT, STEPHEN G. "On Assessing the Size of Forced Concentration Camp Labor in the Soviet Union 1929–56," *Soviet Stud.,* Apr. 1981, *33*(2), pp. 265–95.

———. "Toward a Thorough Analysis of Soviet Forced Labor Statistics," *Soviet Stud.,* Apr. 1983, *35*(2), pp. 223–37.

WILES, PETER J. D. *Distribution of income: East and West.* NY: American Elsevier, 1974.

——— AND MARKOVSKI, STEFAN. "Income Distribution under Communism and Capitalism," *Soviet Stud.,* Part 1, Jan. 1971, *22*(3), pp. 344–69; Part 2, Apr. 1971, *22*(4), pp. 487–511.

YANOWICH, MURRAY. *Social and economic inequality in the Soviet Union.* White Plains, NY: M. E. Sharpe, 1977.

Part II
Growth

6

Soviet Technological Progress

Among the diverse factors determining the future growth of the Soviet economy, the rate of technological advance that is attained must be one of the more decisive. Awkwardly that is also a matter that is inherently rather conjectural.[1] Perhaps I can narrow the range of uncertainty, however, by inquiring summarily into past trends and the forces that have shaped them. Inquiry into these matters hopefully will provide a basis for speculation in the concluding section, about future prospects of Soviet technological advance.

Technological progress has been understood variously. Traditionally reference has been to the introduction and spread of new production methods that enable the community to increase output at a given resource cost. The new production methods often involve use of new sorts of capital goods or physical processes; but other changes in production modes, such as extension of intrafactory specialization, are also envisaged. Whatever their nature, the new methods enlarge the technological "opportunity set" of a production unit, thus generating a larger output at the same resource cost.

Output may expand at given resource cost, however, not only through such variations in production methods but also in other ways; for example, through a reform in labor incentives. Lately technological progress has often been understood to embrace such an institutional change as well. Indeed, technological progress has come to refer to output expansion at given resource cost on any and all accounts.

As between these concepts of technological progress, the last one perhaps has an advantage, for — and this has not always been considered — it is sometimes difficult, even in principle, to draw the line between the introduction and spread of new technologies and other causes of output expansion at given resource cost. Depending on the development stage, for example, amelioration of a historically distorted resource allocation in the process of industrialization may be a significant source of increase in output at the same resource cost. Such a gain is very often treated as technological progress apart from introduction and spread of new technologies. But a transfer of, say, labor from agriculture to industry serves in effect to extend the scope of advanced production methods. From that standpoint, it might be viewed more as a form of technological diffusion, albeit of a rather indirect sort. True, the advanced technologies applied may not be especially novel in any period considered, but that may also be true of technologies whose application is being extended more directly elsewhere in the economy.

I propose nevertheless to focus primarily on technological progress in its traditional and more limited sense. In fact, where a choice is open, I interpret the traditional concept as being less, rather than more, inclusive. A principal concern, however, is to assess quantitatively the pace of technological advance. In attempting that, it is difficult to do otherwise than view such progress, at least in the first instance, in a more inclusive way. That should be to the good, though, for technological progress in the inclusive sense that has come lately into use is also of interest. Thus where the concept in question needs to be distinctly stated I refer to technological progress in the less inclusive sense, relating to new production methods only, as technological progress proper (TPP), and in the more inclusive sense, which embraces also other causes of output expansion at given resource cost, as technological progress extended (TPE).

In either usage, the touchstone of advance is the increase in output at given resource cost. That, strictly speaking, still leaves open the question which treatment is to be accorded to introduction of novel products for household and other final consumption, and the resulting gains in final user values at given resource cost. Although such gains are obviously to be included in any complete accounting for technological progress, the advance realized exclusive of such gains has an interest of its own. Western quantitative research on technological progress has properly often focused on the more limited concept. As rarely noted, it is rather problematic how completely the statistical measures that are compiled do in fact exclude consumers' gains from new final products. But that is an intricate matter that cannot be disposed of in this essay. I compile measures for the USSR, however, that are of a sort usually compiled for Western countries. As will appear, there are reasons to at least be alert to the question regarding the coverage of consumer gains as posed above.

Productivity Growth

Technological progress, by its very nature, is manifest in productivity growth. An attempt to appraise the tempo of such progress, therefore, properly turns to that aspect. Measurement of productivity growth in a way that is indicative of technological progress has generally proven to be a difficult task, and the USSR is no exception to that rule. But the increase of productivity can still serve as an illuminating benchmark. Of particular interest are trends in factor productivity as indicated by the comparative growth of output and factor inputs. Such calculations have by now often been made for the USSR, but it is best to approach the matter afresh here.

I have compiled data on Soviet factor-productivity growth both for the whole economy and for a somewhat less comprehensive sphere. To refer first to the measures for the whole economy, as indicated in Table 1, these relate the growth of GNP to the growth of three major factor inputs, labor, capital and agricultural land. The calculations are made for most part in a usual way. Among other things, they entail the imposition of a Cobb-Douglas production function with assigned factor-input coefficients and neutral technological progress on underlying data on factor inputs and output.[2] The calculations also yield more or less usual results for the period studied: factor-productivity growth, not especially rapid to begin with, slows in successive intervals — and indeed is negligible in the final period considered.

This is not the place to reopen the perennial issue concerning the reliability of Western measures of real national output in the USSR, but it should be observed that the Greenslade (1976) measures that I use are compiled in terms of ruble weights (depending on the level of aggregation, prices or factor costs) which generally relate to 1970 or a nearby year. That is an appropriate weight year for our present purpose of calculating output growth for the latter part of the interval studied, but there might be much to be said for referring instead to a weight year more nearly contemporary to earlier intervals when their output growth is calculated. For well-known reasons, such a computation should yield higher growth rates than Greenslade's for those earlier intervals. For years since 1950, index-number relativity in measurement of aggregative Soviet output appears to be quite modest, indeed so much so that it is hardly perceptible in some relevant data.[3] But the Greenslade series probably does understate the retardation in output growth since the fifties. There must also be a corresponding understatement of retardation in productivity growth as calculated from those data.

Inquiries into the sources of Soviet post-war growth very often proceed without reference to penal labor. That is understandable in view of the uncertain nature of both the numbers and quality of such workers. But, by all accounts, there was a substantial reduction in the penal labor force in the early post-Stalin years. Even though I must resort to rather arbitrary figures, it seems appropriate now to explore the impact on my computations of an allowance of penal labor varying in this way: 1950, 3.5 millions; 1960, 1.5 millions; and 1970 and 1975, 1.0 million. In Table 1 the parenthetic figures for employment are obtained after addition of a penal labor force of these magnitudes.

I also show parenthetically the impact on variations in working hours of an allowance for changes in their quality. Although it is of a rule-of-thumb sort, the allowance probably does not differ very much from that indicated by Denison's (1967) well-known, more careful procedures. Also shown parenthetically is the joint effect of the

Table 1   Average Annual Rates of Increase of Output, Factor Inputs, and Factor Productivity, USSR, 1950–75* (percent)

	All Sectors			Material Sectors		
	1950–60	1960–70	1970–5	1950–60	1960–70	1970–5
Gross Product	5.89	5.26	3.83	7.55	5.53	3.92
Factor Inputs, Total	3.95 (3.92)	3.69 (3.75)	3.72 (3.66)	3.78 (3.72)	3.63 (3.71)	3.65 (3.56)
Labor	1.16 (1.11)	1.74 (1.84)	1.79 (1.70)	.98 (.90)	1.28 (1.41)	1.37 (1.25)
Employment	1.55 (1.30)	2.08 (2.01)	1.63 (1.60)	1.43 (1.12)	1.67 (1.60)	1.17 (1.15)
Hours	−.38 (−.19)	−.33 (−.17)	.16 (.10)	−.44 (−.22)	−.38 (−.19)	.20 (.10)
Capital	9.49	8.00	7.86	9.47	9.06	8.73
Farm Land	3.33	.18	1.04	3.33	.18	1.04
Factor Productivity	1.87 (1.90)	1.51 (1.46)	.11 (.16)	3.63 (3.69)	1.83 (1.75)	.26 (.35)

* Output for all sectors is the gross national product, and for material sectors, the gross national product less the gross product (i.e. net product plus depreciation) of housing and diverse services, chiefly health care, education, science, repairs and personal care, and government administration, including the armed forces. Factor inputs are also calculated separately for the whole economy and for the material sectors as defined above.

Fixed capital is taken to represent capital generally, and the sown area to represent farm land. On the parenthetic figures on employment and hours, and the corresponding data on factor inputs and productivity, see the text and the Appendix. Factor inputs are aggregated by use of a Cobb-Douglas formula with the following "earnings share" weights: for all sectors, labor .62, capital .33, and farm land .05; for material sectors, labor .62, capital .32, and farm land .06.

For further sources and methods, see the Appendix.

allowances for penal labor and changes in quality of hours on the rates
of growth of labor and factor inputs and factor productivity.

Turning to factor-productivity growth of the "material" sectors, I
refer in Table 1 to the whole economy less housing and diverse
services. Productivity of the "material" sector varies broadly, as it
does for the whole economy, but the initial rate of growth in the
1950–60 period is there much higher, so that its overall deceleration is
more marked than for the economy as a whole.

I use essentially the same procedures for the material sectors as for
the whole economy, and also the same sorts of data. That means that
for output I again rely on Greenslade's (1976) calculations in 1970
rubles, so that the slowdown in factor-productivity growth relative to
earlier periods should again be somewhat understated. The allowance
for penal labor that was made previously is now assigned entirely to the
material sectors. Hence, it has a more pronounced effect in these
sectors than in the whole economy.

Some Methodological Issues

I have been referring to calculations where a Cobb-Douglas production function with assigned factor-input coefficients is imposed on
factor inputs and output. Given that production function, the elasticity
of substitution (σ) between factor inputs is unity. In post-World War II
years there have been a number of econometric inquiries concerning
the production function of the USSR. These different inquiries do not
seem to converge to any clear and reliable consensus on either the
general form of the production function or the magnitudes of
parameters that are presupposed (see Bergson, 1979). The econometric studies do alert us, however, to diverse possibilities.

It is of interest, therefore, that if, in place of the Cobb-Douglas

Table 2   *Alternative Computations of Average Annual Percentage
Rate of Growth, Factor Productivity, USSR 1950–70, for Alternative
Elasticities of Substitution (σ) and Rates of Return on Capital (ρ)*

| Period | *Percentage Rate of Growth of Factor Productivity* | | | |
	$\sigma=1.0$ $\rho=.12$	$\sigma=0.5$ $\rho=.12$	$\sigma=1.0$ $\rho=.06$	$\sigma=0.5$ $\dot\rho=6.0$
	All Sectors			
1950–60	1.87	.01	2.66	.87
1960–70	1.51	1.12	2.14	1.73
1970–5	.11	.32	.70	.81
	Material Sectors			
1950–60	3.63	1.40	4.47	2.38
1960–70	1.83	1.14	2.59	2.00
1970–5	.26	.50	.94	1.11

formula, we impose a CES production function with σ equal to, say, 0.5, the trends in factor productivity for the whole economy are somewhat changed. The rate of growth remains modest, indeed for years prior to 1960 it is distinctly lower than before (see Table 2, columns for which $\rho = .12$). As a result the sixties now bring some acceleration, but the rate of growth again slows in the seventies. For material sectors, with the shift to $\sigma = .5$, the earliest rate of growth is likewise much reduced, but remains relatively high, so that growth decelerates over the whole period as before.[4]

To judge from the econometric inquiries, $\sigma = 0.5$ is within the realm of possibilities. An even lower elasticity has sometimes been observed. As it turns out, however, even $\sigma = 0.5$ implies a notably high factor share and rate of return for capital in the early years. If only on that account, results of the econometric inquiries may perhaps be properly discounted at this point.[5]

Factor-input coefficients in the Cobb-Douglas formula are supposedly given by income shares that are imputable to the factors when earnings rates correspond to relative marginal productivities. In the CES formula, a similar correspondence is supposed to prevail between factor-input coefficients that appear there and such imputable income shares in the base year. In applying both formulas here, I obtain the needed coefficients from income shares indicated when the rate of return on capital is 12%. That was in a 1969 Soviet official methodological release the lower limit allowed for "normative coefficients" for appraisal of investment projects (Gosplan SSSR . . . , 1969).[6] How closely actual returns might have approximated that limit, however, is an interesting question.

Here, too, therefore, experimentation with alternative assumptions is in order. For this purpose, I consider a possible reduction in the postulated rate of return on capital to 6%. With that, as was to be expected, factor productivity grows somewhat more rapidly, but the variation in growth rate over time is essentially as before (in Table 2, compare columns for $\rho = .12$ and .06). These results hold for both the whole economy and for the material sectors by themselves.

Farm land in the USSR is publicly owned but made available without charge to those who till it.[7] Here too the earnings share is imputed rather arbitrarily, but I take as a benchmark Western, especially US, experience. Unless the resulting share (5% of the GNP and 6% of gross material product) is implausibly wide of the mark, any error at this point could only affect our results very marginally.

Factor productivity growth during 1970–5 is found to be especially slow. That is true regardless of the computation, although with σ as low as .5 the all-sector rate of growth during 1950–60 is even lower than that for 1970–5. For present purposes, the most recent Soviet performance is of particular interest, but the interval 1970–5 is a very brief and somewhat dated one from which to gauge any enduring trends. The terminal year of that interval was marked by a harvest failure that was severe even by Soviet standards. For that reason, too,

Table 3   *Average Annual Rate of Growth of Factor Productivity,*
USSR, Selected Periods* (percent)

Period	All Sectors	Material Sectors
1950–60	1.87	3.63
1960–70	1.51	1.83
1965–75	.94	1.32
1966–76	.86	1.22
1967–77	.76	1.12
1968–78	.57	.91

* The calculations proceed essentially as in Table 1. Additional data for 1965–8, for output and employment, from sources of corresponding data in Table 1, armed forces being taken as constant at the 1965 level. For capital stock and farm land, see TSU (1968, p. 61; 1969, p. 334; 1970, p. 45). For 1976–8, for often rough extrapolations from 1975, I rely mainly on data in CIA (Aug. 1979, pp. 64–5); Feshbach (1978); TSU (1978, pp. 40–41, 224).

the 1970–1975 growth rate is difficult to interpret. It should be observed, therefore, that the recent growth of factor productivity continues to be depressed, though not as much as in Table 2 if we refer to ten-year periods terminating in very recent years (Table 3). However, a tendency towards further retardation in growth is also evident as the interval considered advances in time.

In trying to gain perspective on future prospects of technological progress in the USSR, one might wish to know about trends in factor productivity not only in post-World War II years but in earlier times. Of particular interest is the pre-World War II peacetime interval that commenced with the initiation of the First Five-Year Plan in 1928. Unfortunately, the violent shifts in economic structure that this plan initiated had a statistical consequence that bedevils any attempt at incisive appraisal of these trends. I refer, of course, to the extreme dependency of aggregative measures of performance on the valuation year considered. There are nevertheless reasons to discount the high rates of growth of factor productivity obtained when valuation is in "early" ruble prices. In that case the 1928–40 performance may not have been much superior to that of the fifties, and possibly even inferior (see Bergson, 1978(c), pp. 117ff; p. 168, n. 21).

To return to the post-World War II years, I more or less implied that productivity growth in the USSR has been undistinguished by Western standards. Although the concern of this essay is with Soviet technological progress, comparison with Western experience can put Soviet trends in perspective. Hence, it should be observed that in respect of productivity growth such a comparison is in fact unfavorable to the USSR. The Soviet performance falls within the range of Western experience, but in the West the rate of productivity growth since World War II has tended to vary inversely with the stage of economic development as manifest by one or another conventional indicator (the level of output per worker, GNP per capita, and the like). For well-known reasons relating to "advantages of backwardness," such an inverse relation is not at all surprising.

If, as thus seems proper, we allow for the Soviet development stage, we find the Soviet performance in regard to productivity growth sub-standard. Over protracted post-World War II periods, the Soviet growth tempo surpasses those of the United States and United Kingdom, two relatively advanced countries, but falls short of those of Italy and Japan. The latter countries were both, midway through the interval we consider here, at development stages more or less comparable to that of the USSR. The USSR also underperforms in comparison with two more advanced countries, Western Germany and France. Here are data on the annual percentage growth of output per unit of inputs during 1955–70 that are broadly comparable to those for the whole economy in Table 1: USSR, 2.4; USA, 1.6; France, 3.9; Germany, 3.4; United Kingdom, 1.8; Italy, 4.4; Japan, 5.9 (Bergson, 1978(c): chaps. 9–11; also Bergson, 1968; Cohn, March 1976). These results rest on use of the Cobb-Douglas formula with a 12% return imputed to Soviet capital, but the Soviet performance is still undistinguished when alternative methodologies are employed (Bergson, 1979).

I have been considering productivity growth in the USSR both for the economy as a whole and for the material sectors. Western productivity research has very often focused on the first of these two spheres, but, for familiar reasons revolving around the conventional practice of measuring service output by inputs, the second is decidedly of more interest for us. To sum up to this point, then, in respect of Soviet productivity increase in material sectors, the rate of growth has declined in post-World War II years to a quite modest level. That is indicated by my initial calculations (Table 1). I shall rely primarily on these results in this essay, but deceleration is also evident, though in somewhat different degrees, in the alternative computations that we have considered. How the Soviet performance during post-World War II years compares with that under the pre-World War II five-year plans is uncertain; but it does not seem to compare well with contemporary Western achievements.

Productivity Growth and Technological Progress 1950–75

I have been referring to factor-productivity growth. Our more ultimate concern is with technological progress. In so far as technological progress is manifest in a divergence between the increase of output and factor inputs, the resultant "residual" is properly taken (as it often is) as an indicator of such progress. As usually calculated, however, the residual also reflects other forces.

Labor Quality

To begin with, the period we consider witnessed a marked advance in

Table 4   *Factor Productivity Growth (annual percentages)*

	Without Adjustment of Employment for Educational Attainment	With Adjustment of Employment for Educational Attainment
1950–60	3.63	3.26
1960–70	1.83	1.29
1970–75	.26	− .21

the educational attainment of the Soviet labor force. If we now adjust the growth in employment for the resultant increase in labor quality in the well-known way pioneered by Denison, we still observe the previous downward trend in the rate of growth of factor productivity. The growth tempos throughout, moreover, are appreciably reduced. And during 1970–75, there is now an absolute decline instead of a very modest annual percentage increase in factor productivity.[8]

In proceeding here in a Denison-like way, I also apply to the USSR indexes of the value of different levels of educational attainment that Denison derived for the United States. The results would be little affected, however, if instead reference were made to indexes reflecting Northwest European experience. Denison's educational-value indexes are, as is well known, rather arbitrary even in respect of the countries he was concerned with; their application to the USSR has to be read in that light.[9]

Labor quality can vary also as a result of shifts in the sex composition of the labor force. Trial calculations similar to those made for education suggest that such shifts were not a consequential element in the variation in Soviet factor productivity over the period in question.[10]

The omission of labor-quality improvement due to advances in educational attainment means that, as originally computed, factor productivity growth was overstated. This is so, rather, in so far as such growth is taken as an indicator of technological progress.

Farm land and Natural Resources

From the same standpoint, another source of bias in our computations, though with opposite effects, is the failure to allow in the case of farm land for the undoubted deterioration that occurred as the cultivated area was expanded. If only climatically, the deterioration must have been particularly marked under Khrushchev's famous New Lands Program, with its attendant great increase in the cultivated area in Kazakhstan and Siberia. However, in view of the limited share of farm land in total output the resultant distortion in our data must be slight.[11]

By similar reasoning we may also discount, I think, a comparable distortion due to the failure to account for deterioration of inputs of mineral resources. The distortion is comparable to the one in the case of farm land, for there must also often have been a qualitative deterioration. That would occur simply as resort is had to less rich deposits, but economically the result is the same when extraction must proceed to increased depths or to deposits that are less favorably located geographically. In common parlance, all these circumstances alike give rise to "diminishing returns." Although that is not the preferred analytic usage, the effect is nevertheless a tendency towards higher costs and lower productivity of labor and capital as output expands.

One need not subscribe fully to the more pessimistic Western appraisals of Soviet oil resources that lately have been published to conclude that such diminishing returns have indeed come to prevail, at least lately, in oil extraction (see CIA, June 1977; NATO, 1974). In the USSR diminishing returns have also been encountered in respect of numerous minerals other than oil.

For the magnitude of the resultant distortion of factor productivity, we may obtain some indication if we consider that in the USSR, on the average over the years studied, the ratio of mineral-resource inputs to GNP, exclusive of selected services, should not have been far from 9.3%, that being approximately the magnitude of the ratio in 1966. The real cost per unit of mineral output increased perhaps about 1.5% yearly, or by 45% overall, during the period 1950–75.[12] What this may have meant for factor productivity can most readily be seen by reference to an ingenious model that Solow (1979) has used in a similar context. Imagine that over the period studied the USSR produced no mineral resources but had to import all of them. The rising real cost of such production accordingly translates itself into a corresponding increase in real import prices. Then, Soviet final output net of resource costs would have grown by 0.14 of a percentage point (i.e., .015 × .093) less than if the real price of resources had been constant throughout. The USSR, of course, does not import, but produces domestically, the great bulk of its mineral resources, but the Solow (1979) model may still be applied on the understanding that reference is to the real price of mineral resources in terms of final product that must be foregone in order to free factors for their production.

The foregoing do not comprise all the forces other than technological progress that might have contributed to the productivity residual that we computed, but we may conclude, I think, that technological progress probably was somewhat less rapid than indicated by the residual. The pace of technological advance also declined more or less as the residual does.

In the previous section I compared post-World War II productivity growth in the USSR with that in pre-World War II years. In view of the uncertainties regarding that comparison, it would be foolish to try to extend it now to allow for aspects of the sort just considered. I also concluded that Soviet post-World War II productivity growth has been undistinguished by Western standards. The comparative Soviet performance becomes even less impressive (cp. Cohn, 1976a) when factor productivity is adjusted to allow for improvement of labor quality. Because of their greater participation in world trade, Western countries until recently have probably been less affected than the USSR by diminishing returns in extractive industries. Thus, calculated productivity growth may understate Western less than Soviet technological advance on that account. All things considered, Soviet technological progress should compare only a little, if at all, more favorably with the West than our calculated productivity residual might seem to indicate.

Technological Progress Proper

I referred at the outset to two sorts of technological advance: technological progress proper (TPP) and technological progress extended (TPE). TPP occurs through introduction and spread of new production methods that enlarge the technological opportunity sets of production units. On that basis, a larger output is produced at a given resource cost. TPE embraces output expansion at given resource cost that is achieved not only through use of such new technologies, but also through other causes. The data on factor-productivity growth that we have considered thus far should reflect output expansion at given resource cost due to any cause, and thus bear more immediately on TPE than on TPP. Allowance for resource-cost variation due to causes discussed in the previous section should make calculated productivity growth the more congruent with TPE. Results of my calculations, summarized in Table 5, are hopefully more or less indicative of what such allowance might come to. Our primary concern, however, is TPP. How might the pace of TPP have compared with that of TPE?

Farm–Industry Labor Transfer

As we saw, the two sorts of technological progress are not easily delineated one from another even in principle, but on the narrow construction of TPP that is favored here, a principal cause of its divergence from TPE in the West has often been the transfer of "surplus", that is, relatively unproductive farm workers, to more productive uses in industry, which occurs as industrialization proceeds. As a result, output produced in the two sectors together at given resource cost increases. While contributing in this way to TPE, these transfers do not affect TPP.

Transfers of farm labor to industry have been occurring in the USSR in the years studied, and very likely have involved shifts from less productive to more productive uses. Allowing for possible differences in skill levels, average farm earnings perhaps have not been inordinately low compared with those in industry. That seems so even if an adjustment, such as described above, is made for the difference in sex

Table 5   Measured Factor-Productivity Growth and Technological Progress, USSR, 1950–75

Average Annual Growth, Factor Productivity, Material Sectors as in Table 2.1, percent	Adjustment to Obtain TPE, percentage points, to Account for: Labor Quality Improvement due to Educational Advance	Natural Resource Exhaustion	Farm–Industry Labor Transfers	Adjustment to Obtain TPP, percentage points, to Account for: Economies of Scale	Weather	Planning Reforms; Other Changes in Working Arrangements
1950–60	3.63 (3.69)	–.37		–.39	–.13	...[a]	...
1960–70	1.83 (1.75)	–.54	} +.14	–.33	–.12	...	...
1970–75	.26 (.35)	–.47		–.30	–.12	+.65	...

[a] Assumed negligible

Table 6   *Average Income per Worker, 1970 (rubles)*

	Without Adjustment for Sex	With Adjustment for Sex
Farm	1473	1787
Nonfarm	1761	2073

structure of the farm and nonfarm labor force.[13] Farm–city price differences favor the farmer in the USSR as they do in the West, though probably to a lesser degree.

But Russia began industrialization with a vast agricultural labor force, and in 1950 farmers still constituted nearly three-fifths of all workers. In such circumstances in the West, the productivity of marginal farm workers has often been low relatively to that of marginal industrial workers, whatever the comparative levels of average earnings. Despite its nonmarket economy, the USSR should not be an exception to that rule.

Soviet industrialization has been notable, however, for the relatively limited contraction occurring in the farm labor force. Although the farm labor force was accordingly still large in 1950, transfers of farm labor to industry have still been comparatively restricted more recently (Table 7). The resulting gains in output relative to resource cost should have been reduced on that account.

We must try, though, to assess the gains quantitatively. To do so, I apply separately to farm and nonfarm sectors Cobb-Douglas production functions corresponding to the one already employed for the two sectors together. On this basis I compare the actual growth of factor productivity for the two sectors together with what it would have been if in each interval considered inputs in each sector were constant at their initial levels. Thus, there are no transfers of either labor or capital and, indeed, no changes in the proportions in which the two factors are allocated between sectors. Calculated in this way, factor productivity growth in the two sectors together is simply an average, with initial-year weights, of the tempos of growth achieved in the two sectors separately.

The indicated reduction in the rate of growth of factor productivity

Table 7   *Farm and Nonfarm Employment, USSR, 1970–5* (millions)*

	1950	1960	1970	1975
Farm	41.4	38.4	36.4	34.8
Nonfarm	29.4	43.2	60.1	67.5
All	70.8	81.6	96.5	102.3

* The data relate to material sectors, and exclude services. They are essentially from sources of employment data cited in the Appendix.

compared with the rate of growth originally computed (Table 5) is much less than the related magnitude — 1.04 percentage points — obtained by Denison (1967, pp. 202ff, 300ff) in analyzing productivity growth in Italy during 1950–62. That reflects to some extent the relatively more limited farm—industry labor transfers in the USSR, but, more importantly, in my calculation the marginal productivity of farm labor is in effect well below, but still a sizable fraction (in 1970, 46%) of, that of nonfarm labor. Denison assumes the marginal productivity of farm labor in Italy to be zero. Curiously, my adjustment at this point turns out to be of a similar order to Denison's related imputation for Northwest Europe during 1950–62, .46 of a percentage point.[14]

In the West, depending on the stage of development, labor may be in "surplus" not only in agriculture but elsewhere. Accordingly, transfers of such labor too can be a source of growth of output at given factor cost. In so far as they are, they contribute to TPE but might properly be excluded, along with farm—industry transfers, from TPP. A major instance in the West, however, has been transfer of labor from family enterprises in trade, crafts and the like. In the USSR, such enterprises were already largely eliminated under the early plans. Resultant gains in output, therefore, should have been realized before the years on which we focus.

Economies of Scale

In economics texts, exploitation of economies of scale is usually assumed to be quite another thing from application of a novel technology that enlarges the opportunity set of a production unit. The distinction is not always easy to make in practice. However, scale economies are considered here as falling outside of TPP and are thus a further source of divergence of TPP from TPE. With a GNP of $330 billion 1978 dollars, the Soviet economy of 1950 was already rather big by any standard. Reflecting the Stalinian proclivity for giantism in earlier years, the typical industrial firm was also already large compared with those in the West. As early as the fifties, plant size often approached or exceeded least-cost levels as determined by Bain (1962).[15] Scale economies, then, should not have been very consequential in the period studied. Econometric inquiries, such as those of Weitzman (1970) and Desai (1976), seem to point in the same direction, for scale economies are found to have little, if any, explanatory power regarding the growth of post-World War II Soviet industrial production.

Soviet plant scale, however, has continued to increase in size, and so too has the Soviet economy. According to serial data available for diverse industries, the increase in plant size since the fifties might have accounted for a major fraction of the growth of output in industry.[16] Gains from scale economies, therefore, should not be ruled out altogether. I assume that one-half of the growth in factor inputs of material sectors as a whole has been of a sort generating such economies, and that a scale coefficient such as the one inferred for Norway by Griliches and Ringstad (1971, p. 63) from Norwegian data applies here as well. The resultant adjustment (see Table 5) is small, and should, if anything overstate economies of scale. Because of the relatively modest size of Norwegian enterprises, such gains should have been more consequential there than in the USSR.[17]

Weather

The weather affects TPE but is clearly outside the range of TPP. I impute the difference between productivity growth during 1970–5 and 1968–78 entirely to subnormal weather during the former interval (see Table 5). Weather during 1950–60 and 1960–70 is taken to be normal. According to the CIA (Oct. 1976), though, weather in the USSR tended to be relatively favorable to agriculture during much of the sixties. In Table 5, perhaps some downward correction of TPE would be in order for the period 1960–70.

Productivity performance during 1968–78 no doubt differed from that of 1970–5 to some extent because of factors other than the weather, but by adjusting for the entire difference between the two intervals in respect of productivity growth we should obtain a closer approach to more persistent aspects. For our purposes, that should be to the good.

Working Arrangements; Planning Reforms

The period studied witnessed a host of changes in Soviet economic institutions and policies or "working arrangements." Many of these shifts were intended to stimulate the introduction and spread of new production technologies. So far as they had such an effect, they would have contributed to both TPP and TPE. Discussion of these particular shifts is postponed to page 59 of this chapter, *Conditioning Factors: The Innovation Process.*

Many changes in working arrangements, however, could have affected output relatively to resource cost quite apart from their impact on the introduction and spread of new technologies. In so far as they did, these shifts are properly considered as affecting TPE alone, and would be still another cause of divergence of TPP from TPE. I refer to the almost innumerable shifts that have occurred in arrangements bearing on labor and managerial incentives, organizational structure, coordinating procedures and the like.[18]

Most, if not all, of the changes were initiated, at least in part, out of a concern to remedy acknowledged deficiencies in existing working arrangements. In the process, the system's directors (to refer in a convenient way used elsewhere to those with ultimate economic responsibilities) clearly sought to increase output relatively to resource cost. It would be surprising if in the upshot there had not been a gain in that respect, yet the Soviet economy has become ever more complex in terms of the numbers of production units and varieties of products to be coordinated, and technological specifications to be met. Were it not for the shifts in working arrangements, performance measured by output relative to resource cost could even have retrogressed. We must, I think, consider seriously this possibility in any event at least in some sectors. Diminishing returns in petroleum extraction for example, must have been compounded by the particular policies pursued in oil development and extraction (see CIA, June 1977, July 1977).

Where in reforming working arrangements aims other than economy of resource cost have been pursued, they must sometimes have conflicted with the latter: a concern for equity, for example, could have been counter-productive in respect of output at given resource cost. At any rate, the period studied was marked by successive wage reforms resulting in a distinct compression of wage differentials that must have affected labor incentives adversely. One reform in working arrangements has sometimes only cancelled another out. The reorganizations of industry by Khrushchev and his successors are the outstanding but not the only case in point. Proverbial aberrations and oddities in planning and management continue to be a subject of complaint in the USSR long after the initiation of measures designed to remedy them.

In order to round out my calculations, I assume that shifts in working arrangements, on the one hand, and offsetting tendencies in complexity and the like, on the other, more or less balanced each other, and together have had no impact to speak of on output at given resource cost (Table 5). Should there have been a positive effect, I suspect it would have been modest. Possibly, as suggested, there could have been some retrogression. But any evaluation of the complex matter at issue must be speculative, and mine is clearly no exception. That should be borne in mind.

That completes my accounting for possible sources of divergence, first between TPE and factor productivity as initially calculated, and, now, between TPP and TPE. Table 8 gives the results, in terms of annual percentage growth rates.

The adjustments that have now been made to my initial calculations of factor productivity and TPE are glaringly crude, but even so a sharp deceleration in growth of TPP is clear. The presumption is that growth of TPP, along with that of TPE and productivity, has slowed in the course of time to quite a low level.[19]

Table 8   *Annual Growth Rates, Material Sectors (percentage)*

	Factor Productivity	TPE	TPP
1950–60	3.63	3.40	2.88
1960–70	1.83	1.43	.98
1970–75	.26	−.07	.16

Previously I compared Soviet performance with that of the West. In respect of TPP, that is especially difficult to judge. Suppose, as I have reasoned, that the Soviet performance in respect to TPE has been substandard. We must still consider that TPE may sometimes have been buoyed up in the West more than in the USSR by forces other than those contributing to TPP. With due regard for the development stage, for example, that may have been so regarding farm–industry labor transfers.

Concerning comparative Soviet and Western TPP, however, we have some further evidence. Taking Boretsky (1966) as a point of departure, Amann, Cooper and Davies (1977) (hereafter A–C–D) have compiled post-World War II data for the USSR and several Western countries on a number of technological indicators that are deemed especially significant. The import of each measure as a barometer of technological progress could be the subject of quite a discourse by itself; as might be expected, the comparative Soviet performance varies with the measure. But the Soviet rate of advance (Table 9) seems generally no more impressive than my comparative factor productivity would suggest. Relative to the USA and the UK, the USSR does less well than might have been expected.

The data in Table 9 refer to the period 1960–1973. A–C–D have also compiled figures for some indicators for 1955–60 and for subintervals of the period 1960–73. These depict a fluctuating Soviet performance rather than any clear trend.

A–C–D have also compiled comparative data for the USSR and the West on the dates of first prototype or commercial production or first industrial installation for some novel technologies and products. They have determined for each country the length of time taken for the new technology of the product in question to represent a given share or output. The resulting indications of leads and lags for one country relatively to another bear immediately on relative technological levels. What counts for comparative TPP is the degree to which such relative levels are changing over time; a systematic difference in level would be consistent with a persistent corresponding difference in TPP. From that standpoint the A–C–D data in question (Table 10) seem broadly in accord with the technological indicators in Table 9, though perhaps somewhat more favorable to the USSR. In their inquiry A C D focus mainly on industry, and in that sector on a limited sample of technologies in basic branches. As they observe, the technologies covered are ones "in which the USSR is normally believed to be in a strong position." Their findings must be read accordingly.

In respect of TPP, I conclude provisionally that the USSR has tended to underperform relatively to the West at a similar development stage. The pace of TPP in the USSR probably has tended also to slow in the course of time. Why has the tempo of TPP in the USSR been modest by Western standards and why has it slowed? I turn now to these questions.

Table 9 Comparative Indicators of Technological Change, USSR and Western Countries, 1960–73

Item	1960[a]					1973/1960[b]				
	USSR	USA	UK	FRG	Japan	USSR	USA	UK	FRG	Japan
1 Electricity Consumed per Person Employed in Industry and Construction, thous. kwh	7.80	20.33	5.66	5.96	5.94	1.7	1.6	1.7	1.9	2.5
2 AC Transmission Lines of 300 kv and Above, Share of Total, percent	5.3	2.4	...[c]	2.1	n.a.[d]	2.0	n.a.	n.a.	2.7	n.a.
3 Nuclear Power, Share of Total Electricity Output, percent	.31	.32	8.32	.07	.02	4.1	13.4	1.2	56.1	136.0
4 O_2 Steel, Share of Total Steel Output, percent	3.8	3.4	1.7	2.7	11.9	5.6	16.3	27.8	25.1	6.8
5 Continuously Cast Steel, Share of Total Output, percent	1.3	0.8	1.4	2.1	1.0	4.1	n.a.	2.1	7.8	20.7
6 Metal-forming Machine Tools, Share of Total Stock in Machinery and Metal-working, percent	16.2	23.9	16.1	n.a.	n.a.	1.1	1.0	.9	n.a.	n.a.
7 NC Machines, Share of Total Metal-cutting Machine-tool Output, percent	.03	1.14	0.11	0.36	.04	59.0	.8	5.7	2.4	32.5
8 Plastics and Synthetic Resins, Per Capita Output, kg.	1.46	15.77	11.20	17.39	7.91	6.4	3.0	3.2	5.9	n.a.

9 Chemical fiber, All, Per Capita Output, kg.	.98	4.28	5.12	5.07	5.92	3.4	3.9	2.6	3.2	2.9
10 Synthetic (noncellulose) Fibers, Per Capita Output, kg.	.07	1.70	1.16	.94	1.26	16.4	8.0	7.0	13.9	9.6
11 Synthetic Rubber, Per Capita Output, kg.	2.1	8.1	1.8	1.5	0.2	1.7	1.3	3.1	4.3	33.5
12 Telephones per Thous. of Population	20	411	156	108	59	2.7	1.5	2.0	2.5	5.4

Source: Amann, Cooper and Davies (1977, pp. 67ff.).

[a] For nuclear power, O_2 steel, and NC machines, 1965; for metal-forming machine tools, 1962.

[b] For electricity consumed and AC transmission lines, 1972/1960; for nuclear power and NC machines, 1973/1965; for metal-forming machine tools, 1973/1962.

[c] . . . = negligible.

[d] n.a. = not available.

Table 10   *Comparative Timing of Introduction and Diffusion of New Technology, USSR and West*

Item	USSR	USA	UK	FRG	Japan
1 Oxygen Steel Making					
First industrial installation	1956	1954	1960	1955	1957
Years to 20% of steel output	16	12	5	11	5
2 Continuous Casting of Steel					
First industrial installation	1955	1962	1958	1954	1960
Years to 5% of steel output	17	7	16	14	10
3 Synthetic Fibers					
First commercial production	1948	1938	1941	1941	1942
Years to 33% of chemical fiber output	25	21	23	23	21
4 Polyolefins					
First commercial production	1953[a]	1941	1937	1944	1954
Years to 15% of plastics output	17	15	18	21	9
5 HVAC (300 kv and over) transmission lines					
First line	1956	1954	1962	1955	n.a.[b]
Years to 10% of lines over 100 kv	14	16	7	18+	n.a.
6 Nuclear Power					
First commercial station	1954	1957	1956	1961	n.a.
Years to 2.0% of electric power	21	14	6	9	n.a.
7 NC Machine Tools					
First prototype	1958	1952	1956	1958	1958
Years to 1.0% of machine-tool output	13	13	12	15+	15

Source: Amann, Cooper and Davies (1977:55ff.).

[a] Estimate.

[b] n.a. – not available.

Conditioning Factors: R and D versus Technological Borrowing

In order to advance technologically a country need not always be inventive. It may instead be able to import new technologies from abroad. Yet importing technologies takes time. Some domestic R and D effort can scarcely be avoided, if only to adapt imported technologies to local circumstances. The nature of the adaptation often determines the resultant economic benefit. Although imported technologies tend to be of a dramatic sort, technological advance must also turn on more pedestrian innovation, which may not be made at all unless prompted by domestic R and D.

Granting all this, a country at an early stage of development may

Table 11 *Expenditures on R and D, Selected Countries[a] (percent of GNP)*

Country	All Outlays		All Outlays Excluding Those for Defense and Space	
	ca. 1967[b]	1975	ca. 1967[b]	1975
United States	2.9	2.2	1.2	1.4
France	2.2	1.5	1.5	1.1
West Germany	1.8	2.2	1.6	2.1
United Kingdom	2.7	2.1[c]	1.9	1.6[c]
Japan	1.8	2.0[d]	1.8	2.0[d]
Italy	0.6	.9–1.0[c]	n.a.[e]	n.a.
USSR	2.9	3.7	1.4	n.a.

[a] For Western countries, see National Science Board (1977, pp. 184–7; for the United Kingdom and Italy, OECD (1967, p. 15) and OECD (1979, p. 42). For USSR, R and D from TSU (1976, p. 744); for defense and space R and D, mid-point of range of percentage shares in Nimitz (1974, p. vii). Soviet GNP from National Science Board (1977, p. 185).
[b] Reference is to these years: USA 1966–7; France, 1967; West Germany, 1966; United Kingdom, 1966–7; Japan, 1969–70; Italy, 1963; USSR, 1965.
[c] R and D as share of GDP.
[d] 1974.
[e] n.a.: not available.

find it economical to limit domestic R and D and to rely for technological advance primarily on imports of technology from abroad. As economic development proceeds, however, an inadequate or ineffective domestic R and D effort can become costly. How different countries compare in respect of technological progress, therefore, could turn in part on the relative magnitudes and effectiveness of their domestic R and D efforts. Differences in these respects should affect not only technological progress generally but TPP.

In trying to understand the substandard Soviet performance regarding TPP, then, it should be observed that the Soviet R and D effort, rather than being deficient in magnitude, appears to have been notably large. Available data on Soviet and Western R and D outlays are not fully comparable in scope, but in relation to GNP the Soviet expenditures have clearly matched or surpassed those of even many advanced Western countries (Table 11). Lately, as manifest in related manpower data (Table 12) the Soviet effort probably has even surpassed that of the United States.[20]

Our concern, however, is with TPP, and not all R and D outlays contribute to that process. Indeed, productivity measurements, as they have been considered in this essay for the USSR and Western countries, are often understood to exclude a major result of R and D: creation of new products yielding increased final-user values at given resource cost. To what extent that is so is a matter that perhaps merits more attention than it has received; but one need not probe too deeply to conclude that the productivity measures are at best apt to embrace only very partially final-user gains, which are especially relevant in the case of one sort of consumer: defense.

In pondering the import for TPP of comparative Soviet and Western R and D outlays, therefore, we must consider how much of the funds going to R and D in the USSR is assigned to defense. That is a matter on which the Soviet government is highly secretive, but, according to a careful inquiry of Nimitz (1974), defense, together with space, absorbed as much as one-half of all Soviet R and D outlay in the sixties. That is the same share of R and D as has gone to defense and space in the United States, but the Soviet defense and space component has been inordinately large compared with that in Western countries other than the United States.[21] The margin of superiority that the USSR enjoys over Western countries as to the share of R and D in the GNP is largely, if not entirely, obliterated when reference is made to civilian R and D alone (Table 11).

The Soviet margin of superiority is reduced the more if allowance is made for the familiar fact that a ruble is not always a ruble. Especially in the case of military expenditures it is often more than a ruble. In respect of both manpower and supplies, priorities for the military sector of one sort or another mean that the effective share of defense in R and D outlays in the USSR is greater than data on R and D outlays in rubles might indicate (Ofer, 1975).

In seeking to understand the sluggish technological progress in the USSR, then, Western analysts have rightly stressed the Soviet preoccupation with R and D for defense. R and D is devoted, however, to creation not only of new weapons but also of new products for household consumption. Here available productivity measures perhaps are not as incomplete as often assumed in their coverage, but

Table 12   *Scientists and Engineers Employed in R and D, USSR and USA**

Year	Thousands		Per 10,000 Workers in Whole Economy	
	USSR	USA	USSR	USA
1950	125.2	158.7	14.7	26.2
1955	172.6	254.3	18.5	39.0
1960	273.0	380.9	27.5	55.8
1965	474.5	494.5	42.6	67.0
1970	661.9	546.5	54.2	66.8
1975	873.5	534.8	66.0	61.5

*Scientists and engineers in United States excluding humanities specialists in all sectors and social scientists and psychologists in industry; and in the USSR, excluding humanity specialists. See Nolting and Feshbach (1979, p. 746). On employment in the whole economy in USSR, see Appendix; in USA, *Economic Report of the President* (1978, pp. 288, 290).

no doubt they are incomplete. Moreover, there is something of a counterpart in the West to the inordinately large Soviet allocation of R and D to defense. Of the continuing vast flow of new models of consumers' goods that is a proverbial feature of a Western mixed economy, a good part requires no R and D to speak of to produce them but a still significant fraction of R and D must often go to the generation of new goods for households (see National Science Board, 1977, pp. 29, 251–3; Denison, 1962, pp. 241–4). As for the USSR, varieties of consumers' goods are often observed to be still relatively limited, and so, too, is the frequency of introduction of style and model changes, and in fact of new products generally. Marginal changes are often reported, but many of these apparently are a means to evade price controls and entail hardly any R and D.

Available data on R and D outlays for both the USSR and Western countries can at most reflect only very fractionally the activities of independent inventors. Although not as important as they once were, independent inventors continue to play a significant part in the creation of new technologies in the West: in a limited sample of inventions made during 1953–73 and deemed "important", independent inventors accounted wholly or in part for 17% in the United States, 16% in France, 34% in West Germany, 2% in the United Kingdom and 7% in Japan (Gellman Research Associates, 1976, pp. 69–72; see also Jewkes et al., 1959, pp. 91 ff). Independent inventors are also active in the USSR, but at most their contribution probably only rivals that in those Western countries where independent inventors are relatively inactive. Reportedly they account for no more than 7% of all inventions that are awarded a certificate in the USSR, the Soviet counterpart of the Western patent (see Martens and Young, 1979, p. 477; Berliner, 1976, pp. 108–11).

To conclude, the precise magnitudes of Soviet and Western R and D efforts that might contribute to TPP is uncertain. The USSR, however, does not enjoy an advantage over the West such as their notably large outlays for R and D of all sorts might suggest.[22]

So much for magnitudes. In respect to R and D, effectiveness also matters, and a substandard performance in that regard must be a source of Soviet sluggishness in respect of TPP. So at any rate we are led to conclude by a number of Western studies of Soviet R and D administration. Apparently costly shortcomings, parallel to those in Soviet planning generally, have abounded. The system's directors have been by no means oblivious of or indifferent to such features. Over the period studied they have sought to counter them, but dubious practices somehow persist and R and D administration continues to be a subject of complaint.[23]

The deficiencies are by now fairly familiar. The following seem to be among the more noteworthy: imperfect, though as a result of successive reorganizations probably improving, integration of R and D with production, with a resultant tendency of R and D proposals to be of doubtful practicality; a tendency towards dubious incentive arrangements for R and D (especially in earlier years these seemingly provided R and D personnel with little, if any, inducement to be concerned with ultimately successful application, a paper "for the shelf" being a not unusual end result); a further tendency, related to the foregoing features, towards underemphasis on development work, particularly preparation of prototypes; the lack of competition in R and D work; overspecialization of R and D personnel and agencies; and bureaucratic obstacles to collaboration among agencies in different ministries.

This comment by *Pravda* (Oct. 19, 1973; quoted in Parrott, 1980, p. 86) indicates some of the more persistent deficiencies:

> The essential criteria for evaluating the activity of institutes and design offices must be the newness, promise and significance of their inventions and discoveries, the economic effect of their application and the number of licenses sold ... The various possibilities for this have yet to be fully exploited. Some institutes remain for years outside of public and administrative influence and criticism. The lack of differentiation in terms of material incentives still persists. At times ... those who provide our science and technology with original achievements and those who only repeat what is already known receive equal compensation. Bonuses are usually given out for all machinery and equipment that is developed or put into production, even if it is really not at all new. As a result, sizable funds are wasted as rewards for the redevelopment of equipment and technology from the past.

Sales of licenses referred to must be those made to foreign concerns; in the USSR inventions are made available domestically without charge.

A comparative study of Soviet and Western R and D administration has yet to be made. R and D administration in the West doubtless has its limitations, but whether overall those limitations can compare with those of R and D administration in the USSR is doubtful.

All of this, of course, is not to say that the USSR has suffered any corresponding lack of new technologies. A shortfall in the output of domestic R and D can in a degree be compensated for by borrowing technology from abroad. As explained, however, inordinate reliance on technological borrowing could be a source of sluggishness in TPP. Where — as in the USSR — considerable funds are actually expended on TPP and relevant R and D, inordinate borrowing from abroad must also put the effectiveness of the R and D administration in doubt. For the USSR that would tend to compound already existing misgivings.

Of interest, therefore, is a massive inquiry by Sutton into the origins of Soviet technology. Sutton (1973, p. 370) summarizes his findings on the sources of technologies employed in some seventy-six activities in a wide range of industries as follows:

> In the period 1917 to 1930 no major applied technologies originated in the USSR. In the period 1930 to 1945 only two such processes originated in the USSR, but in another five areas the Soviets developed and applied

some major technology and we find both Soviet and Western processes used. In the period 1945 to 1965 three processes were of Soviet origin and again five technical areas used both Soviet and Western processes.

If the USSR borrowed foreign technologies extensively during the period in question, it was not alone in doing so. Since World War II the USA by all accounts has been by far the chief contributor to the world's technological pool. Not only the USSR but most Western countries have borrowed foreign technology extensively, with the USA as a principal source. It seems doubtful, however, that the borrowing by Western countries could have matched that by the USSR, as depicted by Sutton. In any comparison between the USSR and the West, due regard must be paid to the still not very advanced Soviet stage of development. Reliance on borrowing might be expected to be greater the less advanced the country. But also to be considered is the large size of the Soviet economy, as indicated by a GDP in 1960 of over half that of the United States and several times that of such countries as France, Western Germany, the UK, Italy and Japan. Other things equal, comparative contributions of domestic inventive activity and technological borrowing from abroad should vary with size.

Sutton's findings are sometimes questioned, but, after a careful review of Soviet chemical technology, A–C–D (1977) conclude only that Sutton may overstate the degree to which the USSR has imported equipment embodying Western technology. As they acknowledge (pp. 43, 275–6), "the Soviet Union alone in this entire group of countries [the USSR, USA, FRG, UK, France, Italy and Japan] has never been the original innovator of a major plastic material or chemical fiber . . . . " A–C–D findings as to the first introduction of new technologies (Table 7) also seem consistent with Sutton's findings on the origins of Soviet technologies.

I conclude that limitations in the effectiveness, though not the volume, of Soviet R and D probably contributed to the relatively sluggish pace of TPP in the USSR. We would also wish to know to what extent, if at all, the decline in the growth rate of Soviet TPP since the fifties may have originated in the same factors. The known facts are readily stated. As a share of GNP, Soviet R and D outlays rose sharply over the period in question (Tables 11, 12; Greenslade, 1976: 273, 297). The share of such outlays devoted to defense must also have risen. But it is difficult to discover at this point any reason for the slowdown in TPP. Similarly, in R and D, as in planning generally, reform in the USSR has again and again only been a prelude to more reform, while familiar complaints about underperformance have continued. The effectiveness of R and D, however, should not have deteriorated; there might well have been some improvement. Here, therefore, no explanation can be found for the slowdown in TPP.

I turn next to the Soviet innovation process. Perhaps we can gain some insight there into the slowdown as well as further understanding of the relatively slow pace of Soviet TPP.

Conditioning Factors: The Innovation Process

Innovation, which embraces not only the first introduction but also the later spread of new technologies, is generally agreed to be a flawed process in the West. Most importantly, patents may be used to prevent dissemination of new technologies. Even if that is not done and licensing is allowed, the fees charged must be viewed as an economic disadvantage (for, as the primers teach, new technological knowledge is, from a social standpoint, ideally distributed as a free good). In the absence of patents, moreover, commercial secrecy can still constitute an effective barrier to the spread of new technologies.

In the USSR, restrictive patents are practically unknown[24] and commercial secrecy, too, although sometimes reported, can be of only relatively limited significance. The Soviet innovation process, however, has limitations of its own, and these could easily be an important cause of the relatively modest pace of TPP in the USSR.

The limitations relate in part to the behavior of the individual enterprise (*predpriiatie*). The enterprise under Soviet centralist planning, of course, has only restricted autonomy, but, with responsibilities typically limited to a single production unit, its management possesses detailed knowledge of technologies in use. How vigorously potential innovations are pursued and what is achieved by their introduction necessarily depends on the management's interest in engaging in such activities. That interest is very often weak at best. Evidence of this began to surface long ago, but owing chiefly to Amann, Berry and Davies (n.d.) and Berliner (1976) we now grasp more clearly than we could before the main underlying causes: proverbial bureaucratic hurdles attendant on obtaining clearances and interdepartmental cooperation for a new technology, with its associated variations in inputs and outputs; uncertainty as to results, an inevitable feature anywhere, that seems often compounded under centralist planning, particularly if novel kinds of equipment or supplies are required; relatively modest material rewards compared with those obtainable if the risky innovation is not undertaken.

Here as elsewhere the system's directors have been aware of and have struggled to alleviate deficiencies, but apparently with only limited success. Writing in 1977, for example, the distinguished Soviet economist, Academician A. G. Aganbegian, had this to say on the Soviet innovation process:

> ... The introduction of many experimental systems is being held up by the excessive complexity of the instructions concerning the rights and possibilities of enterprises in this regard. Every change, even an insignificant one (in table of organization, pay, personnel assignments), requires paperwork of such proportions as to make even the most optimistic executives lose their taste for change.

Here is how Z. Sirotkin, Chief Design Engineer of the Belorussian Motor Vehicle Plant and USSR State Prize Laureate, viewed matters regarding incentives as recently as 1974 (quoted in Berliner, 1976, p. 490):

> Unfortunately the "mechanism" of the Economic Reform has proved insufficiently effective when applied to the question of putting new equipment into production. After all, for production workers, the manufacture of a new machine means, first of all, new concerns and difficulties. The work rhythm is disrupted, and many new problems appear. Under the existing situation, this causes the performance indicators to decline and the enterprise incentive funds to grow smaller. It is for this reason that some plant executives brush aside innovations proposed by science.
>
> ... This is especially true if the plant has achieved a stable work rhythm and high-quality output and has all the benefits the Economic Reform provides; as for material incentives to induce changes, there are none.
>
> In a time of general well-being the plant manager would have to be a very farseeing person indeed to feel any concern or anxiety and to undertake the preparatory work for producing a new model of the machine. For in the next few years that promises many difficulties.

As is often the case with Soviet "self-criticism," Sirotkin exaggerates the inadequacy of incentives for innovation. But, having probed carefully the intricate arrangements that prevail, Berliner (1976) concludes, perhaps too cautiously (p. 490):

> Our guess is that the differential reward for innovation, relative to the reward for competent but non-innovative management is too small to induce a high rate innovation, and that the small differential is a major obstacle to innovation.

Berliner focuses on managerial-bonus arrangements. Soviet policy and practice regarding promotion, demotion and dismissal of managerial personnel have yet to be explored in any depth, but an adverse impact on career prospects must be among the possible penalties for failure that are of concern to enterprise management when pondering potential innovations. The adverse impact must be the greater in an economy where ultimately there is only one employer. On an abstract plane, Bergson (1978c) has shown that, for risk-averse personnel, even modest career penalties might discourage risk taking unless success were rewarded not only with corresponding career gains but with bonuses possibly much exceeding the basic wage. Existing rewards for successful innovation in the USSR are the less effective when seen in that light.

In the West an enterprise is penalized when an innovation turns out awry, but it may also be penalized for not innovating, for a more venturesome competitor may encroach on the market of a less venturesome one. The competitive threat that is thus posed must be a major spur to innovation generally. And so far as there are laggards, and the threatened encroachment on their markets by innovative firms materializes, that in itself represents a way in which new technologies may spread. The fact that this spread is only indirect, via the supplanting of lagging by innovative firms, makes it not less effective, and must be a significant source of TPP in the West.

To what extent similar forces are operative under Soviet centralist planning is yet another relatively unexplored aspect of that system, but the counterpart to the Western competitive process must be slender at best. The consequences for TPP must have been and are correspondingly adverse. True, determination of technologies of *new* firms is essentially the province of superior authorities rather than of managers of existing enterprises, and superior authorities have not been lacking in initiative in that sphere. The systematic introduction of advanced technologies in new enterprises became a hallmark of Soviet development under the earliest five-year plans and has remained so ever since.

That is an important fact in itself. But for it Soviet TPP would have been even more sluggish than it has been. The resultant threat to and encroachment on the "markets" of older enterprises, however, must have been comparatively limited in an economy where superior authorities themselves are continually pressed to achieve intensive utilization of capacity in the interests of fulfilling taxing output goals. No doubt partly for this reason, enterprise liquidation is, clearly, an extraordinary rarity. Because of a concern to limit involuntary unemployment, staff curtailment which might free labor in older firms for employment in newer ones also encounters legal and administrative obstacles: even the venturesome firm might find it difficult effectively to exploit an innovation.[25]

So much for the domestic counterpart in the USSR, such as it is, of the competitive process that is so important to innovation in the West. In the West that process also embraces active foreign competition. With imports as a spur and direct investment from abroad as a carrier, innovation proceeds all the more expeditiously. Not the least of the reasons for a sluggish TPP in the USSR, therefore, must be the state trading monopoly, which carefully controls and mediates foreign access to Soviet markets and excludes altogether direct investment from abroad.

I have been discussing working arrangements regarding innovation in the USSR. In gauging Soviet performance in this sphere, reference should again be made to the comparative data of A–C–D that I discussed earlier (Tables 9, 10). Some of these data bear particularly on innovation, though, as noted, they relate more to relative technological levels than to changes in those relative levels over time. The latter are more immediately indicative of comparative TPP.

Also illuminating, though with the same caveat, are comparative data compiled by Martens and Young (1979) on "lead" times between application for a patent (in the USSR, certificate) and recorded first introduction of an invention. The data for different countries are admittedly not fully commensurate, but it is still of interest that among samples considered for different countries the Soviet lead time tended to be relatively long: at the end of two years, only 23% of Soviet inventions had been implemented. The corresponding figure for the United States was 66%, and Western Germany, 64%.

Results of a survey of the experience of British exporters of machine tools and chemical technology to the USSR (Hanson and Hill, 1979) bear immediately on technology transfer but are also indicative of the functioning of the Soviet innovation process more generally. In both industries, the time elapsing between receipt of an inquiry and final commissioning was found typically to be distinctly longer than for comparable transfers to Western countries: in machine tools, "an estimate of two and three times" that required for a comparable transfer to a Western country "would not appear to be too inaccurate"; in chemicals, lead-times averaged 6 years and 10 months, or "3½ to 4 years longer than a characteristic West European lead time." For machine tools, Soviet performance is compared with that of "advanced" Western countries. The particular West European countries considered in the case of chemicals are not indicated. In both cases, an explicit comparison with less advanced Western countries would also be of interest.

I have been focusing on aspects of the Soviet innovation process that prevailed more or less generally during the period studied. Like the facts set forth previously on R and D, those that have been considered regarding innovation appear to fit in with our prior finding on the likely substandard Soviet performance regarding TPP. We also inferred previously, however, that the pace of TPP in the USSR has slowed. We discovered no explanation for this slowdown in the sphere of R and D. I turn therefore for an alternative explanation to aspects of the innovation process that might have caused its performance to vary over time. These admittedly do not act in only one direction, but on balance they could have produced a slowdown in TPP.

One feature affecting the Soviet innovation process over time has already been alluded to: reforms in working arrangements bearing on coordination and managerial incentives. These apparently have not been especially effective, but should at least have been more a source of acceleration than of retardation of TPP. The reforms in managerial compensation, for example, should have been to the good, though incentives for risk-taking must still be weak.

The impact on the Soviet economy of technology transfers to the USSR that have been occurring under detente since around the mid-sixties has become a somewhat controversial issue. It is also a matter not to be settled here, but our concern in any event is with the long-term variation in Soviet performance regarding innovation. From that standpoint, it should be observed that Soviet technological borrowing is not exactly novel. It is true that transfers lately have, more often than previously, been of a turnkey or otherwise negotiated sort, but Soviet borrowing of technology in one form or another has been occurring on a wholesale scale ever since the earliest five-year plans.

Moreover, whatever the impact of detente, technology transfers if anything should have been more consequential in earlier post-World War II years. If so, the down-trend in transfers could have been a source of slowdown in TPP.

I refer particularly to the impetus to Soviet technology borrowing provided by the backlog of new Western technologies that must have been available to the USSR for exploitation immediately after World War II. Gains from "catching up" in that sphere would have been compounded by the possibility of applying advanced technologies in the restoration and reconstruction of partially destroyed industrial works. Although the USSR in 1950 had already exceeded its pre-war output (GNP in 1950 was 124% of 1940; Bergson, 1961, p. 210), much of the vast war-time destruction remained to be made good.[26]

Even according to an optimistic view the impact of technology transfers under detente appears to be rather modest overall, though significant in some industries. Thus, a hypothetical reduction of imports of Western machinery over the years 1968–73 that cumulatively came to some 16% of the entire stock of such machinery on hand in the USSR in 1973 would have meant a reduction of but 0.1 of a percentage point in the yearly rate of growth of the GNP during 1968–73 (Green and Levine, 1977). Reference, however, is only to technology transfers associated with imports of machinery. Although "indirect effects" through diffusion are supposedly also represented, the underlying statistical analysis can hardly have captured these fully. The above calculation is, moreover, not intended to and could not represent gains to the USSR from any and all technological borrowing, whether occurring through machinery imports or otherwise. But, to repeat, the gains from such borrowing in pre-detente years could well have been even greater. In this view, detente may only have arrested a downtrend that was already in process as post-World War II "catch-up" opportunities became progressively exhausted.[27]

In the course of time, opportunities for borrowing technologies from abroad should have declined in any event, but they should have diminished also as a result of the slowing of technological progress in the West. In the United States, the chief contributor to the world's technological pool, the slowdown has been marked. It seems to have occurred, however, primarily since 1973 (Denison, 1979, p. 105). Soviet TPP would have been affected, but only in the most recent years.

To the extent that new technologies are embodied in and require introduction of new sorts of capital goods, the innovation process is in part but an aspect of capital-replacement policy. We must record as one more source of sluggishness in Soviet TPP, therefore, the tendency in the USSR to discount obsolescence as a factor warranting capital replacement, and to seek rather to prolong service lives through continuing maintenance and repairs. As a result, service lives probably have often been unduly lengthy by Western standards (Cohn, 1976b; 1979). Obsolescence, however, while neglected in earlier years, has been accorded increasing attention in the course of time, and service lives have been correspondingly reduced. That by itself should have tended to accelerate TPP. But a related offsetting factor has been the progressive slowdown in the growth of gross investment in fixed capital, from 12.6% annually in the fifties to a planned increase of only 3.6% annually in the late seventies (Bergson, 1978a, p. 232). The resultant retardation in TPP, however, was probably well below .4 of a percentage point annually.[28]

The sharp decline in the rate of growth of investment volume since the fifties is part of a larger process that has been unfolding since Stalin and that has embraced also persistently rapid growth of consumption (Bergson 1978a). Although defense outlays have also tended to expand more or less in step with the growth of GNP, expansion of industries primarily serving the investment and defense sectors has come to be much more nearly in balance with expansion of those primarily serving consumption. I offer it as a hypothesis which I cannot try to verify here that in the USSR TPP has traditionally been more rapid in the former than in the latter industries. If so, the structural change that has occurred could be one more reason for a slowdown in TPP in the economy generally.

Conclusions

I have distinguished between two concepts of technological progress: technological progress proper (TPP), representing in a restricted way the introduction and spread of new technologies enabling the community to increase output at a given resource cost, and technological progress extended (TPE). The latter embraces not only the foregoing causes of an increase in output at given resource cost but also others, such as incentive reforms, amelioration of a historically distorted resource allocation, weather fluctuations, and so on.

In this essay I have focused primarily on TPP, but technological progress of either sort should be manifest in corresponding variations in output per unit of factor inputs, or factor productivity, as such a coefficient has come to be called. For purposes of quantitative appraisal, therefore, I first compiled data of a conventional sort on the growth of factor productivity. After allowing for changes in factor inputs not initially accounted for, I obtained measures of TPE. By adjusting additionally for the impact of causal aspects other than the introduction and spread of new technologies, I also derived measures of TPP.

The initial computation of factor productivity is flawed by limitations in both underlying data and methodology, while further adjustments to derive TPE and then TPP are often conjectural at best. In the upshot, however, TPP is found to have generated these annual percentage increases in output per unit of factor inputs in material sectors of the Soviet economy: 1950–60, 2.88; 1960–70; .98; 1970–5,

.16. Granting all the limitations of the computations, TPP probably has slowed to quite a low tempo over the period studied.

In respect of TPP, the Soviet performance appears to have been within the range of Western experience, but inferior to that expected of a Western country at a comparable stage of development.

The ultimate concern of this essay is with prospects for the future. Turning finally to that aspect, on such a complex matter the inclination must be simply to opt for the "naive" hypothesis that past trends will continue. On reflection, some such outcome does seem likely, but perhaps we can gauge prospects more clearly and with a better grasp of probabilities if we consider that a substandard Soviet performance hitherto could be a ground for optimism. There is clearly room for improvement.

And, while reforms in relevant working arrangements do not appear to have been especially effective thus far, numerous revisions were initiated only in the latter part of the period studied. They may require more time fully to bear fruit. It would be surprising if the years ahead are not also marked by still other reforms that have yet to be initiated or even conceived.

Yet, among all the sources of difficulty that the Russians have experienced in respect of TPP, three or four appear to stand out as relatively decisive: bureaucratic obstacles attendant on multiple clearances and organization of interdepartmental cooperation for a new technology; the weakness of domestic and foreign competition, that might spur innovation; impediments to labor transfers from lagging to more technologically advanced enterprises, and inadequate incentives.

While subject to amelioration, the first two aspects are more or less integral to the system of centralist planning that in essentials has now been in effect in the USSR for over six decades. There is no indication now of its prospective demise. Impediments to labor transfers originate chiefly in a commitment, apparently deemed fitting in a socialist society, to minimize involuntary unemployment. As for incentives, the system directors hitherto have proceeded with distinct caution in this regard. The USSR today is not notable for egalitarianism, but large and conspicuous managerial bonuses, such as might be needed to induce more adequate interest in innovation, probably are felt to be politically, if not ideologically dubious.

The slowdown in TPP is not due to any deterioration in working arrangements — as indicated, these should have improved. Rather, the reduced pace of TPP probably reflects the unfolding of other forces, principally the progressive exploitation of "catch-up" opportunities present after the war and the shift in the course of time towards a structurally more nearly balanced growth. By now these forces have practically run their course and should not be a further source of slowdown of TPP in future.

Encouragement afforded to technology transfers from the West by detente must have served to dampen somewhat the slowdown in TPP, but, as Afghanistan reminds us, such transfers can be discouraged as well as encouraged. Soviet technological borrowing from the West must suffer in any event should the recent slowdown in Western technological advance persist.

We can only speculate as to the sum of the diverse forces determining the future pace of Soviet TPP. A distinct acceleration is not precluded, but more likely advance will continue at a slow pace more or less comparable to that which has prevailed lately. A negative rate of TPP, although imaginable, is presumably not among the contingencies to be seriously reckoned with.

Although TPE was derived primarily as an element in the computation of TPP, it has an interest of its own. Given prospective TPP, the corresponding TPE now follows from a reversal of adjustments such as I made previously to derive TPP for the past years. In calculating TPP for 1970–5, however, one of the adjustments made to TPE was an addition to allow for abnormal weather (Table 4). In reversing the previous computation, no corresponding deduction from prospective TPP is to be made as we are now concerned with TPE in the long run.

With that understanding, TPE might, by projection of past experience, be expected to exceed TPP by from .4 to .5 of a percentage point. A larger differential than that is possible in the future, but does not seem very likely when it is considered that a deduction made previously from TPE for economies of scale probably overstated gains from that source. Reversal of the previous deduction now should be even more of an overstatement, for gains from scale economies are usually supposed to diminish as scale increases.

Still another deduction from TPE was made previously for output gains from farm to industry labor transfers. By Western standards such transfers have been inordinately low, and the farm labor force of the USSR has come to be notably large for a country at the Soviet stage of development (as measured, of course, by indicators other than that of the share of agriculture in the total labor force; say, by GNP per capita). There is thus a potential for increased output gains from this source. But additional costs for urban housing and infrastructure needed to accommodate transferees probably have caused the government to limit its exploitation previously. They should continue to do so in future. In deriving TPP from TPE I made no allowance one way or the other for the impact of changes in economic working arrangements apart from those bearing on R and D and innovation. Any gains in respect of output at given resource cost, in other words, were supposed to be offset by planning difficulties associated with increasing economic complexity and the like. If that supposition should be projected to the future, it must be understood that at this point an error is possible in either direction.

Note that TPE was obtained in turn by deducting from factor productivity as initially computed, an allowance for labor quality improvement due to educational advance. I also added to factor productivity as initially calculated an allowance for natural-resource exhaustion. Since the former adjustment exceeded the latter, factor productivity as initially computed exceeded TPE: by .2 to .4 of a percentage point. In the future, the educational quality of the labor force can change only slowly, but if the CIA is at all reliable on oil extraction, natural-resource exhaustion should be decidedly more costly to the USSR in the years ahead than it has been hitherto. The margin between these two aspects, therefore, should dwindle if it does not vanish altogether.[29]

In considering the sources of past productivity growth I made no allowance for labor-quality variation that may have occurred on account of the rapid increase experienced in consumption standards. Standards tended to increase practically throughout the period studied, but the gains over the low levels that prevailed under Stalin could have been particularly favorable to worker morale and productivity in the earlier post-Stalin years. If they were, that would have been a further source of divergence of factor productivity as initially computed, from TPE. In any event, in appraising prospects we must consider that any marked deceleration in consumption standards might have an adverse impact on productivity growth in the future. Hence, calculated productivity would then be further depressed relatively to TPE. Such a deceleration of growth in consumption standards seems a distinct possibility (Bergson, 1978a).[30]

In sum, if my projection of TPP is not too far from the mark, the USSR should find it difficult in the future to raise the rate of growth of calculated factor productivity much above the very modest tempo that has prevailed lately: .91% yearly.[31] More likely there will be further decline from this tempo.

I have been referring to productivity in material sectors. It should be recalled, therefore, that for the entire GNP productivity growth has been distinctly slower than for material sectors alone: during 1968–78, .57 compared with .91% annually. Productivity growth for the entire GNP has for some time been drifting downward relatively to that for material sectors (see Table 3). There is no basis to think that this trend will be reversed in the future.

I have now ventured well beyond TPP, the primary concern of this essay, and often into areas that are being explored in other contributions to this volume. Even a very provisional appraisal, however, may facilitate juxtaposition of my results with related findings of others.

To return to TPP, I tacitly omitted the possibility that in order to accelerate TPP, the government might increase the relative volume of resources devoted to civilian R and D. Although such outlays are already sizable, they could still be increased. Without a radical improvement in working arrangements for R and D and innovation, the resultant gains in TPP would likely be modest, but doubtless there would be gains. The gains would be more substantial if the increase in civilian R and D were at the expense of military R and D, for, as indicated, ruble-for-ruble the resources devoted to military R and D must be higher-powered than those devoted to civilian R and D. On any scale, however, a shift from military to civilian R and D is apt to occur only as part of a larger reallocation of resources from defense to civilian uses generally. That contingency and also the further possibility of a shift in resources from consumption to growth, including capital investment and civilian R and D, I must leave for a separate inquiry.

Civilian R and D might also be increased at the expense of investment. To what extent that might be appropriate must depend on the comparative returns to the two sorts of outlays. That is a matter on which Soviet authorities themselves are probably not too clear. Expenditures on all R and D, military as well as civilian, on the one hand, and investment, on the other, have varied closely together in the course of time.[32] Perhaps that reflects a policy decision that will not be abandoned easily.

In discussing prospective TPP and TPE, I assumed that in the future Soviet planning will continue to be of the centralist sort. Should that system of planning finally be abandoned, the alternative presumably would be some form of market socialism that would allow relatively ·great autonomy to the enterprise and involve extensive use of markets as a coordinating device. With such a change in working arrangements, the presumption must be that both TPP and TPE could be affected favorably. That eventuality must also be left for another inquiry.[33]

The subject of this essay, Soviet technological progress, is a familiar one. To my profit, I have been able to draw here on much previous research by Western scholars. It is striking, however, how much remains unsettled. That is inherently so regarding prospects for the future, but uncertainties also abound regarding past trends. To resolve such doubts I have often been able to offer conjectures. Hazardous as such a procedure must be, it may serve at least to underline the need for still more research on an important theme.

Appendix: Sources and Methods for Table 1

1. Gross product

On the growth of the GNP, see Greenslade, 1976, p. 273. For material sectors, gross product is obtained by deducting from GNP the output of services, as given in Greenslade, p. 271. His index numbers for GNP and sectoral outputs are converted to ruble figures; see Greenslade, p. 284.

2. Labor

(a) *Employment.* For all sectors, this is civilian employment plus the armed forces, as given in Feshbach and Rapawy (1976, pp. 132, 135) and Feshbach (1978). For material sectors, I deduct the armed forces, and also employment in services, as given in Feshbach and Rapawy (p. 135), but then restore employment in trade, public dining, and material technical supply, sales and procurement, as in Rapawy (1976, pp. 28–29).

In the foregoing, I refer to data outside parentheses. As to parenthetic figures, reference is to totals inclusive of an allowance for penal labor amounting in 1950 to 3.5 millions, in 1960 to 1.5 millions, and in 1970 and 1975 to 1.0 million. On these magnitudes, see Bergsòn (1961, pp. 443ff).

(b) *Hours*. For material sectors average annual hours per worker are obtained from civilian employment as above in 2(a) and corresponding data on such employment in man-hours in Feshbach and Rapawy (1976, p. 138), for all sectors. I also allow for hours of military personnel averaging 1780 a year, or the same as that indicated for civilian workers in 1970. For both all sectors and material sectors, I assume that hours in 1975 averaged the same as in 1974. For all sectors, I also adjust the resulting variation to allow for the fact that in the case of services changes in hours tend to have no effect on calculated output.

Data in parentheses are intended to allow for changes in the quality of hours associated with a change in their length. For the decade in question, I assume that with 1970 as base the variation in hours, after allowance for such qualitative changes, is simply one-half that without such allowance. For the decade 1950–60, when hours changed most, the result seems to come to much the same thing as might be indicated by more elaborate computations such as Denison's.

3. Capital

For all sectors, reference is to fixed capital as represented by Soviet official end-of-the year data on *osnovnye fondy* in TSU, 1961, p. 85; 1971, p. 60; 1973, p. 60; 1978, p.41. The Soviet data refer to fixed capital gross of depreciation and cover, among other things, draft and productive livestock. For material sectors, reference is to fixed capital as represented by corresponding official data for "productive" sectors.

4. Farm land

This is sown area as given in TSU, 1961, p. 387; 1966, p. 284; 1978, p. 224.

5. Factor-share weights

The underlying absolute data, which are intended to refer to 1970, are in Table 13. For all sectors, the labor share is obtained as the income of households, currently earned, less imputed net rents, plus social-security charges, as given in CIA (Nov. 1975, pp. 3, 10). For capital, I allow a 12% return on net fixed capital, as given in CIA, (Nov. 1975, p. 80). I allow only 6%, however, on the net fixed capital in housing, and no return on net fixed capital in services. The data on fixed capital in the cited source are in 1955 rubles. In the light of conflicting official and Western (e.g. Becker, 1974) data, I rather arbitrarily allow for a 15% increase in prices of capital goods from 1955 to 1970.

Table 13   *Factor-Share Weights, 1970 (billions of rubles)*

	All Sectors	Material Sectors
Labor	202.1	161.2
Capital	105.2	84.1
Farm Land	16.1	16.1

Interest at 12% on inventories is given in CIA, (Nov. 1975, p. 80). I also allow this rate on livestock for fattening and young livestock, as given there, too, pp. 59, 80, 81, 83.

The factor share for capital is intended to be gross of depreciation. On the basis of Moorsteen and Powell (1966, pp. 11–12), I allow for depreciation at the rate of 3.5% on the gross stock of fixed capital. The latter is given in CIA (Nov. 1975, p. 80), though again an upward revaluation of 15% seems indicated.

As for farm land, with US experience as a benchmark, I take agricultural rent to be 30% of farm-labor earnings as indicated in CIA (Nov. 1975, pp. 3, 10).

For material sectors, for labor I deduct from labor's share for all sectors, military pay and subsistence, social security on such earnings, and service-wages and other service earnings and corresponding social security as given in CIA (Nov. 1975, pp. 3, 10, 76).

I allow for a 12% return on the net fixed capital stock and inventories in all sectors, less the corresponding amounts in housing and services as indicated in CIA (Nov. 1975, pp. 80, 83). In the case of fixed capital I revalue capital as was done above. Depreciation is again taken to be 3.5% of the gross fixed stock. The latter is calculated in the same way as the net stock from data in CIA (Nov. 1975, p. 80).

Notes

1 To my profit Simon Kuznets kindly read and commented on an earlier version.
2 I thus apply the familiar formula:

$$Y = Ae^{\rho t} \; E^{\alpha} \, K^{\beta} \, L^{1-\alpha-\beta} ,$$

where E, K and L are inputs of labor, capital and land; α, β and $1-\alpha-\beta$ are corresponding factor-input coefficients; ρ is the rate of technological advance, and Y is output.
3 On the comparative growth of Soviet GNP since 1950 in terms of alternative valuation years, reference may be made to these alternative measures of annual percentage rates of growth: for 1950–55, in Bergson (1961) in 1937 prices, 7.6, and in 1950 prices, 7.6; in Cohn (1970), as revised in Bergson (1974), in 1959 prices, 6.3, and in Greenslade (1976), 6.0; for 1950–60, in Cohn (1970) as revised in Bergson (1974), 6.3; and in Greenslade (1976), 5.9; and for 1960–70, in Cohn (1970), as revised in Bergson (1974), 5.5, and in Greenslade (1976), 5.3. Unfortunately, differences in results from different sources are difficult to interpret because the calculations differ not only in valuation years but in other ways. Moreover, valuations are sometimes only partially made in the year to which they supposedly refer.

According to further computations, the observed divergence for 1950–60, between Cohn (1970), as revised in Bergson (1974), and Greenslade (1976) could be due practically in ite entirety to the difference iin the nature of the weight imputed to "services," particularly the reduced interest allowed on housing and the exclusion altogether of interest on other fixed capital in the former computation. For purposes of compiling data that are comparable to those available for Western countries, however, there is much to say for the Cohn (1970)–Bergson (1974) procedure, and the Greenslade tempo of growth for 1950–60 might be considered as somewhat understated at least on that account.
4 For both the whole economy and industry, use of $\sigma = .5$ instead of 1.0 evidently reduces the rate of annual growth for pre-1970 and raises it for post-1970 years. Recall that 1970 is our base year. As explained elsewhere (Bergson, 1979, p. 124), with factor inputs growing at different rates, a reduction in σ must have such contrary effects on factor productivity in pre- *and* post-base years.

5 Whether $\sigma = 1.0$ or .5, the earnings share imputed to capital in the base year is, for the whole economy, .52 of that for labor, and, for the material sectors, .54 of that for labor. With $\sigma = 1.0$, of course, the same shares obtain for 1950. With $\sigma = .5$, however, the corresponding ratios in 1950 are 2.1 and 2.4. On the rates of return on capital that such earnings shares might imply, see Bergson (1979).

6 In order to determine the earnings share of capital, therefore, it seemed appropriate to apply this assumed rate to the capital stock in prevailing rubles. In the USSR, however, ruble prices cover not only labor costs but a variety of additional and often more or less arbitrary charges, principally turnover taxes, subsidies and profits. At the same time, no systematic charge is made for interest and rent. If for comparison with rates of return familiar in the West we revalue capital to exclude Soviet nonlabor charges and to include interest and rent the assumed 12% return would rise to 13.6%. With the total of interest and rental charges taken to be the same as initially allowed, the revaluation assumes that the price of capital goods changes in proportion to the price level generally. Similarly a 6% return on capital in prevailing rubles translates into an 8.2% return on capital when that is revalued to conform to Western pricing.

7 More precisely, without explicit charge. Under the government's complex arrangements for procuring farm products, Soviet farmers, of course, have by no means been allowed to retain for themselves the entire proceeds of their labor.

8 Here and below, unless otherwise stated, factor-productivity data cited relate to material sectors.

9 To be more precise, I apply educational-value indexes which are adapted from those Denison derived for the United States and represent slight revisions of those in Bergson (1964, p. 371). I assume that the educational attainment of workers in material sectors in 1950 is the same as that of employment in all sectors and in later years the same as that of the entire labor force. Data that are needed on the distribution of employment and the labor force by educational attainment are from DeWitt (1962, p. 136) and CIA (June 1979, pp. 10, 14). On the comparative impact of use of United States and Northwest European educational-value indexes, see the CIA publication above.

10 I assume one female worker to be equal to .7 of a male worker. Earnings of female workers appear to have averaged about that amount relatively to those of male workers in the USSR. See Riurikov (1977, pp. 118–19). Taken together with available Western and official data on the branch and sex structure of the labor force, the indicated discount means that with adjustment for changes in sex composition employment growth would on the average be compounded by .05 of a percentage point yearly over the period 1950–75.

11 A discount for quality of one-half applied to the increase in cultivated area in the fifties, when the New Lands Program was in full swing, would raise factor-productivity growth during that decade by one-tenth of one percent.

12 The volume of mineral-resource inputs relatively to GNP in 1966 is inferred chiefly from data in Treml et al. (1973, pp. 46, 116) indicating that the gross output, less net exports, of minerals in 1966 amounted to 15.4 billion rubles at producers' prices. This represents, I believe, a nearly comprehensive total, but, improperly for our purposes, includes some processing and also limited inputs of minerals into the mineral-extraction branches themselves. In the light of Becker (1969, pp. 477–8), I raise the indicated total to 18.9 billion rubles in order to allow for subsidies. This is 9.3% of the Soviet 1966 GNP (exclusive of services) which, taken from data in diverse sources, amounted to 204 billion rubles at factor cost.

As for the real cost of mineral extraction, for purposes of the Solow Model (see below) reference is made appropriately to the trend over time in the comparative real cost of mineral extraction, on the one hand, and of final output in the economy generally, on the other. The cited average annual increase of 1.5% is intended to represent the trend in mineral-extraction costs in that comparative sense, and results from a somewhat impressionistic summarization of official price-index numbers in different extractive branches, as given in TSU (1971, p. 175; 1978, p. 142), and comparative trends in average money wages and output per worker in material sectors as a whole. On money wages, see TSU (1978, p. 385); output per worker in material sectors is calculated from data compiled in this essay. I use the implied measures of wage cost per unit of output to deflate nominal price changes in extractive branches, and so to obtain an indication of changes in real costs in the desired sense. The official prices considered are net of turnover taxes, but are still distorted by subsidies; how these may have varied over the period studied is conjectural.

Regarding the underlying calculation of the impact of the increase in the real cost of minerals, let Y be net output of the final good, Then

$$Y = Q - PR,$$

where Q is the corresponding gross output, R is resource imports and P the price of such imports in terms of the final good. We also have

$$Q = F(L, K, R),$$

where L is the labor and K the capital employed in producing Q. Finally,

$$\dot{Y} = (Q/Y)\,\dot{Q} - (PR/Y)\,\dot{R} - (PR/Y)\,\dot{P},$$

where $\dot{Y}$, $\dot{Q}$, $\dot{R}$ and $\dot{P}$ are the relative rates of growth.

13 Aggregate farm and nonfarm household earnings from CIA (Nov. 1975); corresponding employment data from Table 7. On the adjustment for sex, see note 10.

14 To be more specific, I assume Cobb-Douglas functions for the farm and nonfarm sectors whose coefficients for capital and labor are proportional to those in the Cobb-Douglas function that I applied to the two sectors together. With farm-land rent amounting as before to 16.1 billion rubles, or 23% of farm output in 1970, the resulting labor and capital earnings shares are for agriculture 51% and 26%, and for industry 66% and 34%. On labor inputs, see Table 7. On corresponding capital inputs, see sources and methods cited in the Appendix for such inputs in the two sectors together. On farm and nonfarm outputs, see Greenslade (1976).

With inputs and outputs as thus determined, I find that the marginal productivity of labor in 1970 is 960 rubles per worker in agriculture and 2110 rubles in nonfarm sectors. Note that the computation also implies a higher marginal productivity of capital in agriculture than in nonfarm sectors in 1970, but the difference is slight: 16.7 compared with 14.9%.

15 I am indebted to Leon Smolinski for allowing me to see results of his unpublished study of the size of the firm in the USSR.

16 For the industries in question, the rate of growth of plant size seems to average out at about 5% annually over the years 1956–65. Among industries for which Smolinski could compile serial data on plant size (I rely again on his unpublished study) I refer to 28 nonmachinery branches. Regrettably, among the machinery branches, only two industries—motor vehicles and tractors, with rates of growth of plant size of (-) 2.1 and 7.4% respectively — are covered. During 1956–65, industrial output grew by 7.7% yearly.

17 Of 20,944 mining and manufacturing establishments counted in the Norwegian census of 1963 (Griliches and Ringstad obtain their basic data from this source), only 73 had 500 or more employees. In the USSR in 1970, the *average* enterprise employed 644 workers.

18 Among the more noteworthy: the progressive transformation of agriculture through the liquidation of the Machine Tractor Station; the increasing stress on the state-farm compared with the collective-farm form of organization; introduction of wage-like payments in the collective farm itself and the sharp post-Stalinian increases in procurement prices; successive reorganizations of industry, with the traditional preeminent industrial ministry being superseded by regional councils under Khrushchev and then reestablished as the preeminent entity by his successors; the fluctuating responsibilities of the industrial enterprise (*predpriiatie*) under the 1965 planning reform and its evolving implementation; since 1973, the progressive shift to the association (*ob'edinenie*) as the basic operating agency in industry; the successive revisions of incentives for industrial management under and after the 1965 planning reform; the reforms in the industrial wage system and structure in the late fifties

and more recently; the successive reforms of industrial wholesale prices; and last but no doubt not least the progressively increased application of mathematical techniques and computers to planning.

19 The shifts in working arrangements were rather spread out over time, but I suspect any favorable impact on productivity would have been more pronounced in later than in earlier years. With allowance for such gains, therefore, TPP might, if anything, decline more sharply than I calculate. On the other hand, allowance for possible biases referred to below, n. 26 and p. 67, would have a contrary effect. In the summary tabulation in the text, I assume that the adjustment rate for natural-resource exhaustion that was derived for 1970–5 applies to each subinterval considered.

20 A chief source of incomparability in the R and D expenditure data is the exclusion of outlays for new investment from US totals. Depreciation, however, is apparently included in R and D outlays of the US business-enterprise sector. With the exclusion of investment in construction, the Soviet R and D ratio for 1965 falls to 2.4% and for 1975 to 3.2%. The Soviet totals also include social-science R and D in higher education. Such outlays are omitted from data for the United States and some other Western countries. On the other hand, the Soviet data are probably less inclusive than most Western data in respect of outlays for the development of prototypes. On the comparative scope of Soviet and Western R and D data, see Nimitz (1974); Nolting (1973); OECD (1967; 1979); Campbell (1978).

21 For Western countries, reference is to defense and space R and D that is government funded and supposedly represents activities that are "directly related to military purposes." Just what this means is not entirely clear. One wonders whether, in addition to work on new weapons, some funds do not go to activities of sorts that might raise the output of old weapons, and so clearly contribute to TPP. In compiling data on Soviet defense and space R and D, however, Nimitz has sought to achieve comparability with Western data. The result should be broadly indicative of the size of Soviet allocations to defense and space relatively to those in the West.

22 To return to the issue regarding the inclusion, in the productivity measures above, of increased values relative to resource cost that final users obtain from new products, note that such values would indeed be completely omitted if new products were included in underlying data on aggregate output at their long-run resource cost. Furthermore, such a valuation of new products is clearly the desideratum where the output data are taken, as is often the case, as observations on the community's "theoretic" production possibilities. Should the new products be valued at prices that include above-normal profits, however, the resulting productivity measures are apt to reflect to a degree additional final-user values at given resource cost. That could be so whether reference is to market prices or factor cost, for the latter as well as the former might include above-normal profits.

To what extent do underlying output data reflect additional user values as described above? This is a complicated question. I can only record here that, regarding output data for Western countries, it would be surprising if above-normal profits generated by new final products did not often have an imprint on calculated output. As for output data for the USSR, I have used those of Greenslade where valuation is supposedly at an imputed factor cost that is exclusive of any and all profits. In fact, Greenslade's valuation procedure (1976, p. 284) is decidedly more complex than that, and one wonders whether enhanced user values from new products may not sometimes have an impact even here.

Although I have focused on new products, all that has been said applies as well to quality changes. Indeed, it is difficult to know where one leaves off and the other begins. Note, though, that the question at issue here concerns the degree to which output measures reflect additional user values relative to resource cost. In discussion of quality changes, reference is often simply to the degree to which output measures reflect such variations. The question whether there are additional values surpassing additional resource cost may often not be addressed.

On previous discussion of final user values and productivity measures, see Denison (1962, pp. 156–7; 1967, pp. 27–9; 1979, p. 124).

23 See particularly Amann, Berry and Davies (n.d.), Nolting (1973, 1976, 1978), Nimitz

(1974), Campbell (1978), Parrott (1980). Also informative on the Soviet R and D process generally is Germashev (1962).

24 I refer to patents issued to Soviet citizens. Although such patents are legally obtainable, and theoretically confer a restrictive entitlement on the recipient, Soviet inventors practically always find it expedient to apply rather for a "certificate of authorship." The invention is then available without cost for general use, though the persons responsible for it are suitably rewarded.

25 A principal obstacle to staff curtailment is the need to find alternative employment for released workers. See McAuley (1969, pp. 121ff), Berliner (1976, pp. 158ff), Granick (1979), also Manevich (1971, pp. 17, 20), Mikul'skii (1979, pp. 116, 249). I am indebted to Dr Tibor Vais for the last two references.

26 The catch-up process also must often have involved restoration to full operation, with relatively limited commitment of new-capital, of plant and equipment that had been largely or entirely written off. That, however, would only nominally boost TPP, for there would then be one more reason, additional to those considered in Section 2.3, why calculated productivity growth would have failed to allow accurately for the actual growth of inputs.

27 It remains to say that Soviet imports of Western machinery have been relatively very small through much of the period studied, though there has been some increase since 1955. Here are some benchmark estimates by Hanson (1976, p. 796) of the percentage relation between imports of Western machinery and domestic machinery investment: 1955, 1.0–2.0; 1960, 1.7–3.4; 1965, 1.1–2.2; 1970, 1.7–3.4; 1975, 2.4–4.8.

Note that Green and Levine (1977) refer to imports of Western machinery, exclusive of transport equipment. On the impact of technology transfers under detente, see in addition to the essays of Green and Levine, Hanson (1976), Weitzman (1979), Green (1979), and Toda (1979).

28 An upper limit of .4 of a percentage point follows from an assumption that the capital stock consists of a single kind of asset with a service life of 25 years. I also assume that as of 1950 the capital stock had an average age such as would have materialized if *prior* to that year gross investment had grown steadily for at least 25 years at a rate of 12.6% annually, and that as of 1980 the capital stock had an average age such as would have materialized if *prior* to that year gross investment had grown steadily for 25 years at a rate of 3.6% annually. The resultant average ages are 6.18 and 10.57 years. Hence, over the 30-year interval 1950–80 the average age of capital stock increases by 4.39 years, or by .146 of a year per calendar year. A decline of .4 of a percentage point in TPP is indicated by that degree of aging if we suppose that the entire increase in TPP during 1950–60, 2.9% annually, was of an embodied sort that occurs simply with the introduction of successive new vintages (i.e. .4 = .146 × 2.9).

29 As readily seen, it would vanish if the growth of employment due to educational advance should continue at the 1960–75 rate, and, should the Solow (1978) model of the cost of mineral-resource exhaustion apply, with mineral output rising from 9.3 to 15% of the GNP. Also the real cost of mineral extraction, which I assumed previously to increase by 1.5% yearly, is now supposed to increase by 3.0% yearly.

I have been referring to factor productivity as initially computed for material sectors. For comparative data on such productivity for the whole economy, see Table 1.

30 Consumption standards depend in part on government policy on resource allocation, particularly the division of national income between consumption, investment and defense. In a sense, then, the variation in these consumption standards might be viewed as one more aspect of the changing working arrangements that I discussed above. That might be the more so since the government's policy on consumption did in fact undergo a significant change in the period studied (Bergson, 1978a). But consumption trends are evidently determined by much more than policy, so that their classification with changing working arrangements could be confusing.

31 I refer to material sectors and, to allow for weather fluctuations, again cite the 1968–78 rate of growth.

32 Here are the annual percentage rates of growth of "science" and new fixed investment respectively: 1950–60, 10.5 and 11.5; 1960–70, 7.7 and 6.5; and 1970–5, 6.1 and 4.8. See Greenslade, 1976, pp. 275, 297.

33 Among existing socialist economies, only one, that of Yugoslavia, can be taken to exemplify market socialism, but the Yugoslav performance in respect of TPP and TPE has yet to be systematically studied. The Yugoslav experience is in any event made rather special by the prevalent system of "labor self-management."

Of more interest as a possible prototype for a reformed Soviet planning system is the New Economic Mechanism that the Hungarians have been operating since 1968. Although legacies of the previous system of centralist planning seem too numerous for the NEM to qualify fully as a form of market socialism, the Hungarian system represents a substantial shift in that direction. Here too the impact on TPP and TPE remains to be studied, but Hungarian economists themselves do not appear to claim any major gains in respect to such macroeconomics aspects. Rather the contention is that there have been improvements in quality, assortment and availability. For a survey of the Hungarian experience with NEM, see Portes (1977).

References

Aganbegian, A. G., "How to Outwit the Idler." *Current Digest Soviet Press*, June 8, 1977.

Amann, Ronald, Berry, M. J., and Davies, R. W., *Science and Industry in the USSR*. Part 5, no place, no date.

Amann, Ronald, Cooper, Julian, and Davies, R. W., eds., *The Technological Level of Soviet Industry*. New Haven, Conn.: Yale Univ. Press, 1977.

Bain, Joe S., *Barriers to New Competition*. Cambridge, Mass.: Harvard Univ. Press, 1962.

Becker, Abraham S., *Soviet National Income, 1958–64*. Berkeley: Univ. of California Press, 1969.

Becker, Abraham S., "The Price Level of Soviet Machinery in the 1960s." *Soviet Studies* **26**, 3: 363–79, July 1974.

Bergson, Abram, *The Real National Income of Soviet Russia Since 1928*. Cambridge, Mass.: Harvard Univ. Press, 1961.

Bergson, Abram, *The Economics of Soviet Planning*. New Haven, Conn.: Yale Univ. Press, 1964.

Bergson, Abram, *Planning and Productivity under Soviet Socialism*. New York: Columbia Univ. Press, 1968.

Bergson, Abram, *Soviet Post-War Economic Development*. Stockholm: Almquist & Wicksell, 1974.

Bergson, Abram, "Conclusions," in *The Soviet Economy in the Eighties*. Brussels: NATO, 1978a.

Bergson, Abram, "Managerial Risks and Rewards in Public Enterprise." *J. Comp. Econ.* **2**, 3: 211–25, Sept. 1978b.

Bergson, Abram, *Productivity and the Social System — The USSR and the West*. Cambridge, Mass: Harvard Univ. Press, 1978c.

Bergson, Abram, "Notes on the Production Function in Soviet Postwar Growth." *J. Comp. Econ.* 3, 2: 116–26, June 1979.*

Berliner, Joseph S., *The Innovation Decision in Soviet Industry*. Cambridge, Mass.: M.I.T. Press, 1976.

Boretsky, Michael, "Comparative Progress in Technology, Productivity and Economic Efficiency: U.S.S.R. versus U.S.A.." In *New Directions in the Soviet Economy*, IIA. Papers, Joint Econ. Comm., US Congress. Washington, DC: Govt. Printing Off., 1966.

Campbell, Robert W., "Reference Source on Soviet R & D Statistics 1950–1978." Mimeo. Washington, DC: National Science Foundation, 1978.

CIA, "USSR. Gross National Product Accounts, 1970." A(ER) 75–76. Washington, DC: Nov. 1975.

---

* See Chapter 7.

CIA, "USSR. The Impact of Recent Climate Change on Grain Production." ER 76–10577U. Washington, DC: Oct. 1976.

CIA, "A Discussion Paper on Soviet Petroleum Production." Washington, DC: June 1977.

CIA, "Soviet Economic Problems and Prospects." ER 77–10436U. Washington, DC: July 1977.

CIA, "USSR. Trends and Prospects in Educational Attainment, 1959–85." ER 79–10344. Washington, DC: June 1979.

CIA, "Handbook of Economic Statistics 1979." ER 79–10274. Washington, DC: Aug. 1979.

Cohn, Stanley H., "General Growth Performance of the Soviet Economy", in *Economic Performance and the Military Burden in the Soviet Union.* Papers, Joint Econ. Comm., U.S. Congress. Washington, DC: Govt. Printing Off., 1970.

Cohn, Stanley H., "The Soviet Path to Growth: A Comparative Analysis." *Rev. Inc. & Wealth* **22**, 1: 49–60, March 1976a.

Cohn, Stanley H., "Deficiencies in Soviet Investment Policies and the Technological Imperative," in *Soviet Economy in a New Perspective.* Papers, Joint Economic Committee, US Congress. Washington, DC: GPO, 1976b.

Cohn, Stanley H., "Soviet Replacement Investment," in *Soviet Economy in a Time of Change,* Vol. 1, 1979.

Denison, Edward F., *The Sources of Economic Growth in the United States.* New York: Comm. Econ. Developm., 1962.

Denison, Edward F., *Why Growth Rates Differ.* Washington, DC: Brookings, 1967.

Denison, Edward F. *Accounting for Slower Economic Growth.* Washington, DC: Brookings, 1979.

Desai, Padma, "The Production Function and Technical Change in Postwar Soviet Industry." *Amer. Econ. Rev.* **66**, 3: 372–97, June 1976.

DeWitt, Nicholas, "Costs and Returns in Education in the USSR." Unpubl. Ph.D. Thesis, Harvard University, March 1962.

Economic Report of the President 1978. Washington, DC: Govt. Printing Off., 1978.

Feshbach, Murray, and Rapawy, Stephen, "Soviet Population and Manpower, Trends and Policies," in *Soviet Economy in a New Perspective,* 1976.

Feshbach, Murray, "Employment Trends and Policies in the USSR." Mimeo, Aug. 1978.

Gellman Research Associates, "Indicators of International Trends in Technological Innovation." PB–263738. Washington, DC: US Dept. of Commerce, Nat. Techn. Information Service, April 1976.

Germashev, A. F., ed., *Izobretatel'stvo i ratsionalizatsiia.* Moscow, 1962.

Gosplan SSSR, Gosstroi SSSR and Akademiia nauk SSSR, *Tipovaia metodika opredeleniia ekonomicheskoi effektivnosti kapital'nykh vlozhenii.* Moscow, 1969.

Granick, David, "Labor Markets in the USSR", 78. Mimeo. Washington, DC: Kennan Institute, 1979.

Green, Donald W., and Levine, Herbert S., "Macroeconomic Evidence on the Value of Machinery Imports to the Soviet Union," in John R. Thomas and V. M. Kruse-Vaucienne, eds., *Soviet Science and Technology: Domestic and Foreign Perspectives.* Washington DC: George Washington University Press, 1977.

Green, Donald W., "Technology Transfer to the USSR: A Reply." *J. Comp. Econ.* **3**, 2: 179–80, June 1979.

Greenslade, Rush V., "The Real Gross National Product of the USSR," in *Soviet Economy in a New Perspective,* 1976.

Griliches, Zvi, and Ringstad, V., *Economies of Scale and the Form of the Production Function.* Amsterdam: North Holland, 1971.

Hanson, Philip, "International Technology Transfer from the West to the USSR," in *Soviet Economy in a New Perspective.* Papers, Joint Economic Committee, US Congress. Washington, DC: GPO, 1976.

Hanson, Philip, and Hill, Malcolm R., "Soviet Assimilation of Western Technology," in *Soviet Economy in a Time of Change,* v.2. Papers, Joint Economic Committee, US Congress. Washington, DC: GPO, 1979.

Jewkes, John, Sawers, David, and Stillerman, Richard, *The Sources of Invention*. New York: St Martin's Press, 1959.

McAuley, Mary, *Labour Disputes in Soviet Russia, 1957–1965*. Oxford: Clarendon, 1969.

Manevich, E. L., "Vosproizvodstvo rabochei sily i puti uluchsheniia ispol" zovaniia trudovykh resursov v SSSR," in E. L. Manevich, ed., *Osnovnye problemy ratsional'noga ispol'zovaniia trudovykh resursov v SSSR*. Moscow, 1971.

Martens, John A., and Young, John P., "Soviet Implementation of Domestic Inventions," in *Soviet Economy in a New Perspective*, 1979.

Mikul'skii, K. I., ed., *Effektivnost' sotsialisticheskogo proizvodstva i khoziaistvennyi mekhanizm*. Moscow, 1979.

Moorsteen, Richard, and Powell, Raymond P., *The Soviet Capital Stock, 1928–1962*. Homewood, Ill.: Irwin, 1966.

National Science Board, National Science Foundation, *Science Indicators 1976*. Washington, DC: Govt. Printing Off., 1977.

NATO, Directorate of Economic Affairs, *Exploitation of Siberia's Natural Resources*. Brussels: NATO, 1974.

NATO, *The USSR in the Eighties*. Brussels; NATO, 1978.

Nimitz, Nancy, "The Structure of Soviet Outlays on R & D in 1960 and 1968." R–1207–DDRE. Santa Monica, Calif.: RAND, 1974.

Nolting, Louvan E., "Sources of Financing the Stages of the Research, Development and Innovation Cycle in the U.S.S.R." FER—3. Washington, DC: US Department of Commerce, Bur. Econ. Analysis, Sept. 1973.

Nolting, Louvan E., "The 1968 Reform of Scientific Research, Development and Innovation in the U.S.S.R." Fer—11. Washington, DC: US Dep. of Commerce, Bur. Econ. Analysis, Sept. 1976.

Nolting, Louvan E., "The Planning of Research, Development and Innovation in the U.S.S.R." FER—14. Washington, DC: US Dep. of Commerce, Bur. Econ. Analysis, July 1978.

Nolting, Louvan E., and Feshbach, Murray, "R & D Employment in the USSR," in *Soviet Economy in a Time of Change*, vol. 1. Papers, Joint Economic Committee, US Congress. Washington, DC: GPO, 1979.

Organization for Economic Cooperation and Development (OECD), *The Overall Level and Structure of R and D Efforts in OECD Member Countries*. Paris, 1967.

OECD, *International Statistical Year 1975*. Paris, March 1979.

Ofer, Gur, "The Opportunity Cost of the Non-Monetary Advantages of the Soviet Military R & D Effort." R–1741 DDRE. Santa Monica, Calif.: RAND, 1975.

Parrott, Bruce, "Organizational Environment of Applied Research." In Linda L. Lubrano and S. G. Solomon, eds., *The Social Context of Soviet Science*. Boulder, Co.: Westview Press, 1980.

Portes, Richard, "Hungary: Economic Performance, Policy and Prospects." In *East-European Economies Post-Helsinki*. Papers. Joint Econ. Comm., US Congress. Washington, DC: Govt. Printing Office, 1977.

Rapawy, Stephen, "Estimates and Projections of the Labor Force and Civilian Employment in the U.S.S.R. 1950 to 1990." FER–10. Washington, DC: US Dep. of Commerce, Bur. Econ. Analysis, Sept. 1976.

Riurikov, Iu. B., "Deti i obshchestvo." *Voprosy filosofii*: pp. 111–21, no. 4, 1977.

Solow, Robert M., "Resources and Economic Growth." *Amer. Economist* 22, 2: 5–11, Fall 1978.

Soviet Economy in a New Perspective. Papers, Joint Econ. Comm., US Congress. Washington, DC: Govt. Printing Office, 1976.

Soviet Economy in a Time of Change. Papers, Joint Econ. Comm., US Congress. Washington, DC: Govt. Printing Off., 1979.

Sutton, Antony C. *Western Technology and Soviet Economic Development 1945 to 1965*, vol. 3, Stanford, Calif.: Hoover, 1973.

Toda, Yasushi, "Technology Transfer to the USSR." *J. Comp. Econ.* 3, 2: 181–194, June 1979.

Treml, Vladimir G., Kostynsky, B. L., Kruger, K. W., and Gallik, D. M., "Conversion of Soviet Input–Output Tables to Producers' Prices: The 1966 Reconstructed Table."

FER–1. Washington, DC: US Dep. of Commerce, Bur. Econ. Analysis, July 1973.

TSU (Tsentral'noe statisticheskoe upravlenie), *Narodnoe khoziaistvo SSSR* (v 1960 g.–1977 g.). Moscow, various years, 1961–78.

TSU. *Narodnoe khoziaistvo SSSR za 60 let*. Moscow, 1977.

Weitzman, Martin L., "Soviet Postwar Economic Growth and Capital–Labor Substitution." *Amer. Econ. Rev.* **60**, 4: 676–92, Sept. 1970.

Weitzman, Martin L., "Technology Transfer to the USSR." *J. Comp. Econ.* **3**, 2: 167–77, June 1979.

7

The Production Function in Soviet Postwar Industrial Growth

I

The sources of Soviet postwar industrial growth have by now been the subject of a number of systematic econometric inquiries, but the underlying production function relating inputs, output, and "technical change" still appears to be rather unsettled.[1]

Thus, Weitzman (1970), Desai (1976), Rosefielde and Lovell (1977), and Gomulka (1977) all consider that variations in Soviet industrial inputs and output may properly be represented by a production function of the CES sort. These authors diverge, however, with regard to further specifications. Although there are also some differences regarding the precise time period covered and the underlying data, differences in specifications do contribute materially to some marked differences in results.

Among other things, Weitzman, Desai, and Rosefielde and Lovell all find the elasticity of substitution (σ) between labor and capital much below unity[2]: for Weitzman, it is 0.430; for Desai, 0.2771, and for Rosefielde and Lovell, 0.1830. On the other hand, Gomulka concludes that σ "could easily be anywhere in the range from 0.1 to 1.2." For purposes of further inquiry, Gomulka (1976, 1977) simply takes σ equal to unity; he thus refers, in effect, to the Cobb–Douglas variant of the CES production function.

As for the further specifications, divergencies relate chiefly to technological progress. Weitzman and Desai both assume a constant rate of Hicks-neutral technical change. Rosefielde and Lovell likewise take

7

---

[1] I have benefited from discussions with Gary Chamberlain and Martin Weitzman, and from unidentified readers' comments. Weitzman suggested among other things, one of the two computations of rates of return on revalued capital that I refer to in the rate-of-return calculations in Section II. I am, needless to say, solely responsible for any deficiencies.

technical change to be Hicks-neutral but assume that the rate varies linearly with time. Gomulka, however, distinguishes between capital- and labor-augmenting aspects; moreover, he makes a further distinction among three major time intervals for which relevant causal forces are believed to differ.

Gomulka seeks to allow in this way for diverse aspects, including the varying quality of a labor hour when the length of working time changes. His complex procedure is perhaps not the most felicitous one that might be used for that purpose, but from 1955 to 1961 (an interval that all cited studies cover), weekly working hours in Soviet industry fell by as much as 15.3% (Rapawy, 1976, p. 45). Denison (1967, pp. 59ff.), who probably has devoted as much attention to this matter as anyone, has compiled coefficients indicating that more than half of such a reduction in hours might have been offset by an opposite change in output per man-hour. Denison's coefficients are admittedly rather arbitrary, but Weitzman, Desai, and Rosefielde and Lovell all take employment as represented simply by man-hours. With technical change also specified as they specify it, their results, one must suppose, could be significantly distorted. It is only fair to add that Weitzman (1970, pp. 687–688) is aware of the shortcomings of his procedure, but judged by Gomulka's findings, they probably are more important than he supposed.

II

Magnitudes found for parameters other than σ also often differ markedly, and some of these findings seem a priori open to question, quite apart from the divergencies between different analyses. Weitzman, for example, finds that the imputed earnings share of capital varies in this way:

1950	86%
1960	65%
1969	44%

As Weitzman would be the first to affirm, such estimates are necessarily crude, but even so, the capital share for earlier years is notably large by Western standards.

In explanation, it has sometimes been argued that Western standards simply do not apply to the USSR. Perhaps that is the moral we must draw, but further computations seem to confirm Brubaker's (1972) undocumented contention that implausibly high rates of return on capital are

---

[2] Here and later, unless otherwise indicated, where an author makes alternative computations, I refer to an explicitly preferred variant, or to one on which he focuses attention.

implied by Weitzman's estimates. Here is how the indicated marginal productivity of capital varies over the years in question:

Rate of return (%)

	With capital in prevailing rubles	With capital revalued
1950	199	38; 44
1960	38	23; 29
1969	6	6

The computations underlying the above table are noted below. Essentially taking labor as a numeraire, I determine total earnings of capital from the earnings share that Weitzman imputes to that factor, and from the actual wage bill. Rates of return on the left side relate total earnings of capital to the Soviet capital stock in prevailing ruble prices. As determined in the well-known Soviet ways, however, such prices hardly conform to textbook norms. It would only be a coincidence if they should cover charges for capital corresponding to its marginal productivity. On the right side above I show, according to crude estimates, what the rates of return indicated by Weitzman's computations might be if capital goods themselves were revalued to reflect his factor shares.[3]

Should Weitzman's computations be valid, rates of return such as those that result without revaluation of capital goods should be observable in the USSR. They should be manifest particularly in investment-project ap-

[3] Rates of return with capital in prevailing rubles are derived from these data:

	Imputed capital earnings, net of depreciation (billion rubles)	Net capital stock (billion rubles)
1950	79.8	40.1
1960	40.8	108.1
1969	15.7	254.1

Capital earnings, as indicated, are inferred from ratios of imputed capital to imputed labor-income shares, as given in Weitzman (1970, p. 682), and from the industrial wage bill. The latter for 1960 is calculated from Weitzman (1970, p. 687). The industrial wage bills for 1950 and 1969 are extrapolated from that of 1960 by reference to workers employed, as in Weitzman (1970, p. 687), and average monthly wages, as in Tsentral'noe statisticheskoe upravlenie (1968, pp. 138–139). Since the capital stock for 1969 could be calculated only in 1960 prices, reference is to the wage bill in 1969 at 1960 wage rates.

As initially computed, capital earnings seem properly construed as gross of depreciation. In order to obtain the corresponding net income, I allow for depreciation at the rate of 4.2% of gross fixed capital: see Weitzman (1970, pp. 689, 691).

praisal when the project makers are considering capital–labor substitutions, at least when this appraisal is of a systematic sort, as under the "coefficient of effectiveness" procedure. It is of interest, then, that there seems to be no record of the Russians, when employing that procedure, ever using a norm that requires a coefficient approaching anywhere near 199%, the rate of return implied by the Weitzman calculations for 1950. Even the corresponding return found for 1960, 38%, is high when we consider that standard coefficients that were established

---

On the stock of fixed capital, gross and net of depreciation on January 1, 1960, see Kaplan (1961, pp. 104, 106). In order to obtain corresponding data for July 1, 1960, I allow for a 6.5% increase over the half-year interval in question. Stocks as of July 1, 1950, and July 1, 1969, are extrapolated by reference to index numbers of the gross stock in Weitzman (1970, p. 677). As thus obtained, stocks for all years are in July 1955 prices. Corresponding figures for 1950 and 1960 in current rubles and for 1969 in 1960 rubles are derived by reference to deflators inferred from Moorsteen and Powell (1966, pp. 389–391).

Although fixed capital is the only capital input in Weitzman, I also include in the capital stock inventories, as obtained for 1960 from Moorsteen and Powell (1966, pp. 456–457). For present purposes, inventories for other years are extrapolated by reference to Weitzman's index numbers for fixed capital.

As for rates of return with capital revalued, the lower results for 1950 and 1960 and the single result for 1969 are obtained by application to capital in prevailing rubles of the ratio of two coefficients: (i) the ratio of total factor charges (labor plus capital) to labor charges alone, as indicated in Weitzman, and (ii) the ratio of ruble factor charges (labor plus nonlabor) in Soviet industry to labor charges alone. The latter ratio is taken to be 1.68 in 1960 and 1969 from data for 1959 in Bergson (1974, p. 79). Partly by extrapolation, I take the corresponding ratio for 1950 to be 1.38. The higher earnings rates for 1950 and 1960 with capital revalued are obtained as the ratio of the following coefficients: (i) capital's share in total factor (labor plus capital) earnings as indicated in Weitzman (though after allowance for depreciation), and (ii) the ratio of the net capital stock to net output in nonfarm nonresidential sectors of the USSR, or 1.93 in 1950 and 2.15 in 1960. These coefficients, chiefly determined from data in Moorsteen and Powell (1966, pp. 335, 362–363, 389–391, 585 ff.), are intended to be in current rubles, although no allowance is made for the increase in prices for nonfarm output from 1950 to 1960.

Of the foregoing two recomputations of rates of return, I evidently assume in the first as a crude approximation that the capital–labor ratio in the capital-goods industries is the same as that in all industry. In the second, I proceed similarly. Thus, I in effect assume that industrial output has been revalued to correspond to the sum of the wage bill and Weitzman's corresponding capital charges. The capital stock is supposedly revalued in the same proportion, so that in the upshot the industrial capital-output ratio is unaffected by the revaluation.

In view of the nature of Weitzman's computations, his data on factor shares, I believe, are properly construed as in "base year" prices. I have nevertheless treated his shares for 1950 as if they were in current prices, but it can be shown that the results would be the same if the calculation were made initially with capital and labor valued in 1960 prices. The resulting rate of return, representing the rate at which 1950 capital in 1960 prices substitutes for labor in 1960 prices, must then be translated into the corresponding rate of return representing the same substitution with capital and labor valued in 1950 prices.

as part of a regularization of the coefficient-of-effectiveness technique in that year varied only from 15 to 30%.[4]

While the rates of return obtained *before* revaluation of capital goods must provoke misgivings, the corresponding returns *after* such revaluation presumably must be considered in any comparison with Western experience. For earlier years these returns are much reduced, but are still high, at least for 1950. True, reconstruction of war damage was still in progress in the USSR in the early fifties. For well-known reasons, returns to capital might have been relatively high in such circumstances. In the early fifties, however, reconstruction of war damage was also still in progress in the West, but it is difficult to find any near parallel to returns such as are here under consideration. In West Germany, for example, the rate of return on capital in 1950 indicated by national income data might have been on the order of 9%. If in the USSR in 1950 investment was in fact yielding as much as 38 to 44% the reasons are quite obscure.

III

One need perhaps not be a perfectionist to feel that questions are also in order regarding the underlying data. With respect to output, Weitzman, instead of using Soviet official data on the gross production of industry as a whole, reaggregates official sectoral index numbers with imputed value-added weights. The reaggregation is certainly to the good, and the official sectoral series that Weitzman uses for 1950 and after must be more reliable that the proverbially distorted ones of the early 5-year plans. But, in view of the work of Greenslade (1972, 1976) and Becker (1974), it is difficult to avoid the conclusion that the meaning of some of the official sectoral series is still highly problematic, to say the least. Weitzman is to be commended, therefore, for considering alternative Western measures of Soviet industrial output. Although one may wonder at his decision to treat this computation only in a subordinate way, with the results confined to a footnote, it still is of interest that the resulting σ is but 0.274, or even lower than that where output is based on the official sectoral series.

Comparison of the alternative computations is difficult, however, insofar as, in using Western output measures, Weitzman focuses on industry in an extended sense, comprising the entire nonfarm sector except various services. He does so, in order to be able to relate the Western output data to available Western measures of capital services of similarly broad scope. A computation employing Western data on

[4] See Bergson (1966, pp. 241 ff., and the sources cited on p. 250, n. 8).

the output of industry in a restricted sense, however, together with corresponding Soviet official data on capital stock, would also be of interest. As for reliability, Soviet official data on capital stock seem to be much superior to the official output measures.[5]

Desai has also improved on the official all-industry series by the double deflation of current ruble data on materials inputs and gross output. She uses as deflators, however, official price indexes whose meaning seems just as problematic as that of the official production indexes.[6] For

[5] As is not always understood, to return to the official output measures, a principal source of distortion under the early plans still is apt to be deleterious. In measuring output in "constant" prices, the Russians apparently often still include, as they did in early years, new products at prices established when such commodities were introduced. Although the price inflation that formerly made this procedure especially suspect has lately been much dampened, the initial prices of new products, predictably, are often notably high, and many such products are reportedly of doubtful merit, serving essentially as a device to circumvent controlled prices. The government tends to change such prices only at long intervals. As Soviet economists themselves affirm, the resultant "concealed" price increase of machinery in particular has been an important source of rising costs of investment.

The new products must also often be overpriced in the official measures of output in "constant" prices. The overpricing admittedly has been manifest more where "productivity" than where "costs" are the valuation yardstick. In measuring real output, the latter standard perhaps merits theoretically some priority over the former (Bergson, 1975), but it is difficult to exculpate the Soviet statistical treatment of new products on that basis.

On the overpricing of new machinery products as a factor affecting Soviet investment costs, see especially Becker (1974). With due allowance for such overpricing, Becker conjectures that over the years 1958 to 1970 machinery prices rose by 25%. According to Soviet official measures, machinery prices rather fell by 11.5% during that period. Soviet official indexes of machinery production more or less approximate physical-volume measures obtained by applying the corresponding indexes of prices as deflators to output in current rubles. We may infer that that is so from Lee (1977, Appendix B), though the precise manner of compiling the price index numbers has apparently varied in the course of time (Bornstein, 1972, pp. 358 ff.; Becker, 1974, p. 374). A downward bias regarding prices, therefore, should be mirrored in an upward bias regarding production. The meaning of Becker's results is, however, from this standpoint somewhat beclouded. As he points out, the indexes of machinery prices that he advances must relate primarily to civilian machinery. The official index number of such prices, however, may well reflect trends in weapons prices as well.

For reference below, note that Soviet official index numbers of prices and physical volume also tend to be broadly congruent for sectors other than machinery. Curiously, though, use of the official price indexes as deflators yields more often than not indexes of physical volume that exceed the corresponding official measures: see Desai (1973).

[6] See n. 5, above; Bornstein, (1972). Desai's principal concern throughout is to explore inclusion of materials, along with labor and capital, as factor inputs. Desai's calculations may well shed light on that interesting matter despite the dubious nature of the output series she relies on.

purposes of determining the Soviet production function, Desai in any case, apparently on technical grounds, finally favors a computation in which the Soviet official all-industry series is used to measure output.

Rosefielde and Lovell, too, contribute by experimenting with a number of variants of Weitzman's reaggregated official series, each obtained by use of a different set of sectoral weights. Among these, weights representing final demand appear particularly novel and interesting. The sectoral volume series, however, are again the Soviet official ones, so here also the meaning of the results is in doubt.

Output is represented in Gomulka (1976, 1977) by Weitzman's reaggregation of official series to 1966 and the Soviet official all-industry series from 1967 to 1975. Here, too, therefore, the data employed must provoke misgivings.

For the period 1950–1969 considered by Weitzman the series on working hours used by him fits in well enough with the careful compilation in Rapawy (1976). In extending the calculations first to 1973 and then to 1975, however, Gomulka (1976, pp. 10–13; 1977, p. 39) takes hours worked to have increased after 1966; in 1973 they are considered to be 7.6% longer than in the earlier year. Rapawy, on the other hand, shows that working hours after 1966 stayed essentially the same as in that year. Let us hope that this divergence between Gomulka and Rapawy can be resolved. Depending on who is right, the rate of growth of employment during 1966–1973 is either 2.1 or 3.1% annually. Such a difference could have some impact on Gomulka's results. On post-1966 hours, Gomulka follows Desai. Since Desai's computations go only to 1971, however, they should be less affected by the divergence on hours with Rapawy.

IV

Although the foregoing comments are sometimes critical, I hope they will be seen as constructive. That is certainly their primary intent. For purposes of analyzing Soviet postwar industrial growth, econometrics is obviously here to stay. With continued careful efforts it should be possible to gain further perspective from its application. Indeed, despite the uncertainties that have been discussed, we have already benefited, I think, by having been made aware of a wider range of possibilities than we might have contemplated otherwise. That is so even if we should discount some of the more extreme results.

Pending the completion of more definitive studies, therefore, it is of interest to consider what the practical import of such a broad spectrum of possibilities might be. I focus particularly on some normative comparisons of Soviet and Western industrial growth that I have made previously (1974, 1978). My concern there was to compare the rate of "technical change" in the nonfarm sector (exclusive of selected services) in the USSR and different Western countries over the years 1955–1970. In the studies cited, I sought to do this by application, to the USSR and the Western countries, of a production function of the Cobb–Douglas form, i.e.,

$$Y(t) = Ae^{\lambda t}K(t)^{\alpha}L(t)^{(1-\alpha)}, \tag{1}$$

where A is a dimensional constant; $Y(t)$, $K(t)$, and $L(t)$ are output, capital, and labor inputs, respectively; α is the gross-earnings share of capital; and λ is the rate of technical progress. I thus assumed a constant rate of Hicks-neutral technical progress, although for the Cobb–Douglas production function, of course, Harrod-neutrality holds as well.

In applying Eq. (1) to Western countries, rather than derive λ and α econometrically, I determined α in a Denison-like way from national-income and related data, and in fact partly from data compiled by Denison. For the USSR, I imputed a 12% return to Soviet capital. (This rate apparently has come lately to be something of a standard one in Soviet investment-project appraisal, though for the year chosen in my calculation of capital's earning share—1960—higher yardsticks may have been applied.) Since in Eq. (1) α corresponds to gross earnings, I also allowed for depreciation. Given α, I then computed λ from (1) and available data on $Y(t)$, $K(t)$, and $L(t)$. In Table 1, I show the magnitudes of α that were obtained, and also, for the columns headed $\sigma = 1$, the resulting magnitudes of λ.[7]

I have previously experimented to some extent with alternative assumptions regarding the production function, and, in the case of the USSR, the rate of return to capital. In the light of the econometric inquiries cited, I now extend the scope of the variants considered. Specifically, as an alternative to (1), I consider a CES production function of the form

$$Y(t) = Ae^{\lambda t}[\delta K(t)^z + (1 - \delta)L(t)^z]^{1/z}, \tag{2}$$

where δ and $(1 - \delta)$ have the property that their ratio in the base year corresponds to the relative earnings shares of capital and labor. Also,

$$z = (\sigma - 1)/\sigma. \tag{3}$$

With $\sigma = 1$, of course, we again have (1). I experiment now with two further values of σ: 0.5 and 0.25.

---

[7] Assuming discontinuous compounding.

TABLE 1

IMPUTED CAPITAL EARNINGS SHARE (α), 1960, AND AVERAGE ANNUAL PERCENTAGE RATE
OF TECHNICAL PROGRESS (λ), 1955–1970 AND 1960–1970, FOR ALTERNATIVE
ELASTICITIES OF SUBSTITUTION (σ), INDUSTRY, SELECTED COUNTRIES[a]

Item	α	λ (1955–1970)			λ (1960–1970)		
		$\sigma = 1.0$	$\sigma = 0.5$	$\sigma = 0.25$	$\sigma = 1.0$	$\sigma = 0.5$	$\sigma = 0.25$
United States	0.22	1.5	1.5	1.5	2.0	2.1	2.2
France	0.26	3.6	3.7	3.9	3.6	3.8	4.1
Germany	0.27	3.2	3.4	3.6	3.2	3.4	3.8
United Kingdom	0.23	1.8	2.0	2.2	2.2	2.4	2.7
Italy	0.30	4.2	4.4	4.7	4.7	5.0	5.4
Japan	0.31	5.9	6.3	7.0	6.3	7.1	8.4
USSR							
With 12% return	0.33	2.2	2.3	2.1	1.8	2.0	2.5
With 20% return	0.42	1.6	1.7	1.6	1.2	1.6	2.2

[a] For all countries, except Japan, reference is to the nonfarm sector exclusive of selective services (chiefly defense, public administration, education, health care, and housing). For Japan, reference is to the whole economy.

The effect of the change in σ on λ is probably much less than might have been expected. For the period 1955–1970, that reflects a feature that is still not always grasped: given a CES production function and inputs growing at disparate rates, a lower σ means that aggregate inputs grow more slowly *after* and more rapidly *before* the year taken as base in the calculations.[8] Therefore, should the base year be an intermediate one in any interval considered, there must be offsetting effects on the growth of aggregate inputs, and necessarily also on the "residual" representing technical change. I take as a base 1960, the same year as that to which my factor-share data relate. That is also the base year in Weitzman's computations. The use of a lower σ, therefore, raises λ for years after 1960, and lowers it for years before 1960.

But, granting the offsetting effects for 1955–1970, there are no such effects for 1960–1970. Here, as expected, the impact on λ of a reduction in σ is more pronounced, but it tends still to be rather modest. Of particular interest from the standpoint of my previous inquiry, the comparative position of the USSR in relation to Western countries is hardly affected. I con-

[8] That this is so can most readily be brought out if we consider an extreme case where $\sigma = 0$, i.e., input coefficients are fixed. Assuming that both capital and labor are fully utilized in the base year, aggregate inputs in effect reduce to the slower-growing input after the base year. Prior to the base year, they reduce to the input for which the decrease from the base year is the greater. From the outset of the period in question, that is also the more rapidly growing input.

clude that such a comparison is insensitive to σ over a wide range of this parameter. That is certainly to the good, for the magnitude of σ may prove to be difficult to delimit narrowly.

I have been assuming that if σ is low for the USSR, it is correspondingly low for Western countries. That assumption has some basis, for indications of a low σ are by no means confined to the USSR (see Bergson, 1975, n. 6). With σ low for the USSR, however, and unity for Western countries, the relative Soviet standing is still much as before, though there is a limited improvement. Moreover, should σ differ in such a way for the USSR and the West, the question is posed as to why, with capital and labor growing at any given differential rates, there should be more marked diminishing returns to the more rapidly growing factor (realistically, capital) in the USSR than in the West. Should σ be especially low for the USSR, such relatively rapid diminishing returns to capital necessarily would prevail there. If that should be so, this, as well as the comparatively low Soviet λ, would be of normative interest.

For the USSR I have been referring, as in my previous inquiry, to calculations where α is given by a 12% rate of return on capital. I also consider now for the USSR a rate of return on capital of 20%. As might be expected, with this rate the Soviet λ is reduced in all computations (see Table 1). With a rate of return equal to 20% instead of 12%, α rises from 0.33 to 0.42. That is still below the capital earnings share, 0.65, that Weitzman finds for 1960. Further increases in the rate of return on capital and in α, however, would only reduce the more the resulting Soviet λ.[9]

References

Becker, Abraham S., "The Price Level of Soviet Machinery in the 1960's." *Soviet Studies* **26**, 3:363–379, July 1974.

Bergson, Abram, and Kuznets, Simon, eds., *Economic Trends in the Soviet Union.* Cambridge, Mass.: Harvard Univ. Press, 1963.

Bergson, Abram, *The Economics of Soviet Planning,* New Haven, Conn.: Yale Univ. Press, 1966.

Bergson, Abram, *Soviet Postwar Economic Development.* Stockholm: Almquist & Wiksell, 1974.

Bergson, Abram, "Index Numbers and the Computation of Factor Productivity," *Rev. Income & Wealth* **21**, 3:259–278, Sept. 1975.

Bergson, Abram, *Productivity and the Social System.* Cambridge, Mass.: Harvard Univ. Press, 1978.

[9] Curiously, with $\alpha = 0.42$, the λ that I obtain for the USSR for 1955–1970 is very close to the one obtained by Weitzman for 1950–1969 for the nonfarm sector with Western output data: 1.34%. That is so whatever the magnitude of σ. What this congruence means, however, is difficult to say. Not only do Weitzman and I refer to somewhat different time periods, our data on inputs and outputs also differ to some extent for periods during which we overlap. Among other things, I have adjusted labor inputs for hours in a Denison-like way throughout.

Bergson, Abram, "The Soviet Economy in the Eighties," In NATO, *The USSR in the Eighties*. Brussels: NATO, 1978.

Bornstein, Morris, "Soviet Price Statistics." In Treml and Hardt, eds., 1972.

Brubaker, Earl R., "Soviet Postwar Economic Growth and Capital–Labor Substitution— Comment," *Amer. Econ. Rev.* **62**, 4:675–678, Sept. 1972.

Denison, Edward F., *Why Growth Rates Differ*. Washington, D. C.: Brookings, 1967.

Desai, Padma, "Soviet Industrial Production: Estimates of Gross Outputs by Branches and Groups," *Oxford Bull. Econ. & Statist.* **35**, 2:153–171, May 1973.

Desai, Padma, "The Production Function and Technical Change in Postwar Soviet Industry," *Amer. Econ. Rev.* **66**, 3:372–381, June 1976.

Gomulka, Stanislaw, "Soviet Postwar Industrial Growth, Capital–Labor Substitution, and Technical Changes: A Reexamination." In Zbigniew M. Fallenbuchl, ed., *Economic Development in the Soviet Union and Eastern Europe*. New York: Praeger, 1976.

Gomulka, Stanislaw, "Slowdown in Soviet Industrial Growth 1947–1975 Reconsidered." *European Econ. Rev.* **10**, 1:37–49, Oct. 1977.

Greenslade, Rush V., "Industrial Production Statistics in the USSR." In Treml and Hardt, eds., 1972.

Greenslade, Rush V., "The Real Gross National Product of the USSR, 1950–1975." In *Soviet Economy in a New Perspective*. Compendium of papers, Joint Economic Committee, U. S. Congress. Washington, D. C.: U. S. Govt. Printing Office, 1976.

Kaplan, Norman M., "Capital Stock." In Bergson and Kuznets, eds., 1963.

Lee, William T., *The Estimation of Soviet Defense Expenditures*. New York, N. Y.: Praeger, 1977.

Moorsteen, Richard, and Powell, Raymond P., *The Soviet Capital Stock, 1928–1962*. Homewood, Ill.: Irwin, 1966.

Rapawy, Stephen, "Estimates and Projections of the Labor Force and Civilian Employment in the USSR 1950 to 1990." *Foreign Economic Report No. 10*, U. S. Department of Commerce, Bureau of Economic Analysis, Sept. 1976.

Rosefielde, Steven, and Lovell, C. A. Knox, "The Impact of Adjusted Factor Cost Valuation on the CES Interpretation of Postwar Soviet Economic Growth.," *Economica* **44**, 176:381–392, Nov. 1977.

Treml, Vladimir G., and Hardt, John P., eds., *Soviet Economic Statistics*. Durham, N. C.: Duke Univ. Press, 1972.

Tsentral'noe statisticheskoe upravlenie, *Trud v SSSR*. Moscow, 1968.

Weitzman, Martin L., "Soviet Postwar Economic Growth and Capital–Labor Substitution." *Amer. Econ. Rev.* **60**, 4:676–692, Sept. 1970.

8

The Soviet Slowdown: Can It
Be Reversed?

The new Soviet five-year plan,[1] promulgated at the XXVIIth Party Congress, commands decidedly more attention than has been accorded such a program for some years. Elevated to General Secretary only a year ago, on March 11, 1985, Mikhail S. Gorbachev has already demonstrated that, not only is he a relatively youthful occupant of that office, he is a notably vigorous and dynamic one as well.

Since his elevation, Gorbachev has devoted himself to many matters, but has manifestly been preoccupied with the performance of the Soviet economy, which has hardly been scintillating lately. Since he assumed office, Gorbachev has made it evident, in numerous speeches and pronouncements, that reinvigoration of the economy will be a cardinal concern of his administration.

In the twelfth five-year plan (1986–1990), we can see more clearly than before what he is attempting to achieve in that regard. Taken together with related proceedings at the Congress, particularly the lengthy introductory address by Gorbachev himself, the plan also provides us with a better basis to judge what he might accomplish and how, consequently, the Soviet economy might evolve under the Gorbachev administration.

The twelfth five-year plan must have been at an advanced stage of preparation when Gorbachev came to office, but it has since been subject to continuing review, so it seems properly identified with his administration. In approving the new five-year plan, the Party Congress also endorsed supplementary guidelines for the development of the Soviet economy to the year 2000. In gauging Soviet economic prospects under Gorbachev, we must consider those guidelines along with the new plan. The guidelines are of particular interest, since Gorbachev could well have had an even greater impact on them than on the targets for the years 1986–1990.[2]

Table 1
Selected Economic Indicators, USSR, Average Annual Rate of Growth[a] (percent)

	1951–60	1961–70	1971–75	1976–80	1981–85	1986–90 (plan)	1991–2000 (plan)
1. Net material product (NMP)[b], Soviet official	n.a.[c]	6.4	5.1	3.9	3.2	3.5–4.1	5.1–5.3[e]
2. Gross national product (GNP)[d], CIA	5.7	5.1	3.7	2.7	2.0	n.a.	n.a.
3. Gross fixed capital, Soviet official							
a. Investment	12.7	6.9	6.9	3.3	3.5	3.5–4.6	n.a.
b. Stock	9.5	8.0	7.9	6.8	6.0	n.a.	n.a.
4. NMP per worker, Soviet official	8.9	6.3	4.6	3.5	3.1	3.7–4.2	6.7–7.4
5. GNP per worker,[f] Bergson	1.2	1.7	1.8	1.3	n.a.	n.a.	n.a.
6. Factor productivity, Bergson	1.9	1.5	0.1	−0.3	n.a.	n.a.	n.a.
7. Industrial output, Soviet official	11.7	8.5	7.4	4.5	3.8	3.9–4.4	4.9–5.2[g]
8. Industrial output, CIA[d]	9.2	6.4	5.9	3.2	2.0	n.a.	n.a.
9. Agricultural output,[h] Soviet official	n.a.	3.8	2.5	1.8	1.2	2.7–3.0	n.a.
10. Agricultural output,[h] CIA	n.a.	3.0	1.4	0.4	n.a.	n.a.	n.a.
11. Real income per capita, Soviet official	6.5	4.8	4.4	3.4	2.1	2.5–2.8	3.5–4.6
12. Consumption per capita[d], CIA	4.2	3.8	2.9	2.2	1.1	n.a.	n.a.

[a] *Sources.* Soviet official data from TSSU (1985) and earlier volumes in the same series; *Pravda* January 26, 1985; January 26, 1986; November 18, 1985; March 9, 1986. Planned rate of growth for investment for1985–1990inferred from announced goal for increase in total1985–1990volume. For CIIA data on GNP, industrial and agricultural output, and consumption per capita, Pitzer (1982a: 52ff); CIA (1984: 68; 1986: 66ff); JEC (1985: 43); Schroeder and Denton (1982a: 335). Data in Bergson (1983: 37) on labor and factor productivity extended to 1980 by reference to data on labor and capital inputs and GNP in CIA (1984: 68).

[b] "Utilized for consumption and accumulation."

[c] n.a.: not available or not applicable.

[d] For 1951–1980, 1970 ruble factor cost; for 1981–1985, 1982 ruble factor cost.

[e] "Almost."

[f] Adjusted for hours.

[g] "Not less than."

[h] Yearly growth rate of average for indicated period over average for preceding period.

I

For Gorbachev, reinvigoration of the Soviet economy means, above all, acceleration of its growth. That was already a specific concern in his public discussion of Soviet economic performance before the Party Congress. Acceleration of growth is clearly also the cardinal aim of the new plan. On any scale, that is apt to be a difficult task for any economy. There are reasons to think it will be especially difficult for the economy of the USSR.

Contrary to a common supposition, the recently much publicized slowdown in the Soviet economy had by no means brought it to a halt by the time Gorbachev came to office. But the slowdown had long been in process. Indeed, the rate of growth of the economy was already falling markedly in the Brezhnev administration. That is apparent from Soviet official data as well as CIA data on national income (Table 1). Curiously, the decline in growth is nearly as great in the official figures relating to the so-called "net material product" (NMP), as in the CIA figures on the "gross national product" (GNP). The CIA calculations, however, are not only more reliable; they alone conform to accepted Western methodology. For example, the CIA figures, as well known, comprehend diverse services that are omitted from the NMP.[3]

The longevity of the Soviet slowdown in itself suggests that acceleration of growth might be difficult. And it seems even more difficult when we consider the complex causes of the retardation. Growth in the USSR early on was generated in a novel way—primarily by the expansion of labor and capital inputs, and only to a comparatively limited extent, by increases in the productivity of such inputs.

Output per worker, it is true, increased markedly, but that was largely due to economy of labor induced by the extraordinarily rapid expansion of the accumulated capital stock (plant, equipment, and so on) on hand. That expansion was fueled in turn by a sharp increase in the share of new capital investment in the GNP. Output relative to inputs of labor and capital, or "factor productivity" as it has come to be called, grew only modestly. In the West too, at similar stages of development, expansion of capital and labor inputs has been a significant source of output growth, but the increase of factor productivity has often accounted for as much as one-half or more of the increase in output.[4]

According to a Soviet usage, often employed in the West as well, the type of growth stressing expansion of labor and capital inputs, such as experienced in the USSR, is extensive in nature. When factor productivity is comparatively significant, as in the West, growth is referred to as intensive.

The difference in growth process is evidently not immaterial. Originating primarily in advances in technology, factor productivity growth requires outlays for R&D, but the resultant costs of additional output are apt to be not nearly as great as those incurred when output increases through the expansion of factor inputs. In the case of capital, of course, costs are understood not only in terms of the new investment required, but also in terms of the consequent consumer abstinence.

Such costs had hardly been a deterrent in Stalin's day, but the dictator died on March 5, 1953. His successors have felt impelled to ameliorate Stalin's proverbially onerous priorities. They have been concerned with the need to foster morale and work incentives for an increasingly literate and sophisticated labor force. It is worth recalling that initial Soviet affirmations that consumption standards were to be increased were received in the West with a certain skepticism. In view of what had gone on under Stalin that is understandable. But per capita consumption, even according to relatively conservative Western calculations, has risen well above the abysmal Stalinian levels (Table 1).

Consumer benefits, nevertheless, have dwindled as output growth has slowed. In order to provide such benefits Stalin's successors have progressively had to limit further increases in the share of GNP invested. They have carefully avoided cutting the investment share, but growth of the volume of new investment has declined to a level near that of the slowing GNP. As a result, growth of the accumulated stock of capital on hand has also necessarily fallen (Table 1).

It is not always considered that the falling growth rate of the accumulated capital stock has itself contributed to the slowdown in output growth. With investment volume increasing at recent reduced rates, capital stock expansion might be expected to slow still more in the future: as the primers teach, increase of a stock responds only with a lag to varying tempos of a flow.

As a cause of slowing output growth, the falling tempo of capital stock growth is thus compounding the impact of widely noted adverse demographic trends, and the resulting retardation in growth of the labor force. The labor force expanded by 1.4 to 1.8 percent yearly during the sixties and seventies; its growth is expected to average only half or less of those tempos during the eighties and nineties (Feshbach 1983). Those increases that are materializing, moreover, are restricted predominantly to peripheral areas (Central Asia, Kazakstan, Transcaucasus). The population there is by all accounts reluctant to migrate to major industrial centers.

Paradoxically, output expansion has remained of the costly extensive sort. While factor input growth has slowed, factor productivity increases, which were never very noteworthy, have also declined. Recently, according to Western computations, they have been negligible, if not actually negative (Table 1; also CIA 1986:70). As a source of productivity increases, limited technological gains have tended to be offset by diminishing returns in the sphere of resource exploitation.

At any rate, with mineral deposits approaching exhaustion, production costs at older extractive sites have often increased sharply. The Russians have been able to turn to newer sources of minerals, but these are frequently of inferior quality or relatively costly otherwise because of their less favorable location and the resultant transportation and other infrastructure costs (compare Dienes 1983; Shabad 1983). Probably due in part to dubious development policies, the output of oil has recently been declining. It is still too early to conclude that the CIA's controversially pessimistic 1977 forecast at long last has been confirmed (Joint Economic Committee 1977), but, significantly, some three-fifths of the total Soviet petroleum output now comes from Siberia.

Soviet agriculture may have been beset for some time by more than its usual share of unfavorable weather, but here, too, diminishing returns must have been a drag on factor productivity growth. Under programs initiated during the Brezhnev era, agriculture has been absorbing one-fifth or more of all investment funds.[5] Yet output growth has tended to slow (Table 1). The total grain harvest during the last five-year plan actually fell well below that of the preceding one.[6]

The government, as the daily news reminds us, has seen fit to supplement the limited foodstuffs supplied by its ineffective agriculture with imports. The imports have been large scale, averaging for grain and grain products alone some $6.4 billion yearly during 1982–1984 (USDA Economic Research Service 1985). At this point, the contrast with Stalin's day could not be more dramatic: it is well known that the dictator exported grain in the face of acute domestic shortages.

The government for some time experienced little difficulty in making such purchases. Under the impact of successive oil shocks, the USSR found its principal export, oil, yielding a virtual plethora of the hard currency needed to pay for grain imports. Indeed, with the resultant earnings, it could purchase quantities of Western technology as well as foodstuffs (Cooper 1982). With domestic production faltering, however, oil supplies for export have not been as readily available as formerly. And, with the recent decline occurring in world oil prices, the government must now find imports of Western technology as well as foodstuffs not nearly as readily financed as they were in the past. The Soviet economy has thus suffered a hard blow at the very outset of the Gorbachev administration.

II

How, then, is Soviet economic growth to be accelerated? The crux of the answer, as Gorbachev already made clear at the very outset of his adminstration, is that the extensive growth process that Stalin introduced must at long last be abandoned. In its place the Russians must "achieve a decisive turn in the transition of the economy on to the rails of intensive growth" (*Pravda* March 12, 1985).

The need for such "intensification" of growth, as it has come to be called, became a cardinal theme of the General Secretary in one speech after another before the Party and elsewhere. And the same imperative now seems clearly embedded in a new five-year plan which calls for little or no speedup in the growth of investment volume, and yet projects accelerated growth of output.

The plan also projects tempos for output per worker that exceed those for output (Table 1). In the material sectors of the economy that are in question, the disparate acceleration of output and output per worker is even more pronounced in the supplementary guidelines for the period to the year 2000. The government apparently hopes to compensate fully, indeed more than fully, for expected declines in labor force growth through making gains in labor productivity. In time, a wholesale transfer of labor is to occur from material sectors to consumer services. Hitherto such services have been relatively neglected.

With all the stress that Gorbachev has placed on intensification, however, one must wonder to what extent the measures being initiated—whether in the plan or elsewhere—can accomplish that objective. An immediate concern is to accelerate "scientific-technical" progress. Assuring such progress "in every possible way" is rightly held to be "a key political and economic task," and diverse changes in planning arrangements are being made to that end. But thus far one principal change of plans has been essentially to expand the scope of a reform affecting enterprise rights and incentives, a reform introduced experimentally under Andropov. Although not without novel features, the reform is highly reminiscent of previous attempts to "perfect the economic mechanism," notably the Kosygin program of the midsixties. Such measures either proved difficult to implement or appear not to have proven especially effective. The government is also making increased use of interbranch coordinating agencies, and other rearrangements of a similarly limited kind.[7]

At the Party Congress, Gorbachev had reason enough to call for "radical reform" in the planning system. But, as he explained, such a reform must take "not a little time," and, judging from his often cryptic specifications, further changes will continue to be essentially of the "within system" sort. The unbelievably bureaucratic system of centralist planning inherited from Stalin will apparently remain substantially intact. That system has been peculiarly inhospitable to technological innovation. The pedestrian Soviet record on factor productivity would suggest as much, and voluminous Western research (for example, Berliner 1976; see also Bergson 1983) is abundantly corroborative.

To speed scientific-technological advance, the plan further projects, among other things, a sharp increase (by 40–45 percent) in the output of machinery and metalworking branches. Together with that, the plan forecasts, in comparison with the eleventh five-year plan, a doubling of the volume of retirements of superannuated industrial capital. To whatever degree such targets are achieved, the resultant speedup of capital replacement could be for the good of Soviet industrial facilities which are reportedly often obsolescent by Western standards.

III

In his appearances before the Party and elsewhere, Gorbachev has often dwelt on the "human factor" on which the success of his program must depend.

As he has explained, "in the final analysis, everything begins with lofty exactingness toward people, toward executives and toward all of us" (*Pravda* April 12, 1985). Judging by the continuing dismissals, even of top personnel, this is not mere rhetoric. Although Gorbachev has not been in office a full year, some two-fifths of all government ministers and state committee chairmen, and nearly one-third of all Party secretaries at the provincial (*oblast'*) level have been replaced (Radio Liberty Research January 22, 1986). Although the fact is not always made explicit, insufficient "exactingness" on the part of previous occupants of these offices is certainly among the causes for such wholesale removals.

In seeking greater "exactingness," Gorbachev is simply continuing, though apparently with more attention to shortcomings at high levels, a policy of tightening labor discipline that was initiated during Andropov's brief tenure (*Pravda* August 7, 1983; Radio Liberty Research October 16, 1985). Andropov's attempts to curb absenteeism and the like possibly contributed to the very limited acceleration of growth that was noted in 1983. Gorbachev's further efforts in this direction could well be similarly rewarding. Any resultant gains, though, seem almost inherently of a one-time sort, and cannot be expected to provide the long-term acceleration of growth that is now being sought.

In seeking greater "exactingness," the Gorbachev administration has launched a wide-ranging campaign to curtail one chronic source of indiscipline in particular: the well-known Russian proclivity to imbibe alcohol excessively and often inopportunely. Actually, here, too, Gorbachev is only following in the footsteps of Andropov, and the latter's measures aimed at curing alcohol abuse were hardly the first in the USSR. Gorbachev nevertheless appears to be proceeding in this sphere with special vigor. But, if previous experience is any guide, consequential and persistent restrictions on the consumption of alcohol will be difficult to achieve, even in a country where the government is the sole legal source of alcohol (compare Powell, 1985).

Along with the stick of discipline, the government is also offering the Soviet worker a carrot in the form of further gains in consumption. Living standards have risen much since Stalin's time, but labor incentives are, by every report, still impaired by proverbial shortages of the better-quality goods on which the worker might spend additional earnings. The new leadership is by no means oblivious to this situation, and should the Gorbachev administration be able to remedy such deficiencies, that would surely be a noteworthy achievement. While it seeks to accelerate growth, that is only a precondition for the "highest aim of the Party's economic strategy," which "was and remains the uninterrupted rise of the material and cultural level of life of the people" (*Pravda* November 9, 1985). In the light of such rhetoric, however, the consumer gains projected in the five-year plan (Table 1) must seem modest to many Soviet workers.[9] In the long term, the government promises decidedly larger benefits, but it would be surprising if such a program should meet with very enthusiastic response.

In any event, how much is achieved regarding consumption standards must turn on the government's ability to reinvigorate not only the economy generally, but agriculture in particular. Here, as elsewhere, "intensification" of growth is the watchword, and, again, in trying to gauge what might be achieved we must remind ourselves that weather is a deciding factor in Soviet agriculture. Should Gorbachev be favored by a run of good weather, the result would doubtless be a very real increase in per capita farm output. Barring such luck, however, recent and prospective developments provide little basis for optimism.

Thus, with argriculture remaining sluggish, the government has found it expedient in recent years to relax somewhat the long-standing constraints on operations of the renowned farm plots that collective and state farm workers are allowed to operate privately. Under a kind of putting-out system, for example, farm households may contract to raise livestock on behalf of collective and state farms. Such measures proably have been to the good, though their effect is difficult to quantify (*Sel'skaia Zhizn'* January 8, 1981; Radio Liberty Research August 2, 1985). Other more or less novel extensions of private enterprise, such as the itinerant group construction teams, which are of a semilegal nature, are similarly favorable.

Before becoming General Secretary, however, Gorbachev had supervised agriculture, generally on behalf of the Party. In that capacity he tended to identify himself, not with private enterprise, but with the so-called "brigade contract system." This scheme of allowing a degree of autonomy to farm workers is already employed on some scale (Radio Liberty Research February 8, 1984; February 18, 1985). As General Secretary, Gorbachev has emphatically also called for improved management of the vertically integrated "agro-industrial complex" that is now widely prevalent in the USSR (*Pravda* April 24, 1985). Prior to the Party Congress, the Gorbachev administration's most conspicuous action regarding agriculture was establishing a new state committee, under the All-Union Council of Ministers, to take over the responsibilities of five ministries that had hitherto overseen agricultural and related industrial affairs (*Pravda* November 23, 1985). Not very surprisingly, Gorbachev singled out the agro-industrial complex for particular attention at the Party Congress, though further and somewhat more novel shifts in agricultural planning were also hinted at.

IV

With the promulgation of the twelfth five-year plan, Mikhail S. Gorbachev has committed himself to rather ambitious goals for the Soviet economy. Still more ambitious are the targets set for the period at the end of this century.[9] A new, vigorous and purposeful administration may be able, in one way or another, to achieve momentary gains in economic performance. As time passes it could easily be disappointed, however, with what is achieved, and this, in turn, could lead to a reexamination of the course which it is now pursuing.

Indeed, there are reasons to wonder whether a reexamination has not already been initiated. In its annual plan for 1986 the government has adopted the goal of an increase in investment volume of 7.6 percent (*Pravda* November 27, 1985). That is far above the average growth of investment volume projected in the new five-year plan. The government may contemplate a sharp reduction in that tempo after 1986. Certainly, any full-scale reversion to Stalinist economics, with all that it implies, is out of the question at this stage. But perhaps the shift from extensive to intensive growth is not really expected to proceed so expeditiously after all. Correspondingly, the gains in consumer benefits might have to be even more modest than the new five-year plan would indicate, and in consequence gains in labor incentives would be weaker than projected.

The Soviet Union, according to estimates of the CIA (Joint Economic Committee 1985:50), is now spending as much as 13 to 14 percent of its GNP on defense. While promising the "further strengthening . . . of the military power of our native land," the twelfth five-year plan provides no details on prospective defense expenditures. Other goals in the plan might be taken to mean that the defense burden is projected to be no less in future than it is now.

However that may be, Gorbachev would doubtless find his task of accelerating economic growth distinctly easier if he could cut defense spending. He has declared again and again his interest in "halting the arms race," and he has been advancing wisely publicized proposals for arms control which give some substance to his avowals. What will be accomplished in this sphere, though, remains to be seen.

In seeking to speed growth, Gorbachev has called for "radical reform" in the Soviet planning system, but early in this administration *Pravda* editorialists (for example, in the issue of June 6, 1985) saw fit to remind its readers that public ownership and centralist planning continue to be integral features of Maxism-Leninism. Thus far none of the rearrangements that Gorbachev has initiated or projected appears especially at odds with that conception. But perhaps he will be induced to initiate some of the more fundamental planning shifts that many Western observers have long believed necessary. In that way, too, growth might possibly be promoted. Even the more enthusiastic proponents of the market, however, hesitate to guarantee such a result.

As the twelfth five-year plan gets under way, the Soviet economy is not in the dire straits that some Western commentary might suggest. Although growth has been depressed lately, the tempos achieved do not compare unfavorably with the post-oil shock rates of a number of Western countries.

The USSR has sought—and under Gorbachev apparently continues to seek—to assure that its military power is at least on a par with that of its great rival in the West. In pursuing that end, the leadership has doubtless achieved considerable success, but in so doing they have had to impose an onerous burden on an economy with a GNP per capita of little more than one-half that of the United States. And, granting that Western economies have recently not been at their best, the pedestrian economic performance of the USSR has been allowing only meager gratification of its citizens' aspirations for higher living standards. And this performance has hardly been in conformity with official ideological presuppositions concerning the economic prowess of the Soviet social system.

Thus Gorbachev has reason to seek urgently to accelerate growth, and he is not simply indulging in hyperbole when he considers a speedup to be of "paramount political, economic and social importance" (*Pravda* June 12, 1985). At best the program he has initiated would promise only limited success. It will be interesting to see just what further actions he may take and with what results.

Notes

[1] With the publication of the new five-year plan, Bergson (1985) has become rather dated, but I still find it of use.

[2] As approved by the Party Congress, and published in *Pravda* (March 9, 1986), the twelfth five-year plan is technically a "draft" (*proekt*), and has yet to be revised to take account of discussions of the Congress as well as at the meetings of local Party, union, and other groups that were held throughout the country after the draft was first published last November. Other such meetings, no doubt, are still to be held. Judging from previous experience, though, changes in the plan that are introduced henceforth are apt to be less than decisive.

To be precise, the draft emerging from the Party Congress already represents something of a revision of the one that was considered at the local Party and other meetings and at the Party Congress itself. According to a sample check, however, the changes from the latter draft, which appeared in *Pravda* (November 9, 1985), tend to be inconsequential.

The Party's program for consumer goods was initially elaborated upon in a separate document, *Pravda* (October 9, 1985).

[3] National income is the best-known case, but, as Table 1 makes clear, it is by no means the only case where Western scholars have found it necessary to compile data on Soviet economic trends alternative to those released officially. For national income, as well as for other aspects, the Western calculations are, where available, properly accorded priority. I also cite corresponding official data, however, since only they are congruent with published plan goals.

For long viewed exceptionally by Western scholars as reasonably reliable, the official data cited on investment have lately also come under attack. For present purposes, however, we will not be too far off the mark, I think, in referring to them. Western data for investment are more or less in accord with the official figures on that aspect, though regrettably they are not fully independent of them. Official data on the capital stock appear to continue to enjoy acceptance in the West.

On Soviet official statistics generally: Treml and Hardt (1972); on the official investment data, Nove (1981a, b); Cohn (1981); Hanson (1984).*

[4] I have set forth what I believe is a conventional view on comparative sources of Soviet and Western growth. It is not always considered, however, that relevant Soviet experience during the

* See also Chapter 12.

very earliest years of interest (for example, under the first two five-year plans) is much beclouded not only by flawed official data, but also by so-called "index number effects" of an extraordinary sort. That complexity apart, however, comparative sources of growth in the USSR and the West have yet to be studied as systematically as one might wish. See Bergson (1978; chs. 8, 9); Moorsteen and Powell (1966; chs. 9, 10); Cohn (1976); Kuznets (1966; ch. 2).

⁵ One-fifth, according to TSSU (1984; 358–359). Higher figures often cited presumably include investment in industrial branches, such as chemicals, which provide current inputs to agriculture.

⁶ TSSU (1986; p. 209). On the weather as a factor in recent Soviet agricultural performance see Amborziak and Carey (1982b).

⁷Among the shifts that Gorbachev sketched at the Congress, though, one concerning agriculture is perhaps relatively noteworthy, but I come to that below. On planning reforms under Gorbachev: *Pravda* August 4, 1985; October 26, 1985; November 9, 1985; February 28, 1986; Radio Liberty Research, August 1, 1983; April 16, 1984; September 21, 1984; March 27, 1985; October 3, 1985; January 22, 1986; February 11, 1986.

⁸ The near term gains are especially modest if account is taken of limitations in official data referred to above. Compare, for periods for which both sorts of data are available, the CIA figures on household consumption per capita with the official figures on real income per capita.

⁹ How much so is evident from the published goals for growth of output and output per worker, but the long-term goals only seem the more striking when one perceives how much, by implication, employment is to be curtailed in the material sectors in question: as calculated, I think plausibly, by V. Kostakov (as cited in Radio Liberty Research, January 22, 1986), by some 13 to 19 million over the period 1985–2000! Since consumer services employment will supposedly expand concomitantly, such a curtailment would not have to cause any mass unemployment, at least not any of more than a temporary "frictional" sort. But curtailment on any scale is quite at odds with Soviet practice hitherto, and even any sizable "frictional" unemployment would violate the long-standing Soviet commitment to full employment, a commitment only lately reaffirmed by Gorbachev (*Pravda* February 8, 1986).

References

Ambroziak, Russell A. and David W. Carey (1982b). "Climate and Grain Production in the Soviet Union." In Joint Economic Committee, U.S. Congress, *Soviet Economy in the 1980s: Problems and Prospects*. Part 2. Washington, D.C.: GPO.

Bergson, Abram (1978). *Productivity and the Social System: The USSR and the West*. Cambridge, Mass.: Harvard University Press.

—— (1983). "Technological Progress." In Bergson and Levine eds., *The Soviet Economy: Toward the Year 2000*. London: Allen and Unwin, pp. 34–78.*

—— (1985, November/December). "Gorbachev Calls for Intensive Growth." *Challenge*, 28 (5), 11–14.

Bergson, Abram, and Herbert S. Levine, eds. (1983). *The Soviet Economy: Toward the Year 2000*. London: Allen and Unwin.

Berliner, Joseph (1976). *The Innovation Decision in Soviet Industry*. Cambridge, Mass.: MIT Press.

CIA (Central Intelligence Agency) (1984). *Handbook of Economic Statistics 1984*. CPAS 84-10002. Washington, D.C.: CIA.

—— (1986). *Handbook of Economic Statistics, 1986*. CPAS 86-10002. Washington, D.C.: CIA.

* See Chapter 6.

Cohn, Stanley H. (1976, March). "The Soviet Path to Economic Growth: A Comparative Analysis." *Review of Income and Wealth*, 22 (1), 49–60.

—— (1981, April). "Response to Alec Nove 'A Note on Growth, Investment and Price Indexes'." *Soviet Studies*, 33 (2), 296–299.

Cooper, William H. (1982b). "Soviet Western Trade." In Joint Economic Committee, U.S. Congress, *Soviet Economy in the 1980s: Problems and Prospects*. Part 2. Washington, D.C.: GPO.

Dienes, Leslie (1983). "Regional Economic Development." In Bergson and Levine, eds., *The Soviet Economy: Toward the Year 2000*. London: Allen and Unwin, pp. 218–268.

Feshbach, Murray (1983). "Population and Labor Force." In Bergson and Levine, eds., *The Soviet Economy: Toward the Year 2000*. London: Allen and Unwin, pp. 79–111.

Hanson, Philip (1984, October). "The CIA, the TSSU and the Real Growth of Soviet Investment." *Soviet Studies*, 36 (4), 571–581.

JEC (Joint Economic Committee, U.S. Congress) (1977). *Soviet Economic Problems and Prospects*. Washington, D.C.: GPO.

—— (1982a). *USSR: Measures of Economic Growth and Development, 1950–1980*. Washington, D.C.: GPO.

—— (1982b). *Soviet Economy in the 1980s: Problems and Prospects*. Part 2. Washington, D.C.: GPO.

—— (1985). *Allocation of Resources in the Soviet Union and China – 1984*. Washington, D.C.: GPO.

Jensen, Robert G., Theodore Shabad, and Arthur W. Wright, eds. (1983). *Soviet Natural Resources in the World Economy*. Chicago: University of Chicago Press.

Kuznets, Simon (1966). *Modern Economic Growth*. New Haven, Conn.: Yale University Press.

Moorsteen, Richard and Raymond P. Powell (1966). *The Soviet Capital Stock 1928–1962*. Homewood, Ill.: Irwin.

Nove, Alec (1981a, January). "A Note on Growth, Investment and Price-Indices." *Soviet Studies*, 33 (1), 142–145.

—— (1981b, April). "A Reply to Stanley Cohn." *Soviet Studies*, 33 (2), 300–301.

Pitzer, John (1982a). "Gross National Product of the USSR, 1950–80." In Joint Economic Committee, U.S. Congress, *USSR: Measures of Economic Growth and Development, 1950–1980* Washington, D.C.: GPO. 3–168.

Powell, David E. (1985, Fall). "The Soviet Alcohol Problem and Gorbachev's 'Solution'." *The Washington Quarterly*, 8 (4), 5–16.

Pravda.

Radio Liberty Research.

Schroeder, Gertrude E. and M. Elizabeth Denton (1982a). "An Index of Consumption in the USSR." In Joint Economic Committee, U.S. Congress, *USSR: Measures of Economic Growth and Development, 1950–1980*. Washington, D.C.: GPO, 317–401.

Sel'skaia Zhizn'.

Shabad, Theodore (1983). "The Soviet Potential in Natural Resources: An Overview." In Jensen et al., eds. *Soviet Natural Resources in the World Economy*. Chicago: University of Chicago Press, 251–274.

Treml, Vladimir G. and John P. Hardt, eds. (1972). *Soviet Economic Statistics*. Durham, N.C.: Duke University Press.

TSSU (Tsentral'noe Statisticheskoe Upravlenie) (1985, and other volumes in the same series). *Narodnoe khoziaistvo SSSR v 1984g.* Moscow.

USDA (U.S. Department of Agriculture) (1985, April). Economic Research Service, *USSR Outlook and Situation Report* RS-85-4. Washington, D.C.: USDA.

Part III
Planning

9

Entrepreneurship under Labor Participation: The Yugoslav Case

In world affairs, Yugoslavia is often a focus of attention because of its strategic location between East and West and the ruling Communist Party's policy of nonalignment with either side. From an academic standpoint, though, it is perhaps of more interest as a country where the social system is socialist in a rather novel sense. Although private ownership of the means of production has been largely excluded, it has been superseded not by public ownership as commonly understood, but by "social ownership." The precise nature of that category is disputed by Yugoslavs themselves, but the devolution to workers of substantial responsibilities and rights normally associated with ownership is clearly among legal first principles.

Practice in Yugoslavia often diverges notably from legal doctrine, but the resulting social system still represents the most far-reaching application so far of labor participation in industrial administration. As such, it has attracted much attention from Western scholars. Yugoslav scholars too have not neglected their novel scheme; rather, they themselves have long been producing an impressive volume of research on it.

The resultant inquiries have only rarely focused on the impact of the new system on entrepreneurship (clearly a cardinal issue under any form of labor participation). Even though emphases tend to be elsewhere, however, the studies still often bear on that matter. Among other things, administrative and financial working arrangements that have been elucidated from other standpoints can be read, if only provisionally, as indicating entrepreneurial motivation. Not infrequently, they relate to entrepreneurship more generally. A review by a nonspecialist will hopefully provide further insight, while serving to underline knowledge gaps relating to an important theme.[1]

In economics, entrepreneurship means various things, but risk taking by producers is almost always a cardinal feature. Discussion of entrepreneurship in this sense often focuses on innovation (for instance, the intro-

To my profit, Stephen R. Sacks and Oliver E. Williamson commented on an earler version of this chapter. I alone, of course, am responsible for any errors.

duction of new technologies and products) where risk is apt to be especially important. Risk taking, however, is also of interest in other contexts. Here, I consider producer risk taking in general terms, though I refer to innovation as an outstanding case.

Producer risk taking occurs when new production units are established and when existing ones are operated. Of these two sorts of activities, the first is more often innovative than the second, but by inquiring into the operation of existing production units, we can draw on a relatively developed body of theoretical analysis. Here, I focus on risk taking by existing production units, although the founding of new ones cannot be entirely ignored.[2]

The Communist Party (since 1952, the League of Communists) came to power in Yugoslavia immediately after World War II. In economic affairs, the new government began as all other newly communist governments in Eastern Europe were doing: wherever feasible (and sometimes where not especially so), it simply replicated Soviet economic working arrangements. These included the characteristic Soviet hierarchical administrative system, with workers serving as hired employees more or less as in the West.

These arrangements were in effect in the summer of 1948, at the time of the famous break of Tito with Stalin. It was not until 1950–1952 that the government took steps to supplant them with a mechanism stressing labor participation. The system that now prevails, however, could hardly spring into existence full-grown. Rather, it evolved in the course of years, not always in a linear way, and through a bewildering number of reforms. Arrangements for labor participation nevertheless reached a relatively mature form by the mid-1960s. Measures introduced in 1964–1965 and referred to collectively as the "economic reform of 1965" are often cited specifically as initiating such an advanced phase. As it turns out, these measures were hardly definitive, but the experience after they were enacted is of particular interest here.

Our concern is especially with agencies administering production units. The chief of these is the enterprise (*preduzeće; poduzeće*). The enterprise, like a Western firm, is in charge of one or more production units. This has been the primary legal entity administering the Yugoslav economy. Or rather that has been so until the last years. In the ever-evolving Yugoslav system of labor participation, even the status of the enterprise has lately been in flux.

Theoretical Considerations

Labor participation is a theme that lends itself readily to theoretical analysis. At all events, it has often been so treated. Although often inspired by the experience in Yugoslavia, the analysis is notably abstract and is sometimes rather remote from Yugoslav practice. It can still serve here, however, as a point of departure.

Relevant aspects for the most part are by now fairly familiar and need be set forth only briefly. In this type of economy, firms administering production units obtain their inputs (apart from labor) and dispose of their outputs in conventional markets. These are usually envisaged as of a competitive sort. Each firm determines for itself the volume of nonlabor inputs it will purchase. With the labor at its disposal, the firm also determines the volume of its output.

The firm determines labor inputs too, but rather than hire workers in a market, it in effect coopts them as members of the enterprise collective. It is the collective that ultimately controls the firm. For their part, workers are free to seek employment in one firm or another in accord with their preferences and talents. It goes without saying that households are also free to spend their earnings as they wish in the market for consumer goods.

A "labor-managed" firm (LMF)—to use the usual designation for such an enterprise—might be motivated variously. In theoretical analyses, however, attention is most often focused on one particular hypothesis. Workers in an LMF are supposedly claimants to residual income that remains after expenses for nonlabor inputs are met. The individual worker, therefore, receives as his remuneration a share of this residual income rather than a conventional wage. According to the hypothesis referred to, the firm, in conducting its affairs, seeks to maximize residual income per worker.

To be precise, if Y denotes the firm's residual income, then

$$Y = p_x X - \sum_i q_i R_i \tag{1}$$

where X is the firm's output; p_x, its price; R_i, the ith nonlabor input employed; and q_i, the price of R_i. For simplicity, the formula is given for a firm producing a single product. For a durable capital good, q_i must be considered a rental charge, compounded of interest and depreciation. If for the moment the labor force is taken to be homogeneous, the hypothesis is that the firm pursues as a maximand,

$$y = \frac{p_x X - \sum_i q_i R_i}{L} \tag{2}$$

where L is the number of workers employed and thus sharing in residual income. Residual income is also designated as net income, although in that case the earnings in question are understood to be net before any charge for labor inputs.

The behavior produced by the pursuit of *y* as a maximand has been the subject of extensive analysis. Suffice it to say that for the LMF (as for its private-enterprise counterpart) there is generally a determinate equilibrium of inputs and outputs.[3] For nonlabor inputs, the specific conditions for such equilibrium are similar for the two sorts of firms. Thus, as the primers teach, the private-enterprise firm employs each nonlabor input up to the point where the value of its marginal product equals its price. That is so for nonlabor inputs generally, even though for durable capital goods (which tend to be fixed in the short run) the equality can be realized only in the long run. In equilibrium, the value of marginal product and price must also be equal for nonlabor inputs in an LMF.

For a private-enterprise firm, however, that equality also obtains for labor inputs. For the LMF, the corresponding equilibrium requirement has the novel form:

$$p_x \cdot \text{MPL} = y \qquad (3)$$

where MPL is the marginal productivity of labor. This one singular feature is rather consequential. Because of it, the response of the labor-managed firm to changes in the prices of nonlabor inputs and the prices of outputs is apt to be different from that of the private enterprise firm; indeed, often paradoxically so.[4]

The foregoing refers to the equilibrium of the firm. Imposition of the usual requirement that prices are at clearing levels leads at once to the concept of the equilibrium for a market. As was done for a private-enterprise system, conditions are also elaborated for equilibrium for the economy in general. In addition to the simultaneous clearing of all markets, there must be no opportunity for workers to gain by leaving one firm for another that is prepared to coopt them, nor any incentive for firms in one industry to shift to another or for workers to leave firms that employ them in order to create new ones. The opportunity to form new firms supposedly also precludes involuntary unemployment.

In the diverse sorts of equilibria that thus materialize, only one feature, already implied, merits note here: the marginal value product (and hence earnings) of labor may differ in different firms. That is almost inevitable in the short run, when enterprise capital stocks, the particular firms in any industry, and the technologies that they use are given. In time, workers whose earnings suffer because of limitations in the capital goods and technologies they employ have an opportunity to remedy such deficiencies, either within the firms where they are employed or by creating new ones. By shifting their firm's output mix or industry, they might also repair any shortfall caused by the adverse state of demand. Such adjustments, however, might take a very long time.

At this point, then, the labor-managed economy is in dramatic contrast to the private-enterprise economy, where the marginal-value product and earnings of labor tend towards parity in different firms even in the short run. There is also a corresponding contrast of the two systems from the standpoint of efficiency, which requires that marginal-value products of any factor should be the same in all uses. This fact has often been stressed (no doubt properly) in the normative appraisal of labor management, but the comparative efficiency of that system and the private-enterprise economy is a complex and manysided matter that need not be systematically pursued here.[5]

I have been considering an economy with a homogeneous labor force. Since the labor force is homogeneous, all of the workers in any firm share equally in net income. Should income shares vary because of differences in labor skills and tasks, the firm's maximand is usually understood to be net income per standard worker. A standard worker is labor of a particular kind. Other kinds of work are expressed in terms of it by reference to their relative shares in net income per unit of labor. The comparative shares accruing to labor of different kinds might be determined independently by each firm, but in maximizing earnings per standard worker, each firm seeks to employ different kinds of labor so that their marginal productivities are proportional to their relative earnings per unit of labor. Different firms should also be impelled by market forces to align their schedules of relative earnings for different kinds of labor.[6]

Attention has been focused on the competitive case—strictly speaking, the case of perfect competition, in which each firm is too small to have any control over input or output prices. In theoretical analyses, alternative sorts of markets where firms exercise monopoly power have also been analyzed. As might be expected, monopoly power is in itself a source of divergencies of labor marginal products in different firms, but that, of course, is also true in the private-enterprise system.[7]

Attention up to this point has been focused on an essentially static economy. As in the private enterprise firm, the LMF must often decide on matters involving a choice between income in different time periods. The question is thus posed as to whether, and to what extent, income should be retained to finance investment. This question is not central here, but a basic aspect is the nature of the firm's maximand when income accrues over time to a staff whose personal composition may shift. That is also a matter that might be (and in theoretical writings, has been) treated variously, but one hypothesis is especially plausible: the enterprise is administered in the interest of the current collective.

To the extent that different workers might anticipate different tenures and have different time preference rates, the implied maximand could still be complex, but a corollary is fairly evident: the current staff has only limited interest in building up their equity in the firm by plowing back current income. The resulting increase in the capital stock, it must be understood, must remain indefinitely with the firm. In other words, the capital is not vested with the workers who generate it, and so does not accrue to them on their departure from the firm. Hence, if the current staff is to retain and invest earnings, rather than distribute them among themselves, they must earn a rate of return that compensates not only for their time preference but for the nonrecovery of principal.

Formally, let the workers' desired savings S be represented by a function

$$S = F(r) \tag{4}$$

where r is the rate of earned interest. Assuming that the principal is recovered, r also corresponds to the workers' marginal rate of time preference. Then the desired saving can be expressed as a function

$$S = F^*(R) \tag{5}$$

where R is the rate needed to induce S when principal is not recoverable. It can be shown that

$$R = \frac{r(1 + r)^n}{(1 + r)^n - 1} \tag{6}$$

Here n is the expected tenure of the current staff. I refer to a simple case where $S(r)$ and r are constant from year to year. With r as the rate of discount, an income stream of r times a principal sum over any period has a present value equal to the principal—provided the principal is recoverable. Without recovery of principal, the same equality obtains for an income stream of R times a principal sum over the period n. Evidently R (let us call it the adjusted marginal rate of time preference) must exceed r. Depending on n, the margin between the two rates could be wide. The margin declines, however, as n increases.

Should staff members withdraw earnings, they might still have the option, say, of depositing funds in a savings bank at interest. Since the principal presumably would be recoverable in that case, formula (4) indicates the individual savings that would occur in that way for any r equal to savings deposit interest. From formula (6), we see that self-financing would supersede such individual savings only if the rate of return on enterprise investment equals or exceeds the corresponding R.

Even so, self-financing of investment could occur depending on the actual rate of return, but from the standpoint of the current staff, such action might still be groundless if another option were open. If unrestricted credit were available, the current staff would prefer to borrow rather than to finance marginal investments internally whenever the market rate of interest is, for the volume of investment in question, less than R.[8]

I have been considering the labor-managed firm as it functions in a riskless world. For our purposes, the alternative environment where there is uncertainty is of particular interest, but again, what is chiefly in question is the enterprise's maximand. In theoretical writings, attention has focused on a natural extension of the maximand considered in the nonstochastic case: the concern of the firm is to maximize the expected utility of its staff members. Suppose, for convenience, that reference is again to a single period, that members of the collective derive income only from work for the enterprise, and that all have the same von Neumann-Morgenstern utility function, $U(y)$. The maximand of the firm is then[9]

$$y^* = EU(y) \tag{7}$$

One implication is obvious but nevertheless important here. It merits more attention than it has received in theoretical writings to date: In order to choose risky over safe options, the LMF requires a higher risk premium than a comparable private-enterprise one. That is to say, the LMF is more prone to risk avoidance than a comparable private enterprise one. Such a pattern derives from the fact that workers are apt to be less affluent than owners of a private enterprise and should, therefore, be subject to a greater degree of risk aversion on that account. A marked tendency to risk avoidance on the part of the LMF is offset to an extent because losses and gains are distributed over many workers, but a corresponding distribution over many owners is also realized in the corporate form of private enterprise.

Given that kind of organization, owners of a private enterprise are less inclined to avoid risk if they can diversify their investments. To achieve a comparable diversification, workers in the LMF would have to be members of many firms at the same time. Such diversification is not very feasible.

Theory teaches that, other things being equal, the greater risk premium that obtains in choices among stochastic alternatives, the less efficient (in a stochastic sense) is the allocation of the community's resources. Among decision makers with the same utility functions, the higher the risk premium, the greater the degree to which opportunities for costless gains from insurance against risk remain unexploited. The difference between the two sorts of enterprises in posture toward risk, therefore, are in that sense a source of economic waste.[10]

This posture toward risk might be manifest in various forms, but it should be particularly prominent in decisions regarding innovation, for risk is especially important there. Losses due to excessive risk premiums, therefore, should take the form of foregone innovations.

To finance investment out of retained earnings, the enterprise must earn a differential return (possibly a sizeable one) over the rate available to individual workers if the income in question is distributed to them and they deposit it in a savings account. If workers are averse to risk, the premium must be larger, for savings invested in the firm are necessarily at risk.

Theoretical writings are not too explicit about the status of banks in the labor-managed economy, particularly whether they too are to be labor-managed. In whatever way they are organized, the government presumably must reserve for itself revenues generated by the expansion of the money supply. The government will also earn interest on any funds it contributes to capital markets. If, as is appropriate here, natural resources are assumed to be publicly owned, rentals for their use would accrue to the government as well. Should the government require still more revenue, there is, or course, no bar to its levying taxes. As in a private-enterprise economy, however, these ideally must be lump-sum taxes; otherwise inefficiency is unavoidable for well-known reasons. The incidental result is that the government must ideally refrain from varying its levies in such ways as the use of surtaxes on high incomes, which would limit variations in labor earnings and in effect the incidence of risk on workers.[11]

All this, however, presupposes that workers in the LMF are indeed residual claimants to income. As such, like owners of a private enterprise, they become in effect primary risk-bearers, and (at least within presumably wide limits) fully absorb losses and gains from the enterprise's activities. Worker earnings, however, could thus be subject to a correspondingly wide fluctuation. In a community committed to labor management, one inevitably wonders whether such fluctuations would be tolerated.

From the standpoint of realism, one may wonder too about the theoretical neglect of management. By implication, management is simply another kind of labor.[12] In private enterprise, management needless to say often has a critical role of its own, especially where entrepreneurial activity is involved.

I said at the outset, however, that the theoretical analysis of the labor-managed firm is notably abstract. The foregoing queries only underline that fact. At any rate, in inquiring here into risk taking by the Yugoslav enterprise, it seems inappropriate to proceed as tends to be done regarding almost any aspect of Western enterprise behavior, that is, to take a theoretical maximum as a datum and to try to explain or predict the firm's behavior in that light. Rather a principal concern must be to explore the nature of the novel working arrangements in question and to try to gauge on that basis how enterprise motivation might be expected to compare with that depicted in theory. So far as a divergence from theory is indicated, we must also consider what the consequences might be for risk taking.

But, for the Yugoslav no less than for the Western firm, expectations must ultimately be tested empirically. In a review such as this, we must consider not only working arrangements but conduct. That is in order even though research on the latter aspect seems still to be at an especially early stage.

I alluded earlier to very recent shifts in Yugoslav working arrangements. The latest, while partially legislated in 1971, were only implemented on any scale after they were embodied in the new constitution of 1974 (Yugoslavia's third under communist rule) and in further legislation of 1976. These 1974–1976 reforms have still not been fully applied, but even if (as now seems doubtful) they were fully applied, they would often leave previous working arrangements intact. I will refer, however, to those earlier arrangements as the pre-BOAL system (PBS). The Basic Organization of Associated Labor (BOAL) is a cardinal feature of the 1974–1976 reforms.

Recall, though, that among earlier arrangements, those that prevailed after the mid-1960s are of particular concern. Unless otherwise indicated, these will be the ones under discussion. I will first explore PBS in some depth, and then consider how matters of interest may be affected by the 1974–1976 reforms. Among working arrangements concerning the enterprise, of special interest here are those affecting internal authority, external constraints, and income disposition. I consider each aspect in turn, and then examine in the light of such arrangements what is to be concluded as to enterprise motivation and risk taking.

Authority within the Firm

In theoretical analysis, just what is meant by labor management is more often implied than explicit. The presupposition, however, is clearly that workers can impose their will on the firm where they are employed, and so assure that the decisions taken will serve their interests. According to Yugoslav legal doctrine under PBS, the question thus posed is readily settled: authority within the Yugoslav firm under PBS was vested in the workers employed there. The enterprise was supposed to conform to existing law, but within its confines the workers were ultimately in charge.

We must heed here that proverbial legalistic view. The siting of ultimate authority in workers employed in an enterprise is the legal hallmark of the form of industrial organization to which the Yugoslavs came to be committed early on: labor management or, in their parlance, self-management (*samoupravljanje*).[13] Our concern, however, is not so much with doctrine as with practice, particularly the practice under PBS. That practice is by now a familiar theme, but the facts on it are rather complex, perhaps more so than some Yugoslav, as well as Western observers, seem to urge. Even a summary account, therefore, must set forth the available evidence, if only in the briefest terms. When an elusive question such as labor management is at issue, it is not surprising that the evidence is ambiguous, or at least difficult to interpret.

If workers are in fact in control of the self-managed firm (SMF) clearly one requirement is that the political process within the firm must be of a democratic sort. Workers thus must be able to determine freely either the policies pursued or the authorities who act for them. This requirement supposedly was met under PBS by means of the principal instrumentality through which the collective of workers exercised authority, the famous workers' council. Legally established procedures for electing members to the council were, by the mid-1960s, democratic in any usual sense of that word. Thus, voting was by secret ballot on candidates nominated at a general meeting of workers. Four sponsors sufficed for any nomination.[14]

Impressive as these arrangements were, they did not always prevail. For many years the trade union had been authorized to determine nominees for the council. Although a competing slate could be presented on the petition of ten percent of the work force, that had been rare. After the mid-1960s, the union was no longer authorized to shape council elections in this way, but it would be surprising if it thereby lost all of its influence. If it did, it soon regained it in some degree. These developments, however, will be considered later as part of the 1974–1976 reforms. An obvious anomaly under self-management, Yugoslav trade unions were mainly a post–World War II creation. Like the Party, with which they are closely allied, they clearly have a quasi-official status.

While acting in behalf of the collective, the council under PBS, was served in turn by a board of management. Limited in size (a membership of five was legally minimal) and meeting more frequently than the council itself, the management board consisted of members of the council together with the enterprise director, who could not serve on the workers' council. The director apart, the members of the management board had been elected by the council from the earliest days.

As for the designation of the director, here again participation by the collective was initially minimal. However, by 1965 the council had a major part in the process. This included substantial representation on a nomination committee, and the right to determine finally the appointment actually made.[15] On the other hand, the government of the locality or commune where the enterprise was located also participated. Although, under PBS, the government no longer formally had the decisive voice it once had, its factual role (for reasons to be explained) must have been consequential. At least at this important point, then, democracy within the firm was somewhat flawed, though by no means fatally so.

How democratic a political process will be depends also on the information available to the electorate. From that standpoint, self-managment surely qualifies as democratic; in fact, the volume of information made available to workers is a subject of complaint in Yugoslavia. It is held, no doubt with some basis, that the worker can hardly digest the often complex and bulky materials supplied to him.[16] Reference is made particularly to workers on the council, but such materials must also have been available (and no more digestible) to workers generally. Granting that, however, the need to provide such information, and its actual dissemination, must have constituted a constraint on willful executives. It has been plausibly argued (Granick 1975, pp. 378 *ff*) that one of the principal gains of the worker under self-management is his enhanced access to information.

In describing the political process within the SMF, I have outlined the diverse entities (the collective, the workers' council, the management board, and the director) that together were legally responsible under PBS for the operation of the enterprise. In earlier years, the trade union also had an important part in the enterprise's affairs—particularly in the election of council members. Under PBS, the union played a more general role in the enterprise's affairs, though usually it did not have independent operational authority. That was also true of the Party, but representatives of the union and the Party in effect acted for quasi-official organizations of national scope. Further discussion of their role, therefore, is best deferred to the section where I refer to external controls over the enterprise.

What is chiefly in question here, then, is the comparative roles in the enterprise of the different entities legally responsible for its functioning. This has been a subject of inquiry by Yugoslav scholars themselves. Although the scholars deal with power within the firm in general, their studies bear at once on the roles of organizational entities referred to. The precise periods to which reference is made is not always indicated, but the bulk of the inquiries clearly refer, among other things, to circumstances under PBS.[17]

Of particular interest are findings such as those Gorupić (1978) has summarized in this way:

> Empirical investigations thus far conducted on the structure of influence in the enterprise have shown that the formal self-managing structure often conceals concrete relations that are inconsistent with the idea of self-management. The enterprise's professional management has excessive influence, while workers have too little. Research has also shown that workers are not satisfied with their role, and that they demand the realization of their self-management rights (p. 131).

In the studies in question, this gap between formal structure and concrete relations is usually, though not always, found.[18] Sometimes it is distinctly wider than that described by Gorupić. According to Županov (1975), the inquiries even show no difference in the distribution of "executive power" in the surveyed Yugoslav organizations as compared with the American organizations: an oligarchic pattern was found in both of them. This finding in itself should not be disturbing since "executive power in democratic organizations usully is distributed in accord with the pyramid structure of authority." However, basically the same pattern was found in the area of "legislative power" where, according to Katz and Kahn a completely different distribution should be expected; even here the top executives as a group are more powerful than the workers' council. True enough, the workers' council is perceived to have a "medium" amount of power, but further analysis revealed that the two most influential groups within the council itself are top executives and staff experts, while blue-collar workers are the least influential group (pp. 82–83).

Coming from scholars in a society like that studied, these are striking assessments. However, in weighing their import we must consider that none of the studies in question was of a comparative sort, rather, data were assembled on circumstances in the Yugoslav firm alone. Županov's conclusion on the comparative distribution of power there and in the U.S. firm, therefore, represents something of an extrapolation, though certainly an illuminating one from a distinguished sociologist.

The inquiries, moreover, utilize diverse indicators of power distribution, of which the principal one is simply the manner in which that distribution is perceived by workers generally. However, an investigation of authority within the enterprise on that basis has its limitations. One suspects that many workers might perceive executives as possessing cardinal authority even if they performed only delegated functions. Reports to the effect that the executives themselves saw their role as preeminent (Županov 1969, pp. 251–252; Županov 1973) are perhaps more illuminating. Also ambiguous are the results of further Yugoslav inquiries focusing on such aspects as the sponsorship of proposals considered and adopted by the workers' council and the extent to which different groups participated in council discussions.[19] Probably one of the more telling indications, however, of restricted worker influence is the reported wholesale abstention on the part of worker members from voting in the workers' council; however, reference is made only to the experience in a single enterprise.[20]

In Yugoslavia, unlike in much of the socialist world, labor strikes are not illegal. In affirming this, Yugoslav officials also affirm that such strikes are also not legal, but they do occur and not infrequently. Some 1526 were reported as occurring during the years 1961–1969. In 37 strikes during 1967–1969 for which there are data on the number of participants, the number of workers involved totaled 57,597.[21]

Strikes are an obvious oddity where workers are supposedly bosses. Those in Yugoslavia are doubtless properly construed (as they have been even in Yugoslavia[22]) as still another evidence of the breach between principle and practice regarding self-management. Paradoxically, however, they may also indicate that under that system, workers' residual authority is often greater than it might have been otherwise. Thus, though the strikes were typically unsponsored even by unions, they were usually of brief duration. Yet, they very often culminated in the workers' essential demands being met. The reason for such easy success, Županov (1978–A) conjectures, may be that:

> Yugoslav executives are insecure about their power, which is very great in actuality but modest in its institutional definition. Thus, much of their power is illegitimate and makes them extremely vulnerable in case of a strike. That is, a strike puts executives on the spot by exposing publicly and dramatically the illegitimacy of their power; this in turn generates an urgent need to bring the strike to an end quickly regardless of cost (pp. 395–396).

As in the West workers strike most often over money—the amount of their earnings and the manner of their determination. These are matters over which the authority of Yugoslav enterprise executives has been relatively constrained, so the strikes need not always signify the kind of usurpation of power by executives that Županov refers to. Also, even Yugoslav scholars might not take enough into account that Western business enterprises do not characteristically need to bring a "strike to an end quickly regardless of cost." Given such an imperative, however, managerial personnel must be concerned to avoid strikes to begin with. By the same token, workers' interests and attitudes might have to be heeded even when not effectively expressed through formal representational procedures.

Authority within the Yugoslav SMF is among the topics dealt with in several case studies completed by foreign scholars who have visited in that country. It has also sometimes been of concern to foreign journalists. The resulting accounts are at best only suggestive, but a rather intricate pattern seems to emerge. Executive domination is certainly among the situations reported, but a meaningful and effective involvement of workers is not rare.[23]

I have been considering authority within the firm under PBS in general terms. Though we seek only a summary view, we must bear in mind that Yugoslav workers, like workers elsewhere, are more interested in some matters than in others. Judging from Yugoslav inquiries into the subject, ordinary workers have probably been relatively influential in some spheres of particular concern. I reserve for later discussion working arrangements as to income disposition (*raspodela dohotka*), but note that these working arrangements, understandably, were one area where the collective had an enhanced role.[24] Among other such spheres were labor discipline, dismissals, and working conditions.[25]

Županov (1974) has characterized the varying meanings of labor participation in different contexts in a related but different way:

Recent investigations into the problem of participation in industry, though far from being systematic and comprehensive, seem to suggest the following tentative conclusions: (a) intensity of participation is normally higher in a "crisis" than in "normal" circumstances; (b) participation is more extensive when human and "internal politics," rather than functional problems, are under discussion; and (c) participation is more intensive when distribution of personal income, rather than production problems, are in debate (p. 186).

I have referred so far to *the* workers' council. As self-management was organized initially, there usually was, in fact, only a single council in an enterprise. In the course of time, however, councils were set-up in enterprise subdivisions—in different plants, if there were more than one in the enterprise, in departments within plants, and possibly in even more limited sectors.[26] In promoting this development, the government clearly intended to enable the ordinary worker to participate more effectively in the firm's affairs. Evidence adduced here on the limitations of such participation bears, however, on circumstances where the proliferation of workers' councils was already relatively advanced. At any rate, the impact of that trend on the workers' role in decision making has probably been modest (Neuberger and James 1973, p. 275; Granick 1975, p. 378). That will be of interest when we turn to the 1974–1976 reforms.

I have been outlining evidence as to authority within the firm under PBS. The conclusion must be, I think, that power gravitated to executive personnel to a distinctly greater degree than official doctrine allows, though perhaps not quite as much as often held, even by Yugoslav scholars. Ordinary workers were probably more influential in some matters than others. Circumstances also varied between enterprises.

Under PBS, who was the entrepreneur? Such a question is rarely easy to answer in the Western business firm; it is no easier here. In the conduct of any enterprise, Yugoslav or Western, risk taking is likely to be especially characteristic of technological and product innovation. In the West, executives usually play a key role in such matters, and the level of authority engaged is often commensurate with the magnitude of the financial commitment entailed for the firm. In the SMF under PBS, executives could hardly do otherwise. This is inevitable, if only because of their hierarchical status and their resultant command over and ability to construe relevant technical information. Such capabilities are especially important when new technologies and products are in question. Yet innovations might easily impinge on labor staffing and earnings—matters of particular concern to workers generally. Where they did, the collective could become involved, one way or another, in the decision-making process. As illuminating case studies illustrate (Adizes 1971, ch. 4), the involvement might be more than perfunctory.

Here as elsewhere, then, self-management hardly conformed to Yugoslav doctrine. However, granting the cardinal role of executives, workers were by no means impotent. These facts will have to be considered when we turn later to motivation and risk taking.

Enterprise Autonomy

In theory, labor management derives its significance for resource allocation from the fact that the firm itself is an essentially autonomous entity. That is so in stochastic circumstances, among other things. The enterprise must procure inputs and dispose of outputs in markets, but it determines for itself how to respond to whatever trading currents confront it. At this point, then, the labor-managed firm is simply a replica of the firm in a private-enterprise economy.

Turning to the question that this raises concerning Yugoslavia, the government in organizing the economy initially reproduced the economic working arrangements of the USSR. Among these—and basic to all else— was the famous Soviet system of coordinating and directing enterprises bureaucratically through the extensive use of obligatory physical targets. Under these circumstances, enterprise autonomy was limited indeed. However, in turning subsequently to labor participation, the Yugoslav government also dismantled the elaborate controls erected previously. Of concern here, therefore, is not the initial system of centralist planning, but the mechanism that supplanted it.

That, it is often assumed, is a form of market socialism, where coordination and direction are accomplished essentially through market processes. Although economic plans are still formulated, these supposedly are of the indicative sort that excludes obligatory targets for the enterprise. The corollary is that the Yugoslav SMF has in fact approached the LMF of theory with respect to autonomy. Although only rarely explored systematically, such suppositions are doubtless broadly valid with respect to PBS (on which I still focus). Under that scheme, however, the enterprise was still appreciably constrained, and sometimes in ways that could possibly affect risk taking. I again defer discussion of one sphere in which that was so, that of income disposition.

Under PBS, another such sphere was price determination. In theoretical analyses of labor management, prices are generally market determined, but it does not matter for the functioning of the firm if the government determines them instead. If market forces rule, prices are data for the enterprise in any event except where there is monopoly power. Should the government fix prices to clear markets, the enterprise might behave in the same way in one case as in the other.[27]

The stipulation is essential, however. If it is not met, the enterprise might behave rather differently from the way theory envisages. It should be observed, therefore, that although centralist planning had long since been abandoned, the government under PBS still regulated prices. The regulation was of varying, but usually fairly extensive scope. It took diverse forms, including determination of fixed prices and trade margins, ceiling prices, requirement of prior approval of price changes, episodic overall price freezes, establishment of maximum benchmark increases, price rollbacks, and so on.[28]

More concretely, what was involved can be judged from the fact that a principal element of the economic reform of 1965, which ushered in PBS, was a radical restructuring of prices carried out in July 1965. The restructuring followed a brief price freeze. Producers' prices of some 65 percent of industrial output were subject to controls of one sort or another by the end of 1966. Of the total increase in living costs in the first quarter of 1973 (5.5 percent), nearly one-fifth manifested initiatives or approvals of federal authorities, and about one-third, initiatives or approvals of republican or local governments (Organization for Economic Cooperation and Developments, OECD, 1969, pp. 19–21; 1974, p. 18).

Government regulation of prices is of interest here, to repeat, only to the extent that markets are not cleared in consequence. Given the scope and nature of the Yugoslav regulation, it would be surprising if this were not often the case. Observers rarely report the kinds of retail-shop sellouts and queues that are so characteristic elsewhere in the socialist East; however, shortages and informal rationing sometimes occurred even for intermediate products, at least in the early years (Montias 1967, p. 405).

The economic reform of 1965 embraced, along with a revision of the price structure, an extensive reorganization of the banking system. Enterprises, however, continued to obtain the bulk of their new capital (beyond what they generated for themselves) in the form of bank credits. Such credits were used to meet long-term as well as short-term needs. This mode of external financing is in contrast to the traditional Eastern one involving budgetary grants (at least for long-term needs). The Yugoslavs themselves employed the latter form of financing under centralist planning.

Under the circumstances, the government necessarily came to use the banking system, itself of shifting structure, as an instrument for assuring macroeconomic balance. The more or less persistent inflation and sharply fluctuating tempos of change in physical volume testify that the effort was not exactly successful (Horvat 1971; OECD 1974). Of more concern here, however, is another closely related, but still distinct, function that the banking system was called on to perform.

Under PBS, the economic plans of the government were essentially indicative—that is, they did not include obligatory physical targets for the enterprise.[29] In the still imperfect state of planning of the time, one wonders how much of a constraint the plans (especially the longer-range ones) could be even for government entities themselves. The plans nevertheless did embrace diverse sectoral as well as aggregative targets, and banks were expected to heed them in granting credits. Whatever the degree of implementation of plan targets per se, political entities at all levels had development policies that they called on the banks to help promote. Government agencies also called on the banks to administer so-called earmarked funds, whose use might be restricted to particular regions or branches, or possibly to an even more limited sphere. In this way, government agencies could buttress to a degree their plans and development policies.

As for banks, they charged interest on their credits, but the rates levied were subject during the period in question to a ceiling, initially 10.0 percent and, later, 8.0 percent. With industrial producers' prices rising annually an average of 7.3 percent during 1966–1973, the banks (not surprisingly) were often able to impose higher rates, one way or another. For practical purposes, credit rationing was also widespread.[30] Not surprisingly, too, banks came to occupy an important role in the enterprise's affairs. In one Yugoslav empirical inquiry into self-management, banks outrank all other entities as an external influence on the enterprise.[31]

Just what this meant is not entirely clear, but bank credit policy was obviously politicized. Enterprise autonomy must have suffered as a consequence, if only from an expedient concern for orienting investment projects to bank, and ultimately political, interests. That was made more likely by the fact that, whereas the enterprise itself might be among the founders of, and hence have a voice in, the affairs of the bank, that was also true of political entities.

Under PBS, then, bank and political influence on investments must have been a constraint on enterprise autonomy in addition to that represented by price regulation. One of the political entities that had a voice in bank affairs, furthermore, was the commune government. Enjoying, as explained, a special status as a participant in the recruitment of the enterprise director, that agency was also a frequent sponsor of the firm when it was established, and a source of aid when it experienced financial and other difficulties. It was thus in an especially favorable position to influence enterprise investment activity. It apparently had an even larger role than that—it was able, as Županov (1974) put it, "to widen its influence on the business and personnel policies of the enterprise through formal and, to a greater extent, through informal means" (p. 190).

Banks and the commune government were significant constraints on enterprise autonomy, but two other external entities were also influential. Under PBS, one of these (the trade union) no longer had the formal status that it once had. However, it probably still had some role in council elections. Like strikes, a transparent incongruity under self-management, the union also had an impact more generally, if only in informal ways (Wachtel 1973, pp. 77–79).

To the extent that it did, however, it usually acted as a surrogate for another quasi-official body, the Party. As for that organization, it too was generally without legal responsibilities. Indeed, as seen by Edward Kardelj, a principal architect of self-management (quoted in Rusinow 1978, p. 217), the Party was supposed to play only a severely restricted part in the enterprise's affairs:

> The internal decision making and acts . . . of the bodies of self-management in working organizations must not be interfered with by Party organizations and their bodies except by means of political action, i.e., by persuasion, help, by providing information to the public, education, and similar methods.

As rhetoric, Kardelj's 1966 statement on the Party's role under self-management was by no means novel, but reformist currents of the time embraced politics as well as economics. Although the Party was once relatively potent, it clearly experienced something of a decline as PBS was being put in place. That trend encountered resistence within the Party, and was in due course reversed. But while it prevailed, Kardelj's prescription for Party behavior within the self-managed firm was more important than might be supposed.[32] We must read in that light further results of Yugoslav inquiries into the perceptions of power within the enterprise under circumstances prevailing in 1968–1969. The Party was seen as outranked by higher executive personnel. That was the perception of executives themselves, as well as of workers generally.[33]

Such results must in a degree reflect enduring forces. Whatever the larger political currents of the moment, Party activists had to be concerned not only with Party directives in general, but with the material success of the firm. However that might be construed, the Party activists had to temper their strivings for influence. The result, predictably, was that the executive who could manage successfully acquired "great power over the organizational environment."[34]

The director of the enterprise, of course, was himself often a member of the Party (Wachtel 1973, p. 80; Dirlam and Plummer 1973, p. 52; Granick 1975, pp. 441–442; Sirc 1979, p. 186). What is in question, however, is the degree to which the director was subservient to the Party organization in the firm. Often he was not.

The commune government, as noted previously, was a source of outside influence on the self-managed firm under PBS, partly because the commune government often sponsored the fledgling enterprise. More generally, under PBS, a political body at any level might be the founder of a new enterprise—which is to say that, among other things, it either had to arrange for the firm's financing or supply the needed capital itself (Sacks 1973). Service in that capacity, therefore, could be a source of influence for other political agencies as well as the commune. Enterprises, however, were also often founded by other enterprises. In principle, a group of citizens could also found an enterprise, although that procedure was of relatively limited importance.[35]

This chapter is concerned with risk taking. Risk taking is especially important in decisions on investment projects such as those that apply novel technologies or introduce new products. The SMF under PBS, we may conclude, had substantial autonomy, but regarding such investment projects it probably had to defer to some degree to authorities outside the firm, particularly banks and the local government. Even so, enterprise autonomy was much greater than it generally is under Eastern socialism, even in Yugoslavia itself, when it was under centralist planning. That is one of the more important ways in which market socialism, as found in Yugoslavia under PBS, differed from centralist planning. In trying later to gauge how the self-managed firm might behave in the face of risk, we must keep in mind the foregoing facts.

Income Disposition

A basic feature of the LMF of theory is the manner in which labor earnings are determined. Rather than being paid conventional money wages, workers have at their disposal the balance of income after nonlabor charges are met. If they wish, they can save part of this for use by the firm; the rest is available for distribution among them, supposedly in accord with their productive contributions. With all workers acquiring in this way the status of residual claimants, they also become primary risk-bearers, absorbing both gains and losses from varying performance. The behavior of the firm under stochastic conditions is shaped decisively by these arrangements.

Even if the same procedures prevailed in Yugoslavia, a firm there might behave rather differently in the presence of risk. As we have seen, the Yugoslav SMF often differs from the theoretic LMF in two basic spheres: authority within the enterprise and enterprise autonomy. Nevertheless, how labor earnings are determined in the SMF might well affect risk taking there. If we are to gauge risk-taking behavior under PBS, therefore, we must know how the SMF compared with the theoretical LMF regarding income disposition.

Although practice regarding income accounting for the self-managed firm has varied over time, we can grasp the essentials by referring to Yugoslav serial data on revenues remaining after charges for nonlabor operating expenses and depreciation (Table 1). The data relate to revenues "realized

Table 1

Disposition of Net Income of Enterprises in Socialized Sector, Yugoslavia 1966–1971

(percent)

Item	1966	1967	1968	1969	1970	1971
All	100.0	100.0	100.0	100.0	100.0	100.0
Allocated to political-social institutions	40.0	43.0	44.0	43.2	42.9	39.5
Interest on credits	4.1	5.0	5.3	5.7	5.6	5.5
Interest of capital assets	2.5	3.2	3.0	2.8	2.2	0.2
Turnover taxes[a]	10.9	12.7	13.7	12.1	13.0	12.7
Taxes on personal incomes	20.2	19.5	18.8	19.5	19.0	17.6
Other	2.3	2.6	3.2	3.1	3.1	3.5
Retained inome of enterprise[b]	21.6	17.0	15.9	15.5	16.3	19.6
Net personal incomes	38.5	40.2	41.2	41.2	40.7	40.9
Discrepancy	(−).1	(−).1	(−)1.1	—	—	—

Source: SZZS (1973), p. 155. On the scope of the data, see also pp. 20–21.

Note: Reference is to realized income (see text). On the discrepancy see *n.* 36. Other divergencies between sums of indicated items and 100.0 are due to rounding.

[a]In addition to the turnover tax (*porez na pomet*), this includes a special surcharge (*naknada*) on the retail price of gasoline.

[b]Allocations to capital account, reserve funds, and various other accounts.

through the market"—that is, revenues apart from changes in stocks—but for our present purposes, that is just as well. As so understood, net income was devoted in part to paying interest on bank credit.[36] Although made at rates below clearing levels, such payments were simply a further nonlabor factor charge. Hence, there is, in principle, no departure from theory at this point.

Under PBS the net income remaining after the charge for interest on bank credit was divided among three uses: (1) taxes and other obligatory payments to governmental and other public institutions; (2) earnings retained in the enterprise; and (3) incomes paid out to the working staff. Of these three claims, the first had a prior character, whereas under self-management, retained earnings as well as take-home pay are viewed as worker income. Apparently, then, the immediate corollary is that in the SMF under PBS, theory was generally replicated with respect to income distribution. Workers were, in effect, both residual claimants and primary risk-bearers.

Or so it is often reasoned. The conclusion is not very wide off the mark, but for a more accurate appraisal we must also consider that even though taxes and the like are prior charges against net income, they might conceivably vary in ways that might dampen the impact of shifting enterprise fortunes on residual earnings. To the extent they did so, the residual claimant fails to bear the risk experienced by the enterprise as a whole. In fact, among three main sorts of Yugoslav levies,[37] one (yielding the least revenue) was simply a charge on the enterprise's net worth paid in addition to the interest paid to banks. Although likewise referred to as interest (*kamata*), this levy extended to the enterprise's self-financed capital, and is more properly considered a tax. Under PBS, a very low flat rate—for some time, 4 percent—was standard. While there were reductions for some kinds of capital and some industries, no further adjustments were scheduled that depended on the profitability of the individual enterprise.[38]

The so-called turnover tax (*porez na promet*), like the Soviet tax of the same name, was originally levied on sales turnover at different stages. It was transformed in 1965 into little more than a retail sales tax—or rather, a complex of such taxes, with federal, republican, and communal governments each levying charges of its own. Within any locality, however, the total percentage charge was uniform for any commodity—and, to a considerable extent, even among commodities.

Taxes on personal incomes, as recorded in the table, are in Yugoslav parlance "contributions" (*doprinosi*). They include payments by the SMF, not only into governmental budgets as such, but into special funds such as that for social security. What is to be noted here, however, is that under PBS the bulk of such charges were essentially levied as a flat percentage of sums allocated to worker incomes. Taxes were also levied at progressive rates on incomes, reported on individual declaration, but such charges were apparently directed primarily at super incomes. Socialized sector earnings over a wide range extending well beyond the usual income of an SMF director were subject to either a nul, or a relatively low, marginal as well as average rate. In any case, the taxes on income indicated on individual declaration were reportedly evaded in a wholesale way.[39]

The foregoing levies on the enterprise and its workers all differ from lump-sum taxes. To the extent that they do, income disposition under self-management deviates from theory. The divergence, however, has little practical import for our purposes, for such levies can have only a limited effect on the stochastic dispersion of earnings. The latter is what counts for risk taking.[40]

So much for variations in taxes and similar levies as a factor affecting the workers' status as a residual claimant and risk bearer. From the same standpoint, a further question arises concerning the enterprise's retained earnings—particularly the degree to which such allocations are determined by worker time preference. That they are so determined is presupposed by LMF theory. It is only on that basis that retained earnings can be viewed as on a par with take-home pay as worker income. Discussion of this matter is postponed; however, any close correspondence to worker preferences appears unlikely. Departures from worker preferences, moreover, could have served to dampen fluctuations in take-home pay.

Under PBS, then, the worker under self-management diverged to some extent from his theoretical counterpart as a claimant to residual earnings and as a risk bearer. The divergence becomes more pronounced (though still only partial) when we consider that the worker actually received at regular intervals an advance payment (*akontacija*) determined from the estimated income of the enterprise for its accounting period (most often, a year). While frequently referred to as a wage (*plata*), the advance payment was only provisional, for the worker periodically received supplementary payments as well, that represented his share of net income after retention of earnings.

Or rather, he received such supplements if the net income was high enough. If net income instead fell below the projected amount, no earnings might be retained, but there would be no supplements either. On the other hand, the enterprise might be able to maintain worker earnings at the advance payment level for a time, even though net income did not actually suffice for this purpose. To do so, it might draw on reserve funds held for such purposes. It could also possibly draw on corresponding communal funds to which it contributed jointly with other enterprises in the same area. With the support of the communal government, it might be able to extend its bank loans, or even negotiate new ones. It might delay paying its suppliers (a not at all unusual circumstance, especially if the banks themselves became restrictive). For a firm experiencing financial difficulties, tax waivers too were a possibility.[41] In a word, the *akontacija,* rather than being purely residual earnings, might become something like a conventional contractual wage.

The enterprise was obligated in any case to pay workers a legal minimum wage. Should it be unable to do so, the commune government was obliged to make up the shortfall. The minimum at the time in question, however, was not very effective, for it was well below the earning levels in most industries.[42]

A further obligation of the enterprise—established by law—was to maintain its capital intact. If an enterprise failed to meet its obligations, its commune government could place it under receivership. In that case, self-management was suspended, and the enterprise was administered by authorities appointed by the commune government. Alternatively, the enterprise might be declared bankrupt, and liquidated.[43]

In fact, workers tended to receive a modest supplement to their advance payments. These averaged, if we can judge from pre-1965 experience, about 7-12 percent of their total earnings.⁴⁴ However, such earnings varied downward as well as upward, sometimes markedly so. Although the precise magnitude of such drops were rarely indicated, delays in wage payment and reductions in wages were reportedly among the more significant immediate causes of strikes (Jovanov 1978, pp. 366-367). On the other hand, payments at projected levels did often continue for some time in the face of losses, and receiverships and bankruptcies were relatively infrequent. In 1968, for example, bank credit was being relaxed after the severe restraint of 1966-1967, but 36 percent of Yugoslav firms were reportedly unable to meet their contractual obligations. Of the 13,840 enterprises in the socialized sector, however, only 74 were put into receivership and 124 were liquidated.⁴⁵ Bankruptcy was rather rare according to Horvat (1971), "because the commune is obliged to find new employment for workers and so prefers to help the enterprise as long as possible" (p. 105). The commune government might also be required to assume the financial obligations of a defunct enterprise (Tyson 1977a, p. 288).

Let me try to sum up the worker's status with respect to income disposition. In the SMF under PBS, workers generally had only a rather limited part to play in decision making in the presence of risk. Paradoxically, however, they were nevertheless residual claimants to income. While not to the degree envisaged in theory, they necessarily were also risk bearers. More precisely, their earnings might be depressed should the enterprise experience an adverse conjuncture, though in one way or another the impact of such a development was dampened. Worker gains from enterprise successes might also have been limited through involuntary or quasi-voluntary variation in the rates of income retention by the enterprise.

I have been discussing total labor earnings under self-management. On the related question concerning the shares of different workers in that total, only one aspect—executive pay—is of particular interest here. However, it should be observed first that under PBS it was left to the enterprise—particularly the workers' council—to decide at what specific rates different workers should share in the total income available.

As in the socialist world generally, though, an authoritative ideology required that rewards conform to "work done." In implementing that precept, the government formerly intervened in detail in the sphere of labor remuneration, and under PBS, it still prescribed general principles to be observed. It was partly on that account that there was considerable uniformity regarding the essentials of enterprise practice. Thus, the relative earnings rates for different kinds of work were determined in each enterprise in accord with a detailed scale established in advance. Each job was placed in the scale according to diverse criteria, all familiar to a Western observer: skill and educational requirements, effort needed, working conditions, and

the like. In establishing a scale and classifying tasks in it, the workers' council necessarily had to consider how other similar enterprises were dealing
with the same matters. The state of the labor "market" in general might
also be weighed, though with what effect is not too clear.

When the rates for different kinds of work were determined, the relative pay of the individual worker performing one or another job was also
fixed. The worker's pay in a particular job, however, might also vary
depending on his seniority, special proficiency, and so on. In piece work,
which was often employed, the worker's pay also depended on his output.
His pay might also include a bonus for, say, product quality that was determined in accord with established principles.[46]

On the basis of the foregoing procedures, the enterprise determined the
worker's rate of advance payment (*akontacija*). Supplementary distributions might then be made simply in proportion to advance payments,
though not necessarily. Here, particularly, the workers' council might
endeavor to allow for market conditions.[47]

So much for the distribution of earnings among workers generally. As
for executive pay, the main fact of interest becomes evident when we
observe that, for the purpose of determining relative earnings rates, administrative personnel were essentially treated like all other workers. Their jobs
too were classified in the enterprise's earning scale, and with due regard for
the criteria considered in classifying workers generally.

The workers' council might also pay executives bonuses for successful
performance, but special rewards were rather exceptional and, where available, tended to be quite modest.[48] Not very surprisingly, that was also true
of executive incomes overall. In 1969, socialized-sector enterprise directors
earned, on the average, only 3.3 times as much as unskilled workers (*Savezni
Zavod za Statistiku,* SZZS, 1971, p. 271). Executive personnel also benefited
from inevitable fringes, such as the use of a company car (Bajt 1972; Bučar
1978, p. 431). However—at least in self-managed enterprises—Yugoslav
incomes were probably more egalitarian than Yugoslavs themselves often
assumed.[49]

The role and status of executive personnel are rarely considered in the
theory of the LMF. The supposition is that such personnel are simply
another type of labor and, if rewarded as such, can be counted on in general
to pursue the interests of the workers as those interests are conceived in
theory. In the Yugoslav SMF under PBS, as we have seen, executive personnel often were the repository of inordinate power. The manner in which
they were rewarded is, therefore, of particular interest. This has yet to be
fully elucidated, but earnings must have tended to vary, much as did those
of the rest of the collective, with the income of the enterprise. When we
come to the behavior of the SMF with respect to risk, that will be a cardinal
datum to consider.

Although executive pay is of special concern, it should be observed that earnings differentials from firm to firm for workers generally were here too broadly as theory envisages. With differentials apparently of a constricted sort, though, the earnings from different kinds of work are unlikely to have approximated the marginal productivities to which theory equates them.[50]

I have been discussing income disposition, but the deeper concern has been risk bearing and hence risk exposure. From that standpoint, we must consider that in adverse circumstances in the West, not only income but employment (which is not the same thing) can be at hazard for workers and executives alike. That is also true of the staff of the LMF of theory, although that fact tends to be neglected in the analysis of risk taking. In gauging risk exposure in the SMF, therefore, we must be aware that under PBS, as before, staff curtailment was legally a matter for final determination by the workers' council rather than by the administration (International Labor Office, ILO, 1962, pp. 180–185; Blumberg 1969, p. 203). Council members, according to a survey, considered themselves relatively influential in that sphere (Arzenšek 1978, pp. 377–381). In view of likely limitations in council representativeness, that could obviously mean various things. However, under self-management, staff curtailment in the face of an adverse market conjuncture was, in fact, relatively infrequent and limited. That might perhaps be inferred from reports of chronic overstaffing, but avoidance of staff curtailment is also a recurring theme of writings on the SMF.[51] Under self-management, then, while workers experienced risk as residual claimants to income, the additional risk posed by the possibility of dismissal in adverse circumstances was relatively modest. A corollary, though, is that earnings fluctuations must often have been greater than they would have been otherwise.

The foregoing deals with the risk of dismissal for workers generally. For executives, it might suffice to refer to the enterprise director. Under PBS, the occupant of that post was normally appointed for a term of four years and could then be reappointed. He could also be dismissed before completing his term. Here, the workers' council—at least de facto—shared power with communal authorities (Blumberg 1969, pp. 204–205; Granick 1975, pp. 363–364). At all events, dismissal was a possibility as was failure to be reappointed (which comes to much the same thing). That, in fact, was the fate of 15–19 percent of the directors whose terms expired between 1966 and 1970. Some of the persons in question were probably superannuated; others must not have been candidates for reelection to begin with. Directorial turnover during the years considered must also have reflected a Party policy of the time to deprofessionalize cadres.[52] Even without dismissal or failure to be reappointed, of course, the director's career might be impaired should the enterprise experience vicissitudes. In appraising risky ventures, the director had to consider such facts, along with the modest material rewards for success. We must read in that light reports of difficulties in recruiting directors.[53]

Enterprise Motivation and Risk Taking

In preceding sections, I have outlined working arrangements under PBS relating to authority within the firm, enterprise autonomy, and enterprise income disposition. The working arrangements are sometimes similar to, and sometimes different from, those envisaged in the theory of the LMF. We must now consider how risk taking under those working arrangements might compare to that predicted theoretically. Research on the actual behavior of the Yugoslav firm under PBS is still not very advanced, but we must consider whether something can be inferred from such research as well as from the prevailing working arrangements.

Activities of interest turn decisively on the motivation of relevant decision makers. In theory, such motivation in stochastic circumstances is represented by a particular enterprise maximand. A cardinal issue here, therefore, concerns the degree to which that maximand applies to the Yugoslav SMF.

As given by formula (7), however, that criterion is but a variant of an alternative one given by formula (2), which supposedly obtains where risk is absent. Such an environment is an analytic construct rarely encountered in the real world, but for many sorts of decisions uncertainty is often negligible. Whatever can be ascertained as to the applicability of (2) in such circumstances should also bear on the applicability of (7) under uncertainty. Similarly, whereas both formulas (2) and (7) abstract from time, we may be able to judge their relevance better if we consider also how theoretical principles relating to choices over time can be applied to the SMF.

In trying to gauge motivation for risk taking in the Yugoslav SMF under PBS, therefore, it is well to begin with the related issues posed by formula (2), concerning motivation in the absence of risk, and the further theoretical principles, just referred to, for choices over time. Formula (2) simply represents net income per worker—that is, net income after nonlabor expenses are met. In relating such income to employment, due allowance is made for differences in labor quality and conditions. These differences are supposedly reflected in corresponding differentials in earnings. What is in question, then, is the degree to which (2), so understood, represents a maximand that is applicable to the SMF under PBS. Reference is to circumstances where the concern is essentially with nonstochastic alternatives relating to a single time period.

In trying to appraise that matter, we must consider these aspects:

1. Theoretical analyses are rarely explicit on authority within the LMF. The presupposition is that the collective is effectively in charge and is able to impose its will whenever it wishes to do so. As we saw, that was formally true in the SMF under PBS; however, in practice, much power was in the hands of executive personnel, particularly the director.

2. On the other hand, labor earnings were determined more or less as theory posits—that is, as a residual after nonlabor factor charges. Before incomes accrued to workers, deductions were also made for diverse taxes. Since these diverged from the lump-sum taxes of theory, they could have distorted enterprise behavior in familiar ways not central here,[14] but they would not at all bar pursuit of a maximand such as that assumed by theory. Also not envisaged in the theory are diverse Yugoslav arrangements tending to cushion the impact on labor earnings of unexpected declines in enterprise income. However, those arrangements are of only limited interest in the nonstochastic context of immediate concern.

3. I have been referring here to the total earnings bill. Between different kinds of labor, earnings varied broadly (as in theory) depending on labor quality and work conditions. This was true not only of ordinary workers but of executives. In seeking their own pecuniary gain, therefore, executives had reason to seek that of workers generally. It also follows that, despite the inordinate power of executives, enterprise motivation need not have diverged from that in theory.

4. A well-known, yet curious, feature of the theoretical LMF is that, depending on the initial level of operations, maximization of net income per worker might call for a curtailment of the work force. With that maximand, then, some members of the collective could be expected to seek their financial gain by dismissing some of their fellow workers. A virtual corollary is, however, that the realism of the theoretical maximand itself is in question at this point. That is so even if the collective is fully in control, for *a priori,* such staff curtailment is hardly likely in a community where labor management is the rule.

5. In any event, the SMF under PBS could not have been too prone to staff curtailment. As explained, dismissals were relatively infrequent, and overstaffing was reportedly widespread. Thus, the operation of the theoretical maximand applied to the SMF under PBS was subject to a constraint against staff curtailment.

6. A feature of the Yugoslav labor market is chronic unemployment. Under PBS, registered job seekers exceeded 7 percent of the social-sector labor force (Dubey 1975, p. 87). The unemployment doubtless had diverse causes, but it is consistent with a persistent gap between the marginal productivity of labor and its supply price that is understandable in terms of the theory of an LMF economy.

7. A further implication of labor-management, as seen in theory, is that in a short-run equilibrium, earnings of workers doing the same kind of

work in different enterprises can diverge even in the same locality. Because of differences in capital per worker, in technologies, and (in the case of firms in different industries) product demand, the divergence in earnings could be substantial.[55] Such a divergence—so much in contrast with the relatively short-run erosion of earnings disparities expected in a private enterprise economy—is considered a hallmark of an economy where labor-managed firms seek to maximize net income per worker.

In fact, notably large differentials have been reported in Yugoslavia. Horvat, for example, cites Yugoslav data showing that the earnings of workers performing the same kind of job in Belgrade in 1967 differ by as much as 3:1 or 4:1 (Horvat 1971, p. 117).[56] Yugoslav earnings differentials, as analyzed more generally by Estrin (1981), also suggest behavior such as that predicted by LMF theory.

As Jaroslav Vanek (1977) and Vanek and Jovicic (1975) have argued, some of the variation in earnings for similar work could represent rents on capital in excess of the capital tax and bank-loan interest. To that extent, the variation simply reflects the nature of Yugoslav income accounting and in no way confirms the LMF theory. Much of the variation, however, is apparently due to other causes. While the precise nature of those causes is still not clear, the variation is not inconsistent with theoretical expectations.[57]

8. I alluded earlier to other (sometimes paradoxical) implications of the theoretical maximand. One of these is that the firm could find it useful—at least in the short run—to reduce output in response to an increase in its price. Since the prediction is conditional, not much can be settled by referring to one or another instance of actual price-output variation. According to Horvat (1975), however, no pattern of price-quantity variations such as that in question

> . . . *has been observed in the Yugoslav economy.* Increases in prices, as *signals of unsatisfied demand,* have been followed rather quickly by efforts to increase supply (vol. 2, p. 235; his italics).

We may, perhaps, properly demur at Horvat's view that to be satisfied as to the validity of his contention, "it suffices to read newspapers." We should also note, however, that exclusion of short-run curtailment of output comes to much the same thing as the constraint on employment cuts referred to earlier.

I sum up the foregoing considerations in this way: If only provisionally, the theoretical maximand represented by formula (2) can be plausibly ascribed to the SMF under PBS. Such motivation on the part of the SMF was seemingly induced by working arrangements within the enterprise regarding the disposition of income. As a result, executives tended to see their interests as broadly in accord with those of the collective generally, and in that way, in effect, with the theoretical maximand. In the perspective of theory, executive authority in the SMF must be considered inordinate. Without executive incentives to conform to the theoretical maximand, the enterprise could easily be impelled to pursue a rather different end. There is also some indication of motivation like that represented by the theoretical maximand in observed enterprise behavior—particularly in the notably large divergencies in earnings for the same kind of labor in different firms.

Most likely, however, the theoretical maximand had only limited application to the SMF when it called for staff curtailment. The disinclination of the SMF to take such action, though, testifies not so much to a breach with the preferences of the collective as to the lack of realism of the theoretical maximand as an expression of those preferences when staff curtailment is in question.

The LMF of theory pursues its maximand in a market system that functions effectively—that is, prices tend to be at market clearing levels. As we saw, for the SMF under PBS that may not be the case. Government controlled prices can deviate from clearing levels even more than is usual in market systems. It also follows that without being motivated differently from the LMF the SMF might sometimes be led to behave differently from that entity. Such distortions, if they occur, are not observable from the limited information at hand. They will be consequential, however, in a later context.

Similarly, the SMF could diverge from theoretically predicted behavior because of external constraints on its response to market conditions. Here, too, available data are not illuminating. However, at least one source of external pressure on the firm, the commune government, has sought ends that were more harmonious with than in conflict with those we impute to the SMF. Thus, other things being equal, that agency had diverse specific concerns (Neuberger and James 1973, p. 270). One of these was to expand its tax revenue. With rates subject to substantial federal constraint, that objective should have been broadly consistent with increasing net income—though not necessarily net income per worker. The latter could dictate a reduction in employment and total income. The commune government could be expected to oppose such action, however, to the extent that a further concern of that agency was to expand employment within its locality. The enterprise, in any case, was probably not inclined to curtail staff.

Available evidence as to the motivation of the self-managed firm under PBS, however, is rather limited as yet. That also implies that we cannot really rule out some hypotheses, rather different from LMF theory, that have been advanced mainly by Yugoslav economists. Among these, the chief is that of Horvat: the enterprise seeks to maximize, not net income per worker as understood here, but net income after deduction of labor charges at some target pay rate. This explains at once the asserted absence of a backward-sloping short-run supply curve; on the other hand, that is equally excluded by a constraint on staff curtailment. Horvat apparently considers such a constraint as applying in any case. Also, the resulting analysis is incomplete in that no explanation is provided of the target pay rate, or, more basically, for the earnings differentials observed among workers doing similar work in different enterprises.[58]

Enterprise choices among time periods (to come to that aspect) are involved in a sense in every decision on investment, but central to all such decisions is that on enterprise savings. To the extent that savings are invested and investment in the real world inherently entails risk, in exploring enterprise savings we cannot continue to exclude risk as we have done so far. Systematic discussion of risk taking, however, is still deferred.

When savings are in question, as we saw, the maximand of the theoretic LMF can become rather complex. From the standpoint of the current collective, however, the case for retaining income within the LMF, rather than distributing it, could clearly be rather attentuated.

To recall analytic essentials: the current staff will engage in self-financing only so far as the rate of return matches or exceeds an adjusted marginal rate of time preference, R. The latter rate exceeds the marginal rate of time preference because the required return must also compensate for nonrecovery of principal by the current staff. The excess over the time-preference rate depends on the expected tenure of the current staff. If workers have the option of depositing in savings accounts at interest sums that they save individually, the rate of return must also match or exceed the R for which the marginal rate of time preference equals savings-deposit interest. Finally, even if the rate of return matches or exceeds R, the current staff should prefer to finance investment through credits, should the credits be available at a rate of interest less than R.

What all this meant for the SMF under PBS, we can discern when we consider that interest rates on savings deposits over the years in question ranged from 5.0 to 7.5 percent (Dubey 1975, p. 228). With a marginal rate of time preference equal to, say, 6.0 percent, the corresponding R would vary as follows depending on the expected worker tenure:

Expected tenure (years)	(percent)
1	106.0
5	23.8
8	16.1
10	13.6
20	8.7

Under PBS, interest on bank credit was subject to a ceiling of 8.0–10.0 percent. With industrial producers' prices rising at an average rate of 6.4 percent, however, banks could often impose above-ceiling rates, while credit rationing was widespread.

Nevertheless, unless workers looked forward to a relatively long tenure, they had little incentive to engage in self-financing. If bank credit were available, there was instead a case for recourse to such funds to finance investment. Savings deposits too must very often have been relatively attractive.

The incentive to invest would have been low even if investment in the enterprise posed no risk. To the degree that there was risk, the rate of return required to induce self-financing would have exceeded R by an appropriate risk premium. Recourse to bank credit would be more appealing on that account.

Under PBS, enterprises nevertheless retained 15.5–21.6 percent of their income (Table 1), or 27.4–35.7 percent of their disposable income (that is, income after taxes and other payments to political-social institutions). These totals include allocations both to investment and to diverse other purposes. However, investment allocations alone came to about 17.2–24.5 percent of disposable income.[59] By Western standards, such shares represent a notably high propensity to save for a country at the Yugoslav level. That is so even though, in the West, principal is recoverable. Yugoslav enterprise savings, moreover, were superimposed upon appreciable private savings by households (Dubey 1975, pp. 220–221, 227–228; SZZS 1973, p. 176).

One wonders, therefore, whether enterprise motivation at this point is not different from that posited theoretically. For well-known reasons, enterprise executives in the West often find it to their interest to promote growth, and retain profits to that end. If Yugoslav executives were similarly motivated, they could have sought, by use of their authority, to influence the enterprise to act accordingly. Their immediate financial rewards for promoting growth would be modest, but the resulting gains in status and prestige (Jan Vanek 1972, p. 205) could have been appealing.

Still, granting the possibility of such countertheoretical motivation, there were causes enough to explain the inordinate savings. Here again, markets were not as envisaged in theory. At this point, the divergence must have been consequential. I refer particularly to the limited availability of credit, and to the fact that the banks usually financed fixed investments only if the enterprise supplied some of the required funds. At least, that was the practice in earlier years, and apparently it persisted under PBS to some degree (Furubotn and Pejovich 1971, pp. 72, 87; Jan Vanek, p. 264).

Then too, before the economic reform of 1965, the division of enterprise income between retained funds and worker take-home pay was the subject of rather specific government guidelines. Under the reform, such regulation was abandoned, but informal external control of one sort or another can hardly have been entirely lacking. At any rate, preform patterns sometimes persisted. Reinstitution of quasi-official (if not official) controls over earnings retention and worker take-home pay has been a feature of the most recent reforms, and some steps in that direction were already being taken as PBS waned.[60]

In short, the capital market was flawed, and the enterprise was constrained in ways favorable to high rates of savings. However, the enterprise for its part could still have been motivated as theory posits.

Under PBS, the share of income that the self-managed firm saved was impressive throughout, but it tended to decline over the course of time (Table 1). The reason must have been the indicated shift regarding external controls. While informal constraints probably persisted after 1965, the abandonment of governmental guidelines doubtless stimulated an increased payout. In the process, enterprise savings should have come to diverge less widely from theoretical expectations.

Although the savings share was generally large, among different firms it tended to be larger the higher the level of worker take-home pay—or so we infer from industry data on income-retention rates (Wachtel 1973, p. 114 *ff*). Such a relation between savings and income is familiar in the West, and in itself need not represent any departure from theoretical expectation. In the Yugoslav case, however, the differential savings rates might have reflected the need of less prosperous firms to compete for labor with more prosperous firms. If so, workers weighing employment in different firms must have discounted enterprise savings relative to take-home pay. Theoretically, that would be understandable only if savings exceeded those that conform to workers' preferences. We have found reasons enough for this to be the case. The same causes that gave rise to the excess, furthermore, probably had much to do with the differential savings rates between firms with different levels of worker take-home pay.

Thus, it is not surprising that the egalitarian tendencies in earnings differentials between workers in different occupations operated here as well to limit the payout of more prosperous firms (Comisso 1979, pp. 107–108). Another related doctrinal strand bore more expressedly on earnings retention: the enterprise should exclude from workers payout unearned gains such as those derived from a price increase. A tendency for the individual firm to plough back a larger share of earnings when business is good (Jan Vanek 1972, p. 246) would also have contributed to the variation in enterprise savings ratios with the level of worker take-home pay. That, however, could easily have occurred without any external constraints.

Policies and practices such as the foregoing have an immediate corollary for the main theme of this chapter: Given the apparent constraints on enterprise saving, workers' gains from stochastic variations in enterprise income should have tended to be restricted. There probably was thus a kind of symmetry involved—a high level of worker earnings was trimmed back, just as sharp cuts in pay were avoided.[61]

This brings us finally to risk taking. In choosing among stochastic alternatives, the LMF of theory would be notably prone to risk avoidance because, with workers ultimately in charge and primary risk bearers, the concern would be to maximize the expected utilities of the collective in general. Members of the collective will ordinarily be at income levels that are characterized by marked risk aversion. Unlike stockholders in the usual Western corporate enterprise, workers in the LMF will also be unable to limit risk through diversification.

In gauging to what extent the SMF under PBS was similarly prone to risk avoidance, our point of departure must be the tentative view of its motivation to which we have arrived thus far. Although the SMF contrasted sharply with its theoretical counterpart with regard to executive authority, under the existing income-disposition arrangements, executives and workers had an incentive to pursue ends more or less as theory postulates. Viewed as a hypothesis, the prevalence of such motivation can sometimes be discerned in enterprise behavior with respect to nonstochastic alternatives relating to a single time period. The theoretical maximand tends to lose effect, however, where staff curtailment is in question. As for choices among time periods, as manifest in enterprise savings, the enterprise diverges from theoretical expectation at this point, but the causes could be other than failure to pursue the relevant theoretical maximand.

In short, to the extent the hypothesis is valid, enterprise motivation in the face of risk must turn on how workers and executives in the SMF under PBS compare with the collective as a whole in the theoretical LMF in their degree of aversion to and exposure to risk. Should all those groups experience the same degree of risk aversion and exposure, the SMF is no less and no more a risk avoider than its theoretical counterpart. Should workers and executives in the SMF be adverse and exposed to risk in different degrees, the extent to which the enterprise seeks to avoid risks would depend additionally on the comparative influence of the two groups when risk taking was in question.

Turning to those matters, the essentials are readily stated so far as they are known. Workers in general are presumably equally risk averse, whether employed in the SMF under PBS or the LMF of theory. On the other hand, the SMF differed markedly from its theoretical counterpart regarding the exposure of the collective to risk, especially with respect to enterprise adversity. Unfavorable consequences for worker take-home pay were cushioned in one way or another, particularly in the short run. Repercussions on employment were also limited to the extent that there was a constraint against staff curtailment, although earnings fluctuations were correspondingly magnified. The worker was by no means completely sheltered from downside risk, but overall, his exposure was distinctly mitigated. Through more or less imposed variations in the retention of enterprise earnings, the workers' participation in gains from enterprise success was also circumscribed, but overall, workers in the SMF had less reason to be risk avoiders than those in the theoretical LMF.

With higher incomes than those of workers in general, executive personnel should have experienced somewhat less risk aversion than the latter. Their exposure to enterprise risk should have been broadly similar to that of the collective as a whole. Should the enterprise come upon adversity, however, executives might be affected inordinately—whether through dismissal, failure to be reappointed, or some other form of career impairment.

What can be said about the comparative influence of the collective as whole and executives in particular on decisions on questions involving risk must already be evident. Such questions arise most often in the case of investment projects that entail the introduction of new technologies and products. Here, to a greater degree than elsewhere, executives, together with their technical aides, tended to be relatively influential in the SMF under PBS.

Just what the foregoing facts mean as to the tendency of the SMF under PBS to avoid risk must to some extent be conjectural. This tendency, however, should not have been nearly as great as could be expected to characterize the LMF of theory.

I have tacitly assumed that under PBS workers were not only exposed to risk, but were aware of that fact. Results of a survey of workers in ten enterprises reported on by Županov (1967; 1969, ch. 1) indicate otherwise. When asked about the impact on their own earnings of a decline in the income of their enterprise, a great many responded either that they did not expect their earnings to be affected, or that they did not know what the effect on their earnings would be. The survey was conducted, however, in June 1966. As Županov indicates, it might not fully reflect circumstances following the 1965 reform. The survey questionnaire apparently did not distinguish between a short-term and a long-term reduction in enterprise income. That could be an important aspect, particularly as the first effect of a reduction in enterprise income might be felt only on the supplementary income that the worker received at the end of, say, a year. To the extent that workers were not clear about the downside risk to which self-management subjected them, however, the tendency toward risk avoidance under that form of organization would be less.

I refer to Županov's findings for the collective generally. Županov regrettably does not present any numerical data on the perceptions of managerial personnel alone, but apparently the majority were aware of the downside risk to which not only they, but ordinary workers, were exposed. There is no basis here, therefore, for discounting the tendency to risk avoidance.[62]

However weak or strong that tendency may have been, our ultimate concern is with risk taking. We wish especially to grasp how self-management may have affected decision making regarding innovation, where risk is apt to be relatively important. From that standpoint, although self-management probably did not skew decision making against risk as much as it would in the theoretical LMF, it still entailed significant diffusion of authority within the enterprise. That was true regarding innovation. Here, as elsewhere, decision making was an internal political process as well as a bureaucratic one. Not too surprisingly, the process often turned out to be cumbersome and one whose consummation in any practical action was rather uncertain—in short, a process hardly favorable to innovation. Here again, Županov (1978b) is an eloquent witness:

> Since there are no systematic data on anti-entrepreneurship, one can only cite individual examples from the press. Such argumentation nevertheless rests upon shaky foundations, since one can always find contrary examples. A true picture could be provided only by systematic research that demonstrates how many managers have attempted to behave in an entre-preneurial manner and—encountering disapproval and misfortunes—have abandoned that behavior. The number of defeated and resigned is unlikely to be small. Approximately 73 percent of directors and 62 percent of other managers interviewed expressed the view that new ideas create resistance and conflicts in the organization, making it difficult to predict whether directors would be successful in implementing changes. In any case, the labeling of entrepreneurial behavior with the reprehensible term "managerialism" speaks for itself (p. 83).

Županov is citing here the results of a survey of some 245 executives who attended a 1968 symposium.[63]

The self-managed firm, under PBS, we must again consider, was not entirely autonomous. In the case of investment projects, outside agencies—chiefly the commune government and the banks—played a significant part. If the commune government was motivated as argued above, it would not have discouraged enterprise initiative regarding investment projects, but the additional clearance involved could not have been helpful. Banks were often under the influence of the commune government, but they doubtless tended otherwise—as banks do almost everywhere—to inhibit risk taking, if only through qualitative credit controls.

While limiting downside risk for workers, the prevailing constraint on staff curtailment must also have acted by itself to thwart innovations. Still again, activites entailing risk in a theoretical context must have been even more risky in an environment such as that in Yugoslavia under PBS: an environment, that is, where shifts in working arrangements were numerous and frequent; where the economy itself manifested marked instability (Horvat 1971, pp. 90 *ff*); and where, as indicated, prices must have diverged frequently from clearing levels. Because of the latter, availability of materials for new technologies and products must sometimes have been uncertain.

The net of all forces affecting enterprise risk taking under PBS, considered together, can only be determined by further empirical inquiry. It would be surprising, though, if the SMF were not more entrepreneurial than the LMF of theory could be expected to be. I have been comparing the SMF with its theoretical counterpart, but it would also be surprising, I think, if the SMF under PBS were as entrepreneurial as the typical Western private enterprise firm.

The 1974–1976 Reforms

What I have called the BOAL system of self-management dates essentially from the promulgation of the latest Yugoslav constitution (in 1974) and the subsequent codification and elaboration (principally in legislation enacted in 1976) of the novel arrangements for self-management outlined there. Many features of the new system had already been introduced in June 1971 as a series of amendments to the previous (1963) constitution, but prior to the adoption of the 1974 constitution, these amendments remained largely inoperative. Even after the new arrangements were dealt with in the new constitution and subsequent legislation—most importantly, in the Law on Associated Labor of November 25, 1976—they were by no means put immediately into effect. According to the latest accounts, some legalities have still to be fully implemented. That fact must be kept in mind as we consider the more important of the changes made in working arrangements.[64]

Of these, the chief relates to the internal organization of the enterprise. Organs of self-management began to proliferate within the firm at an early stage. Among other things, there could be further councils in individual works and departments in addition to the enterprise-wide workers' council. That arrangement had already become widespread by the late 1960s, but under the latest reforms, it is being extended further and transformed dramatically. The BOAL, or Basic Organization of Associated Labor, is an administrative entity that can be organized for an enterprise division. It has its own organs of self-management, has gained legal authority over enterprise assets required for the division's functioning, and has become a separate and distinct commercial entity. Its relations with the BOALs established in other divisions of the same firm are supposed to be conducted accordingly. The different BOALs can continue to coordinate their activities and arrange for services to be used in common, such as legal counseling, marketing, and the like. However, that is supposed to be by agreement, and transfers of goods and services between divisions are to take place at agreed-upon prices.[65] At the same time, a BOAL administering a division formerly subordinate to one enterprise can enter into contractual relations with a BOAL adminstering a division formerly subordinate to another enterprise.

The new arrangements are to be established more or less generally in industry. To organize themselves into a BOAL, workers in an enterprise division must be performing labor whose results are expressible "in terms of value within the work organization or on the market," but the stipulation evidently is not highly restrictive. Wherever it is met, workers have not only the right, but the duty, to establish a BOAL.[66]

The mandated restructuring of industrial self-management is dramatic indeed. In effect, the BOAL is to supersede the enterprise as the primary agency for industrial administration. The resulting atomization of multi-divisional enterprises might be the envy of any Western trust-buster. As a mechanism for industrial coordination, however, the new arrangements are obviously quite complex, and what could be achieved by introducing them must have seemed problematic to many concerned. Understandably, the restructuring has also turned out to be often *pro forma*. While instituting the new arrangements on paper, many enterprises have reportedly functioned much as they did before (Comisso 1980, pp. 193, 201–203).

The new scheme has doubtless been widely implemented in a more or less meaningful way (compare Sacks 1980). Even where it has, however, the break with the past has been mitigated by the inevitable feature already mentioned: after divisions of an enterprise are organized into BOALs, they must still coordinate their activities. That is legally obligatory—at least, a BOAL cannot withdraw from the larger "work organization" of which it was a part if that should "lead to a major hindrance or prevention of work" elsewhere in the work organization (Constitution of 1974, art. 37).

In coordinating their activities, the different BOALs can also assign responsibilities to central-enterprise executive authorities and self-managed organs, including the workers' council. The latter is composed of delegates from the different BOALs. Arrangements of this sort must be more or less widely operative, although as a result of the very restructuring that has been in progress relevant statistical data are difficult to construe (Sacks 1980, p. 223).

The government had diverse aims in restructuring self-management in the foregoing manner, but not least was the obvious one of making that system more effective in assuring workers' control. To the extent that the new arrangements have come to operate at all effectively, they must have tended to weaken the authority of central executives in the enterprise (Comisso 1980; Sacks 1980). To what extent, however, the worker has gained in influence is an interesting question. The trend towards divisional self-management that prevailed before the BOAL was instituted apparently yielded the worker at most only limited gains in influence. Although the enterprise is being atomized, the government has also taken steps to assure that the trade unions can participate legally in the process of staffing executive posts in the BOAL and in other affairs of the enterprise. Partly on that basis, the unions (and also the Party) have recovered influence within the enterprise that they lost previously.[67] Yugoslav complaints about the limitations of the workers' role under self-mangement continue; so, on some scale, do strikes.[68]

Under the latest reforms, the government has also initiated a number of shifts affecting the institutional environment within which the enterprise operates.[69] Most importantly, it has sought to reestablish control over income disposition through the system of so-called "social compacts" and "self-management arrangments," early antecedents of which date as far back as 1968. Social compacts have now been concluded countrywide among political, social, and economic agencies at different administrative levels ranging from the federal to the commune. The agencies for a particular region or industrial branch determine in this way the principles of income disposition that are supposed to be implemented by self-management agreements among corresponding BOALs and enterprises.

Although this process is rather different from pre-1965 regulatory procedures, the principles established in the social compacts are apparently obligatory for BOALs and enterprises and must be heeded in their own self-management agreements. The compacts and agreements concluded so far have yet to be studied in any systematic way; however, what they mean for income disposition can be inferred from the fact that the post-1965 decline in the share of disposable income retained by the enterprise has been arrested, if not reversed.[70]

Under the new arrangements, disproportionately high retention rates have been imposed on high-income BOALs and enterprises.[71] That, of course, was to be expected. As we saw, the same pattern probably prevailed already under the informal constraints of the late 1960s. If a 1972 self-management agreement for Belgrade trade workers is at all indicative, though, progressivity has perhaps become more marked: A firm with income per standard worker amounting to as little as 61 percent of the projected Belgrade average could devote as much as 95 percent of its income to take-home pay. Should income per standard worker be as high as 212 percent of the projected Belgrade average, however, the permissible payout fell to 55 percent of income (Furubotn and Pejovich 1973, p. 293 *ff*).

According to the Law on Associated Labor (arts. 115, 128) income disposition within the BOAL is to conform to "common bases and scales" (*osnovi i merila*) established by the self-management agreement among different BOALs in an enterprise. We presumably must read in that light instances reported where extreme variations in income per worker among different BOALs within a firm gave rise to hardly any variations in payout per worker. The differences in earnings, we must infer, go rather to generate widely different rates of earnings retention.[72] The net impact of the BOAL system on executive pay is not clear.[73]

Control over income disposition is the principal, but not the only, use to which the system of social compacts and self-management agreements has been devoted. The government has also been seeking in the last years to use the accords as an instrument of coordination more generally. It has been endeavoring to assure that the plans of political, social, and economic entities will be more fully integrated with each other than was the case previously. To that end, self-management agreements are supposed to cover not only income disposition but matters of mutual interest to the signatories—particularly prices, quantities of goods traded, and joint investment projects. BOALs and enterprises are supposed to reach agreements on these matters with due regard to annual and medium-term plans that they formulate. The plans, in turn, must take into account guidelines established in social compacts. Through an interactive process, the plans of different BOALs within an enterprise are to be brought in harmony with each other, with those of BOALs in other enterprises, and with those of political and social entities.

Shortly after this scheme was introduced in 1976, the mechanism by which it would be implemented was described as "agonizingly vague" (Milenkovich 1977, p. 58). Its workings are still not too clear. The government claims not to have revived centralist planning. This might be true, but planning was not entirely indicative previously, and divergencies from indicative planning have no doubt increased. How fully the plans of different entities are being integrated is another matter, but self-management agreements that fix prices, quantities of goods traded, and investment pooling arrangements are being widely concluded.[74]

To come again to risk taking and innovation, the particulars of the new reforms are often uncertain. In any event, the changes are still in the process of implementation. It is not too early, however, to discern significant tendencies. It is difficult to avoid the conclusion that, overall, risk taking and innovation are probably being adversely affected. This is so despite some aspects that favor such activities—for instance, the fact that the self-management agreements, in effect, establish forward markets. The environment within which the enterprise operates might, in this way, become less stochastic.

Another feature, not yet noted, should have a mixed impact on risk taking. I refer to the explicit prohibition in the Constitution of 1974 (art. 32) and Law on Associated Labor (arts. 177, 213) of staff curtailment to implement technological and other innovations without arranging appropriate alternative employment for the workers affected. Not really very novel, the prohibition would tend to limit downside risk for workers, but even so could sometimes make infeasible otherwise admissible innovations.

Even if the foregoing features together tend to favor risk taking and innovation, still others should more than offset them. For instance, under the new controls over income disposition, the gains from successful outcomes have probably been restricted. Also, the atomization of the enterprise will limit risk pooling, despite such arrangements as those for joint investments by different BOALs. Likewise, under the BOAL system, relatively independent authorities in charge of different divisions of the enterprise must reach agreement on common action. This must often make the process of innovation even more cumbersome than before.

However, such tendencies might or might not persist. The outlook is especially uncertain when one is referring to such extraordinarily complex and sweeping reforms. One wonders how completely the reforms will ever be implemented, and, if they are implemented, how long they will endure before they provoke still further sweeping changes.[75]

Conclusion

This has been a lengthy inquiry. In conclusion, it may be advisable to summarize the discussion. The concern throughout has been with entrepreneurship as manifest in risk taking under the so-called "self-management" form of industrial organization in Yugoslavia. Risk is apt to be relatively important in the case of innovation, and attention has been directed especially to that aspect.

As a form of labor participation, self-management has been subject to extensive theoretical analysis. Theoretical writings refer particularly to an economy in which enterprises are labor-managed in a rather ideal sense. The resulting analysis is highly abstract, but is still serves as a point of departure. Of particular interest is the implication that, with workers ultimately in control and residual claimants to income—and hence primary risk-bearers—the labor-mangaged firm (LMF) should be notably inclined to risk avoidance. Innovation might suffer as a result.

Appraisal of this matter under Yugoslav self-management must consider that the relevant economic working arrangements have been notably fluid. I have focused particularly on the relatively developed system that came to prevail after the multiple institutional shifts known collectively as the economic reform of 1965. Reference was made at first to the pre-BOALs system (PBS)—that is, the economic working arrangements that prevailed prior to further reforms implemented after 1974–1976, and hence prior to the large-scale introduction of the so-called Basic Organizaton of Associated Labor (BOAL).

With respect to PBS, an initial finding concerns the behavior of the self-managed firm (SMF) in circumstances where risk is not consequential and enterprise savings are not in question: The enterprise probably pursued, at least to a degree, the maximand postulated for the LMF of theory. That is, it sought to maximize net income per employed worker. To determine the maximand, employment must be understood as calculated with due regard to differences in labor quality.

Depending on the circumstances, pursuit of such a maximand might theoretically call for staff curtailment. Hardly plausible to begin with in a labor-managed economy, such action could be expected under PBS only rather rarely and in attenuated form. However, sizeable divergencies in earnings for similar labor in different enterprises give reason to think that the theoretical maximand was otherwise pursued. That such divergencies should prevail in at least a protracted short run is an important analytic corollary of maximization of net income per worker.

Working arrangements that might have affected the behavior of the self-managed enterprise under PBS were nevertheless rather different from those assumed in theory. Most importantly, authority within the firm gravitated to a notable degree to managerial personnel, though perhaps not to the extent sometimes assumed in Yugoslav, as well as Western, discussion. Workers, however, generally had more or less the status of residual claimants to income that theory envisages for them. Granting the analytically incongrous authority of executives, such persons still found it to their interest to pursue the theoretical maximand along with workers generally. Under PBS, their incomes were determined essentially like (and varied with) the earnings of other members of the collective.

Under PBS, however, enterprise savings probably exceeded what might have been expected theoretically. Perhaps enterprise motivation at this point was other than theory envisages, but the inordinate savings can be explained otherwise in terms of credit rationing, the requirement posed by banks that enterprises supply matching funds, and the likelihood of informal external constraints on the share of enterprise income paid out to workers.

Under PBS, even if enterprise motivation in nonstochastic single-period choices and in decisions on savings had been such as theory presupposes, the SMF could not be expected to be as prone to risk avoidance as the LMF of theory was. True, in the SMF (as in the theoretical LMF) the collective's status as a residual claimant to income meant that risk-averse workers were also primary risk-bearers. However, for Yugoslav workers, exposure to risk of income curtailment in adverse circumstances was markedly limited by diverse mitigating arrangements. The risk of the loss of employment was also comparatively modest. Informal constraints on income payout probably tended at the same time to limit gains from successful performance, but with due regard to losses as well as gains, the expected payoff from risk taking should have been more favorable to such action than theory might suggest.

I have been referring to the collective generally. Under PBS, the attitude of managerial personnel towards risk was necessarily particularly important to enterprise risk taking. With their higher incomes, however, such persons should have been less risk-averse than workers, while their exposure to risk was broadly similar to that of workers.

Although the SMF was probably not as prone to risk avoidance as its theoretical counterpart, the SMF still was so inclined, perhaps sometimes markedly so. Moreover, however self-government affected attitudes towards risk, it often tended to thwart risk taking in the cardinal sphere of innovation. Granting the often preponderant authority of executives, power was still diffuse, with the result that obtaining clearances for innovations was notably cumbersome and uncertain. Additional clearances that might be required from external authorities, including both banks and commune officials, were not helpful. The constraint against staff curtailment must also have been an impediment.

So much for PBS. The shifts in economic working arrangements referred to as the 1974–1976 reforms have often been implemented only *pro forma* or not at all. To the extent that they have been implemented effectively, they are strikingly complex, and their impact on risk taking and innovation must be uneven, but overall adverse. To refer only to the most outstanding aspect, it is difficult to see how risk taking and innovation could benefit from establishing relatively independent self-management organs, or BOALs, to administer different divisions of the enterprise. Such atomization must tend to limit risk pooling and make the innovation process itself even more cumbersome than before.

Entrepreneurship under Yugoslav self-management is a relatively novel theme. In exploring it here, I have nevertheless been able to draw on much related Western and Yugoslav literature. A principal conclusion, however, is that still more research is needed. That is too evident from the often tentative nature of my findings to need laboring.

Yugoslav self-management is of interest not only for its own sake, but as an outstanding example of labor participation in management. From that standpoint, an inevitable question arises: How relevant is the Yugoslav experience elsewhere? In pondering this complex issue, the reader should consider the special circumstances under which labor participation evolved in Yugoslavia, particularly the relatively early stage of economic development there, the recent peasant origin of much of the labor force, and the nature of the political system—which, if not as authoritarian as elsewhere under socialism, is still authoritarian. If labor participation in Yugoslavia has often turned out rather differently than many proponents hoped, such circumstances are not the least of the reasons.

That must be so, among other things, with respect to the relatively limited role of the ordinary worker in managerial affairs—a denouement so much at odds with both the theory of the LMF and Yugoslav legal doctrine. On the other hand, the additional departure from theory represented by the dampening of downside risk for the worker must be inevitable in any far-reaching scheme of labor participation. Failure to consider that can only signify a lack of realism in the analysis. However, these are properly matters for separate inquiry, and cannot really be pursued here.

Notes

1. Much to the benefit of one who is not far along in his efforts to acquire Serbo-Croatian, a good deal of relevant Yugoslav scholarly work was originally published in English or has been translated.

2. My inquiry, thus, is complementary to that of Sacks (1973), which focuses on the founding of new firms. The latter study is an outstanding exception to the general neglect of entrepreneurial behavior.

3. The proverbial caveat as to scale, which holds in the linear homogeneous case for the private-enterprise firm, applies here as well.

4. See Ward (1958); Domar (1966); Jaroslav Vanek (1970); and Meade (1972).

5. Jaroslav Vanek (1970) provides an extensive discussion, though one that seems incomplete in interesting ways. For an example, see note 6.

To return to the variation in the marginal product of labor in different firms, note that for firms in the same industry applying the same linear homogeneous production function, a difference in capital stock will not cause marginal products to differ even in the short run. (See Jaroslav Vanek 1970, pp. 31–33.)

6. So Jaroslav Vanek plausibly argues. However, a definitive formal demonstration that relative earnings will be the same in equilibrium has yet to be provided.

7. In response to monopoly power represented by a downward-sloping demand schedule, however, the LMF tends to be more restrictive than the corresponding private-enterprise firm (Meade 1972; 1974).

8. The maximand that I assume applies in decisions on self-financing is essentially the one stressed in theoretical writings. Vanek, however, apparently adopted that maximand after first focusing on one of a rather different sort. On this and the conditions determining the volume of enterprise self-financing, see Jaroslav Vanek (1970), pp. 168–171, 296–298; and Jaroslav Vanek (1977), chs. 8–9. See also Furubotn and Pejovich (1974), pp. 227 *ff;* Pejovich (1973); Stephen (1980); and Furubotn (1980).

As indicated above, the LMF, like the private enterprise firm, employs a durable nonlabor input up to the point where the value of marginal product equals the rental charge corresponding to the rate of interest and depreciation. The rate of interest is supposedly that prevailing in the market, but one further assumes that the enterprise does, in fact, borrow at that rate.

For any likely market rate, that will usually be true, but a labor-managed firm might conceivably wish to meet all of its investment requirements out of its own savings. In that case, the rental charge is determined not by the market rate of interest, but by the R corresponding to r for the volume of savings in question.

9. The labor force is again supposed to be homogeneous. On the maximand for the labor-managed firm under stochastic conditions, see Hey and Suckling (1979).

10. I have been referring to absolute, as distinct from relative, risk aversion, and to risk premium in the sense of the excess of expected income over its certainty equivalent in terms of risk-taker utility. Also, in comparing enterprises under different systems, reference is to the risk premium, and hence to the expected return that is required—other things being equal—to induce risk takers to commit themselves to a given marginal project. On the foregoing, I have benefited from discussions with Jerry Green. Compare Arrow (1971), pp. 277-278.

11. From the standpoint of efficiency, however, the lump-sum taxes could also be differentiated between social states. For instance, in agriculture, a higher tax might be levied when there is rain than when there is no rain. Theoretically—though hardly in practice—income variation might be dampened somewhat in that way.

12. A rare exception is Furubotn and Pejovich (1974), pp. 227 *ff*, although reference there is to a nonstochastic environment, rather than to the stochastic one of interest here.

13. See, for example, Horvat et al. (1979), vol. 1, p. 25, and the 1974 constitution.

14. On elections to the workers' council, see Ward (1957); International Labor Office, ILO (1962): pp. 78-81; Blumberg (1969), pp. 196 *ff*; and Wachtel (1973), pp. 64 *ff*.

15. Different sources sometimes differ on the precise nature of the council's authority in selecting the enterprise director. See ILO (1962), pp. 100-104; Horvat (1971), p. 100; Wachtel (1973), pp. 70-71; Sacks (1973), p. 10; Granick (1975), pp. 363-364; and Sirc (1979), pp. 39, 183-184.

16. See *Radio Free Europe Research* (February 20-26), 1980).

17. A principal source here on the studies in question is Obradović and Dunn (1978). Some of the relevant essays by Yugoslav scholars collected in this volume are apparently revisions of papers previously published or otherwise circulated, but the empirical data still generally relate to PBS. On the other hand, the fact that the authors, in republishing their earlier essays, saw no basis to qualify conclusions that clearly followed from such empirical data is a fact to keep in mind when we assess the 1974-1976 reforms.

On the Yugoslav work on power distribution within the firm, see also Wachtel (1973), pp. 86 *ff*; Neuberger and James (1973), p. 276; Županov (1969), ch. 10; and Županov (1973; 1974; 1975).

18. For some dissident and also some corroborative views, see Wachtel (1973): pp. 86 *ff*.

19. As in Obradović (1978) and Vejnović (1978).

20. In Vejnović (1978), pp. 272 *ff*.

21. See Jovanov (1978), the report cited above on a book of the same author in *Radio Free Europe Research* (February 20–26, 1980), and the same serial for June 8–14, 1978.

22. *Radio Free Europe Research* (February 20–26, 1980).

23. See Adizes (1971) and *The Economist* (July 16, 1966; September 16, 1967; August 2, 1969). Although referring to a later period, the following accounts have implications for the PBS arrangements now being discussed: Comisso (1979), chs. 7–9; and *Wall Street Journal* (October 8, 1975).

24. *Raspodela dohotka* has usually been translated as "income distribution." However, in the West, that term is often used to refer to the division of income among individuals or households. For reasons that will become evident, the more general "income disposition" seems more accurate.

25. See particularly Obradović (1978), and Arzenšek (1978) in Obradović and Dunn (1978); also Županov (1969), pp. 248 *ff*; Zupanov (1973); Neuberger and James (1973), p. 280; and Wachtel (1973), pp. 91 *ff*.

26. According to a long-standing practice, however, no workers' councils were organized in very small firms; instead, the entire collective served as its own council.

27. The fixing of market-clearing prices by a Central Planning Board is, of course, an outstanding feature of the market socialism of Oskar Lange.

28. Pejovich (1966), p. 23 *ff*; Horvat (1971), pp. 108 *ff*; Dirlam and Plummer (1973), pp. 90 *ff*; OECD (1966; 1967; 1969; 1974; 1979); and Schrenk et al. (1979), pp. 119–122.

29. In Yugoslav parlance, economic plans are called social plans. Beginning in 1966, the annual plan at the federal level was superseded by a policy statement issued as a parliamentary resolution. On the state of planning at the time in question, see Pejovich (1966), pp. 36 *ff*; Horvat (1971), pp. 87 *ff*; and Dirlam and Plummer (1973), ch. 7.

30. The oft-noted Yugoslav experiment with credit auctions turned out to be just that—an experiment. It was employed only for a limited period after 1954. For more on the investment auctions, the state of post-1965 credit markets, and banking more generally, see Neuberger (1959); Horvat (1971), pp. 130 *ff*; Furubotn and Pejovich (1971); Dirlam and Plummer (1973), pp. 177 *ff*; Dubey (1975), pp. 66, 210 *ff*; Granick (1975), pp. 396 *ff*; and Schrenk et al (1979), chs. 4, 7, 8.

Given the prevailing inflation, the ability of the banks to impose extra ceiling rates and the prevalence of credit rationing do not seem inconsistent with the 9 percent rate of return that Jaroslav Vanek estimates is realized on the depreciated capital of self-managed enterprises.

31. Rus (1978-B), pp. 404 *ff* is not explicit as to the date of the survey data on which he relies. Although an original version of his essay was prepared for presentation to a conference held in August 1974, his conclusion about the status of banks, I believe, could apply to earlier years now of interest.

32. On the Party and self-management, see Wachtel (1973), pp. 79–82; on the Party's role in Yugoslav life more generally, see Rusinow (1978).

33. Neuberger and James (1973), p. 226; and Rus (1978-A), pp. 199 *ff*.

34. Bučar (1978), p. 427. The ascendancy that the executive achieved in this way over Party activists is reminiscent of circumstances long prevailing in other Eastern countries, where the secretary of the enterprise Party cell may find it expedient to collaborate with management even in violation of official norms. Bučar is also highly illuminating on the relation of the Party and trade union of self-management organs, although one wonders whether their control over the latter is nearly as complete as he implies. At any rate, the Party and the union were again on the ascendant in enterprise affairs towards the close of the PBS period, when subsequent arrangements began to come into play. Bučar may be referring particularly to circumstances at that time.

35. Founders, whoever they might be, had the right to repayment of any capital that they supplied. At least for citizen founders, repayment was with interest (Sacks 1973, pp. 12–13).

36. In the source cited, reference is the "net product" (*neto produkt*). However, that category comes to essentially the same thing as "net income" (*neto dohodak*) as that was used in Yugoslav accounting practice by 1969, or rather it is the same except that turnover taxes (exclusive of special charges on retail gasoline sales) are treated as a deduction before deriving net income.

As represented in Table 1, net product is apparently rather different from the category of that name in Yugoslav national income accounting. That is necessarily so, if only because changes in stocks are excluded from net product in the table, but reference there is to initial and terminal stocks at acquisition prices. For purposes of national income accounting, initial and terminal stocks are valued at the prices on the corresponding dates.

Possibly there are other divergencies between the two output categories. At any rate, even apart from the treatment of stocks, net product as given in the table should not be identified with the category of that name as used in Western national income accounting, though there is clearly a broad correspondence.

On Yugoslav SMF and national income accounting, see Gorupić and Paj (1970), pp. 152 *ff;* Furubotn and Pejovich (1972); and Dubey (1975), ch. 9, appendix A.

SZZS (1973) provides no explanation of the discrepancy (*razlika*). It appears only for the three years 1966–1968, and is probably related to the manner of accounting for sales, which was changed in 1969.

37. On enterprise payments to social-political institutions under PBS, see Gorupić and Paj (1970), pp. 139 *ff;* Horvat (1971), pp. 145 *ff;* Dirlam and Plummer (1973), pp. 186 *ff;* Wachtel (1973), pp. 111 *ff;* and Dubey (1975), ch. 9.

38. The 4-percent rate was established along with the 1965 economic reform in July 1965. The tax was levied on the *poslovni fond* (business fond), which essentially corresponded to the net worth of a Western firm even though some self-financed special claims against the enterprise's assets were excluded (for example, so-called "reserve funds" and funds for "communal consumption" and housing. The *kamata* ceased to be levied in 1971. See Lepotinec et al. (1967), pp. 183 *ff;* Furubotn and Pejovich (1972), pp. 276–277; Dirlam and Plummer (1973), pp. 41–45, 192–193.

39. Although the progressive taxes under PBS served as a source of local finance, they were intially levied in accord with the schedule promulgated by the federal government. Subsequently, schedules were promulgated by republican (or sometimes local) governments. A schedule in effect in Croatia circa 1969, however, was more or less typical: annual incomes of up to 20,000 dinars were fully exempt from the tax. Should the taxpayer have any dependents, the exemption rose by 3,000–5,000 dinars per dependent. For incomes exceeding exempt amounts, the marginal rate of tax varied from 3 percent to 80 percent, the latter rate being levied on the excess over 80,000 dinars. For someone earning 45,000 dinars with no dependents, the marginal rate on the last 5,000 dinars earned was 13 percent.

For comparison, the average worker in the socialized sector of the economy earned 11,520 dinars in 1969. The corresponding figure for the director of an SMF was 28,404 dinars. (These figures, of course, represent earnings from employment in the SMF.) Income from outside work were also subject to the tax, although no doubt the tax was frequently evaded. See Jurčec (1969), pp. 77 *ff,* 160; Bakračlić and Stojanovic (1970); SZZS (1971), pp. 268, 271; Dirlam and Plummer (1973), pp. 190–191, and Dubey (1975), p. 250.

40. As a benchmark, it may be useful to consider that for an individual with an income of $100, an even chance to win or lose $10 means that his choice is between the certain income of $100 and the stochastic option of ($90, $110). With a lump-sum tax of, say $10, the alternatives become $90 and ($80, $100); and with a 10-percent income tax $90 and ($81, $99). For a risk-averse person, the stochastic option is somewhat more attractive with the income tax than with the lump-sum tax.

41. On the financing of enterprise losses, see Dirlam and Plummer (1973), pp. 49–51; Sacks (1973), pp. 75–78; and Tyson (1977a).

42. That was clearly so for a minimum fixed by federal law. A com-

mune government could, if it wished, fix a higher minimum for workers within its purview, but the commune rates too were relatively low. See Gorupić and Paj (1970), p. 167; Wachtel (1973), pp. 101–102; and Dirlam and Plummer (1973), pp. 50, 65.

43. Gorupić and Paj (1970), pp. 180–183; Horvat (1971), pp. 104–105; and Dirlam and Plummer (1973), pp. 49–51.

44. In relation to total earnings, supplementary payments in manufacturing and mining averaged in 1956, 7.2 percent; in 1959, 12.2 percent, and in 1961, 9.0 percent [Wachtel (1973), p. 110.] Reason to think that the corresponding relation under PBS may have been similar is found in data available for the socialized sector in Slovenia: supplements there in 1971 constituted 10.4 percent of total earnings. See Miovic (1975), p. 108.

45. Furubotn and Pejovich (1972), p. 280; Dirlam and Plummer (1973), pp. 49–50; SZZS (1969), pp. 128–129.

46. See ILO (1962), pp. 126 *ff*; 218 *ff*; Bajt (1966); and Wachtel (1973).

47. While according to ILO (1962), p. 222, proportionality had been traditional regarding supplementary payments, Wachtel (1973), pp. 108–111, cites data on the relation of full to variable wages for different groups of industrial workers to show that that rule had ceased to apply by the late 1960s. As Wachtel is aware, the highly aggregative data he presents are open to more than one interpretation from that standpoint, but divergencies from proportionality doubtless occurred.

48. Executive incentive payments tend to be neglected in writings on Yugoslav self-management. However, in a textile enterprise that Adizes (1971) visited in 1967, some executives might earn as much as 32 percent over their basic pay if the enterprise's plan were completely fulfilled in specified particulars. There were even bonuses for limited degrees of underfulfillment, while overfulfillment brought still larger rewards. See Adizes (1971), pp. 51–52. This bonus scheme apparently was an exception to the rule enunciated in OECD (1965), p. 36: ". . . managerial categories receive management bonuses which can amount to 10 percent of their salaries."

A further question concerns the extent to which such special bonus arrangements prevailed under PBS. The textile firm referred to is one of two visited by Adizes. He does not indicate whether a corresponding scheme was used in the other. Granick (1975), found that special bonuses were being paid to executives in only one of the eight firms that he visited during 1970 (pp. 358, 365). Professor Alexander Bajt informs me (by letter of February 3, 1981) that bonus schemes such as those described by Adizes are, in fact, exceptional. According to both Slovenian Chamber of Commerce and trade union officials, no more then ten percent of enterprises have special incentive arrangements for executives. Such arrangements were more frequent prior to 1972, a "year of . . . severe political criticisms of managerialism, technicratism, and similar tendencies among managers."

49. Yugoslav income disparities appear to have been rather contracted by Western standards. Among countries at a comparable development stage, they were very much so. See Lydall (1968), pp. 215–219; Wachtel (1973), pp. 126 *ff*; Michal (1973); Granick (1975), pp. 459 *ff*; and Chapman (1977). Brown (1977) finds that Yugoslav labor differentials are somewhat wider than those in Great Britain, but his data do not seem to reach to the top among executives of British firms (pp. 56–58). Among Western countries, furthermore, Britain has for some time been both relatively advanced and relatively egalitarian.

50. A further implication is that any tendency towards the equality between firms and industries of relative marginal productivities of different kinds of labor should have been attenuated.

Such attenuation is inevitable wherever income disposition is shaped in an egalitarian manner. In effect, a firm with superior executive and other highly skilled labor is apt to employ too few unskilled workers relative to a firm less well-endowed with executive and other workers of superior quality.

51. Blum (1970), pp. 182–185; Horvat (1971), p. 105; Adizes (1971), pp. 128–129; Bajt (1972), p. 6; Jan Vanek (1972), p. 240; Neuberger and James (1973), pp. 267–268; Dirlam and Plummer (1973), pp. 49–50, 51–52; and Sirc (1979), pp. 131–137.

52. On the dismissal and non-reappointment of directors, see Brekić (1967), pp. 337–339; and Granick (1975), pp. 339, 352. Sletzinger (1976), cites somewhat different data on the number of directors who were not reelected, but his data relate to socio-political as well as economic organizations, and might be broader in scope than Granick's (pp. 58–59).

53. Granick (1975), p. 355; Sirc (1979), pp. 183–186. See also Županov (1969), ch. 10; and Županov (1973).

54. I refer, of course, to the impact of the taxes on labor effort and the like.

55. The tendency could only be compounded if income distribution were egalitarian, as in Yugoslavia. See above, n. 50.

56. See also Jan Vanek (1972), p. 284.

57. From industry data on net income and capital assets per worker, Vanek and Jovicic inpute a rate of return of 7 or 9 percent to capital (the precise figure depends on whether capital is gross or net of depreciation). Reference is to net income including the capital tax and bank loan interest, but as Vanek and Jovicic point out (though with data somewhat at variance with those underlying Table 1), interest at the imputed rates would exceed such charges. According to their calculations, however, the coefficient of correlation between net income per worker and gross capital assets per worker is only .48. When reference is to net capital assets per worker, the coefficient is only .53.

In a similar analysis, but with interest deducted from net income, Marschak (1968) found hardly any correlation to speak of between net income per worker and capital assets per worker (pp. 581–582). In their calculations, however, Vanek and Jovicic adjust employment for differences in skill; Marschak apparently makes no such adjustment. That could have been a factor in Marschak's relatively low correlation coefficients. Perhaps relevant circumstances in 1969, the year on which Vanek and Jovicic focus, were also rather different from those in 1959 and 1960. Marschak refers to the latter years.

58. In advancing his theory initially, Horvat sometimes took the charge in terms of which labor costs are calculated as corresponding to the *akontacija*. However, elsewhere reference is made to a target that includes supplementary pay. See Horvat (1971), p. 105; Horvat et al. (1975), vol. 2, pp. 234 *ff*. On other Yugoslav theories of the self-managed firm, see Milenkovich (1971), ch. 8.

I referred earlier to special bonuses sometimes paid to executives under PBS. Such bonuses tended to be unusual and, where paid, were rather limited in magnitude. However, to the extent they were paid, they might have affected marginal choices. It is of interest to note, therefore, that in the case described by Adizes (1971), executives were paid bonuses depending on how close they came to fulfilling plan targets for "profit from production," "cost" reduction, and sales (pp. 51–52). Adizes does not give these categories explicitly, but he informed me (by letter of February 12, 1981) that wages were probably not treated as a cost and expense before profits from production. To the extent that wages were not so treated, the bonus scheme represents an argument against the Horvat view of enterprise motivation.

59. The cited figures represent the sum of allocations to the "business fund" and one-half of allocations to the "fund for communal consumption and funds for housing construction." See SZZS (1973), p. 155.

60. Pejovich (1966), p. 31–32, 74; Bajt (1966), pp. 256–258; Furubutn and Pejovich (1971); Jan Vanek (1972), pp. 119–120; Furubotn and Pejovich (1973); and Sirc (1979), p. 138.

61. In the foregoing, I argued that large shares of disposable income saved under PBS must be understood in terms not of a maximand diverging from that of theory, but of market imperfections and external constraints. The latter constraints, though, became weaker in the course of time. Tyson (1977b) has urged a rather different view of PBS enterprise-saving rates. The maximand is still as theory posits, but enterprise savings essentially express propensities of a permanent income sort. For this view, Tyson can cite statistically significant (and often plausible) lagged relations between worker earnings withdrawals and enterprise income for different industrial branches. I wonder, though, if the same lagged relations are not consistent with market imperfections and external constraints that are especially

potent in initial years. If so, Tyson's view is not so very different from mine. Given the legal imperative to keep capital intact, Tyson's inclusion of depreciation in the enterprise's discretionary income also seems questionable.

62. In view of Županov's findings, one might wonder whether workers were subject to any downside risk at all. The evidence that they are, however, rules òut any serious doubts on that score. Županov's findings for managerial personnel alone point to the same conclusion.

63. Reference is particularly to findings given in Županov (1969), pp. 247–248, and Županov (1973), pp. 55–56. In the same survey, the executives were asked to indicate in which of a number of spheres their authority should be increased. While one of the spheres in question was "technological decisions" (*tehnološke odluke*), most of the executives did not cite this as meriting an increase in their authority [Županov (1969), p. 249; Županov (1973), pp. 57–58]. Very possibly, they did not construe the technical decisions in questions as embracing consequential innovations. Although they might have felt that they already had sufficient authority to introduce major innovations, that seems unlikely. Compare, for example, Županov (1978b), p. 83.

64. The Constitution of 1974 and Associated Labor Act are available in English translation. On the latter, see Flanz (1979). For surveys of major facets of the BOAL system, see also Milenkovich (1977); Schrenk et al. (1979); Comisso (1980); Sacks (1980); and Tyson (1980).

65. The use of internal transfer prices among subdivisions of the enterprise has rather early precedents. See, for example, ILO (1962), p. 228.

66. See the Constitution of 1974, art. 36; also Law on Associated Labor, art. 320. The division must also be such that workers can realize "their socio-economic and other self-management rights." This almost lacks content; however, reference is made elsewhere to certain entities, such as units servicing several BOALs, banks, and so on, that are to form "work communities"—agencies similar to, but not the same thing as, BOALs. Among economic agencies, the stipulation is presumably to take cognizance of such exceptional entities. More difficult to interpret, as it has turned out, is another provision that a BOAL should focus on only one sort of activity. See Sacks (1980), pp. 212–213.

67. In the process, both organizations have come to serve as major instruments for imposing more or less novel controls to which I refer below. On the role of the Party and the union in industrial administration under the BOAL system, see the Constitution of 1974, art. 104; the Law on Associated Labor, arts, 36, 504, 505, 509, 590; Milenkovitch (1971), p. 59; Rusinow (1978), ch. 8; Comisso (1979), ch. 6; Comisso (1980); and *Radio Free Europe Research* (September 26, 1980).

68. Jovanov (1978); *Radio Free Europe Research* (April 7, 1977;

March 8, 1978; June 12, 1978; June 14, 1978; December 8, 1978; September 20, 1978; September 26, 1980; November 29, 1978; February 12, 1979; July 11, 1979).

69. The question may be raised, is it meaningful any longer to refer to the enterprise under the BOAL system? The answer is that the enterprise no longer has the clear legal identity that it had previously, but it still exists as a form of relatively close collaboration of BOALs. As such, it still has a status in Yugoslav law, though it is now referred to as a "work organization" or an "organization of associated labor" [compare Sacks (1980), pp. 217 *ff.*]

70. See Schrenk et al. (1979), pp. 151, 329. The apparent reversal, though, seems largely to reflect increments in inventory values caused by price increases. There are limited discrepancies between Schrenk et al., and Table 1 in the data for 1966–1971. The reasons for this are not clear.

71. On social compacts and self-management agreements, see Furubotn and Pejovich (1973); Dubey (1975), pp. 237–239; Comisso (1979), pp. 124 *ff;* Schrenk et al. (1979); pp. 49 *ff,* 147*ff;* Sirc (1979), pp. 137–140; Comisso (1980); Sacks (1980); and Kardelj (n.d.)

72. Comisso (1980), pp. 202–203. In Slovenia, payouts in excess of norms have been made subject to a progressive tax [Dubey (1975), p. 238]. On other recent developments regarding enterprise taxation, see Dirlam and Plummer (1973), p. 193, and Comisso (1979), p. 126.

73. In the 1972 self-management agreement for Belgrade trade workers, differentials generally varied with educational qualifications; however, executives were to be paid 40 percent more than their educational level would indicate [Furubotn and Pejovich (1973), p. 296]. In the machinery firm that Comisso (1979) visited in 1974, the base rate of the director was 3.8 times that of a cleaning woman (pp. 142 *ff*). That spread is little greater than the 3.4 reported by Jan Vanek (1972) for a large undertaking in 1959 (pp. 129–130).

74. In addition to Milenkovitch, see Schrank et al. (1979), ch. 4; Comisso (1980); and Sacks (1980).

75. I have suggested the 1974–1976 reforms might be considered a kind of trust-busting program. The introduction of the BOAL system has also been referred to as a form of divisionalization (Sacks 1980). That characterization doubtless has its merit, but, in commenting on a preliminary draft of this chapter, Oliver Williamson pointed out that the key to effective divisionalization is to recognize opportunities for decomposability. Where there are such opportunities, he argues, operating responsibilities should be assigned to the parts concerned, but a general office should still be maintained that evaluates the performance of the individual divisions and is responsible for strategic resource allocation.

Although Williamson's formulation applies primarily to divisionalization in a Western firm, Williamson is surely right in assuming that there is an economic case for heeding the foregoing principles in respect to the Yugoslav SMF. Have they, in fact, been heeded under the 1974–1976 reforms? I cannot really pursue that matter here, but as Williamson conjectures, his principles have doubtless been violated often under the BOAL system.

References

AER: *American Economic Review*

EJ: *Economic Journal*

OECD: Organization for Economic Cooperation and Development.

QJE: *Quarterly Journal of Economics*

SZZS: Savezni Zavod za Statistiku

JCE: *Journal of Comparative Economics*

SL: *Službeni List SFRJ*

SFRJ: *Socijalistika federativna republika Jugoslavija*

Adizes, Ichak. *Industrial Democracy: Yugoslav Style.* New York: Free Press, 1971.
Arrow, Kenneth J. *Theory of Risk Bearing.* Chicago, Ill.: Markham, 1971.
Arzenšek, Vladimir. "Managerial Legitimacy and Organizational Conflict." In Obradović and Dunn (1978).
Bajt, Aleksander. "Income Distribution under Workers' Self-Management." In Ross (1966).
————. "Managerial Incentives in Yugoslavia." Mimeograph. Milan: Centro Studi e Recerche su Problemi Economico Sociali, 1972.
Bakračlić, Miodraz and Stojanović, Teodosije. *Zbirka propisa o doprinosima i porezima gradana.* Belgrade, 1970.
Blum, Emerik. "The Director and Workers' Management." In Broekmeyer (1970).
Blumberg, Paul. *Industrial Democracy.* New York, Schocken Books, 1969.
Bornstein, Morris, ed. *Plan and Market.* New Haven, Conn.: Yale University Press, 1973.
————. *Comparative Economic Systems,* 3d ed. Homewood, Ill.: Irwin, 1974.
Brekić, Jovo. "Analiza reizbornosti direktora." In Gorupić and Brekić (1967).

Broekmeyer, M.J., ed. *Yugoslav Workers' Self-Management.* Dordrecht, Holland: Reidel, 1979.

Brown, Henry Phelps. *The Inequality of Pay.* Oxford: Oxford University Press, 1977.

Bučar, France. "Participation of State and Political Organizations in Enterprise Decisions." In Obradović and Dunn (1978).

Chapman, Janet. "The Distribution of Earnings in Selected Countries, East and West." Mimeograph. Pittsburgh, (1977).

Comisso, Ellen T. *Workers' Control under Plan and Market.* New Haven, Conn.: Yale University Press, 1979.

————. "Yugoslavia in the 1970's: Self-Management and Bargaining." *JCE,* June 1980.

The Constitution of the Socialist Federal Republic of Yugoslavia. New York: Merrick, 1976.

Dimitrijevic, Dimitrije, and Macesich, George. *Money and Finance in Contemporary Yugoslavia.* New York: Praeger, 1973.

Dirlam, Joel B., and Plummer, James L. *An Introduction to the Yugoslav Economy.* Columbus, Ohio: Charles E. Merrill, 1973.

Domar, Evsey. "The Soviet Collective Farm." *AER* 56, 4 (September 1966):734–757.

Dubey, Vinod. *Yugoslavia: Development with Decentralization.* Baltimore: Johns Hopkins University Press, 1975.

The Economist. Various dates.

Estrin, Saul. "Income Dispersion in a Self-Managed Economy." *Economica* 48, 190 (May 1981):181–194.

Flanz, Gisbert H. *Constitutions of the Countries of the World: Special Supplement: Yugoslavia.* Dobbs Ferry, N.Y.: Oceana Publications, 1979.

Furubotn, Erik G. "Bank Credit and the Labor-Managed Firm: Reply." *AER* 70, 4 (September 1980):800–804.

Furubotn, Erik, and Pejovich, Svetozar. "The Role of the Banking System in Yugoslav Economic Planning, 1946–1969." *Revue Internationale d'Histoire de la Banque.* Geneva: Librairie Droz, 1971.

————. "The Formation and Distribution of Net Product and the Behavior of the Yugoslav Firm." *Jahrbuch der Wirtschaft Osteuropas* vol. 3. Munich, 1972.

————. "Property Rights, Economic Decentralization and the Evolution of the Yugoslav Firm, 1965–1972." *The Journal of Law and Economics* 26, 2 (October 1973):275–302.

————. "Property Rights and the Behavior of the Firm in a Socialist State: The Example of Yugoslavia." In Furubotn and Pejovich (1974).

Furubotn, Eric G., and Pejovich, Svetozar, eds. *The Economics of Property Rights.* Cambridge, Mass.: Ballinger, 1974.

Gorupić, Drago. "The Worker-Managed Enterprise (I): Stages of Institutional Development." In Obradović and Dunn (1978).

Gorupić, Drago, and Brekic, Jovo, eds. *Direktor u samoupravnim odnosima*. Zagreb, 1970.

Gorupić, Drago, and Paj, Ivan. *Workers' Self-Management in Yugoslav Undertakings*. Zagreb 1970.

Granick, David. *Enterprise Guidance in Eastern Europe*. Princeton, N.J.: Princeton University Press, 1975.

Hey, John D., and Suckling, John. "The Labor-Managed Firm under Price Uncertainty." Discussion paper 38, University of York, November 1979.

Horvat, Branko. "Yugoslav Economic Policy in the Post-War Period." *AER* 61, 3, part 2 (June 1971):71–169.

Horvat, Branko; Markovic, Mihailo; and Supek, Rudi, eds. *Self-Governing Socialism: A Reader*. vols. 1 and 2. White Plains, N.Y.: International Arts and Sciences Press, 1975.

ILO. *Workers' Management in Yugoslavia*. Geneva: ILO, 1962.

Jovanov, Neca. "Strikes and Self-Management." in Obradović and Dunn (1978).

Jurčec, Mijo, ed. *Zbirka propisa o doprinosima in porezima gradjana*. Zagreb, 1969.

Kardelj, Edward. *The System of Planning in a Society of Self-Management: Brioni Discussions*. Belgrade, n.d.

Komentar zakona o udruženom radu. Belgrade, 1980.

Lepotinec, Slavko; Djačić, Milan; Plivelić, Marijan; Šunjić, Ivo; and Vrsalovic, Berislav. *Zbirka propisa o sredstvima i dohotku*. Zagreb, 1967.

Lydall, Harold. *The Structure of Earning*. Oxford: Oxford University Press, 1968.

Marschak, Thomas A. "Centralized versus Decentralized Resource Allocation: The Yugoslav 'Laboratory.'" *QJE* 82, 4 (November 1968):561–587.

Meade, James. "The Theory of the Labor-Managed Firm and of Profit Sharing." *EJ* 82, 325S (March 1972):402–428.

———. "Labor-Managed Firms in Conditions of Imperfect Competition". *EJ* 84, 336 (December 1974):817–824.

Michal, Jan W. "Size Distribution of Earnings and Household Incomes in Small Socialist Countries." *Review of Income and Wealth* 19, 4 (December 1973):407–428.

Milenkovitch, Deborah D. *Plan and Market in Yugoslav Economic Thought*. New Haven, Conn.: Yale University Press, 1971.

———. "The Case of Yugoslavia." *AER* 67, 1 (February 1977):55–60.

Millikan, Max F., ed. *National Economic Planning*. New York, N.Y.: Columbia University Press, 1967.

Miović, Peter. *Determinants of Income Differentials in Yugoslav Self-Managed Enterprise.* Ph.D. thesis, Cornell University, 1975.

Montias, John M. "Economic Planning in Yugoslavia: Comment." In Millikan (1967).

Neuberger, Egon. "The Yugoslav Investment Auctions." *QJE* 73, 1 (February 1959):88–115.

Neuberger, Egon, and James, Estelle. "The Yugoslav Self-Managed Enterprise: A Systemic Approach." In Bornstein (1973).

Obradović, Josip. "Participation in Enterprise Decision-Making." In Obradović and Dunn (1978).

Obradović, Josip, and Dunn, William N., eds. *Workers' Self-Management and Organizational Power in Yugoslavia.* Pittsburgh: University of Pittsburgh Press, 1978.

OECD. *Economic Surveys: Yugoslavia.* Paris: OECD, various dates.

Pejovich, Svetozar, *The Market-Planned Economy of Yugoslavia.* Minneapolis, Minn.: University of Minnesota Press, 1966.

———. "The Banking System and the Investment Behavior of the Yugoslav Firm." In Bornstein (1973).

Radio Free Europe Research.

Ross, Arthur M., ed. *Industrial Relations and Economic Development.* London: Macmillan, 1966.

Rus, Veljko. (A) "Enterprise Power Structure." In Obradović and Dunn (1978).

———. (B) "External and Internal Influences on Enterprises." In Obradović and Dunn (1978).

Rusinow, Dennison. *The Yugoslav Experiment 1948–1974.* Berkeley, University of California Press, 1978.

Sacks, Stephen R., *Entry of New Competitors in Yugoslav Market Socialism,* Berkeley: University of California Press, 1973.

———. "Divisionalization in Large Yugoslav Enterprises." *JCE* 4, 2 (June 1980):209–225.

Schrenk, Martin; Ardalan, Cyrus; and El Tatawy, Nowal A. *Yugoslavia: Self-Management Socialism and the Challenges of Development.* Baltimore: Johns Hopkins University Press, 1979.

Sirc, Ljubo. *The Yugoslav Economy under Self-Management.* New York: St. Martin's, 1979.

Sletzinger, Martin C. *The Reform and Reorganization of the League of Communists of Yugoslavia, 1966–1973.* Ph.D. thesis, Harvard University, 1976.

Stephen, F.H. "Bank Credit and the Labor-Managed Firm: Comment". *AER* 70, 4 (September 1980):796–799.

Službeni list SFRJ.

SZZS, SFRJ. *Statistički godišnjak Jugoslavije 1971,* Belgrade 1971.

SZZS, SFRJ. *Privredni bilansi Jugoslavije, 1966–1971.* Belgrade, 1973.

Tyson, Laura D. (A) "Liquidity Crises in the Yugoslav Economy: An Alternative to Bankruptcy?" *Soviet Studies* 29, 2 (April 1977):284–295.

————. (B) "A Permanent Income Hypothesis for the Yugoslav Firm." *Economica* 44-176 (November 1977):393–408.

————. *The Yugoslav Economic System and Its Performance in the 1970's.* Berkeley: University of California Press, 1980.

Vanek, Jan. *The Economics of Workers' Management: a Yugoslav Case Study.* London: George Allen & Unwin, 1972.

Vanek, Jaroslav. *The General Theory of Labor-Managed Economies.* Ithaca, N.Y.: Cornell University Press, 1970.

————. *The Labor-Managed Economy.* Ithaca, N.Y.: Cornell University Press, 1977.

Vanek, Jaroslav, and Jovicic, Milena. "Capital Market and Income Distribution in Yugoslavia." *QJE* 89, 3 (August 1975):432–443.

Vejonić, Milos. "Influence Structure in a Self-Managing Enterprise." In Obradović and Dunn (1978).

Wachtel, Howard M. *Workers' Management and Workers' Wages in Yugoslavia.* Ithaca, N.Y.: Cornell University Press, 1973.

The Wall Street Journal. Various dates.

Ward, Benjamin, "Workers Management in Yugoslavia." *Journal of Political Economy* 65, 5 (October 1957):373–386.

————. "The Firm in Illyria: Market Syndicalism." *AER* 58, 4 (September 1958):566–589.

Županov, Josip. "The Producer and Risk." *Eastern European Economics* 7,7 (Spring 1967).

————. *Samoupravljenje i društvena moć.* Zagreb, 1969.

————. "Is Enterprise Management Becoming Professionalized?" *International Studies of Management and Organization.* Fall, 1973.

————. "The Yugoslav Enterprise." In Bornstein (1974).

————. "Participation and Influence." In Horvat et al., vol. 2 (1975).

————. (A) "Two Patterns of Conflict Management in Industry." In Obradović and Dunn (1978).

————. "Egalitarianism and Industrialism." In Obradović and Dunn (1978).

10

Annual Plan Fulfillment in Soviet Industry, 1961–1985

Under centralist planning, plan fulfillment must yield to other more basic matters, such as growth of output and productivity, and growth of consumption levels, which are normative indicators of the system's economic performance. How nearly plan targets are met, however, is of interest in itself because it measures the degree of accomplishment of declared goals. Normative appraisal apart, one also turns to plan fulfillment in seeking to understand centralist planning, its nature and its manner of functioning.

Of particular interest is the immediately operational annual plan. We are fortunate, therefore, to have, as a result of the indefatigable efforts of Eugene Zaleski (1971; 1980), extensive and detailed tabulations on Soviet performance regarding annual plan fulfillment for the pre-World War II years. Thus far, however, the record for post-World War II years appears to have been subject to only limited inquiries, the chief amongst them being that of David Granick (1980) for the years 1969–1977.

The resultant gaps in our knowledge of Soviet annual plan fulfillment is unhappily not easily remedied. In pursuing his researches for pre-World War II years, Zaleski could draw on quite substantial releases on annual plan targets. The publication of inclusive and detailed annual plans was interrupted by the war and has never been resumed since. The releases that the government has issued, never too informative, tended over time to become progressively less so.

On such an important matter, however, even limited information can be of value. The attempt made here to delineate tentatively trends in annual plan fulfillment in the crucial industrial sphere over the years 1961–1985 should be viewed in that light. At the risk of compounding uncertainties, I also speculate about the causes of the shifts that are discerned.

Table 1
Annual Plan Output Targets and their Degree of Fulfillment (DOF) Selected Industrial Products, 1933–37 and 1961–85[a]

Item	1933–1937[b]	1961–1965[c]	1966–1970[d]	1971–1975[e]	1976–1980[f]	1981–1985[g]
Number of targets	41	41	34	34	33	29
Average target, percent of previous year	128.7	114.3	108.5	106.1	106.3	104.1
Targets fulfilled:						
Number	13	28	20	28	6	9
Average DOF, percent	105.8	102.2	101.0	101.1	100.9	101.4
Targets underfulfilled:						
Number	28	13	14	6	27	20
Average DOF, percent	88.0	96.8	97.5	99.1	96.9	98.2

[a] Except as noted, products covered are coal, oil, natural gas, electric power, steel, rolled steel (all or finished only), mineral fertilizer, cement, and plastics. *Sources:* For 1933–1937: Zaleski (1980: 550ff), with mineral fertilizer represented essentially by cited phosphoric varieties and 1932 actual from TSSU (1964). For 1961–1985: plan goals, *Pravda*, Dec. 21, 1960 and corresponding annual issues in later years. Some goals for 1964 interpolated from planned increases, 1963–1965. Minor conflicts sometimes noted between stated output target and corresponding target inferred from projected increments, where both are given, are generally resolved in favor of the former. For all 1961–1985, actual, TSSU (1963) and corresponding volumes for other years; annual economic reports in *Pravda*.

[b] Omitting for natural gas, 1933; plastics, 1933–1935.

[c] Omitting for coal, 1965; mineral fertilizer, 1961; cement, 1964–65.

[d] Omitting 1968; for mineral fertilizer, 1966; cement, 1967.

[e] Omitting 1972; for mineral fertilizer and plastics, 1973.

[f] Omitting 1977; for steel, 1979; cement, 1978; plastics, 1980.

[g] Omitting 1982; for natural gas, 1981; steel, 1981 and 1983–1985; cement, 1983; plastics, 1981.

I

In compiling the data set forth on annual plan fulfillment (Table 1), I referred only to the targets reported to the Supreme Soviet that were included in the initial version of each plan. The degree of fulfillment (DOF) that is achieved is thus unaffected by any revisions made in targets as the plan was implemented.[1] The targets considered also have the virtue that they are all expressed in physical units, so their DOF can be gauged on that basis. Where goals and output are in ruble terms, incongruities between the two sorts of data preclude accurate appraisal of the DOF (CIA 1980).

Inconveniently for our purposes, the official post-World War II releases on plan targets have not only been relatively restrictive, they have also been notably erratic in scope: a target for any particular product is often reported very irregularly; frequently just for one or a few years. The nine products on which I focus (coal, oil, natural gas, electric power, steel, rolled steel, mineral fertilizer, cement, and plastics) appear to be practically all the non-food industrial goods for which targets for output in physical units are reported with any considerable regularity. (For present purposes, harvest-sensitive food products would seem to be rather special.) Even for the nine goods considered there are sometimes gaps, and several years are not represented at all in my compilation.[2]

The targets in question are evidently industrywide, and are also highly aggregative with respect to product assortment. Even at that level of aggregation, the indicated products constitute but a small fraction of the number of commodities produced by Soviet industry. They are, nevertheless, cardinal outputs of the sectors that account for a major part of Soviet industrial non-food production (41.7 percent in 1970, Ray Converse 1982:190). A number of the products considered are also basic inputs virtually throughout industry. Regarding trends, if not levels, of DOF, the nine products should represent much more than themselves.

For familiar reasons, target overfulfillment under centralist planning is by no means apt to be an unmitigated good, but, manifestly, it is not to be equated to underfulfillment. Accordingly, I record separately the two sorts of cases. In a sense, though, divergencies from plan in either direction represent a form of malfunctioning in planning, and it may not be amiss to explicate the record of performance in that light.

For comparison with my data 1961–1985, I have compiled corresponding measures for the years 1933–1937 (the years of the last complete pre-World War II five-year plan) from Zaleski (1980). Referring momentarily to the post-World War II performance during the first three of the five-year plan periods covered, that is, the years 1961–1975, the contrast to that of pre-World War II years is striking. Among the nine products considered, targets during the sixties and early seventies are fulfilled relatively much more often and correspondingly underfulfilled relatively much less often than during the years

1933–1937 (Table 1). Where targets are underfulfilled, the shortfall tends to be markedly less in the later intervals than in the earlier one.

So far as targets are overfulfilled, performance also evolves markedly and in a corresponding way. Output systematically falls nearer the mark and exceeds targets less frequently during the period 1961–1975 than during the pre-World War II period.

The nine products considered are all important, but not equally so. It is of interest, therefore, that from the pre-World War II years to the years 1961–1975, the shift in performance when the products are considered as a group, is also generally manifest for individual products (Table 2; I focus at this point on plan underfulfillment). There are, though, some striking variations. Among the nine products, oil, for example, is one of the worst performers in the period 1933–1937 and it performs the very best for the years 1961–1975.

I conclude, if only provisionally, that in respect of plan fulfillment a shift, broadly similar to that manifest for our nine products, occurred among industrial goods more generally. In the sixties and early seventies, plan fulfillment among such goods should generally have been superior, possibly very superior, to that of the years 1933–1937.

The sorry performance of plan fulfillment during the period 1933–1937, manifest in my summary data for the nine products, only epitomizes a record of egregious divergencies from targets which has already been made evident in the more inclusive data of Zaleski (1980).[3] Such results for Soviet pre-World War II planning could come as no great surprise. The indication of a marked improvement in performance by the years 1961–1975 is also not surprising. That result, though, may merit underlining. Presuppositions as to Soviet annual plan fulfillment originally formed in relation to the pre-World War II experience often seem to color thinking about plan fulfillment more generally, and with little regard to actual performance in later periods.

If we judge from the results of my limited sample, though, the post-World War II improvement proved to be, to a degree, only temporary. Here, too, there have been ample indications of the shift that is now indicated (Table 1). Gertrude Schroeder's (1985) exposition of the vicissitudes attendant on the 1976–1982 slowdown is especially illuminating in this regard.

It still seems useful to see in quantitative terms the retrogression that occurred in respect to plan fulfillment during the period 1976–1985. Compared to the sixties and early seventies, fulfillment and overfulfillment of targets are, again, relatively rare and underfulfillment is quite frequent. There is no longer any pronounced difference in either case, however, regarding the average DOF. As before, too, the shift in respect of fulfillment is general, and for all nine products studied, the frequency of underfulfillment increases markedly (Table 2).[4]

I referred above to Granick's 1980 inquiry into plan fulfillment. Referring to industrial ministry, rather than product targets, Granick (see also Gorlin and Doane 1983) finds that during the years 1969–1977, there were two years

Table 2
Underfulfillment of Annual Plan Targets, by Product, for Nine Industrial Goods, 1933–1937 and 1961–1985[a]

Products	1933–1937			1961–1975			1976–1985		
	No. of targets	No. underfulfilled	DOF[b] (%)	No. of targets	No. underfulfilled	DOF (%)	No. of targets	No. underfulfilled	DOF (%)
Coal	5	5	92.9	12	2	98.8	8	7	97.3
Oil	5	5	90.7	13	1	99.7	8	8	98.7
Gas	4	4	90.7	13	6	98.6	7	0	n.a.[c]
Electric power	5	1	89.4	13	3	98.3	8	3	98.9
Steel	5	3	87.8	13	3	98.9	3	3	97.3
Rolled steel	5	2	82.2	13	3	98.9	8	8	97.5
Mineral fertilizer	5	3	90.8	10	4	96.6	8	6	95.3
Cement	5	4	76.3	10	3	98.0	6	6	98.2
Plastics	2	1	88.7	12	8	95.0	6	6	96.5
All	41	28	88.0	109	33	97.5	62	47	97.5

[a] *Sources:* See Table 1.   [b] Degree of fulfillment.   [c] n.a. = not applicable.

in which 29 percent of the ministries missed their output targets. For the remaining six years, out of the 157 cases that were observed there was only one instance of ministry underfulfillment of a target. Granick is referring to targets for "realized output" or "sales" in ruble terms. For reasons indicated above, the DOF for that aspect is of doubtful meaning, but his finding is not inconsistent with the generally favorable performance of plan fulfillment that I observe for the years 1971–1975.[5] Referring to the same sort of targets, Granick also finds a significant improvement in ministerial performance when the period 1969–1977 is compared with the years 1949–1956.

II

What is the reason for the temporal variation in plan fulfillment we have discerned? Plan fulfillment in the USSR is by now a familiar topic, but seemingly the causes of divergencies from targets have yet to be explored in any systematic way. That is a deficiency that is not easily repaired, but there is no basis here to dissent from what I judge is a prevalent view: to a significant extent, the dismal record of fulfillment observed during the years 1933–1937 reflected the fact that the plans for those years tended to be notably taut to begin with; notably taut, that is, in the accepted sense that, under likely circumstances, the probability of fulfillment of their targets tended to be low (compare Kornai 1980:49ff).

For pre-World War II plans, this seems to be an unavoidable conclusion; and if it is granted that the plans were unlikely to be fulfilled it is but an easy step to the further conclusion that the improvement in plan fulfillment observed by the years 1961–1975 very likely reflected a tendency on the part of the "system's directors" to formulate less taut plans than those characteristic of the years 1933–1937. The sharply reduced rates of growth that were projected (Table 1) are in themselves highly suggestive, though not conclusive evidence, on that score.

But, while targets very likely did become less taxing, it would be wrong to infer, as one is tempted to do, that this factor alone accounts for the much improved performance regarding plan fulfillment. During the years 1933–1937, centralist planning in the USSR was still at an early stage, and from a technical standpoint it was also, not surprisingly, relatively primitive. Much Western research before Zaleski (1980) demonstrated how primitive centralist planning was, but his detailed account graphically underlines the pervasive inadequacies.

The corollary is that even should Soviet planners have wished to avoid tautness, it might have been difficult for them to do so. The alternative desideratum presumably would have been feasibility, but in an uncertain world miscalculations are unavoidable. With the information and procedures for processing it that were available to Soviet planners during the years 1933–1937, miscalculation would have been great indeed. True, the resulting divergencies from plan targets would have been in the direction of over- as well as underfulfillment, but in the case of intermediate products especially, underfulfilled targets tend to have "secondary effects," which only give rise to more underfulfilled targets.

In fact the Soviet planners sought tautness in preference to feasibility, but *in the foregoing ways* the technical incapacity of centralist planning should have contributed to the egregious performance regarding plan fulfillment during the years 1933–1937. The infrequent instances of overfulfillment as well as the very frequent instances of underfulfillment are properly read in that light.

Our concern is not so much with plan fulfillment during the years 1933–1937 as with its marked improvement observed by the years 1961–1975. If technical deficiencies contributed to the extraordinary divergencies from plan targets during the years 1933–1937, however, an amelioration of those deficiencies should have been, along with reduced tautness, a factor in the comparatively near approximation to targets during the years 1961–1975. Soviet centralist planning was hardly unflawed at the outset of that period, and despite much publicized reforms, it was still flawed at the end of that period. It would be surprising, however, if there had not been some improvement over the rudimentary pre-World War II procedures.

We know a good deal about the cause of the abrupt fall-off in growth that occurred in Soviet industry beginning in 1976 (Levine 1983; Schroeder 1985), but why that should have been associated with a deterioration in the performance as to plan fulfillment (to come finally to that shift) is less clear. Since the government progressively lowered its targets for industrial growth over the period 1976–1985, one hesitates to assume that Soviet planners consciously opted for greater tautness, but in seeking to limit the slowdown, they could well have done so.[6]

Even if planners did opt for greater tautness, they must have been surprised by the extent of the retardation, so there is perhaps also some indication here of a decline in their technical proficiency. The circumstances of an abrupt decline in growth, however, must have complicated their task. More generally, during the years 1976–1985 the government continued the effort they had initiated during the years 1961–1975 to "perfect" the planning system. Even the skeptically inclined must concede that the various measures adopted, if not to the good, should not have been especially to the worse.

One wonders, however, whether there is not evidence in the worsened record of fulfillment that the task of programming Soviet industrial expansion has become particularly onerous at the present stage. I am thinking, of course, of the difficulties posed under centralist planning by the ever increasing numbers of enterprises and products, and the ever more refined specifications that have to be dealt with under centralist planning. Such difficulties must have become formidable for an economy where there are 44,000 industrial enterprises (TSSU 1981:121); in the electro-technical industry alone there are some 250,000 commodities of distinct specifications (Ellman 1971:61).

We still have much to learn about the Soviet experience in respect of plan fulfillment. From available facts, though, we can perhaps better understand the commitment of a new leadership to a planning shift more sweeping than any yet undertaken since Stalin.

Notes

* Martin Weitzman made helpful comments on an earlier draft.

[1] Also excluded from the accounting are any revisions to the targets, made in the Council of Ministers, in response to discussion at the Supreme Soviet. In the case of targets, such as those considered here, such revisions, I believe, are rarely consequential. For comparison with the 1961–1985 experience, below I utilize data drawn from Zaleski (1980) on plan fulfillment during the years 1933–1937. It should be noted that the process of governmental review of an annual plan has evolved somewhat, at least formally, in the course of time. The goals cited by Zaleski, nevertheless appear to be essentially comparable, in respect of the stage of the review progress represented, to the post-World War II goals considered here. They sometimes reflect, however, subsequent revisions. One might suppose, as a result, that the DOF should tend to be improved. In the circumstances of the thirties, though, a contrary bias is perhaps not precluded.

[2] None of the goals of interest here were reported for industrial products in 1972, and it seemed just as well to omit also those for 1968, 1977 and 1982, though a goal for electric power was reported in each case. Such extensive withholding of annual plan targets need not have any deep meaning. For 1972, for example, probably a decisive factor was that the plan for that year was reported to the Supreme Soviet concomitantly with the five-year plan for the years 1971–1975.

[3] In his exhaustive 1980 inquiry, Zaleski was able to compile data on plan ful@lment during 1933–1937 for as many as 74 industrial non-food products. Zaleski himself processes his data in a more or less summary way (1980:270ff). While his procedure differs from mine, we need not reprocess his figures to arrive at a reassuring though not very unexpected result: for his lengthy list of products, performance of plan fulfillment must have been, if anything, even less impressive than for the nine products on which I focus.

For each of his 74 industrial non-food products, Zaleski calculates the average DOF for targets in the five annual plans issued for the years 1933–1937. From these data, we may calculate that the average DOF for my nine products, taken together, is 93.8 percent. The corresponding figure for all of the products that Zaleski covers is 89.0 percent. In these calculations, as I did for my own compilation (Table 1), I consolidate the two kinds of mineral fertilizer that Zaleski distinguishes into one commodity. I also extend his list to include the plastics, which he omits from his summary data, presumably because only two years are covered. As before, I draw here on Zaleski (1980:550ff).

[4] My serial data for nine selected products hardly constitute random samples, but it is still of interest to note that the indicated gain in DOF from the period 1933–1937 to that of 1961–1975 yields a Chi-square, 16.22, that easily attests significance at the 1.0 percent level. Similarly, the reversal in DOF from the period 1961–1965 to that of 1976–1985 yields a Chi-square of 31.13. I apply the Chi-square test in corrected form to my comparative data on fulfillment and non-fulfillment of plan targets (Table 1), without regard to the magnitude of the DOF.

For the 28 targets underfulfilled during 1933–1937, the mean DOF was 88.0 percent (Table 1). Aggregating results previously recorded for five-year intervals, we find that for the 33 targets underfulfilled during the years 1961–1975 the mean DOF was 97.5 percent, which was also the mean DOF for 47 targets that were underfulfilled during the years 1976–1985. Among targets underfulfilled, it may also be of interest that the median DOF for the years 1933–1937 was approximately 88.5 percent; for the years 1961–1975, 97.0 percent, and, for the years 1976–1985, 97.0 percent.

[5] According to Granick, the two years when ministerial plan underfulfillment was relatively frequent were 1969 and 1972. For 1969 I found that targets for six of my nine products were underfulfilled. I omitted 1972 from my compilation because of lack of data.

[6] For my nine products, the reduction in planned growth rates does not occur until the years 1981–1985 (Table 1), but I think the tempos projected for industrial growth in general under the tenth five-year plan (1976–1980: 6.5 percent) and the eleventh five-year plan (1981–1985: 4.9 percent) are more relevant at this point. Under the ninth five-year plan (1971–1975) the corresponding tempo was 8.0 percent, while the tempo realized was 7.5 percent (CIA 1986:64; Converse 1982:201). As Soviet planners must have been to some degree aware, the last figure, indicated by official data, must have been an inflated one. According to the CIA's calculations, Soviet industrial output grew during the years 1971–1975 by but 5.4–5.7 percent yearly.

References

Bornstein, Morris (1985, January). "Improving the Soviet Economic Mechanism." *Soviet Studies*, 37 (1) 1–30.

Central Intelligence Agency (CIA) (1980, August). *Comparing Planned and Actual Growth in Centrally Planned Economies*, ER-80-1046, Washington, D.C.: CIA.

—— (1986). *Handbook of Economics Statistics, (1986)*. CPAS, 86-10002. Washington, D.C.: CIA.

Converse, Ray (1982). "An Index of Industrial Production in the USSR." In Joint Economic Committee, United States Congress, *USSR: Measures of Economic Growth and Development, 1950–80*. Washington, D.C.: GPO.

Ellman, Michael (1971). *Soviet Planning Today*. Cambridge: Cambridge University Press.

Gorlin, Alice C. and David P. Doane (1983, December). "Plan Fulfillment and Growth in Soviet Ministries." *Journal of Comparative Economics*, 7 (4), 415–531.

Granick, David. (1980, September). "The Ministry as the Maximizing Unit in Soviet Industry." *Journal of Comparative Economics*, 4 (3), 255–273.

Pravda (1960, December 21).

Schroeder, Gertrude (1972, July). "The 'Reform' of the Supply System in Soviet Industry." *Soviet Studies*, 24 (1), 97–119.

—— (1985, January–March). "The Slowdown in Soviet Industry, 1976–1982." *Soviet Economy*, 1 (1), 42–74.

Tsentral'noe Statisticheskoe Upravlenie (TSSU) (1963). *Narodnoe khoziaistvo SSSR v 1962 godu*. Moscow.

—— (1981). *Narodnoe khoziaistvo SSSR v 1980 godu*. Moscow.

—— (1964). *Promyshlennost' SSSR*. Moscow.

Zaleski, Eugene (1971). *Planning for Economic Growth in the Soviet Union, 1918–1932*. Chapel Hill, NC: University of North Carolina Press.

—— (1980). *Stalinist Planning for Economic Growth, 1933–1952*. Chapel Hill, NC: University of North Carolina Press.

11

The Geometry of
COMECON Trade*

1. Trade relations within COMECON are by now the subject of numerous scholarly Western studies, but the analytic import of this work is not always easy to grasp. An attempt to interpret the empirical findings more systematically than is often done from a theoretic standpoint may be of value. As it turns out, knowledge of some cardinal matters still seems uncertain, but to be clear about that may serve at least to help focus further research.

Of particular interest is the relation of COMECON trade to neo-classical principles familiar in Western trade theory. COMECON trade obviously must often diverge from such principles, but it remains to consider the nature and degree of the departures and the resulting economic gains and losses to participants.

COMECON,[1] an organization originally set up as something of a response to the Marshall Plan but more recently concerned to coordinate economic policies and promote economic integration among communist countries, embraces the USSR, Bulgaria, Czechoslovakia, East Germany (GDR), Hungary, Poland and Rumania. Mongolia is also a member, Cuba has been too since 1972, and Vietnam became a member in 1978. Yugoslavia and North Korea are affiliated as observers.

I focus on trade between the USSR and Eastern European COMECON member countries (to be referred to as EE). That aspect has long been of particular interest.

2. For present purposes, some international trade geometry adumbrated early on by Meade (1952) is still helpful. I show in fig. 1 hypothetical offer curves of the USSR and EE. The schedule for the USSR is constructed in a

*A reference below (note 9) to Jagdish N. Bhagwati will only begin to indicate my indebtedness to his detailed and penetrating comments on an earlier version of this essay; as the same note may suggest, I have also benefited from thoughtful advice of Edward A. Hewett. The comments of an anonymous reader are gratefully acknowledged. Of course, I alone am responsible for any remaining errors.
[1]Council of Mutual Economic Assistance.

usual way from Soviet production possibilities and prevailing domestic indifference curves. For purposes of this inquiry, the latter, in the case of the USSR, are envisaged as given by some objective function of the Soviet system's directors. (Whether any coherent objective function such as is in order is properly imputed to such persons is admittedly an interesting question.) For example, with, say, n as origin Soviet production possibilities are represented by hh'. With terms of trade such as indicated by the line mOn, the USSR maximizes its utility on indifference curve, I_s, producing the

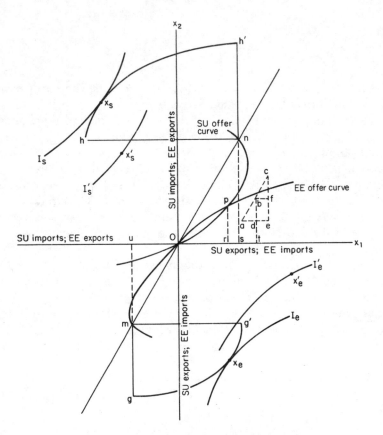

Fig. 1. Hypothetical model of COMECON trade.

output mix x_s (with n as origin). It exports Os of x_1 in return for imports of sn of x_2.

For EE, the corresponding offer curve might properly be derived by aggregating offer curves of the individual countries in question. The offer curve for each country would be obtained, just as is that for the USSR, by reference to the country's production possibilities and some objective function. For present purposes, though, I assume simply that there is for EE as a whole some aggregate production possibilities schedule, such as gg' with m as origin, and some corresponding collective preference map. With terms of trade indicated by the line mOn, EE maximizes its utility on indifference curve I_e. There it produces an output mix x_e (with m as origin), exporting Ou of x_1 and importing um of x_2.

As constructed, the offer curves of the USSR and EE represent how these areas would trade should the economies of the countries in question be of the perfectly competitive private enterprise sort familiar in Western textbooks. Their governments, it must also be understood, do not intervene to limit or encourage trade in any way, for example, by use of tariffs or subsidies. Barring such intervention, offer curves such as have been constructed would show how, under perfectly competitive private enterprise, the two partners would respond to any given world prices.

In the USSR and EE, enterprises are in fact predominantly publicly, rather than privately, owned. In place of perfect competition there is generally a rather bureaucratic system of economic control that has come to be known as centralist planning. Yet the same offer curves as before represent for each partner the most efficient way to conduct its foreign trade. By responding in the prescribed manner to opportunities to trade at prevailing world prices, each partner could reach the highest utility level open to it. That is so apart from the possibility that one partner or the other might occupy a sufficiently large place in world markets to be able to exert monopoly power over trade terms. Should either partner have such power, it could achieve a still higher level of utility by exploiting it. Otherwise, though, the offer curves indicate for each partner the optimal response to any given trade terms. To what extent either the Soviet Union or EE achieves maximum efficiency in this sense is a question to be considered, but the desideratum still can serve as a convenient benchmark.

I have referred to efficiency in the conduct of trade. That is but an aspect of, indeed presupposes, efficency in the economy generally. Thus, in an optimum the community, as well known, must realize its production possibilities. It must also determine its product mix and trade so that the marginal rate of substitution (MRS), given by the objective function, equals the marginal rate of transformation (MRT), given by the production possibilities schedule. Both coefficients must correspond in turn to the foreign trade–price ratio. In the figure all these requirements are met for the two commodities and foreign trade price ratio in question.

For present purposes, however, the degree of realization of production possibilities is only of limited interest. It may not be amiss, therefore, to suppose that that schedule is fully attained throughout; or perhaps more realistically that production conforms to some 'feasibility locus', that is, production possibilities after due allowance for inefficiency in its attainment. I accordingly take hh' to represent the Soviet and gg' to represent the EE feasibility locus. With MRT and the offer curves reinterpreted correspondingly, the latter schedules still represent an efficient response to foreign trade terms, though now apart from the contingency that production possibilities may not be fully achieved. I shall say of trade that is efficient in this qualified sense that it conforms to 'competitive norms'.[2] Exports per unit of imports that are indicated by an offer for a given volume of imports will be designated as the 'competitive demand price' for that volume of imports.

Should the terms of trade actually be such as represented by mOn, then, and offer curves of the two partners be shaped as depicted, trade conforming to competitive norms would also be as shown. I assume provisionally that these conditions on trade terms and offer curves are indeed met, or at least sufficiently so that the resulting trade is of the parallel sort shown: that is, with trade conforming to competitive norms, each area exports x_1 to and imports x_2 from the world, and engages in no trade either way with the other area.

Depending on world prices, such a trade pattern could emerge from comparative Soviet and EE production possibilities and preferences, and hence offer curves, of diverse sorts. I am assuming a substantial similarity in these aspects.[3] I do not suppose, however, that they are the same. Hence, should trade at world prices be completely excluded, the two partners would trade with each other to some extent. Thus, with competitive norms obtaining, the USSR would export Or of x_1 to EE in exchange for pr of x_2. EE trade, of course, would simply be the mirror image of that of the USSR.

Our two-dimensional geometry mandates that reference be to only two commodities. So far as there are many commodities, and competitive norms are observed, the USSR would almost inevitably export at world prices numerous goods that EE would import and conversely, but the share of such divergent flows in the total trade of the two areas should be smaller the more similar are their offer curves.

I have been referring to trade conforming to competitive norms. Provisionally to complete the figure, I take trade between the USSR and EE actually to be rather different from what it would be at competitive norms, even should trade at world prices be excluded. Although the commodity structure of exchanges is broadly of the sort indicated by such norms, the volume is distinctly larger than the norms would require. The terms of trade are for the USSR inferior and for EE superior to those afforded by world prices. To refer again to our two-dimensional figure, then, I show trade between the two partners as entailing an exchange of Soviet exports of Ot of x_1 for EE exports of bt of x_2. The resultant volume of trade evidently

[2]To be at all realistic, the EE production possibilities schedule would have to be understood in any event to reflect some constraints on inter-country transfers of productive factors. The concept of feasibility locus has its limitations, but I don't think these need to be expatiated on here.

[3]In the case of offer curves, similarity refers to the degree to which the NE segment for one area corresponds to the SW segment of the other.

exceeds that which would prevail should the two partners simultaneously conform to competitive norms and trade exclusively with each other. Trade terms are also related to world prices as assumed.

While trading with' each other, the two partners are understood also to trade with the world at large at world prices. Such trade tends to be structurally parallel, as it would be if all trade were at world prices and conformed to competitive norms. Hence, in the figure, the USSR exports, say, *bf* of x_1 in exchange for *cf* of x_2. EE exports some *ad* of x_1 in exchange for *bd* of x_2.

In the figure, the USSR pays for its imports from EE and the world an average price in exports that is higher than its competitive demand price, i.e., at '*c*' the USSR is beyond its offer curve. At '*a*', however, EE is favorably situated relative to its offer curve, and ir paying for the imports it receives from the Soviet Union and the world an average price in exports that is lower than its competitive demand price. These circumstances need not actually obtain, but should the terms of Soviet and EE trade with the world have been the same as their terms of trade with each other, the Russians would be paying more and EE less than their respective competitive demand prices.

3. Or so I assume, and the question is whether this and other suppositions that I have made are in fact at all near the mark. Let me explain that, while I have sought to distill here results of recent Western research, often my assumptions, far from being substantiated, are intended only as conjectures calling for further inquiry. By far the most striking proposition is that concerning the relatively unfavorable nature of Soviet–EE trade terms from the Soviet and their relatively favorable nature from the EE standpoint. On this, I rely primarily on Hewett (1977, pp. 111 ff.). Drawing on Hungarian input–output data on factor inputs into traded goods of COMECON countries. Hewett finds that the factor costs of Soviet exports to EE in 1960 and 1970 exceeded the factor costs of domestic substitutes for the goods imported from EE. This holds for Soviet trade with EE generally, and for Soviet trade with individual EE countries except Bulgaria and Rumania. On the other hand, all the EE countries, except Rumania, devote less resources to their exports to the USSR than are required for production of domestic substitutes for goods imported from the USSR.

The underlying computations are of a familiar sort and subject to familiar limitations. As Hewett would be the first to acknowledge, such limitations are often compounded in his results. Probably most important, factor costs as calculated consist only of direct and indirect labor and depreciation. No allowance is made for interest on capital or for rents which must arise where average and marginal costs differ. The latter charges, however, should be especially great in extractive industries, and the Soviet exports to EE are heavily weighted with the products of those industries (see below). On a more correct accounting for factor costs, therefore, Soviet–EE trade terms should be as Hewett's data might suggest: exports per unit of imports for the USSR are above and for EE below the corresponding *MRT* in each area.[4]

I assumed, however, that Soviet–EE trade terms are such that exports per unit of imports for the USSR are above and for EE below their respective competitive demand prices for the goods they import both from each other and the world. That is not quite the same thing as the relation just indicated of Soviet–EE trade terms to the *MRT* of each partner, but there is at least a presumption that such terms are also related similarly to competitive demand prices.[5]

Should they be so, Soviet–EE trade terms still need not be less favorable for the USSR and more favorable for EE than world prices. From further data compiled by Hewett (1977, pp. 106 ff., 117), however, this appears to be the case. COMECON foreign trade prices supposedly are consistent with world prices. In fact, for purposes of determining COMECON prices, world prices are taken as a point of departure, but the results often diverge from world prices, and in varying degrees for different sorts of products. Thus, COMECON foreign trade prices tended during the sixties (to refer again to that period) to be relatively high for machinery and equipment and

---

[4]In the case of extractive industries, allowance must also be made for royalties. The latter, understood as charges for withdrawal of an exhaustible resource, are difficult to fit into the conceptual apparatus of fig. 1, but they evidently are to be reckoned as a factor charge nonetheless.

In recasting trade theory in terms of a feasibility locus instead of the conventional production possibilities schedules, we cannot ignore here that one way in which a shortfall from the latter occurs is that where the marginal technical rate of substitution between factor inputs varies in different industries. Given such divergencies, the appropriate valuation of factor inputs becomes somewhat problematic, and references to a net charge for capital and rents and royalties must be read accordingly. So far as Soviet export and EE import industries are preeminently ones in which there are diminishing returns to reproducible capital and labor, however, the presumption remains that Hewett's data on resource costs should tend, if anything, to understate the rate at which export can be transformed into import goods domestically in the USSR. There should be a corresponding overstatement for EE. I assume, however, that the average reproducible capital–labor ratio in extractive is not markedly higher than in other industries.

[5]The feasibility locus is taken to be, like the usual production possibility schedule, concave from below. At Soviet–EE trade terms, then, should the USSR be trading exports for imports at a rate above the coeresponding *MRT*, competitive norms would dictate that the USSR reduce its output of export goods. Given that, the rate in exports that the USSR pays EE for its imports would be certain to exceed its competitive demand price in a simple case: The Soviet–EE trade terms apply as well to their trade with the world and *MRS* corresponds to those terms in each area. Under these conditions, the indicated shifts in domestic output would necessarily bring an increase in real income. Unless the Soviet export product is an inferior good, imports would also have to decline. At the prevailing Soviet–EE trade terms, it also follows that the Russians are paying more than their competitive demand price for their imports.

In the same simple case, and on similar reasoning, EE may be shown, at the prevailing Soviet–EE trade terms, to be paying less than its competitive demand price for its imports. When we go beyond the case in question, anything is possible, but there would still seem to be a presumption in favor of the stated relation of Soviet–EE trade terms to competitive demand prices.

manufactured consumer's goods and to be relatively low for agricultural products and, at times, for fuel, mineral raw materials and metals. From Montias' careful reconstruction of COMECON trade data, we see that during the sixties, the latter low-priced sorts of goods tended to constitute a distinctly larger share of Soviet exports to than of Soviet imports from EE. At the same time, the higher priced products constituted a larger share of EE exports to than EE imports from the USSR (table 1). Note that the bulk of the Soviet exports of foods are of a raw sort.

Although Hewett here too is able to draw on Hungarian work, his findings evidently are rather paradoxical. In the process by which foreign trade prices

Table 1

Structure of Soviet trade with Eastern Europe, 1960 and 1967 (percent).[a]

	ETN no.[b]	1960	1967
Soviet exports			
All		100.0	100.0
Machinery and equipment	1	14.1	23.1
Fuels, mineral raw materials, metals	2	39.1	39.2
Chemicals, fertilizers, rubber	3	3.4	3.7
Building materials	4	0.2	0.6
Agricultural products, except food	5	12.8	10.5
Raw foodstuffs; food products[c]	6–8	17.1	10.7
Manufactured consumers' goods	9	3.6	2.6
Special group[d]		9.7	9.6
Soviet imports			
All		100.0	100.0
Machinery and equipment	1	42.0	42.4
Fuels, mineral raw materials, metals	2	20.7	12.2
Chemicals, fertilizers, rubber	3	3.4	3.7
Building materials	4	0.6	0.6
Agricultural products, except food	5	4.6	3.3
Raw foodstuffs; food products[c]	6–8	8.0	9.4
Manufactured consumers' goods	9	18.2	24.3
Special group[d]		2.4	4.1

[a]Montias (1974, p. 667). Discrepancies between totals and sums of items due to rounding.
[b]COMECON classification.
[c]Includes live animals not for slaughter.
[d]Probably munitions.

are generated from world prices, there necessarily is often much room for negotiation in respect of more highly fabricated goods, particularly machinery and equipment, which are frequently of very differentiated and special sorts. In contrast, world prices must usually be relatively constraining for fuel, raw materials and such, which tend to be more standardized. It is puzzling, however, that the process of negotiation should tend to operate to the disadvantage of both the latter products and the USSR. Hewett (1974, pp. 54 ff.) offers a plausible explanation of this oddity, but price comparisons such as are in question are notoriously difficult to make. Further investigation here should be to the good.

So much for the terms of trade between the USSR and EE. However advantageous such terms are to one partner or the other, the commodity structure of trade might conceivably still conform to or deviate from competitive norms in varying degrees. In assuming that there is a very broad conformity, I consider the structure of Soviet–EE trade as just indicated, particularly the comparative stress on raw materials, fuel and the like in Soviet exports to EE, and the fact that the USSR by all accounts is relatively well endowed with natural resources. Data on comparative factor costs of different exports that underly Hewett's calculations on gains from trade [Hewett (1977, pp. 112–115)] also suggest a broad conformity of commodity structures of intra-COMECON trade to competitive norms. Here again, however, the exclusion from resource cost of any allowance for interest on capital and rents makes interpretation difficult.

Also of interest is Rosefielde's (1973) inquiry into Soviet trade structure as manifest in Leontief statistics. A Leontief statistic is understood in a usual way as given by the formula

$$\Omega = (^{k}m/^{1}m)/(^{k}v/^{1}v), \tag{1}$$

where ^{k}m and ^{k}v are the direct and indirect capital inputs into import-replacements and exports respectively, and ^{1}m and ^{1}v are corresponding labor coefficients. Rosefielde refers to a given ruble volume of import-replacements and exports structured to correspond to Soviet trade with a country in question. Focusing particularly on the period 1955–1968, he finds that the Leontief statistic for Soviet trade tends to vary directly with the capital–labor ratio of Russia's trading partner. Soviet trade with partners having a higher capital–labor ratio than the USSR also tends to show a 'capital-intensive import bias' (i.e., $\Omega > 1$). Similarly, there is a 'capital-intensive export bias' (i.e., $\Omega < 1$) in Soviet trade with partners having a lower capital–labor ratio than the USSR.

These results hold for Soviet trade with COMECON as well as less-developed and Western countries. According to Rosefielde, they indicate that the structure of Soviet trade in general tends to conform to the Heckscher–Ohlin theorem. If it does, it evidently should also tend to conform to competitive norms, so Rosefielde's finding appears to fit in with other evidence that has been cited. Conformity with the Heckscher–Ohlin theorem, however, is assured theoretically only under rather ideal conditions, including identity, as between trading partners, of linear homogeneous production functions, and possibly also of homothetic preferences. In view of the manifest unreality of such conditions in the case of the USSR and its trading partners, East and West, one wonders whether a pattern of Leontief statistics such as Rosefielde observes may not be more of a coincidence than evidence of competitive norms.[6]

Rosefield uses as a surrogate for a country's capital–labor ratio its GNP per capita. For limited data available, GNP per capita varies rather differently from the capital–labor ratio between countries (table 2). At least among Western countries, a relatively large Leontief statistic no longer seems

Table 2

GNP per capita and capital–labor ratio (K/L), selected countries (USSR = 100).[a]

| | Average Leontief statistic (Ω) 1955–68 (1) | Average GNP per capita 1955–68 (2) | Capital–labor ratio, 1960[b] | |
			With labor unadjusted for quality (3)	With labor adjusted for quality (4)
USSR	1.0000[c]	100	100	100
United Kingdom	1.3968	164	103	87
W. Germany	1.3352	164	106	96
France	1.1663	149	132	116
USA	n.a.[d]	275	294	222

[a]Sources: For cols. (1) and (2), Rosefielde (1977, pp. 52, 134); for cols. (3) and (4), Bergson (1978, p. 101).

[b]Capital stock per worker is calculated from reproducible fixed capital and employment in the economy generally, exclusive of selected final services: health care, education, government administration, defense and housing. Labor is adjusted for hours in both cols. (3) and (4), and also for education and sex in col. (4).

[c]In Rosefielde's analysis, scaled as unity.

[d]Not available.

readily explicable in Heckscher–Ohlin terms when the capital–labor ratio replaces Rosefielde's surrogate for it, per capita GNP. The surrogate, however, might possibly be more nearly valid for COMECON than for Western countries. EE countries, taken together, might be more like the USSR in respect of the relation of the capital–labor ratio to per capita GNP.

[6]Rosefielde is applying the Heckscher–Ohlin theorem to bilateral exchanges in a many-country world. His application of the theorem in terms of Leontief statistics is plausible, but even under ideal conditions does not yet seem to have been clearly justified theoretically. In an *n*-country world, with factor prices *not* equalized Deardorff (1978) deduces a pattern of bilateral exchanges that appears congruent with the one on which Rosefielde focuses, but for Deardorff there is virtually complete specialization. Given that, practically no import replacements such as the Leontief statistic requires would be in production. Note also that Deardorff focuses on direct rather than direct and indirect factor requirements, and shows that the Heckscher–Ohlin pattern could be upset by trade impediments. With factor price equilization, Horiba (1974) deduces bilateral exchanges that are again related to but apparently of a different sort from Rosefielde's.

In exploring the 'Leontief paradox' for socialist countries, Rosefielde has opened up a very interesting line of inquiry. It should be pursued further.

If the commodity structure of COMECON trade does correspond at all to competitive norms, the correspondence must only be broad. Under the Soviet-type system of centralist planning that has been traditional in COMECON countries, a cardinal preoccupation in respect of foreign trade has been simply to offset domestic deficits and surpluses. Lately central planning has been subject to some reform, and trade administration has become increasingly sophisticated. But optimization such as full conformity to competitive norms requires, if sought at all, seems still to be a remote and elusive desideratum. Among other things, notably distorted domestic prices continue to obstruct any attempts at meaningful cost calculation. Efforts to correct for the distortions in an *ad hoc* way, which have increasingly been exerted in the course of time, are no doubt to the good but also underline the difficulties [Hewett (1974, ch. 4) and Holzman (1976, pp. 26 ff.)].[7]

Turning to the volume of Soviet and EE trade, the total foreign trade of the USSR and of EE with all countries has greatly expanded since the early fifties. That is so not only absolutely but in relation to the GNP, so foreign trade participation rates are higher than they used to be. Such rates formerly were notably low, however, and they probably still are often more or less depressed by Western standards [Bergson (1968), Pryor (1968, pp. 163–164), Holzman (1976, pp. 24 ff.)].

I have, nevertheless, assumed that trade between the USSR and EE exceeds the volume that might conform to competitive norms even in the absence of trade with other partners. I could be wrong on this, but no question the volume of Soviet–EE trade has been inordinately great by Western standards. That is already suggested by the extraordinarily large share that each region occupies in the other's trade: in 1970, for example, 55 percent of Soviet trade was with EE, and 50 percent of EE trade (exclusive of that among EE countries themselves) was with the USSR [CIA (1977, pp. 59, 62)]. In view of their dated character, figures for pre-WWII years, when EE was not yet communist, cannot serve as much of a benchmark, but it is still of interest that in 1938 only 1.9 percent of EE imports (exclusive of those from EE countries) came from the USSR. Of Soviet imports, 5.5 percent came from EE [Holzman (1976, p. 70)].

On Soviet–EE trade, we may also draw on results of an analysis by Hewett (1976). Using a 'gravity flow' model, Hewett finds the volume of trade between the USSR and all EE countries to be equal to or greater than the amount that might be expected among Western trading partners. The expected volume takes account of distance as well as other factors that might

---

[7]One of the more significant recent developments in COMECON foreign trade planning is the increased use of so-called 'efficiency indexes', but application of such indices is necessarily handicapped by the dubious domestic prices, the more so since, as Desai and Bhagwati (1978) point out, in such calculations all tradeables (and not just those commodities that happen to be traded) properly are evaluated at world prices.

determine trade among Western countries. Of the six EE countries considered, the volume of trade of four with the USSR ranges from 64 to 371
percent above the amount indicated by Western experience. Hewett takes as
a benchmark here Western trade as it would be apart from custom-union
effects. EE trade with the USSR is often not in excess of that characterizing
trade in Western customs unions, particularly EEC and EFTA.

Although the USSR and EE trade preponderantly with each other, they do
trade with non-communist counteries.[8] I have assumed a substantial parallelism in the commodity composition of this trade. In support of this
supposition, I can cite the striking correspondence in the structure of Soviet
and EE imports from non-communist countries by broad commodity categories (table 3). For exports, too, if we group together relatively resource-
related categories (food, beverages, tobacco; crude materials, fats and oils;
fuels and related products), there is also a striking correspondence in
structure. by broad categories. Among the resource-related products, however, there are significant disparities.

Table 3

Structure of Soviet and East European trade with non-communist countries, 1965
(percent).[a]

	Exports of		Imports of	
	USSR	EE	USSR	EE
All	100.0	100.0	100.0	100.0
Food, beverages, tobacco	5.9	24.7	26.6	22.3
Crude materials; fats and oils	27.5	11.1	22.8	20.0
Fuels and related products	26.9	9.6	0.1	0.7
Chemicals	2.4	7.3	6.6	10.8
Machinery; transport equipment	12.2	12.4	22.9	20.0
Manufactures	21.1	29.3	20.1	24.6
Other	3.9	5.6	0.8	1.7

[a]Eastern Europe includes Albania. For purposes of this table, Yugoslavia is
included among non-communist countries. Exports are c.i.f. and imports f.o.b.
Discrepancies between indicated totals and sums of indicated items due to
rounding. *Source*: U.S. Department of State (1968).

These data also suggest that should Soviet and EE trade at world prices
be unconstrained by their preoccupation with each other, there might again
be a substantial, though hardly complete, parallelism in their trade. In fig. 1, I
also assumed that would be so if the trade should be in conformity with
competitive norms. I have already conjectured that any such conformity that
actually obtains in the case of Soviet–EE trade must be broad at best. On

[8]They also conduct a significant volume of trade with Cuba and the communist countries of
Asia.

the same reasoning, that should also be true of the trade of each partner with non-communist countries. The observed parallelism in structure of such trade, therefore, may not have too much to do with competitive norms, but for the broad categories in question some congruence with such norms seems plausible when we consider the still not highly advanced stage of development of the areas in question. In 1960, *GNP* per worker in the USSR was but 30 percent and in the countries of EE but 17–42 percent of that of the USA [Bergson (1978, p. 200)]. The USSR, as well known, has greatly reduced the relative factor costs of many types of machinery in the course of the five-year plans, but deficiencies in quality and service availability still hamper machinery sales to the West. Such deficiencies are also obstacles to EE machinery sales to the West, and there what has been accomplished in respect of the reduction of resource costs is less clear than in the case of the USSR. When seen in this light, the relatively limited volume of Soviet and EE machinery exports to non-communist countries appears more in accord than in conflict with competitive norms. That still seems true when we consider that the bulk of the machinery exports go in any event to less-developed countries rather than to the industrial West.

The parallelism of Soviet and EE trade under competitive norms nevertheless could easily be overstated. Among other things, as noted, there are significant structural differences of natural resource endowments of the two partners. If only on that account, significant trade could still take place between them even should competitive norms prevail. By the same token, there could be appreciable divergencies in their exchanges with the West.

4. Is COMECON to be regarded as a customs union? Holzman (1974; 1977) has argued cogently that it is. If we do view COMECON in that way, we must consider that the common external tariff of the usual Western customs union is here replaced by a complex of quotas imposed under centralist planning. The resultant degree of restriction on trade must vary not only by commodity but between member countries. Planned quotas also supercede free trade within COMECON. No question, however, COMECON is characterized by what is at least in a degree a usual feature of a Western customs union: trade diversion. Indeed, in view of facts that have been set forth, the diversion probably has proceeded to an extraordinary extent. True, intra-COMECON trade is not notably large in the perspective of trade between members of Western customs unions (see above), but there are reasons to think that the intra-COMECON trade would be especially limited in the absence of the political constraints that COMECON imposes. I refer particularly to the broad similarity already noted in the structure of Soviet and EE trade at world prices. The attenuated trade between the USSR and EE in pre-COMECON days is also illuminating.

Though hardly to be taken literally, then, the portrayal of the resultant trade diversion in the two dimensional geometry of fig. 1 may not be altogether far-fetched. Thus, with trade politically unconstrained at world prices, trade between the USSR and EE is shown as nil. Any trade between them, therefore, represents trade diversion. In fig. 1, politically unconstrained trade at world prices is supposed to conform to competitive norms. As a benchmark for gauging the impact of COMECON, perhaps we should imagine that in the absence of that entity's political constraints there would still be some tariffs levied on Soviet and EE imports. Short of being prohibitory, such a tariff would 'contract' the Soviet and EE offer curves in a familiar way. As a result, trade at world prices would decline, but in our two-commodity world exchanges between the USSR and EE would still be zero. Of course, even without COMECON'S political constraints, Soviet and EE trade might still be subject to planned quotas, but, as suggested, the parallelism of trade at world prices that appears in fig. 1 might still not be wholly unrealistic. Hence, the conclusion as to the substantial nature of COMECON trade diversion remains valid.

Our geometric analysis may also help us to approach the recurring question of who gains and who loses from COMECON trade. The terms of trade between the USSR and EE are less favorable to the USSR and more favorable to EE than world prices. So at least Hewett finds. Should his conclusion be accepted, the question posed might seem to be answered, for at least marginally the USSR loses and EE gains from trading with each other rather than at world prices. As not always considered, however, each could still gain or lose from trading with each other as an alternative to not trading at all. How has each fared from that standpoint?

With Soviet–EE trade terms related in the manner we have surmised to the corresponding *MRT* of each partner, evidently the USSR must gain and EE must lose from a marginal contraction in their trade. That must be so even if the trade of each at world prices were unchanged, for with the marginal contraction the USSR would have at its disposal, after all trade, more of both products. EE *per contra* would have less of both products. That must be so should Soviet–EE trade terms be unchanged. Should such terms change, of course, the impact of trade contraction must depend on that aspect too.

I have referred separately to two sources of Soviet and EE gains and losses from COMECON trade (the divergence of Soviet EE trade terms from world prices and from the *MRT* of each partner) and only to marginal variations. Under COMECON, how have the two partners fared overall? The answer as portrayed in fig. 1 is that both partners experience a loss of utility. I refer to a loss compared with what might have been achieved under competitive norms. Thus, in fig. 1 intra-COMECON trade leaves both partners at 'b'. Even with the addition of trade at world prices, each side is at a lower utility level than might have been achieved: for the USSR, at x'_s on I'_s, instead of x_s on I_s; for EE, at x'_e on I'_e instead of x_e on I_e. In order not to complicate the chart unduly, I have left it to the reader to shift appropriately the production possibilities of the Soviet Union (to '*c*' as origin) and EE (to '*a*' as origin).

Should Soviet–EE trade terms be as described, this outcome is inevitable for the USSR but not for EE. Thus EE gains so far as Soviet–EE trade terms are relatively favorable to EE but loses from the substantial redirection of trade that COMECON requires. In the figure the loss outweighs the gain, but the results could be otherwise.

In the figure, I assume that, whatever the volume and structure of trade, $MRS = MRT$. The loss in utility in question, then, occurs from an inefficient determination of volume and structure of trade and *ipso facto* of domestic output, in response to world prices. The loss, as indicated, may be offset or compounded by differential trade terms within COMECON. As so delimited, the loss in utility may have a conceptual interest of its own, for it might be viewed as representing the impact on welfare of the conduct of trade as such, as distinct from resource allocation generally. In fact, however, MRS and MRT hardly can be equal in the USSR and EE. A discrepancy between these coefficients could not very well be avoided when trade is conducted as described. It is also an inevitable counterpart of well-known aberrations of centralist planning generally, as found in the USSR and EE.

It should be observed, therefore, that so far as $MRS \neq MRT$ the loss of utility is necessarily greater than has been depicted. That is so for both the USSR and EE. For the latter, however, there could still be a gain overall.

The indifference curves I_s and I_e represent the highest levels of utility that the Soviet Union and EE can attain, should they conform to competitive norms. So far as they have any monopoly power in world markets, however. they could attain still higher utility levels by exploiting that power. The losses that the Soviet Union and EE suffer through trade must be seen accordingly.

The conclusion that COMECON entails a loss in utility for the USSR contradicts a frequently encountered presupposition, but the result must follow if Soviet–EE terms and Soviet trade flows are as has been depicted Should EE too lose because of COMECON, that too would be somewha surprising. While COMECON is widely thought to have been costly to EF in earlier years, relatively favorable trade terms are supposed to have made i profitable to EE more recently. Such reasoning seems to neglect the costs to EE of the significant redirection of trade that COMECON imposes, but witl due regard to that aspect the possibility that EE gains rather than loses fron COMECON is not precluded.[9]

[9] I am indebted to Jagdish Bhagwati for this interesting point. In fig. 1, I show EE selling t the West the same kind of product as it imports from the USSR. By implication, EE could b regarded as serving as an arbitrageur between the USSR and the West, and gaining in th process. Here again the figure must not be taken too literally, but, as Hewett has explained t me, such EE arbitrage does indeed take place on an appreciable scale, though in an indirec way, with EE exporting to the West, not the products that it imports from the USSR, but good processed from such products.

This essay is concerned with the long-run. Losses and gains from trade must be viewed accordingly. In view of adaptations that have been made to COMECON in the course of time, both sides presumably fare better under its constraints when reference is only to the short-run.

The reader is reminded of the frequently conjectural nature of my analysis. My principal moral clearly must be that more research is needed on COMECON.

The moral is the more in order if we go beyond the sixties, the period on which I have focused, for much of the relevant Western research on COMECON relates to that interval. Much of what has been said probably applies more generally, but that is not always so. For example, COMECON terms of trade, as implied, may have favored the USSR rather than EE in earlier years. That, however, seems to be a controversial matter [Holzman (1974, chs. 11, 12)]. The Russians have also benefited from the rise in oil prices in the seventies. Where that leaves their terms of trade with EE is not yet very clear.

I have assumed that trade of the USSR and EE with each other and the world at large was in balance. That was more or less true during much of the sixties, but lately both the USSR and EE have gone increasingly into debt to the West. Some capital flows are also occurring between the USSR and EE, probably chiefly in the form of EE investments in the USSR on concessionary terms. On the other hand, for some years after World War II the USSR was receiving unrequited exports from EE in the form of reparations. These facts too must be considered in extending our analysis to either earlier or later years than the sixties.

References

Bergson, Abram, 1968, On prospects of communist foreign trade, in: Alan A. Brown and Egon Neuberger, eds., International trade and central planning (University of California Press, Berkeley, CA) 384–392.

Bergson, Abram, 1978, Productivity and the social system (Harvard University Press, Cambridge, MA).

Central Intelligence Agency, 1977, Handbook of economic statistics, ER77-10537, Sept. (Central Intelligence Agency, Washington, DC).

Deardorff, Alan V., forthcoming, Weak links in the chain of comparative advantage, Journal of International Economics.

Desai, Padma and Jagdish N. Bhagwati, 1978, On inferring the rationality of foreign trade of the CPE's, Processed.

Hewett, Edward A., 1974, Foreign trade prices in the Council for Mutual Economic Assistance (Cambridge University Press, London).

Hewett, Edward A., 1976, A gravity flow model of CMEA trade, in: Josef C. Brada, ed., Quantitative and analytical studies in East–West trade (International Development Research Center, Bloomington, IN).

Hewett, Edward A., 1977, Prices and resource allocation in intra-CMEA trade, in: Alan Aboucher, ed., The socialist price mechanism (Duke University Press, Durham, NC).

Holzman, Franklyn D., 1974, Foreign trade under central planning (Harvard University Press, Cambridge, MA).

Holzman, Franklyn D., 1976, International trade under communism (Basic Books, New York).

Horiba, Y., 1974, General equilibrium and the Heckscher–Ohlin theory of trade: The multi-country case, International Economic Review 15, 440–449.

Meade, James E., 1952, A geometry of international trade (Allen and Unwin, London).

Montias, J.M., 1974, The structure of COMECON trade and the prospects for East-West exchange, in: Joint Economic Committee, United States Congress, Reorientation and commercial relations of the economies of Eastern Europe (US Government Printing Office, Washington, DC).

Pryor, Frederick, 1968, Discussion, in: Alan A. Browm and Egon Neuberger, eds., International trade and central planning (University of California Press, Berkeley, CA).

Rosefielde, Steven, 1973, Soviet international trade in Heckscher–Ohlin perspective (Heath, Lexington, MA).

US Department of State, 1968, The Battle Act report 1967 (US Department of State, Washington, DC).

Errata:

(i)   On p. 293, in the 2nd complete paragraph, after the first sentence, insert the following:

'In that case, of course, reference must be to offer curves derived from domestic indifference curves that correspond to consumer preferences. I need not expatiate here on the well-known complexities of that notion.'

The sentence following should then begin:

'The governments of the two regions, it must also be understood,...'

(ii)   On p. 293, in the third complete paragraph, change the third sentence to read:

'Yet offer curves constructed in the same way as before, though now from indifference curves given by the objective function of the system's directors, represent for each partner the most efficient way of conducting foreign trade.'

Part IV

Problems of Measurement

12

On Soviet Real Investment Growth

AMONG Soviet official statistics on real volume, those relating to real fixed investment have long enjoyed a relatively privileged status in the West. While in other spheres such Soviet data have again and again been held to be distorted, those on fixed investment volume have usually been considered as at least broadly reliable.

True, the CIA has nevertheless seen fit to compile measures of its own on that matter, but in doing so it accepts, for its purposes, data released by the Soviet TsSU on a major component, producers' durables investment. Moreover, so far as its measures on real fixed investment as a whole tend to be similar to the official data, that has been widely taken to be reassuring regarding the CIA as well as the TsSU calculations.

If the two sets of measures stand together, though, they must also fall together. It might now seem that the latter is indeed their proper fate. TsSU data on real fixed investment, it has been urged by such reputable authorities as Nove (1981A, B; 1983), Wiles (1982) and Hanson (1984A, B), are afflicted after all with the same kind of distortion as so often affects its measures of real volume in other spheres. Here as elsewhere, concealed inflation has, at least lately, caused a gross upward bias. While attention has been focused primarily on the TsSU figures, those of the CIA expressly or by implication are also clearly indicted.

Cohn, however, early on (1981) demurred at such a negative appraisal, but apparently with little impact on the subsequent discussion. According to a further assessment attempted here, as I may as well say at once, there are indeed troubling uncertainties affecting the TsSU and CIA measures. But perhaps those data are not as wide of the mark as Nove, Wiles and Hanson argue.

The issue that is posed as to real investment growth in the USSR is rather important. The CIA compiles its widely used measures of Soviet GNP in the first instance by sector of origin rather than final disposition. Hence, should its data on fixed investment prove to be in error, that would not immediately necessitate any revision of its GNP figures. But those figures would still be vulnerable, for the CIA calculations of the contributions of the industrial and construction sectors to the total GNP would almost certainly come into question. More importantly, fixed investment is a cardinal source of output expansion. Should the TsSU and CIA data on fixed investment growth be radically inflated, we surely would have to rethink our views on the Soviet growth process. Since attention is directed particularly to the recent experience, a reconsideration of the causes of the much-discussed Soviet slowdown would at once be indicated.

Fixed investment, as reported by TsSU, consists predominantly of construction and investment in producers' durables. That is also true in the case of the CIA calculations, and for both agencies reference is to gross investment, i.e., investment prior to any allowance for depreciation. The TsSU measures on which attention has been focused, however, relate only to new investments, and hence do not cover so-called 'capital repairs' (Moorsteen and Powell, 1966, p. 33; Pitzer, 1982, pp. 117ff). The CIA, for its part, compiles data on both new fixed investment and capital repairs, but only the former data are now of concern.[1]

I

If in respect of fixed investment TsSU has hitherto been accorded more credence than it usually is for its measures of real volume, that is not without reason. In fact, the case that can be made out for such special treatment may be at some points weightier than has been supposed. In reappraising the TsSU data, and with them those of the CIA, it is well to begin by considering what that case is.

Regarding TsSU measures of real volume, concealed inflation is a shorthand expression that has come to be used for distortions in the aggregation procedures TsSU employs. Reference is especially, though not exclusively, to distortions occurring in the valuation of new products. Such distortions could in principle lead to biases in more than one direction, but seemingly tend in practice towards overstatement rather than understatement of growth.

In the case of a fixed investment, it may be well to remind the reader, TsSU avowedly values different products in 'comparable prices' corresponding to 'estimate prices' that are used in planning investment projects. The particular estimate prices used, though, have been revised from time to time. Thus, for data such as are considered by N–W–H (I trust it will not be amiss often to refer thus to Nove, Wiles and Hanson collectively; their critiques overlap substantially) reference is made, according to TsSU (1984, p. 346), to 'estimate prices of 1 January, 1969, account being taken of the new wholesale prices of equipment introduced on 1 January, 1973 and the reduced norms for construction-assembly work introduced on 1 January, 1976'.

That is, needless to say, a rather complex standard, but, if only elliptically, valuation might be said to be in terms of prices relating to a base year. Hence, the results, summarily set forth here (Table 1) along with corresponding CIA figures, apparently should be serial data on real investment of a more or less conventional Laspeyres kind.

That, however, could also be said of the frequently dubious TsSU data on real volume in other spheres, but for those on fixed investment the calculations in question arguably could be quite different from those that apparently have given rise to major distortions elsewhere. Any resultant upward bias should not be comparable, for example, to that usually assumed to affect TsSU measures of the gross output of machinery and metal working (MBMW) industries in 'comparable prices'.

Cohn (1981) evidently considers that the use of 'estimate prices' in itself significantly distinguishes the TsSU investment data from its data on gross MBMW output. The import of the distinction is not self-evident but in calculating the estimate price of a project TsSU apparently refers to estimate prices of standard intermediate components, e.g., a cubic metre of brick masonry, a cubic metre of reinforced concrete, a square metre of plastering, etc. Use is also made of official handbooks providing simplified formulae for the cost of a cubic metre of a structure in relation to its intended purpose, size and location and the materials employed (CIA, 1976; Krasovsky, 1979, p. 68).

Valuation of investment in estimate prices so obtained manifestly could mean that the resulting measures fail to reflect adequately relevant qualitative trends. But while the Soviet economy seems to experience difficulties in advancing in that respect, no one urges that it is in a decline, so there is no basis to suppose an upward bias at this point. What is more to be stressed, in any event, is that the standardization involved could by itself much reduce the dimensions of the new product valuation problem. The procedures in question are presumably applicable on any scale only in construction, but at least in that sphere systematic distortions due to improper valuation of new products should be relatively limited. In the case of the TsSU measures of MBMW output, it is usually supposed that overvaluation of new products has been especially consequential.[2] The different approach to new products in the case of construction is one way in which the TsSU calculation for investment volume would seem to score over those for MBMW output in respect of reliability. There are also others, among them the fact that the latter data relate to gross output as determined by the 'factory method', and so are affected by any change in industrial integration. While the resultant double-counting could cause a downward rather than an upward bias, it is still to the good that the TsSU data on fixed investment relate to final dispositions, and hence should be free of such a bias.

II

But granting such comparative virtues of the TsSU calculations of investment volume, one admittedly would hesitate to accord them much credence were it not for a very interesting fact: after adjustment for net imports the producers durables component of investment, as calculated by TsSU, has for some time been more or less congruent with measures of producers' durables output that the CIA has obtained as a component of its own computation of real MBMW output more generally. That is despite the fact that the CIA computation yields growth rates far below those indicated by the corresponding ones of TsSU for all MBMW output (Table 1).

As the CIA (Converse, 1982) acknowledges, its data for producers' durables output have their limitations. Probably most importantly, for numerous types of machinery, it had to utilize TsSU serial data on values in 'comparable prices'. Should there be concealed inflation in those series, though, the failure of other serial data in physical units to allow for qualitative gains should be something of an offset. Among a number of illustrative cases considered by the CIA, one assuming for physical quantity series a one percentage point understatement and

TABLE 1

GROSS FIXED INVESTMENT AND MACHINERY PRODUCTION, USSR, AVERAGE ANNUAL RATES OF GROWTH, 1951–1980[a] (%)

	1951–55	1956–60	1961–65	1966–70	1971–75	1976–80
Gross fixed investment[b]						
TsSU	12·3	12·8	6·2	7·6	7·0	3·4
CIA	12·4	9·9	7·2	6·4	4·8	3·8
Construction						
TsSU	n.a.[c]	n.a.	4·1	7·0	5·8	0·8
CIA	11·6	9·7	5·1	6·4	5·1	1·7
Gross investment in producers' durables						
TsSU	n.a.	n.a.	10·4	7·6	8·7	6·5
CIA	10·8	13·4	10·4	7·6	8·7	6·5
MBMW output						
TsSU	16·7	14·2	12·4	11·7	11·6	8·2
CIA	9·6	7·9	7·4	6·9	7·9	5·4
Producers' durables						
Investment, TsSU, adjusted for net imports	14·6	10·0	9·6	7·7	9·1	5.2[d]
Output, CIA	11·8	12·4	8·9	7·8	8·6	{ 5·8 / 6·3[d] }

Notes: [a]*Sources:* CIA data, Pitzer (1982, p. 68); Converse (1982, pp. 201, 206, 207). TsSU data, TsSU (1961, pp. 590–1; 1966, p. 529; 1981, p. 334; 1983, p. 356); Pitzer (1982, pp. 118, 120); Converse (1982, p. 201).
[b]On the scope of fixed investment, see text.
[c]n.a.: not available.
[d]1976–79.

for value series a three percentage point overstatement in annual growth would seem to be conservative. For the 1970s it yields a rate of growth 1·6 percentage points below that indicated by the principal CIA computation, and correspondingly a 1·4 percentage point overstatement in the adjusted TsSU measures of producers' durables investment (Converse, 1982, pp. 216–8; compare Cohn, 1981).

Hanson (1984A), nevertheless, supposes that the overstatement in the CIA measures of producers' durables output growth could be much greater than that the cited illustrative computation might indicate. The congruity of the CIA output with the TsSU investment data accordingly is not seen as at all reassuring as to the reliability of the latter.

Curiously, Hanson (1984A, pp. 576–7) cites approvingly independent computations of Khanin (1981) that apparently indicate for the 1970s an annual rate of growth of MBMW output of 5·7–6·9%. That is indeed well below the tempo claimed by TsSU, 9·9%. But, as Hanson seems not to have noticed, the CIA calculations for MBMW output yield a tempo, 6·6%, which is within the range delineated by Khanin. Thus, while underlining an upward bias in TsSU measures for MBMW output, Khanin in effect provides some support for the CIA's corresponding calculations, and also by implication for its supposition that TsSU measures for producers' durables investment are not very wide of the mark. Nove (1983, pp. 14–16) also fails to note that implication of Khanin's calculations, though he, too, cites them to indicate the upward bias in TsSU data on MBMW output.

As Khanin makes clear, his recomputation of MBMW output is crude. As well as being broadly reassuring, however, it is the more germane here since, as will appear, it is somehow construed by Hanson to indicate the concealed inflation in the TsSU measures of producers' durables investment as well as in those of MBMW output![3]

Although the CIA was able to adjust TsSU measures of producers' durables investment in order to allow for net imports, it apparently prefers to rely on the unadjusted TsSU measures rather than make a corresponding adjustment of its own data on producers' durables output. Difficulties encountered in making the adjustment, one gathers, were a factor in that decision. The congruity of the adjusted TsSU measures for producers' durables investment with the CIA data for producers' durables output must be read in that light.[4]

III

In elucidating the case for the TsSU and also the CIA data for real fixed investment, I noted above that at least in respect of construction TsSU may have been able under its valuation procedure to grapple relatively effectively with new products. The CIA (Pitzer, 1982, pp. 23ff, 117ff), as indicated, has nevertheless chosen to make its own calculations of investment in construction. Essentially, the volume of such investment is taken to vary in proportion to the volume of construction materials employed, the latter being estimated from data on the output of different sectors supplying materials to construction and on the shares of such output going to construction. Such shares are calculated from input–output tables. Construction volume as thus determined includes capital repairs, but price indices that are implied are then used to deflate new construction in current prices. With that capital repairs are excluded.

As the CIA recognizes, the underlying assumption that construction volume varies proportionately with materials employed is open to question. Such a simplification nevertheless has often been employed in the calculation of construction volume, and in the light of US experience it should not be wide of the mark (Pitzer, 1982, p. 84). It seems all to the good, then, that here, too, the CIA results have for some time been reasonably close to those that TsSU obtained from its calculations in 'comparable prices'.

Viewed simply as measures of the volume of material inputs into construction, however, the CIA data may still be faulted. On close scrutiny, the estimates of materials supplied to construction by different industries are themselves subject to error. A further computation, though, is reassuring on that feature. I have tabulated here (Table 2) the price indices which the CIA found to be implied in its calculation of construction volume, and which it then used to obtain by deflation investment in construction, exclusive of capital repairs. Also shown is the corresponding implied deflator indicated by the TsSU measures of construction in 'comparable prices'. As was to be expected, these two series, in their relation to each other, are essentially mirror images of the CIA and TsSU measures of construction investment already discussed.

TABLE 2

CONSTRUCTION INVESTMENT PRICES AND FACTOR COSTS, USSR,
1960–78[a]

(1970 = 100·0)

	Implied deflator, CIA (1)	*Implied deflator,* TsSU (2)	*Synthetic ruble factor cost* (3)
1960	80·1	78·6	80·8
1965	79·2	81·6	81·1
1970	100·0	100·0	100·0
1975	103·4	99·9	101·1
1978	102·6	99·9	99·9

[a]*Sources:* Col. (1): Pitzer (1982, p. 87); Col. (2): derived from current price data in Pitzer (1982, p. 120) and 'comparable price' data in TsSU (1981, p. 334; 1984, p. 356); Col. (3): see text.

The third series tabulated, however, is novel. Consider the following expression

(1) $RFC_{oi} = P_{oi}[(1+\lambda_i)/(1+\lambda_o)][(1+\pi_i)/(1+\pi_o)]$.

Here λ_o and λ_i are the ratios of non-material to material construction costs in years o and i respectively; π_o and π_i are corresponding ratios of profits to costs in construction, and P_{oi} is the index of construction materials prices over the interval in question. The term RFC_{oi}, as readily seen, is on one assumption an index of ruble factor cost per unit of output in construction. The assumption is simply that of the CIA: construction output per unit of materials inputs is constant.[5]

In applying the formula, I take λ_i to be constant over the period covered. Available official data indicate a slight decline in the share of materials in construction costs, but the outlays in question include some wages, e.g., for labour engaged in transporting materials, while inclusive data for the principal non-material costs, wages, indicate a slight decline in their share (Table 3). The cited profits ratios follow from Soviet data on the 'gross social product' of construction in current prices and corresponding current ruble profits. In respect of officially reported construction costs and gross output there should be little

TABLE 3

ELEMENTS IN CALCULATION OF RUBLE FACTOR COST, USSR, 1960–78[a]

	Construction materials prices (1970 = 100·0) (1)	*Share of materials, inc. some wages, in construction costs* (%) (2)	*All wages, as share of construction costs* (%) (3)	*Profits ÷ costs, construction* (%) (4)
1960	83·8	56·3	36	3·6
1965	83·8	55·6	34	4·1
1970	100·0	55·6	32	7·5
1975	98·5	55·0	32	10·3
1978	98·5	53·8	32	9·0

[a]*Sources:* Col. (1): TsSU (1973, p. 199; 1979, p. 139). Cols. (2) and (3), TsSU (1971, pp. 502–3; 1979, p. 360). Col. (4), calculated from data in TsSU (1966, p. 757; 1973, pp. 59, 701; 1979, pp. 41, 519).

'double counting' such as afflicts such releases for MBMW.[6] For P_{oi} I use the TsSU index numbers of wholesale prices of construction materials. For MBMW prices such TsSU data, like its measures of MBMW output, have long been suspect. For products such as construction materials, however, there is little basis to suppose that they are wide of the mark. They are often accepted on that basis.

As computed, the index of ruble factor cost in construction is nevertheless inexact. The striking correspondence with the other two deflators, however, adds to the weight of evidence in support of both the TsSU and the CIA measures of the construction component of investment. Indeed, one is led to wonder whether TsSU may not itself be taking the volume of materials inputs as an indicator of investment in construction.

IV

In holding the TsSU measures of real fixed investment to be distorted by concealed inflation, Nove, Wiles and Hanson all alike stress particularly the role of the TsSU treatment of new products. As in the TsSU calculations of MBMW, it is held, so in those for real fixed investment, such products are systematically overvalued. Nove and Hanson, however, also urge that in respect of valuation TsSU may well be off the mark regarding old as well as new products. Indeed, far from constituting a Laspeyres-type series, the TsSU data on investment very possibly are simply in current prices.

It must already be evident that such a view is untenable if affirmed in any general way. With valuation at current prices the corresponding implied deflator must be constant. At least for construction, as we saw (Table 2), the deflator implied by TsSU measures in comparable prices varies widely in the course of time. Hanson, it is true, focuses on years since 1970, and the implied deflator for construction for those years does turn out to be virtually constant. But so, too, does our index of ruble factor cost. So far as concerns construction, therefore, it would seem neither surprising nor damaging to the TsSU calculations if Hanson were correct.

Hanson, however, is referring to the TsSU data for all fixed investment, including producers' durables as well as construction. For that reason, it is well to pursue somewhat further the question at issue. I repeat (Table 4) the evidence

TABLE 4

FIXED INVESTMENT, GOVERNMENT AND COOPERATIVE, USSR[a]
(billion rubles)

	Investment in	
	Comparable prices	'Current prices'
Year	(1)	(2)
1970	71·4	71·9
1975	100·4	102·3
1980	120·2	120·8
1981	125·2	125·6
1982	129·6	129·6

[a]*Source:* Hanson (1984A, p. 574). Collective farm investment not included.

that Hanson (1984A, p. 574) adduces for his conjecture. In col. (1) are data on investment in 'comparable prices' that TsSU (1983, p. 335) reports. In col. (2) are corresponding figures immediately derived by Hanson from two related series of TsSU (1983, p. 347), one on unfinished construction in rubles and another on the percentage relation of such construction to the volume of fixed investment. Since the ruble figures given for unfinished construction are said to represent the 'factual value for the builder' (*po fakticheskoi stoimosti dlya zastroishchika*), the derived figures, Hanson reasons, must have a similar meaning. Given the close accord of cols. (1) and (2), he also infers, values at 'comparable prices' must essentially come to the same thing as 'factual value', or in effect value at current prices.

This argument is easily seen, however, to be fallacious. The agreement between cols. (1) and (2) could possibly mean that, as Hanson reasons, comparable and current prices are one and the same thing. But it could also mean that a not too meticulous TsSU staff member, in deriving the reported percentage relations of unfinished construction to investment volume, simply referred, for the latter, to the TsSU data in comparable prices.

And confirmation for that hypothesis is quickly obtained when we consider the relatively sizable discrepancy for 1975 between the two sets of data that Hanson juxtaposes. The discrepancy vanishes when for 1975 reference is made to the figure on investment volume in comparable prices, 102·3 billion rubles in TsSU (1976, p. 502). At the time that that yearbook appeared, TsSU was declaredly using as comparable prices the estimate prices of 1 January, 1969, but without the extensions introduced in TsSU (1983, p. 335), the source that Hanson uses.[7]

Some time before the cited essay by Hanson appeared, Nove (1981A) also argued, from rather different evidence, that the TsSU data on fixed investment in 'comparable prices' might in fact be in current prices. Cohn (1981) disputed that, but apparently unconvincingly for Nove (1981B). In view of the evidence that has now been presented, it should not be necessary to dwell longer on this matter.

V

In arguing that TsSU, in its calculations on real investment, overvalues new products, N–W–H are not too explicit as to how precisely such products should have been valued. There probably will be no dissent, however, if for present purposes I take the desideratum in that respect to be this: relatively to prices of old products, those of new ones should be commensurate with their ruble factor cost (RFC). I refer to RFC not as actually incurred when the new product is produced, but as might have been incurred had the new product been produced in the base year. The costs in question, though, are preferably such as might obtain after some modest batch had been produced, and hence such as would reflect some learning experience and initial economies of scale, should there be any.

I assume that real fixed investment is to be envisaged as a component of real

GNP. In Soviet circumstances, strictly speaking, not RFC, but 'adjusted factor cost' (AFC), has come to be accepted as the valuation standard appropriate to such a calculation. The two standards, as is well known, are not one and the same. In the present context, the limitations of RFC from that standpoint are for the most part of only secondary interest but, as will become evident, cannot be ignored.[8]

As perhaps should also be noted, the hypothetical base year RFC, to which the price of a new product is to be related, might presumably be calculated from a knowledge of base year technologies and factor charges. That is apt to be a taxing task, however, and for the valuation of a new product, Western practice sanctions diverse expedients of a familiar sort. Such procedures too should be kept in mind.[9]

Although N–W–H do not expatiate on how TsSU should have valued new products, it is clear enough how, in their view, that agency has in fact deviated from the foregoing principles. Essentially, as they see it, TsSU has valued new products simply at prices prevailing around the time of their introduction. That in itself could be a source of overvaluation so far as costs are generally rising, or might possibly relate to unduly small initial output batches. Much more stressed, however, is the further contention that under Soviet price-fixing practices new product prices might be expected to be inordinately high in any case.

For these propositions and the gross distortion that is said to result, N–W–H adduce diverse sorts of evidence. To begin with, there are the dubious TsSU releases on the growth of MBMW gross output. The precise import of allusions made to those TsSU data is not always clear, but the apparent presence in them of gross concealed inflation seems to be viewed, at least by Nove and Hanson, as indicative of its presence in the TsSU data on real fixed investment as well. Indeed, as we saw, Hanson (1984A) takes as one benchmark of the concealed inflation in the producers' durables component of TsSU fixed investment measures the upward bias in that agency's data on MBMW output. I refer to the bias indicated by an independent recomputation by Khanin.

There is much we still do not know about the way in which TsSU compiles its data on real fixed investment. But, especially for the construction component, reasoning by analogy with the TsSU measures of MBMW output seems clearly unwarranted. I have already explained why that is so. As for Khanin's recomputation, as explained, that appears if anything to support, rather than to invalidate, the TsSU data on real investment in producers' durables.

VI

The possible analogy with the TsSU measures of gross MBMW output is one kind of evidence advanced for substantial concealed inflation in the corresponding measures of real fixed investment. Another is found in a number of Soviet scholarly inquiries into recent trends in the sphere of capital formation in the USSR. The principal theme is the 'increasing costliness' (*udorozhanie*) of output in terms of capital. That certainly could be germane to concealed inflation, but the Soviet writings in question are unhappily often problematic; as witness the fact that an intriguing passage in Krasovsky (1980) has been construed in three quite different ways by Nove (1981A), Cohn (1981) and Wiles (1982, pp. 289–90). Hanson, probably wisely, does not refer to the passage at all.

For present purposes, I doubt that there is much to be gained by further exegesis of any inclusive sort. Rather I propose to focus on just one of the Soviet inquiries in question. Fal'tsman and Kornev (1984) became available only at a late stage of Western discussion of the TsSU investment data. Among contributors to the discussion, Hanson alone has referred to it, and he did so only rather briefly (1984B) after his main critique (1984A) of the TsSU data had appeared.

Among Soviet writings on *udorozhanie*, however, F–K (1984) are apparently regarded by Hanson as providing 'the most systematic evidence' that has yet been made public on concealed inflation in the TsSU investment data. The essay is, I think, relatively informative on aspects of *udorozhanie* such as N–W–H have noted in Soviet writings on that theme. While it, too, is sometimes difficult to construe, we should be able to gauge from it what additional evidence for concealed inflation may be extracted from relevant Soviet writings more generally.

In inquiring into *udorozhanie*, F–K (1984) range widely. Of particular interest are results they report of a special investigation into the experience of producers of 130 products in eight branches of industry (coal, iron and steel, chemicals, machinery, timber, construction materials, light manufactures, food processing). For those products, taken together, Fal'tsman and Kornev find that the 'capital coefficient' (*kapitaloemkost'*) in respect of output during 1971–75 was 9% above that for 1966–70, and during 1976–80 101% above that for 1971–75. As the context makes clear, the coefficient in question is none other than the incremental capital–output ratio (ICOR) familiar in Western parlance, i.e., the ratio of investment to the associated increment in output.

On the basis of the same investigation, Fal'tsman and Kornev also report on trends in a corresponding capital coefficient in respect of production 'capacity'. Relating investment to the associated increment in production capacity, this coefficient is in effect the incremental capital–capacity ratio (ICCR). It is found to increase by 28% from 1966–70 to 1971–75 and by 43% from 1971–75 to 1976–80.

Fal'tsman and Kornev also present data on various sources of the increase in the ICCR from 1971–75 to 1976–80 (Table 5). They also cite results of a related inquiry into the prices of 37 types of domestic machinery that are said to constitute about 40% of all investment in machinery of Soviet origin. For these products, prices per unit of 'design productivity' (*pasportnaya proizvoditel'nost'*) are found to have been on average during 1971–75 7% higher than during 1966–70. The corresponding increment for 1976–80 compared with 1971–75 was 15%.

What follows as to concealed inflation? Evidently nothing at all unless we assume, as Hanson (1984B) tacitly does, that the investment data in terms of which F–K (1984) gauge *udorozhanie* are consistent with those, in comparable prices, which TsSU releases. But while it seems advisable to be explicit on that

TABLE 5

SOURCES OF INCREASE IN INDUSTRIAL INCREMENTAL CAPITAL-CAPACITY RATIO (ICCR), USSR,
1976–80 OVER 1971–75[a]

Item	Increase, 1976–80 over 1971–75 (%)
Investment in machinery, per incremental unit of 'capacity' (*moshchnost'*)	72
Of which:	
Increased costliness of domestic machinery per unit of 'productivity' (*proizvoditel'nost'*)	11
Disproportionate increase in procurement of machinery not directly connected with introduction of capacity to produce final output	32
Increase in volume and costliness of imported machinery	21
Other factors	8
Increase in 'estimate value' (*smetnaya stoimost'*) of construction, per cubic metre	23

[a]*Source:* Fal'tsman and Kornev (1984, pp. 38, 42).

score, I do not really wish to challenge Hanson on it. Fal'tsman and Kornev, themselves, are nowhere explicit as to the nature of their investment data, but Hanson's is the only plausible way to interpret them, and there is in fact some specific support for that construction.[10]

As for concealed inflation, in expatiating on that Hanson (1984B) refers among other things to the data just cited on domestic machinery prices. He considers that those data provide 'strong evidence of concealed inflation in Soviet investment arising from domestic sources, chiefly padding of new product prices to increase bonuses'. Similar data reported in Soviet writings on *udorozhanie* that appeared before F–K (1984) were viewed in a like manner in Wiles (1982) and Hanson (1984A).

But to return to Hanson (1984B) he evidently is assuming at this point that the price increases in question are embedded in Fal'tsman and Kornev's, and hence also in TsSU, investment data. Here, too, he is doubtless correct. Fal'tsman and Kornev do not explain how they computed sources of the 72% increase, for 1976–80 compared with 1971–75, in machinery procurements per incremental unit of capacity (Table 5), and their characterizations (fairly literally rendered in the table) of the different sources are sometimes cryptic, to say the least. But, on any likely reading the imputations made probably do take into account the cited increase, 15%, in domestic machinery prices for 1976–80 compared with 1971–75.[11]

The F–K (1984) findings on domestic machinery price increases, I must also agree, could indicate concealed inflation in the TsSU data on investment, as they relate to such machinery. If they do, however, the degree could easily be overestimated. Note, to begin with, that reference is to the price of machinery per unit of design productivity. Productivity here is clearly measured in terms of machine output. Hence no account is taken at all of any gains that one or another machine may achieve through economy of labour, materials, fuel and power, environmental amelioration or through other qualitative features.

As Fal'tsman and Kornev also make clear, much is amiss with Soviet machine building. Resources embodied in producers' durables again and again in diverse ways fail economically to serve their purported functions. That is a familiar theme, and doubtless a corollary is that resultant labour economies and other non-output gains are not commensurate with the additional resource outlays they entail. Measured real investment, however, still properly reflects such resource outlays (compare Cohn, 1981). Any corresponding price increases, it also follows, cannot be considered as concealed inflation.

As commonly assumed, machinery is extensively produced to order rather than serially in the USSR. Through incorporation of novel features, such production provides a means whereby the producer may evade price controls and increase his profits and bonuses. So Hanson indicates, and so F–K (1984, pp. 41–42) in effect confirm. So far as there are such inordinate profits, moreover, there would be no corresponding resource inputs. To that extent, then, resultant price increases must in fact represent concealed inflation. Curiously, though, the profit margin on MBMW output in current prices, while it seems to have trended upward until 1970, has apparently declined more recently. In relation to final output, in current prices, less profits, these are the margins in question (%): 1960, 18·9; 1965, 22·4; 1970, 26·0; 1972, 23·7; 1975, 20·9.[12] Perhaps the contribution to inflation of profit padding on new products is not as great as has been supposed.

In brief, per unit of design productivity, the prices of domestic machinery are found in F–K (1984) to have increased by 1·4% annually from 1966–70 to 1971–75, and by 2·8% annually from 1971–75 to 1976–80. Without more information, the meaning of these findings for concealed inflation must be opaque. Should there be such inflation, however, it very probably proceeds at distinctly lower tempos than those at which, according to F–K (1984), prices per unit of design productivity increased. One must wonder also whether the acceleration of price increases per unit of design productivity that is reported by F–K (1984) may not be largely, if not entirely, a reflection of increased outlays for design features other than machine output, especially labour economy. The lately much discussed decline in labour availability was already well under way in the 1970s (CIA, 1985, p. 68). Inefficient as Soviet machine designers may be, it would be surprising if they were not responding to that fact.

Of the 72% increase in machinery procurements, per incremental unit of capacity, that is found to occur from 1971–75 to 1976–80, Fal'tsman and Kornev attribute 21 percentage points to the increased volume and costliness of machinery imports (Table 5). Here, again, Hanson (1984B) finds evidence of concealed inflation, and Wiles (1982) too apparently sees rising machinery import prices as contributing to that phenomenon. They could be right, and the inflation admittedly could be appreciable. Imports accounted for only a very limited part of Soviet investment in machinery in the early 1970s, but they became more consequential as the decade progressed. Reflecting the world inflation, domestic prices for imports rose apace; indeed, under the established Soviet procedures for converting foreign currency into domestic ruble prices, the latter prices for machinery imports must have risen essentially as their foreign currency counterpart did (Treml and Kostinksy, 1982). As a result, machinery investment overall could have been inflated by as much as, say, one-half a percentage point yearly during 1971–75 and perhaps by as much as 2·0 percentage points yearly during 1976–80.[13]

In all this, though, I assume, as Hanson does, that in the calculation of investment in comparable prices, machinery imports are simply included at current domestic prices. That could be so, though it is troubling that Fal'tsman and Kornev nowhere expressly say it is. While *udorozhanie* occurs here as elsewhere, reference is to costliness per incremental unit of capacity, and more or less as before the increase in costliness could reflect increased outlays for design aspects not manifest in capacity, i.e., economy of labour and materials and so on. On the other hand, the underlying measures of foreign currency prices of machinery imports on which my calculations rest supposedly take account of such features.

So much for concealed inflation in machinery investment. As further explanation of the 43% increase in the ICCR in 1976–80 compared with 1971–75, Fal'tsman and Kornev indicate that the 'estimate value' (*smetnaya stoimost'*) of a cubic metre of industrial construction shows a corresponding increase of 23% (Table 5). That is said to be due partly to the 'revision' (*peresmotr*) of estimate values and for the rest to higher levels of technical equipment and amenities, and shifts in construction to eastern, northern and seismic regions. Revision of estimate values is a familiar feature in Soviet construction and may or may not signify any increase in estimate prices of similar projects that would become embedded in measures of investment in comparable prices (compare Cohn, 1981, p. 297; CIA, 1976, pp. 3–4). Hanson does not offer grounds for one view or the other, and it is difficult to find in F–K (1984) any basis to do so.

I have referred to concealed inflation as it might occur in different components of investment. For purposes of judging such inflation overall, might not the increasing ICCR itself serve as an indicator? Hanson (1984B) nowhere urges that it might, but in his earlier essay (1984B) he seems to construe shifts of a like sort broadly in that way.

As he is aware, such trends nevertheless could originate quite otherwise, but it may be well to underline what already must be evident: on any reasonable construction, the data in F–K (1984) make it clear that concealed inflation could at most be only a very partial cause of the increasing ICCR.

Such a result does not seem very surprising when one ponders the diverse familiar purposes beyond the increase in capacity that investment serves: purposes, that is, such as already alluded to in the discussion of the relation of prices and machine design productivity. Much as before, too, one surmises that a resultant disproportionate increase in investment could easily become more so in the course of time, as F–K (1984) report that it does. Here, however, such a trend must be compounded by a factor not previously considered: the increase in investment needed to offset diminishing returns in extractive industries.

If the ICCR cannot serve as an indicator of concealed inflation, manifestly still less can the ICOR. If only for completeness, however, it should be noted that the shifts observed, in F–K (1984), in the ICOR relatively to the ICCR must simply reflect variations occurring incrementally in respect of capacity utilization. Thus, the increment of output associated with successive increments of capacity apparently increased during 1971–75 relatively to 1966–70 and then fell off markedly during 1976–80 relatively to 1971–75.[14]

It remains to refer to an intriguing feature of the ICCR as computed by Fal'tsman and Kornev. In aggregating capacities to produce different products, as they explain, they make calculations in both constant and current prices. Capacity grows faster with the latter than with the former valuation. That is not surprising, but, considering that differential, Fal'tsman and Kornev adjust their final measure of capacity increase upward by 10% in order to allow for a 10% improvement in quality. They apparently refer to the quality of products rather than of the capital goods producing them, but in view of their adjustment they can hardly be construed as holding new product pricing in the USSR to be all to the bad!

VII

This has been a rather lengthy paper. In conclusion, I try to set forth essential results summarily. Real fixed investment, according to TsSU, grew at annual average rates of 7·0% during 1971–75 and 3·4% during 1976–80. As calculated by the CIA, the corresponding tempos were 4·8% and 3·8% respectively (Table 1).[15] In both agencies, the indicated tempos are far below corresponding ones computed for early post-WW II years, but, according to Nove, Wiles and Hanson, they are nevertheless grossly distorted by concealed inflation. For Wiles (1982), one gathers, the yearly increase of Soviet real fixed investment during 1966–76 might, in fact, have been about 1·0%. Hanson (1984A) apparently leans to a similar figure, though he refers rather to 1976–80. As seen by Nove (1981A), Soviet real fixed investment volume lately has been declining rather than increasing, so the rate of growth, if anything, has been negative.

Fixed investment is understood by both TsSU and CIA as consisting predominantly of construction and investment in producers' durables. For construction, TsSU and the CIA have lately been more or less in accord. Yearly growth rates for 1971–75 and 1976–80 were, for TsSU, 5·8% and 0·8% respectively, and, for the CIA, 5·1% and 1·7%. The evidence on these measures that has been assembled in this essay is somewhat conflicting, but seems on balance to point to their being of the right order. At least, the CIA should not be far off the mark in calculating what it in effect has sought to do: the variation in investment in construction as indicated by the volume of construction materials utilized to that end. That already appeared to be so before the present inquiry was undertaken but the validity of the CIA calculation has, I think, been buttressed here by the striking agreement of a derived index of ruble factor cost per unit of materials utilized with the deflator implied by the CIA calculation.

On the further question concerning the reliability of the volume of utilized materials as an indicator of the volume of construction, my inquiry has shed no new light. But reference to materials utilization in that way is a familiar expedient in computations of construction, and has some support in US experience. Such a procedure, however, is manifestly subject to error. For that reason, there is little basis to choose between the CIA measures and those of TsSU, which, to repeat, move closely with those of the CIA.

For investment in producers' durables, the CIA has found it in order essentially to replicate the TsSU data which show rates of growth of 8·7% and 6·5% for 1971–75 and 1976–80 respectively. Nove, Wiles and Hanson tend to direct their fire more to these data than to those on construction. Their strictures apparently turn in part on an assumed analogy between the TsSU data on producers' durables investment and its further data on gross MBMW output. The latter, by all accounts, are indeed affected by concealed inflation, but, as not always considered, the TsSU calculation of producers' durables investment is apparently different from that of MBMW output; as witness the fact that the TsSU measures of producers' durables investment are highly congruent with results of CIA calculations of MBMW output. The latter allow in effect for substantial concealed inflation in the corresponding TsSU data.

On concealed inflation in the TsSU measures of producers' durables investment, however, Nove, Wiles and Hanson also cite as evidence a number of Soviet scholarly writings on the 'increasing costliness' (*udorozhanie*), in terms of capital, of further increases in output. On close scrutiny, the import of such evidence for concealed inflation often seems problematic, but the TsSU measures could possibly incorporate the inflation which has lately occurred in Soviet machinery import prices, and which was especially pronounced during the latter part of the 1970s. We must also reckon perhaps with a degree of concealed inflation owing to overevaluation of new domestic machinery, though the evidence on that is particularly opaque. It would, I think, be surprising if the resultant overstatement overall in annual producers' durables investment growth was more than one percentage point for 1971–75 and three percentage points for 1976–80.[16]

In sum, that the TsSU and CIA data on real fixed investment are subject to concealed inflation has yet to be conclusively demonstrated. But we must, I think, reckon those measures to be very possibly so affected. Should they be, the rate of growth cited above for 1971–75 might have to be discounted by a fraction of a percentage point. For the tempo cited for 1976–80, the corresponding discount might be, say, a full percentage point.[17] With the latter reduction, the rate of growth of gross fixed investment during 1976–80 becomes low indeed, but still hardly at the vanishing or near-vanishing levels allowed by Nove, Wiles and Hanson. For 1971–75, the tempo remains, as it was previously, rather impressive.

Whether discounted or not, investment in producers' durables is found by both TsSU and CIA to grow distinctly more rapidly than construction. The disparity is manifest during the 1970s generally, but becomes especially marked in the latter part of the decade. Such an incongruity perhaps could in itself be considered a count against the TsSU and CIA computations, but note that it is not unprecedented in Soviet post-WWII development (see Table 1). More to the point, the disparity seems understandable when we consider that the government found it expedient during the 1970s to increase sharply the share of investment devoted, not to establishment of new enterprises, but to 'reconstruction, extension and re-equipment' of existing ones (see Rumer, 1984; TsSU, 1976, p. 509; 1981, p. 339). While the resultant economy of new construction was not always consequential, the shift towards investment in producers' durables should have been marked.

As a factor affecting the TsSU and CIA measures of real fixed investment, concealed inflation, if operative at all, is found here to be primarily so in the late 1970s, and then primarily because of the impact of rising machinery import prices. Although evident, it may be well to underline that in that respect concealed inflation could prove to be rather transitory. World prices of machinery, which rose at extraordinary rates in the post-oil shock years of the 1970s, have more recently been increasing at relatively modest tempos.

On concealed inflation in the TsSU and CIA measures of real fixed investment, I have found it necessary to differ from Nove, Wiles and Hanson, but the present inquiry manifestly is hardly definitive. Let us hope that with further research we can gain additional insight into the important question at issue. In vigorously compelling attention to it, Nove, Wiles and Hanson have put fellow students of the Soviet economy much in their debt.

Notes

James Noren kindly clarified for me some aspects of the CIA calculations on investment volume growth, and he and Boris Z. Rumer helpfully called my attention to some pertinent Soviet writings.

[1] While for both TsSU and the CIA construction and investment in producers' durables dominate fixed investment, the two agencies appear to diverge in respect of lesser items that are also included in that category. Thus, the CIA includes in fixed investment net additions to basic livestock herds, while TsSU omits that item from its corresponding total. On the other hand, TsSU includes in fixed investment various other minor items, such as certain design and exploratory work. The CIA may include such items nominally, but variations in its totals over time seemingly are determined only by changes in construction, producers' durables investment, and livestock herds. Although TsSU and the CIA are broadly in accord on real fixed investment, there are, as will appear, sometimes marked incongruities. For that, the difference in treatment of lesser items is apparently a partial cause. On the scope of fixed investment for TsSU and the CIA: TsSU (1976, p. 801), Pitzer (1982, pp. 117ff).

[2] On the TsSU calculations of MBMW output: Greenslade (1972), Converse (1982).

[3] In view of the implications regarding the degree of upward bias in the TsSU data on MBMW output, Khanin is understandably cryptic regarding his findings. I accept here Nove's (1983) interpretation of them. That includes their dating. In the passage in question, Khanin, writing in 1981, compares official and his own calculations of MBMW growth for the 'last two-three five year plans', and at that point he may well be extrapolating relations derived originally for years before 1970. Hanson apparently construes Khanin in the same way as Nove. He cites, however, only the lower of the two figures I have given for the resulting rate of growth of MBMW output. Khanin makes a number of alternative recomputations of MBMW output, but averages the results in order to obtain a single figure on its growth. The two figures that I have cited originate from the oblique way in which he reports his findings rather than from his alternative computations.

[4] In Table 1, I have presented TsSU data on producers' durables investment only for years since 1960. The CIA extended its series for producers' durables investment years prior to 1960 mainly by reference to corresponding TsSU data for state (as distinct from collective farm) investment.

[5] Exclusive of profits, ruble factor cost per unit of construction output in any year i is simply: (1a) $RFC_i = P_i a + NMC$, where a is the materials input coefficient in construction, P_i is the price of materials per unit and NMC is all non-material costs per unit of construction output. Hence, (1b) $RFC_i = P_i a (1 + \lambda_i)$. Formula (1) follows at once with adjustments for profits. Profits, of course, are properly included here in ruble factor cost.

[6] Less profits, the gross social product (GSP) reported for 1972 was 60.75 billion rubles.

According to a nearly inclusive accounting, material purchases by construction in that year came to an estimated 36·2 billion rubles (Pitzer, 1982, p. 85), or 59·6% of the GSP, less profits. That is somewhat above the officially reported share of materials, inclusive of wages, for 1972: 55·4%. The apparent incongruity could arise in various ways. For example, the CIA computation of materials inputs very possibly includes some products that are classified otherwise by TsSU. But there is evidently little room for double-counting here.

[7] In TsSU (1976, p. 502) investment in comparable prices for 1970 is 72·7 billion rubles, yielding a slightly greater discrepancy from col. (2) than Hanson observed. But here and elsewhere in the calculations in question rounding errors could easily cause such a small discrepancy in either direction. To return to the deflators for construction (Table 2), an intriguing feature of those implied by the TsSU calculations in 'comparable prices' is that the underlying current and 'comparable price' figures for 1978 are almost the same: 83·1 and 83·2 billion rubles respectively. Since the comparable prices are purportedly derived from estimate prices of 1969, that may seem odd. Even if comparable prices generally are not current prices, one might wonder whether there is not an indication here that all is not as it should be. Perhaps it is not, but note that a post-1969 cross over of comparable and current prices is unavoidable in view of the modifications noted above that TsSU makes, in 1969 estimate prices, in deriving comparable prices.

[8] Of course, AFC itself is something less than ideal theoretically, but what is more to be noted here is that reference to the AFC standard presupposes use of real GNP in appraisal of 'production potential'. As theory primers teach, that is but one of two alternative uses to which real GNP might be put. Should the concern instead be 'welfare' appraisal, it is understood that AFC is superseded by its analytic twin, the 'welfare' standard.

Quite apart from that option, though, we must consider that real investment might be viewed not as a component of GNP but as a productive input. Curiously, however, valuation for new products at AFC is still indicated, though for old products a 'productivity' standard is then appropriate. At least, that is so where, as is usually the case, the final concern is through a calculation of factor productivity to appraise technological progress: Bergson (1975, reprinted 1982).

[9] On Western norms for valuation of new products in aggregative physical volume measures: United Nations, (1979, pp. 24ff). Of course, some expedient such as alluded to must be adopted should production of the new good require use of a technology that was not known in the base year. Calculation of costs by reference to base year technologies and factor prices, though, has a formal counterpart in the methodology used by the CIA in deriving its famous estimates of Soviet defence expenditures in dollar prices. On that, and on a related but distinct principle that might preferably be applied in such a context, see Bergson (1983).

[10] For the 130 products and eight industrial branches that they study, Fal'tsman and Kornev find that investment during 1971–75 was 39% greater than during 1965–70, and during 1976–80, 25% greater than during 1971–75. According to TsSU (1983, pp. 338–9) the corresponding increments for all industry were 40·8% and 29·9% respectively.

[11] That increase is presumably relevant in particular to the imputation of 11 percentage points to the increased costliness of domestic machinery per unit of productivity. Relatively to the 15% price increase, the computation could be of the right order provided the latter is taken to represent investment in all domestic machinery; which is to say all investment in machinery other than imports. On the latter, see below, n. 13.

[12] Final output derived from Steiner (1978, pp. 78, 83); profits from TsSU (1973, p. 699; 1976, p. 727; 1979, p. 517).

[13] With the data at hand, the calculations underlying these figures must be rather notional. It may suffice to say that in the light of Bogomolov (1984, p. 91) I take the share of imports in machinery investment in the early 1970s to be 15%. Bogomolov refers only to industrial investment, and his figure could possibly be high for all sectors. For the later 1970s I take the import share to average out to 23%. I consider here the indication in Fal'tsman (1983, p. 16) that the share was nearly one-third by the end of that interval. Of the total imports, I assume that those from the West accounted for 30% in the early 1970s and 35% in the later 1970s. The balance would come from Comecon. Compare Köves (1985, pp. 165ff). Domestic prices, in the case of imports from the West, are taken to vary with US machinery prices, as given in the US Council of Economic Advisors (1983, p. 227). For imports from Comecon, they are taken to vary similarly but the index for any year is supposed to reflect the shifting system of Comecon averaging described in Hewett (1980, p. 324). In the upshot domestic prices of imports from the West are calculated to rise an average of 5·0% yearly from 1966–70 to 1971–75 and 8·9% yearly from 1971–75 to 1976–80. The corresponding rates of price increase for imports from Comecon are 2·4% and 8·7% respectively. I make no allowance for changes in the Soviet foreign currency coefficients. For machinery imports they appear from 1972 on simply to have varied so as to offset changes in the dollar-ruble exchange rate. Possibly, though, the

price increases for 1971–75 over 1969–70 should be adjusted upward somewhat to take account of that aspect: see Treml and Kostinsky (1982).

[14] To return to the ICCR, for both investment and production capacity, reference is to increments gross of retirements, but variations in the latter should affect the numerator and denominator of the ICCR correspondingly. On the other hand, the retirements would affect only the numerator of the ICOR, so that coefficient has to be read in the light of trends in retirements. On that, see below.

Also to be noted in respect of both coefficients is the fact that investment includes any increase in unfinished construction. Curiously though, that probably was not a consequential factor over the years in question. If we may judge at all from flawed comparative data such as already referred to (TsSU 1981, pp. 334, 345), the total volume of unfinished construction rose markedly during the 1970s, but the increment of such construction remained a small and somewhat declining share of investment, i.e., in %, during 1966–70, 6·6; during 1971–75, 4·9, and during 1976–80, 4·5.

[15] On apparent incongruities between indicated comparative growth of TsSU and CIA measures for all fixed investment, on the one hand, and its two major components, construction and producers' durables investment on the other, see above, n. 1.

[16] I allow for the possible impact of inflation of import prices at rates suggested above, i.e., one-half a percentage point during 1971–75, and two percentage points during 1976–78. The balance of the indicated overstatement for each interval is simply one-half of the rates of increase in domestic machinery prices, per unit of design capacity, as indicated in Fal'tsman and Kornev, and discussed above. I also allow, though, for the shortfall of domestic from total machinery investment, as indicated in n. 13.

I referred earlier to two computations of the output of producers' durables: one made by the CIA as part of its calculation of MBMW output, the other derived by the CIA from the TsSU measures of investment in producers' durables. The derivation entails adjusting those measures to exclude net imports. The two series, as indicated, are broadly in accord. The agreement is nevertheless not exact, but oddly for 1975–79 the CIA calculation of producers' durables output shows somewhat faster growth than the adjusted TsSU series—6·3% compared with 5·2% annually. If the TsSU series includes imports at current prices, one would expect the reverse to be true, for in adjusting that series for imports, I understand, the CIA calculated imports at constant prices. Possibly the explanation is simply that the CIA series errs at this point. Since it is based on a sample, that is certainly possible. Possibly, though, there is further reason to doubt that, in calculating investment in producers' durables, TsSU really includes imports at current prices.

[17] Investment in producers' durables constituted in 1970 30% and in 1975 33% of all gross fixed investment. I refer to the TsSU (1981, p. 334) data. In the CIA (Pitzer, 1982, p. 67) the corresponding figures are about the same.

References

Abram Bergson, 'Index Numbers and the Calculation of Factor Productivity', *The Review of Income and Wealth*, Series 21, No. 3 (September 1975), pp. 259–78.

——. *Welfare, Planning and Employment*, Cambridge, Mass., 1982.

——, 'On the Measurement of Soviet Real Defense Outlays', in Padma Desai ed. *Marxism, Central Planning and the Soviet Economy* (Cambridge, Mass., 1983).*

O. T. Bogomolov, 'O vneshneekonomicheskikh svyazyakh SSSR', *Kommunist*, 1974 no. 5, pp. 89–99.

CIA (Central Intelligence Agency), *Ruble-Dollar Ratios for Construction*, ER 76–10068, (Washington, DC February 1976).

——, *Handbook of Economic Statistics, 1985*, CPAS 85–10001, (Washington, DC 1985).

Stanley H. Cohn, 'Response to Alec Nove, A Note on Growth, Investment and Price Indexes', *Soviet Studies*, XXXIII no. 2 (April 1981), pp. 296–9.

Ray Converse, 'An Index of Industrial Production in the USSR', in US Congress, Joint Economic Committee, *USSR: Measures of Economic Growth and Development, 1950–80*, (Washington, DC 1982), part 2, pp. 169–244.

V. K. Fal'tsman, 'Narodnokhozyaistvennyi zakaz na novuyu tekhniku', *EKO*, 1983 no. 3, pp. 1–19.

V. Fal'tsman, and A. Kornev, 'Rezervy snizheniya kapitaloemkosti moshchnostei promyshlennosti', *Voprosy ekonomiki*, 1984 no. 6.

Rush V. Greenslade, 'Industrial Production Statistics in the USSR', in Vladimir G. Treml and John P. Hardt eds. *Soviet Economic Statistics*, (Durham, NC 1972), pp. 155–94.

Philip Hanson, 'The CIA, the *TsSU* and the Real Growth of Soviet Investment', *Soviet Studies*, XXXVI no. 4 (October 1984) (A). pp. 571–81.

* See Chapter 13 in this book.

Philip Hanson, 'New Evidence about Soviet Investment', *Radio Liberty Research*, 13 September 1984 (B).
Ed. A. Hewett, 'The Impact of the World Economic Crisis on Intra-CMEA Trade', in Neuberger and Laura D. Tyson eds. *The Impact of International Economic Disturbances on the Soviet Union and Eastern Europe*, (New York, 1980).
G. I. Khanin, 'Al'ternativnye otsenki rezul'tatov khozyaistvennoi deyatel'nosti proizvodstvennykh yacheek promyshlennosti', *Izvestiya Akademii Nauk SSSR, Seriya ekonomicheskaya*, November–December, 1981, pp. 62–73.
A. Köves, *The CMEA Countries in the World Economy*, (Budapest, 1985).
V. Krasovsky, 'Investitsionnyi kompleks: planirovanie i rezervy', *Voprosy ekonomiki*, 1979 no. 1, pp. 59–69.
Richard Moorsteen and Raymond P. Powell, *The Soviet Capital Stock, 1928–1962*, (Homewood, Ill., 1966).
Alec Nove, 'A Note on Growth, Investment and Price Indices', *Soviet Studies*, XXXIII no. 1 (January, 1981) (A), pp. 142–5.
——, 'Reply to Stanley H. Cohn', *Soviet Studies*, XXXIII No. 2 (April 1981) (B), pp. 296–9.
——, 'Has Soviet Growth Ceased?', *Manchester Statistical Society*, 15 November, 1983.
John Pitzer, 'Gross National Product of the USSR, 1950–80', in US Congress, Joint Economic Committee, *USSR: Measures of Economic Growth and Development, 1950–80*. (Washington, DC), part 1, 1982, pp. 3–168.
Boris Z. Rumer, *Investment and Reindustrialization in the Soviet Economy*, (Boulder, Col., 1984).
James E. Steiner, *Inflation in Soviet Industry and Machine Building and Metalworking (MBMW) 1960–75*, (Washington, DC 1978).
TsSU (Tsentral'noe Statisticheskoe Upravlenie), *Narodnoe khozyaistvo SSSR v 1983*. (Moscow, 1984), and other volumes in the same series.
United Nations, *Manual on National Accounts at Constant Costs, Statistical Papers*, Series M, no. 64, (New York, 1979).
US Council of Economic Advisors, *Economic Report of the President*, (Washington, DC 1983).
Peter Wiles, 'Soviet Consumption and Investment Prices and the Meaningfulness of Real Investment', *Soviet Studies*, XXXIV no. 2 (April, 1982), pp. 289–95.

13

On the Measurement of
Soviet Real Defense Outlays

This essay focuses on some conceptual issues concerning calculations of Soviet real defense expenditures by the Office of Strategic Research (OSR) of the Central Intelligence Agency (CIA). The resulting measures of real defense expenditures of course take the form of index numbers, and the issues that are to be considered essentially lie within the realm of index number theory. The nature of the relevant principles and their application to Soviet defense outlays, however, may not yet have been sufficiently explored.

Measurement of Soviet real defense outlays is a theme that seems only rarely to be examined from a theoretic standpoint.[1] By providing further analytic perspective on that important matter, this essay will perhaps serve as a fitting tribute to Alexander Erlich, who has done so much to illuminate the Soviet economy generally.

The OSR compiles two sorts of measures of Soviet real defense expenditures, one relating to the variation in such outlays over time, and the other, to their volume compared with that of the corresponding outlays in the United States. I focus primarily on the latter, but the main argument is readily extended to apply to measures of Soviet real outlays over time.

In the intelligence community measurement of comparative real outlays in the U.S.S.R. and the United States has come to be called the "sizing" problem. In addressing that problem, an initial question that the OSR had to deal with concerns the appropriate scope of such expenditures. This matter is also perhaps somewhat more complex than might be supposed, but it is not of primary interest here.[2] Suffice it to say that OSR construes military outlays in a broadly conventional way to include weapons procurement, defense construction, military personnel costs, various operational and maintenance outlays, and R and D outlays that are taken to be defense related.[3]

In whatever way defense expenditures are delineated, a comparison of such outlays in different countries must be made in constant prices. In the present case the calculations might be made in dollar or ruble prices. The OSR has focused especially on the derivation of comparative data in dollar prices.

Obtaining appropriate data on U.S. outlays can pose no problem for the OSR, at least none in principle. As for the corresponding figures for the U.S.S.R., the OSR has elucidated in numerous unclassified reports the general nature of the procedures it employs in deriving such measures.[4] By now the so-called "building-block" method it applies must be broadly familiar. Essentially, the concern is to establish insofar as possible the physical magnitudes of different Soviet defense goods and services and then to value the items directly in dollar prices commanded by comparable defense goods and services in the United States. The OSR also in some instances uses variants of the building-block method, but that is the chief procedure employed.[5]

The building-block method is of course a very usual one in practical work with index numbers. Given data on the quantities of defense goods and services that the Soviet government is procuring, the procedure evidently can be readily applied where dollar prices happen to be quoted in the United States for precisely the same items as are procured in the U.S.S.R. What, however, if, as is often the case, an item in one country is unique and not produced in the other?

The OSR apparently assumes that U.S. and Soviet defense items are often sufficiently similar, and thus dollar prices of the former may still be applied to the latter. Probably the outstanding instances are in the sphere of military manpower, where services of a given rank in the U.S.S.R. are simply valued at the compensation rates, including money pay, allowances and rations, for services in a corresponding rank in the United States.[6]

Whether such a procedure is always warranted is an interesting question that cannot be pursued here. In this chapter I focus predominantly on goods, rather than services, where circumstances are admittedly otherwise: the Soviet defense items have no identical counterpart in the United States, nor even a sufficiently near one to warrant evaluation simply at the dollar prices of U.S. procurements. Such Soviet items must be numerous, especially among relatively fabricated goods such as munitions. Here, according to a statement submitted by the CIA to the Joint Economic Committee, the OSR has proceeded in this way:

> Our dollar concept is the cost of producing the Soviet design in the United States using base year U.S. production technology, input prices, and profit margins. Our ability to reflect the Soviet design depends to a large degree upon our knowledge of the physical and performance characteristics of the

individual weapons. When we have good data, our cost estimates capture the "austerity or complexity" of the Soviet weapon. We have to fall back on U.S. analogs for weapons or components when our knowledge is less complete. In these cases we attempt to adjust the analog results by extrapolating from our general understanding of Soviet design practices.

When we have sufficient information we do engineering cost studies. Most of our costs are derived using cost estimating relationships (CER's) which are based on U.S. weapons costs adjusted to "Sovietize" the weapon. Some weapons—usually lower cost items—are costed on the basis of the nearest equivalent U.S. weapons.[7]

In other words, where there is no U.S. good identical or deemed very close to a Soviet good, an inquiry is made as to what the factor or resource cost (including an appropriate profit margin) might be of replicating the Soviet good in the United States. The Soviet good is valued at that U.S. factor or resource cost. That is the essential principle applied.

On the face of it this principle can be defended theoretically, by extending to the intercountry comparison of real defense outlays the familiar analysis applied when real national income is compared among countries. Theory teaches that in the latter case we obtain an observation on comparative production capacity in the countries in question. I refer to the capacity to produce goods and services with available factor supplies such as labor and capital.[8] In comparing real defense outlays, we must think correspondingly of the capacity represented by factor supplies committed to the production of defense goods and services.

In national income comparisons production capacity may be understood to refer specifically to comparative capacity to produce the same mix of goods and services in the two countries. The mix to be considered as standard in that sense depends on the prices in which output is valued; paradoxically, with valuation in prices of one country the standard mix is the one actually found in the other. Pursuing further the analogy to real national income comparisons, we see that the comparison of real defense outlays may be construed as indicating relative capacities to produce, with resources committed to defense, the mix of military goods and services found in one country, particularly the one other than that whose prices are used in valuing output. With valuation in dollars, then, the standard mix is the one actually produced in the U.S.S.R.

As usually formulated, the theory of real national income comparison relates to circumstances where any good produced in one country is also produced in the other. The analysis may be extended, however, to circumstances where that is not so, and that is true also of the comparison of real defense outlays. In the case now in question the OSR valuation procedure is seen to be an appropriate one. For Soviet defense goods not produced in the United States, valuation at the dollar factor cost of replicating such goods in this country evidently permits us to construe the defense outlay comparison in dollars as before, that is, as providing an observation on the comparative capacity in the two countries to produce the Soviet mix of defense goods, given the respective volumes of resources committed to defense. That applies to the Soviet mix whether or not there are counterparts in the United States.

The OSR procedure is not the only one available, however. An interesting alternative approach may be formulated based on work in a different context by the late Rush Greenslade, the essentials of which were outlined in a brief memorandum he prepared several years ago.[9] I present the approach in somewhat different terms from Greenslade's and with a rather different rationale from the one that he indicated.

As concerns Soviet products not produced in the United States, and on the valuation of those products in dollars, the OSR procedure estimate is the resource or factor cost of replicating the Soviet product in the United States. Reference is apparently to physical replication, but, so far as that is done, the U.S. replica of course will have the same performance characteristics as the Soviet product; if there is complete physical replication, the performance must be the same.

Yet that is not the only way to get the same performance characteristics. In the United States, if we were seeking to replicate the performance characteristics in question, we might choose to produce them with different inputs—materials, labor, and the like—from those used in the Soviet product. Indeed it would be surprising if we should not do so. Given the disparate technologies, labor supplies, materials, and so forth, in the two countries, scarcity relations in the United States differ from those in the U.S.S.R. To achieve certain performance characteristics, we might find it economical to substitute one sort of factor input for another. So there is the possibility that to some degree similar performance characteristics could be achieved at a different and presumably lower dollar cost than would be entailed in replicating physical characteristics.

In the alternative, as in the OSR calculation, one turns to U.S. manufacturers to obtain estimates of cost. The primary stress, however, is on the cost of replicating performance characteristics, although in some cases this might entail replication of physical characteristics as well. More specifically, valuation at a least-cost reproduction of the Soviet performance characteristics would be sought. Ideally, the Soviet defense goods are to be valued in dollars on that basis.

What is the comparative merit of this and the OSR procedure? While there is a conventional, theoretic basis for the OSR calculation, which makes it seem the more obvious one to employ, the proposed alternative merits consideration. Essentially, when defense outlays in the two countries are valued in dollars and the alternative procedure is applied to Soviet goods that lack any near counterpart in the United States, the resulting data would still be indicative of the comparative capacity of the two countries, with the resources committed to defense, to produce the Soviet mix of defense goods. In the case of Soviet goods lacking any counterpart in the United States, however, reference is to U.S. capacity to produce the performance equivalent of the Soviet good rather than the identical physical item.

The result we get by comparing the real defense outlays of the two economies in that way is arguably more significant than the one from the OSR kind of calculation. What we seek to obtain ideally are observations on comparative "military utility." As we need not ponder long to become aware, military utility measurement is a very difficult thing indeed. We hardly have data we can interpret easily from that standpoint.[10] In any event a comparison of production capacity is certainly not the same thing as a comparison of military utility. But as between capacity to produce physical replicas and capacity to produce performance equivalents, the latter would seem closer to the ultimate desideratum.

I have been considering the OSR procedure as it is in principle. In practice OSR must make many compromises, and no doubt they themselves must often take performance characteristics as an indication of physical characteristics. The difference between the two procedures therefore might not be as great as it might seem on paper. But there is an indisputable difference, and the result is that measured U.S. defense capacity tends to be lower relatively to that of the U.S.S.R. than it would be if the alternative stressing performance were employed.[11]

But I have been referring to the comparative magnitudes of index numbers obtained under the alternative procedures. It remains to consider that, as observations on defense production capacity, both sorts of measures are apt to err. In index number theory that is a familiar kind of theme, but we are concerned with it in a rather novel context. It may be well to expatiate on the matter in formal terms.

Whichever of the two approaches is employed, the index number to be obtained is given by this formula:

$$I_{01} = \frac{V^{11}}{V^{01}}. \tag{1}$$

Here V^{11} is U.S. defense outlays in dollar prices, and V^{01}, Soviet defense outlays in dollar prices, which is given by the formula:

$$V^{01} = \sum_{i=1}^{g} p_i^1 q_i^0 + \sum_{j=h}^{w} \bar{p}_j^1 q_j^0. \tag{2}$$

There are w defense items purchased in the U.S.S.R., of which g have identical or near identical counterparts in the United States, and $(w - g)$ have no such counterparts. In obtaining the total Soviet outlays, the quantities of the former, q_i^0, are valued at actual U.S. prices, p_i^1, and the latter, q_j^0, are valued at U.S. replication costs, $\bar{p}_j^1$. Depending on the approach adopted, reference is to the replication of physical counterparts in one case and performance equivalents in the other.

In formula (1), as implied,

$$V^{11} = \sum_{i=1}^{t} p_i^1 q_i^1, \tag{3}$$

where t items are produced in the United States, and p_i^1 and q_i^1 are their actual dollar prices and quantities. Formula (3) applies whether items produced only in the U.S.S.R. are valued at physical replication or performance equivalent cost. For clarity, however, we must also consider alternative hypothetical mixes of defense items that the United States could purchase for the same dollar total:

$$V^{11} = \sum_{i=1}^{g} p_i^1 r_i^1 + \sum_{j=h}^{t} \bar{p}_j^1 s_j^1. \tag{4}$$

Here r_i^1 is a possibly varying quantity of an item procured in the United States that has a near counterpart in the U.S.S.R., while s_j^1 represents a possibly varying amount of the U.S. reproduction of an item produced in the U.S.S.R. that has no near counterpart in the United States. Depending on the approach adopted, reference is either to a physical replica or a performance equivalent, and $\bar{p}_j^1$ is construed correspondingly.

I have referred to resources committed to defense. When a country's overall production capacity is in question, the resources that constrain output are understood correspondingly as those available to the country as a whole. Since our concern is only with the defense sector, one is tempted to try to delineate from the economywide totals the resources committed to that sector alone. That would be conceptually difficult, for the mix of factors employed in defense could be expected to vary with the mix of defense goods and services produced. But we can define at once the country's capacity to produce defense goods and services in a manner appropriate here simply on the understanding that we refer to mixes that can be produced when the

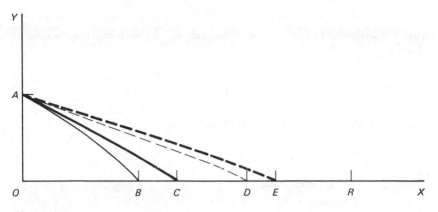

Figure 1
Comparative defense production capacity

quantities of all other goods produced are constant. With economywide resources given, that would seem to represent plausibly our desideratum: the capacity corresponding to a given commitment of resources to defense.

Resulting production capacity frontiers for the United States are illustrated (Figure 1). While actually producing only a single defense item, say, a type Y tank, the U.S. is capable of producing different mixes of that and a corresponding item, say, a type X tank, produced by the U.S.S.R. Feasible mixes are represented by AB, when for type X we refer to physical replicas of that tank, and by AD, when the performance equivalent of that tank is in question. Both frontiers are segments of the economywide production capacity surface on the plane corresponding to constant outputs of all nondefense items. Also shown are U.S. defense "budget" lines delineated by (4). Here AC is given by that formula when the second term on the right refers to physical replicas and AE, when that term refers to performance equivalents.

Relative to Soviet output of the type X tank then, the U.S. capacity to produce its physical replica is given by the ratio

$$C_{01}^* = \frac{OB}{OR},$$ (5)

where OR stands for the actual Soviet output. With (1) to (4) likewise referring in the case of our single Soviet defense item to its physical replica in the United States, I_{01} has the magnitude:

$$I_{01}^* = \frac{OC}{OR},$$ (6)

which should tend to approximate C_{01}^* but need not equal it. Similarly, where reference is to U.S. capacity to produce a performance equivalent of the Soviet tank, the relevant capacity ratio becomes

$$C_{01}^{**} = \frac{OD}{OR},$$ (7)

and the corresponding magnitude of I_{01} is

$$I_{01}^{**} = \frac{OE}{OR},$$ (8)

which should approximate C_{01}^{**}.

Since in the case graphed each country produces but a single item, the standard mix consists of only one item: with sizing in dollars, that is, the item produced in the U.S.S.R. With many items produced in each country, however, formulas (1) through (4) still provide alternative observations on U.S. capacity to produce the Soviet mix. The particular observation depends, as before, on the kind of U.S. reproduction in question for Soviet items.

Figure 1 shows the production capacity frontiers as concave from below, which is of course the way they usually are drawn. Given that curvature, formula (1) overstates U.S. capacity relative to that of the U.S.S.R. That is so no matter which of the two approaches is adopted. For the simple case illustrated, the overstatement under each approach is evident. Should there be economies of scale, however, the production capacity frontier may or may not be concave from below. The direction of bias in (1) is then uncertain. Many sorts of defense goods are of a highly fabricated kind such that economies of scale often obtain.

The foregoing assumes that the U.S. cost of replicating a Soviet defense item is calculated for a small batch. Should reference instead be to a larger batch that exploits scale economies in greater or less degree, there is perhaps some presumption against understatement of U.S. capacity. What bias, if any, obtains, however, would depend on the degree to which scale economies are allowed for over a relevant range of U.S. output variation. That range might itself be a rather complex matter to gauge.[12]

Costs not only may vary with scale; for highly fabricated products they often vary also with time, through a learning experience. There seems to be no way to rule theoretically between different cost levels that might be experienced in such circumstances. A level some distance out on the learning curve, I suspect, would usually be of primary interest.

We must judge, however, how the OSR deals with cost variation from occasional statements, such as this concerning the valuation of a Soviet ICBM:

... the estimated annual dollar costs of this procurement ... is derived by applying the production numbers to an estimate of the cost of the initial unit produced and then bringing the costs down a cost reduction curve which U.S. production experience has led us to believe is appropriate for this kind of hardware.[13]

The production numbers in question apparently refer to the scale of actual Soviet output rather than, as is theoretically indicated, of the hypothetical U.S. output associated with U.S. procurements of a standard, Soviet mix. It is not clear whether the "cost reduction curve" referred to relates only to cost variation with scale or embodies learning experience as well.

So much for the sizing of Soviet defense outlays in dollars. Soviet and U.S. defense outlays can also be compared in ruble prices. U.S. outlays can be translated into rubles in just the same way as the OSR translates Soviet outlays into dollars, with U.S. physical procurement for the most part being valued at ruble prices. So far as U.S. products have no near counterpart in the U.S.S.R., reference might be to the hypothetical factor cost in rubles of replicating those products with respect to their physical characteristics in the U.S.S.R. That evidently would be the mirror image of the procedure used by the OSR to value in dollars Soviet munitions that have no near counterpart in the United States. Or reference might be made to an alternative procedure, such as I have described, where the concern is with replication of performance characteristics. The results again must differ. The procedure stressing physical replication should now result in a measured level of U.S. relative to Soviet defense outlays that is higher, not lower, than the procedure stressing performance. In either case, the measured level then may deviate from comparative defense production capacity in a manner that has been explained.

One may suppose such calculations are possible, but the data would hardly be available in practice. Among other things Soviet manufacturers are not likely to cooperate readily with inquiries into Soviet factor cost of replicating U.S. defense goods. Understandably, the OSR, in comparing defense outlays in ruble prices, must employ rather different methods from those it uses in its dollar comparison. For U.S. products that have no near counterpart in the U.S.S.R., the procedure employed also differs from that emphasizing performance.

Essentially, in calculating Soviet defense outlays in rubles, the OSR values some Soviet defense goods and services directly in ruble prices.[14] For example, military manpower is apparently valued directly in the ruble pay and subsistence of Soviet troops. But for a considerable volume of Soviet defense goods OSR begins with dollar values that have been derived in the manner described earlier. The OSR apparently is also able to refer to ratios of rubles and dollar prices for some defense goods and goods deemed to be similar to defense goods in comparative Soviet and U.S. costs. These ratios provide a basis for translating into rubles the Soviet defense goods initially valued in dollars. As for the calculation of U.S. defense outlays in rubles, the OSR again values some items such as military manpower directly in rubles but begins with dollar procurement values for a large volume of defense goods and translates these into rubles by reference to ruble/dollar price ratios.

This procedure calls for several comments. To begin with, it is fairly obvious that the OSR has to operate with a relatively limited sample of ruble/dollar ratios. Although the sample has grown in time, the ratios themselves must often be inferred from indirect evidence.[15] The calculations in ruble terms therefore must be especially crude. The crudeness is to some extent highlighted by the drastic revision that occurred a few years ago when apparently some additional information became available on ruble/dollar price ratios.[16] The additional information is comforting, but the sensitivity of the results to it is disconcerting.

In fairness, the OSR itself acknowledges the relatively inexact nature of its ruble comparison, and the results have generally been published as a range rather than in single figures. For some time the range for Soviet outlays has been but 11 to 13 percent of the GNP. That allows for a variation of about 20 percent in the defense outlays, but about half of that reflects a difference in concept. One wonders whether the margin of error can be as limited as implied.

However accurate or inaccurate the OSR's calculations in ruble prices may be, as theory teaches and our analysis has clearly implied, production capacity appraisal presupposes that relative commodity prices ideally correspond to "marginal rates of transformation." For well-known reasons one may wonder to what extent dollar prices for defense goods conform to that principle, but the limitations of ruble prices generally are proverbial (see Bergson 1961). Ruble prices of defense goods could not be expected to be an exception to that rule.

Further reference to theoretic principles at this point seems otiose, but a conceptual issue may be worth airing. In compiling ruble/dollar price ratios, suppose that in the case of dollar prices reference for some defense goods must be to the estimated dollar cost of replicating a Soviet product in the United States. Of the two procedures for obtaining such an estimate that I have discussed, which is the more appropriate in determining dollar prices that are to be used in compiling ruble/dollar ratios? For purposes of translating Soviet defense outlays from dollars to rubles, the answer presumably must be that the procedure should be the same as that employed in deriving the dollar values to begin with. For purposes of translating U.S. defense outlays from dollars to rubles, the matter is not so clear, but, the least-cost replication of performance should yield a dollar price that, when compared with a corresponding ruble price, could be more or less indicative of ruble/dollar ratios for defense goods, while a dollar price given by the cost of replicating physical characteristics could easily be off the mark. Actual dollar prices of defense goods should tend to reflect least-cost production of performance characteristics. The market for defense goods, with all of its proverbial limitations, should not sustain for long egregiously uneconomic production of performance characteristics.

In such discussions as have occurred about the rationale behind OSR's methods of sizing Soviet defense outlays, a question frequently raised concerns the treatment of a product of only one country that might be "infinitely" costly to replicate in the other. The main problem here concerns the ruble costs of replicating U.S. high-technology defense goods when sizing is in ruble prices.[17] No satisfactory solution seems to have been found.

Whether there are any products in the United States that would be infinitely costly to replicate in the U.S.S.R. is an interesting issue, but there are doubtless some products whose costs of replication would be so high as to make a literal application of the OSR methodology of doubtful interest. Replication of performance equivalents would to some extent avoid such an outcome.

Recourse is possible, however, to another expedient not yet considered: omit the items in question from the calculation. If one simply excludes from U.S. expenditures the hypothetical ruble outlays on such items, the resulting index would still indicate comparative capacities to produce the U.S. defense mix. I refer, however, to capacities delineated by resources committed to procurement of U.S. items other than those that are infinitely costly to replicate in the U.S.S.R. The U.S. mix that serves as standard must be construed correspondingly. Should any Soviet defense goods be infinitely costly to replicate in the United States, they might be treated similarly in the comparison in dollar terms, with a similarly construed result. In either case the limited coverage must be stressed. With inclusion of the omitted items, comparative outlays of one country or the other become exceedingly large, the country in question being the one whose output is infinitely costly to replicate in the other country.

My discussion of measurement of the comparative volume of Soviet and U.S. defense outlays can be readily extended to the analogous problem of measuring the change in Soviet and U.S. defense outlays over time in constant prices. Usually such a calculation is made in prices of the country concerned, but a choice must be made between early and late prices. Since old products may drop out of and new ones enter the mix of goods produced, here too the problem arises of valuing in one period goods produced in another. At least in principle then we are again confronted with alternative procedures, one stressing physical replication and the other performance. There are also parallel differences in results. With valuation in late prices the procedure emphasizing physical replication should yield a lower measured rate of growth than the one emphasizing performance. With valuation in early prices the relation of the two series of procedures is reversed. Viewed as observations on the change in production capacity over time, both measures are subject to a bias parallel to that obtaining for intercountry comparisons at one time.

The foregoing applies equally to measurements of real defense outlays over time in the U.S.S.R. and the United States. Insofar as the measurements for the U.S.S.R. are in rubles, however, and derived, as in the OSR calculations, through the mediation of dollar values, meaningful application of either of the two procedures must be difficult.

The concept of comparative capacities to produce performance equivalents inevitably calls to mind the so-called "hedonic" approach that lately has come into use in the calculation of the cost of living and real income. While there is an obvious affinity between the two measures, it should be noted that, whether we refer to performance or hedonic equivalents, what is in question is only items within relatively limited commodity categories. As between categories, comparative physical volume is calculated in the one case by use of production cost weights to measure comparative production capacity and, in the other, by use of prices reflecting relative utilities to measure real income changes as they relate to variations in utility.

By considering performance equivalence within categories, I admittedly derive an index of a conceptually mixed character. The result, I believe, is still interesting and meaningful, more so probably than when, as is sometimes done, hedonic equivalents are determined by comparative costs.[18]

Notes

I elaborate here on ideas presented initially in a lecture at the Air Force Academy, Colorado Springs, August 18, 1978. I have benefited from comments of an unidentified reader on an earlier version.

1. An exception, however, is Franklyn D. Holzman, Are the Soviets really outspending the U.S. on defense? *International Security* (Spring 1980). See also Abraham S. Becker, *Military Expenditure Limitations for Arms Control*, Cambridge, Mass.: Ballinger, 1977, ch. 2.

2. Becker, *Military Expenditure*, ch. 2.

3. On the scope of defense outlays as understood by OSR and on the OSR calculations of Soviet defense outlays more generally, see Joint Economic Committee, United States Congress (hereafter, JEC), *Allocation of Resources in the Soviet Union and China—1975*, Washington, D.C., 1975; volumes with corresponding titles for later years that were issued by the JEC in Washington, D.C., in 1976, 1977, 1978 and 1979; Permanent Select Committee on Intelligence, House of Representatives, *CIA Estimates of Soviet Defense Spending*, Washington, D.C., 1980; CIA, *Estimated Soviet Defense Spending in Rubles, 1970–1975*, SR 76-10121 U, May 1976; CIA, *A Dollar Comparison of Soviet and U.S. Defense Activities 1965–1975*, SR 76-10053, February 1976; CIA, *Estimated Soviet Defense Spending: Trends and Prospects*, SR 78-10121, June 1978; CIA, *A Dollar Cost Comparison of Soviet and US Defense Activities, 1966–1976*, SR 77-10001 U, January 1977; and corresponding CIA reports for 1967–1977, 1968–1978, 1970–1979, and 1971–1980 issued, respectively, as SR 78-10002, January 1978; SR 79-10004, January 1979; SR 80-10005, January 1980; SR 81-10005, January 1981. The foregoing CIA reports are cited hereafter by number and date.

4. See note 3.

5. The variants apparently are employed mainly in the case of operation and maintenance and R and D.

6. JEC, *Allocation of Resources in the Soviet Union and China—1975*, pp. 21, 81; Permanent Select Committee on Intelligence, *CIA Estimates*, p. 8.

7. JEC, *Allocation of Resources in the Soviet Union and China—1975*, p. 83. See also Permanent Select Committee on Intelligence, *CIA Estimates*, pp. 2ff, 73ff.

8. For a brief exposition and bibliography, see Abram Bergson, *The Real National Income of Soviet Russia since 1928*, Cambridge, Mass.; Harvard University Press, 1961, ch. 3.

9. Rush V. Greenslade, Resource cost versus performance cost standard in valuing soviet defense (typescript), October 4, 1976.

10. Compare Becker, *Military Expenditure*, ch. 2.

11. Whatever the characteristics considered, the CIA reportedly very often derives the appropriate dollar figure from a regression equation relating dollar costs to those characteristics. Provided the regression equation itself is based on empirical inquiry into U.S. dollar costs, that procedure would seem to be unexceptionable in principle, though as with any such application of regression analysis the result is necessarily subject to error.

Given the nature of the underlying empirical inquiry, however, theory decrees that reference ideally be to dollar costs of the year for which Soviet defense outlays are being sized in relation to those of the United States. Only on that basis can the calculations be read, as theory teaches they might be, as observations on the production capacity frontier. For this reason, Steven S. Rosefielde (in testimony before the Permanent Select Committee on Intelligence, *CIA Estimates*, pp. 10ff) has a point in holding that the CIA's use of 1970 dollar cost relations for other years, would be a further source of error in the agency's calculation's. According to Rosefielde, that has been a usual practice. I for one, though, am unable to grasp why the resulting bias must be as Rosefielde seems to argue in the direction of understating Soviet outlays in post-1970 years. From correspondence with Rosefielde, I have come to wonder whether I have misunderstood him at this point.

12. The shape of the production capacity frontier is affected by U.S. economies of scale not only for Soviet items that lack near counterparts in the U.S. but also for Soviet items that have such counterparts. What is in question for each item is how costs vary over a range defined, on the one hand, by actual U.S. production and, on the other, by the hypothetical output indicated when the U.S. produces a mix conforming to that of the U.S.S.R. To determine that range evidently would require a knowledge of the U.S. production capacity frontier, but it could be approximated so far as formula (4) itself is a near surrogate for that.

To make matters still more complex, where many defense goods are produced, the nature of the least-cost U.S. performance equivalent of any particular Soviet defense good might depend on the mix of defense goods in question. It must be understood therefore that reference is in principle to that U.S. performance equivalent that would be produced at least cost when the United States is producing a mix of defense goods corresponding to the Soviet mix.

13. JEC, *Allocation of Resources in the Soviet Union and China—1975*, p. 23.

14. On the OSR procedures for sizing Soviet defense outlays in rubles, see the items in note 3, especially JEC, *Allocation of Resources in the Soviet Union and China—1975*; the sequels to that volume for 1976 and 1977; CIA, SR 76-10121U, May 1976; Permanent Select Committee on Intelligence, *CIA Estimates*.

15. See Rosefield's testimony in Permanent Select Committee on Intelligence, *CIA Estimates*, p. 14.

16. See CIA, SR 76-10121 U, May 1976.

17. See Holzman, Are the Soviets really outspending, pp. 93–94; Permanent Select Committee on Intelligence, *CIA Estimates*, pp. 9, 45, 76.

18. On hedonic index numbers, see Zvi Griliches, ed., *Price Indexes and Quality Change*, Cambridge, Mass.: Harvard University Press, 1971.

Permissions

Previously published essays that are republished or extensively drawn on in this volume are listed below. I also indicate in each case the holder or holders of the corresponding copyright. Thanks are due to the latter for permission to reprint or draw on the essay in question.

"Comparative Productivity: The USSR, Eastern Europe and the West," *The American Economic Review*, June 1987, *77*, 342–357: American Economic Association.

"Inventories: East and West," in *Socialist Economy and Economic Policy: Essays in Honour of Friedrich Levcik*, New York: Springer Verlag, 1985: Wiener Institut für Internationale Wirtschaftsvergleiche.

"Soviet Consumption in Comparative Perspective," *Economic Notes*, 1982, *2*, 199–218: Monte dei Paschi di Siena.

"Income Inequality under Soviet Socialism," *Journal of Economic Literature*, September 1984, *22*, 1052–1099: American Economic Association.

"Technological Progress," in *The Soviet Economy: Toward the Year 2000*, Abram Bergson and Herbert S. Levine, eds. London: George Allen and Unwin, 1983.

"Notes on the Production Function in Soviet Postwar Industrial Growth," *Journal of Comparative Economics*, June 1979, *3*, 116–126: Academic Press.

"Sovetskaia ekonomika pri Gorbacheve: dvenadtsatyi piatiletnii plan," *Obozrenie*, June 1986, *20*, 22–26: La Pensée Russe and Aleksandr Nekrich.

"Entrepreneurship under Labor Participation: The Yugoslav Case," in *Entrepreneurship*, Joshua Ronan, ed. Lexington, Mass.: Lexington Books, 1983.

"The Geometry of COMECON Trade," *European Economic Review*, November 1980, *14*, 291–306: North Holland.

"On Soviet Real Investment Growth," *Soviet Studies*, July 1987, *39*, 406–424.

"On the Measurement of Soviet Real Defense Outlays," in *Marxism, Central*

Planning, and the Soviet Economy: Economic Essays in Honor of Alexander Erlich, Padma Desai, ed.: Cambridge, Mass.: The MIT Press, 1983.

Index

DATE DUE